Product Cost Controlling with SAP®

 **PRESS**

SAP PRESS is a joint initiative of SAP and Galileo Press. The know-how offered by SAP specialists combined with the expertise of the publishing house Galileo Press offers the reader expert books in the field. SAP PRESS features first-hand information and expert advice, and provides useful skills for professional decision-making.

SAP PRESS offers a variety of books on technical and business related topics for the SAP user. For further information, please visit our website: *www.sap-press.com*.

Shivesh Sharma
Optimize Your SAP ERP Financials Implementation
2008, 696 pp.
ISBN 978-1-59229-160-1

Manish Patel
Discover SAP ERP Financials
2008, 544 pp.
ISBN 978-1-59229-184-7

Aylin Korkmaz
Financial Reporting with SAP
2008, 672 pp.
ISBN 978-1-59229-179-3

Paul Theobald
Migrate Successfully to the New SAP GL
2007, 104 pp.
ISBN 1-978-159229-166-3

John Jordan

Product Cost Controlling with SAP®

Galileo Press

Bonn • Boston

ISBN 978-1-59229-167-0

© 2009 by Galileo Press Inc., Boston (MA)
1st edition 2009

Galileo Press is named after the Italian physicist, mathematician and philosopher Galileo Galilei (1564–1642). He is known as one of the founders of modern science and an advocate of our contemporary, heliocentric worldview. His words *Eppur si muove* (And yet it moves) have become legendary. The Galileo Press logo depicts Jupiter orbited by the four Galilean moons, which were discovered by Galileo in 1610.

Editor Stephen Solomon
Copy Editor Ruth Saavedra
Photo Credit Gettty Images/Don Farrall
Production Editor Iris Warkus
Cover Designer Jill Winitzer
Layout Design Vera Brauner
Typesetting SatzPro, Krefeld (Germany)
Printed and bound in Canada

Contents at a Glance

Contents

Product Cost Controlling allows you to plan costs, collect actual costs and revenues, and analyze and report on the results.

1   Introduction

Most manufacturing or service companies are interested in accurately apportioning their operational and other costs to products or services provided. Comparing these costs with corresponding revenues allows you to determine your company's profitability.

Accurately determining the profitability of products, product lines, and services provided can be surprisingly difficult. This becomes apparent when you start entering the details that SAP requires to accurately set up Product Cost Controlling. For example, the relatively simple task of determining the cost of components depends on the validity dates of vendor quotations, the quantities planned and actually purchased, and freight costs, taxes, customs, and duties. This is not an exhaustive list, but you can see that apparently simple data setup tasks involve more detail than you might realize when initially using a highly integrated system such as an SAP system.

When departments are allowed to determine the costs of processes manually in spreadsheets, there is less scrutiny, questioning, and transparent access to the details behind many of these important figures and calculations. The highly integrated nature of SAP systems increases discipline in keeping data accurate and up to date, and most importantly increases communication within and between departments.

The more complicated task of apportioning labor and general overhead costs to individual products or services is usually a compromise between the accuracy required and the time and effort necessary to gain more accuracy. For example, it's possible to manually enter the actual time to perform each activity when manufacturing an assembly, or you can automatically enter the average time required for each activity. You gain more accurate information by recording actual activity time, but you incur the extra cost of manually entering the time in the system.

One of the aims of this book is to increase your understanding of the detailed reporting and analysis capability possible with Product Cost Controlling. This will allow you to make informed decisions when designing processes and the level of detail you input into the system. This is, of course, determined by the level of costing and profitability reporting detail you require from the system. A great deal of detailed documentation on setting up data and processes in Product Cost Controlling is available online. This book presents many process overviews, examples, and case scenarios to assist you in understanding how the details fit together, understanding the overall processes, and leveraging the investment you've made in your integrated system.

This book is designed to be useful for users, managers, consultants, and anyone interested in gaining a greater understanding the product costing process. It contains easy-to-understand process overviews and detailed master data and configuration setup requirements. You can use this book as a reference, referring to specific sections when needed. For example, during master data setup, you can refer to a specific chapter on master data. Or can may refer to the chapter on costing sheets when configuring overhead.

The screenshots and menu paths in this book are taken from an SAP ERP Central Component, Release 6.0 system. Manufacturing order is used as an umbrella term for production and process orders throughout.

1.1 Structure of this Book

The structure of this book should help you quickly navigate to the sections of particular interest depending on your role and requirements. This book is divided into three parts, each representing major areas within the Product Cost Controlling component as described in the following sections.

1.1.1 Part 1 – Integrated Planning

Integrated planning is the first step in planning and controlling costs for future fiscal periods or years. You create sales plan quantities in Profitability Analysis or Sales and Operations Planning, and convert the quantities to a production plan that you then transfer to demand management. Long-Term Planning accesses these requirements to determine work center loads and purchasing requirements based on production master data. Scheduled activity requirements are transferred to Cost Center Accounting, where planned activity requirements are determined.

▶ **Chapter 2**
We follow a typical best practice integrated planning scenario as described above.

1.1.2 Part 2 – Product Cost Planning

Product Cost Planning is where you plan procurement and production costs and set prices for materials and services. You normally determine the purchase price for externally procured items first and then the manufactured cost for assemblies. The following master data and configuration chapters describe the setup requirements necessary to create cost estimates.

Master Data

Master data is information that stays relatively constant over long periods of time. In these chapters we examine in detail every master data field relevant to Product Cost Planning, including many examples and case scenarios. The following master data is discussed:

▶ **Chapter 3**
We discuss controlling master data including cost elements, cost centers, activity types, and statistical key figures.

▶ **Chapter 4**
We look at fields in material master views including Material Requirements Planning (MRP), Controlling, and Accounting.

▶ **Chapter 5**
We examine logistics master data including bills of materials (BOMs), routings, product cost collectors, and purchasing info records.

Configuration

Most configuration settings are made when you first implement the system. All configuration settings are closely controlled and monitored because they have a major impact on the system process design for your company. Configuration settings are discussed in the following chapters:

▶ **Chapter 6**
We examine costing sheets and how you use them to set up overhead calculation.

▶ **Chapter 7**
We analyze cost components and structures and how they group costs of similar type such as material, labor, and overhead for reporting purposes.

▶ **Chapters 8 and 9**
We examine how you set up costing variants that contain all of the configuration required to create cost estimates.

After setting up master data and configuration, we are ready to create cost estimates as discussed in the next chapters.

Cost Estimates

Cost estimates plan procurement and manufacturing costs. Different types of cost estimates are used for different purposes as discussed in the following three chapters:

▶ **Chapter 10**
We discuss how standard cost estimates are used to update the standard price and revalue inventory. We examine the mark and release process and costing runs, which mass process standard cost estimates.

▶ **Chapter 11**
We cover in detail how preliminary cost estimates calculate the planned costs for manufacturing orders and product cost collectors.

▶ **Chapter 12**

We look at how unit cost estimates are designed for use during the product development phase. They are easily changed because they resemble a spreadsheet format, which is ideal for a development environment.

1.1.3 Part 3 – Cost Object Controlling

Cost Object Controlling allows you to determine planned costs for cost objects, post actual costs, and then analyze variances as discussed in the following chapters.

Planned and Actual Costs

In these chapters we determine how to plan and post actual costs to cost objects:

▶ **Chapter 13**

We analyze how preliminary cost estimates plan costs for cost objects such as manufacturing orders and product cost collectors.

▶ **Chapter 14**

We look at how actual costs such as component and activity costs are posted to cost objects during simultaneous costing.

Period-End Processing

During period-end processing you carry out overhead, work in process, and variance calculation, as well as settlement, as discussed in the following four chapters:

▶ **Chapter 15**

We examine how to carry out overhead period-end calculations based on costing sheet configuration as discussed in Chapter 6.

▶ **Chapter 16**

We look at how work in process is configured and how the period-end step is executed.

▸ **Chapter 17**
We look at production variance configuration, period-end processing, and analysis.

▸ **Chapter 18**
We analyze settlement configuration and period-end processing.

Special Topics

Special topics cover more specialized topics within Product Cost Controlling.

▸ **Chapter 19**
We discuss configuration and period-end processing for sales order controlling, subcontracting, and the material ledger.

Information System

In this section we discuss the standard reporting available for Product Costing Controlling.

▸ **Chapter 20**
We examine the standard reports available for both Product Cost Planning and Cost Object Controlling. We examine how you can drill down from high-level summarization reports to cost-element-based detailed reports and line item reports.

1.2 Looking Ahead

After reading this book you will have a clear understanding of Product Cost Controlling processes including integrated planning, Product Cost Planning, and Cost Object Controlling. Although a great deal of detailed information is available in online help documentation, this book provides an overview of how the many details of product costing fit together in this integrated system.

This book will help you take advantage of the many aspects of controlling costs, by following the product costing process flow from start to finish and explaining in detail the many analysis and reporting options available. This information can increase the profitability of your company by helping you analyze and understand the flow of costs in your system and the reasons for variances between planned and actual costs. Companies that regularly analyze production variances and take immediate corrective action gain a competitive advantage over companies that react only after increased costs or inefficient processes have already decreased profitability.

Readers do not need a detailed knowledge of accounting or production planning to understand the concepts and details discussed in this book.

You can contact the author at *jjordan@erpcorp.com*.

PART I
Integrated Planning

Integrated Planning is the first part of three in this Product Cost Controlling book.

Integrated Planning begins during the budget preparation for future fiscal periods or years. Sales mangers enter planning data into either Profitability Analysis (CO-PA), Sales and Operations Planning, or some other planning component or system. This initial sales planning data is transferred seamlessly to other components such as Long-Term Planning, Material Requirements Planning and Cost Center Planning, where detailed procurement and operations plans are derived from the sales plan.

This planning information is generated from projected sales plans over the next one to three years or longer. This sales information entered into CO-PA can provide a basis for planning future purchasing and production requirements in other components. Standard cost estimates are created from the detailed production plan information that can be transferred back to CO-PA to allow margin analysis based on budget sales and cost information provided by standard cost estimates.

After Integrated Planning is completed, we're ready to begin examining the Product Cost Planning process in Part 2, beginning with controlling the master data setup in Chapter 3.

Then we'll look at the Cost Object Controlling process in Part 3 beginning with preliminary costing in Chapter 13.

So let's get started with Part 1 by looking at the Integrated Planning process.

Integrated Planning allows you to plan production and procurement costs based on planned sales quantities.

2   Integrated Planning

Integrated Planning allows you to take advantage of a fully integrated system such as an SAP system. You can enter a sales plan to determine a production plan and projected manufacturing costs. This together with cost center plan costs allows you to calculate planned activity rates and standard cost estimates, which plan the cost of manufacture for each product. This process, also known as driver-based planning, allows you to plan costs based on sales quantities, which is best practice in the manufacturing industry.

One of the main advantages of using the Integrated Planning functionality is that you can compare planned with actual costs and determine the reason for the difference between them, which forms the basis for variance analysis. You can then use this as an iterative process to improve your sales and production planning period by period and year by year.

There are many alternatives for entering and processing plan data in SAP systems. In this chapter we'll examine entering sales data in Profitability Analysis (CO-PA), and then follow a typical flow from Sales and Operations Planning to Long-Term Planning to Cost Center Accounting. A sales manager typically enters a sales plan either into CO-PA or Sales and Operations Planning, and analyzes multiple sales scenarios. A preferred sales plan is then converted into a production plan, which is then transferred to Long-Term Planning.

The bill of material (BOM) and routing are then accessed by Long-Term Planning to determine component procurement, and cost center capacity, requirements. A BOM is a hierarchical structure of components and subassemblies, whereas a routing lists operations and standard values required to manufacture a finished product.

Activity scheduled quantities are then transferred from Long-Term Planning to Cost Center Accounting, where, together with Cost Center Planning data, activity and overhead rates are calculated. Let's start initial planning by entering a sales plan in CO-PA.

2.1 Profitability Analysis

Sales managers can enter the quantity of finished products they expect to sell in future budget periods with Transaction KEPM or by following the menu path ACCOUNTING • CONTROLLING • PROFITABILITY ANALYSIS • PLANNING • EDIT PLANNING DATA. Enter the operating concern and press Enter to display the screen shown in Figure 2.1.

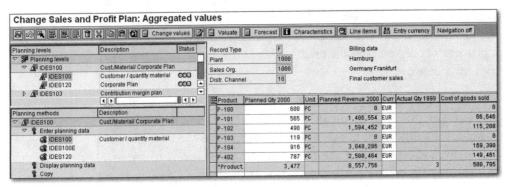

Figure 2.1 Planning Package for CO-PA Planning

Select Planning level and then Planning package, which are both IDES100 in this example. Expand the Enter planning data node (lower left) and then double-click IDES100 to enter planning data on the right side of the screen.

After you've entered sales planning data in CO-PA you can either:

▶ Transfer the data to Sales and Operations Planning (or other components) by following the menu path ACCOUNTING • CONTROLLING • PROFITABILITY ANALYSIS • PLANNING • INTEGRATED PLANNING

▶ Create a planning scenario with Transaction MS31 and access the CO-PA data directly with Long-Term Planning, which we'll discuss further in Section 2.3

We'll follow an example of transferring CO-PA data to Sales and Operations Planning so you can see this additional functionality.

2.2   Sales and Operations Planning

You can enter a sales plan for future periods and fiscal years directly into the Sales and Operations Planning component, or you can transfer the data from other components such as CO-PA. The sales plan can be entered for a product group and disaggregated to lower members or entered directly for individual materials. The production plan is determined from the sales plan and then transferred from Sales and Operations Planning to Demand Planning. If the production plan is determined from the sales plan on a spreadsheet, it can be entered manually into Demand Management instead of the Sales and Operations Planning component.

Enter a sales plan for a material into Sales and Operations Planning with Transaction MC88 or by following the menu path LOGISTICS • PRODUCTION • SOP • PLANNING • FOR MATERIAL • CHANGE. The data entry screen shown in Figure 2.2 is displayed.

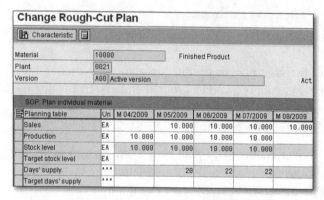

Figure 2.2 Sales and Operations Planning Entry Screen

Sales plan quantities are entered in the Sales row, and production plan quantities are entered in the Production row. Figure 2.2 displays an example of the production plan offset on month forward in time from the sales plan to help ensure that sales plan delivery dates are met. The production plan may also need to be different from the sales plan due to known production capacity requirements. For example, if the sales plan is to sell a quantity of 40 in month 08/2009, you may need to adjust the production plan to manufacture a quantity of 10.000 in the four preceding months.

After the production plan is determined, it is transferred to Demand Management with Transaction MC74 or by following the menu path LOGISTICS • PRODUCTION • SOP • PLANNING • FOR MATERIAL • TRANSFER MATERIAL TO DEMAND MANAGEMENT. The screen shown in Figure 2.3 is displayed.

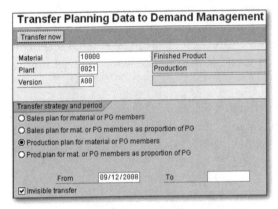

Figure 2.3 Transfer Production Plant to Demand Management

You transfer either the sales plan or production plan, for either an individual material or PG members (product group members) by making the appropriate selection in the Transfer strategy and period section, and then clicking the Transfer now button.

Now that we've converted the sales plan into a production plan and transferred the production plan to Demand Management, let's start working with this information in Long-Term Planning.

2.3 Long-Term Planning

Long-Term Planning allows you to enter medium- to long-term production plans into the system. Medium-term production plans generally involve production quantities between three months and three years into the future. Long-term production plans can plan production quantities as far into the future as you need. The production plan represents planned independent requirements, which are used to meet two downstream prerequisites necessary to create cost estimates:

▶ They generate requirements for purchased items. These can be used to request vendor quotations, negotiate raw material prices, and ensure purchasing info records are current. Purchasing info records are commonly used in cost estimates to determine the estimated planned price of components.

▶ Planned independent requirements can also be used to transfer scheduled activity requirements to cost centers. Cost center planned costs, divided by scheduled activity requirements, provide an estimate of planned activity price used by cost estimates to determine labor costs.

You can transfer the production plan from Sales and Operations Planning, as previously discussed in Section 2.2, or enter it directly with Transaction MD62 or by following the menu path LOGISTICS • PRODUCTION • PRODUCTION PLANNING • LONG-TERM PLANNING • PLANNED INDEPENDENT REQUIREMENTS • CHANGE. The data entry screen shown in Figure 2.4 is displayed.

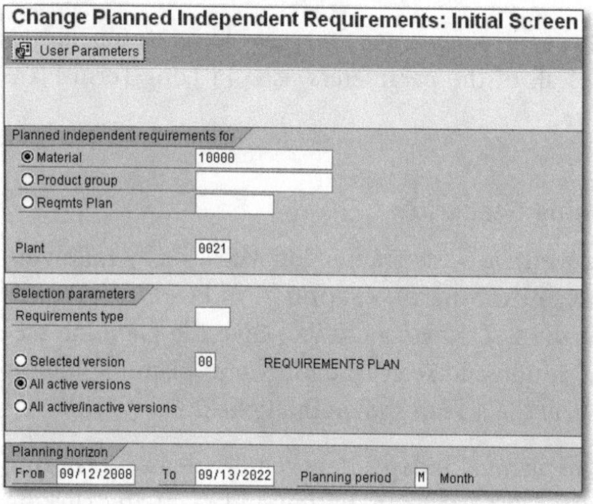

Figure 2.4 Change Planned Independent Requirements Initial Screen

Complete the fields in this screen and press Enter to display the independent requirements planning table as shown in Figure 2.5.

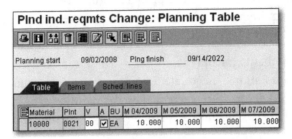

Figure 2.5 Change Planned Independent Requirements

The requirements displayed in Figure 2.5 correspond with the production plan transferred from Sales and Operations Planning shown in Figure 2.2. The requirements can be changed, or additional requirements entered directly. The A (version active) indicator shown in Figure 2.5 determines if the requirements are relevant to operative material requirements planning (MRP). If relevant to operative MRP, requirements will result in generation of planned orders, which can be converted to production orders for in-house production or purchase requisitions for external procurement. The system also explodes the BOM for assemblies produced in-house and generates dependant requirements for material components.

To generate dependent requirements, we first need to create a planning scenario that combines all of the parameters used in Long-Term Planning.

2.3.1 Create Planning Scenario

You create a planning scenario with Transaction MS31 or by following the menu path LOGISTICS • PRODUCTION • PRODUCTION PLANNING • LONG-TERM PLANNING • PLANNING SCENARIO • CREATE. Give the planning scenario a name and description and select the long-term planning indicator. Press Enter to display the screen shown in Figure 2.6.

Assign a version for the planned independent requirements by clicking the Planned Independent Requirements button and plants by clicking the Plants button. After you've checked the control parameters, release the planning scenario for planning by clicking the Release + Save button.

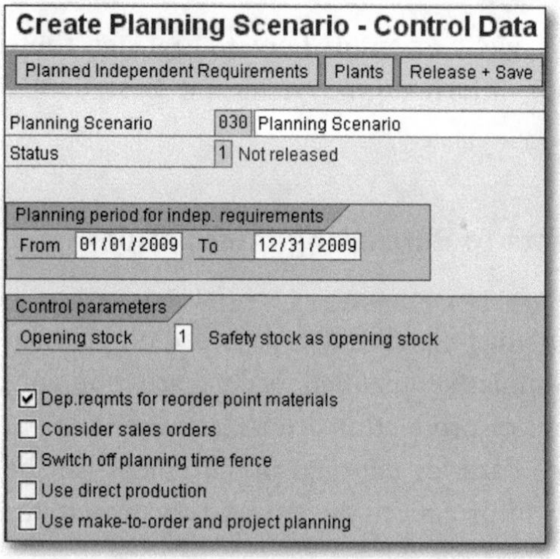

Figure 2.6 Planning Scenario Details

2.3.2 Planning Run

Run Long-Term Planning for a planning scenario with Transaction MS01 or by following the menu path LOGISTICS • PRODUCTION • PRODUCTION PLANNING • LONG-TERM PLANNING • LONG-TERM PLANNING • PLANNING RUN. The screen shown in Figure 2.7 is displayed.

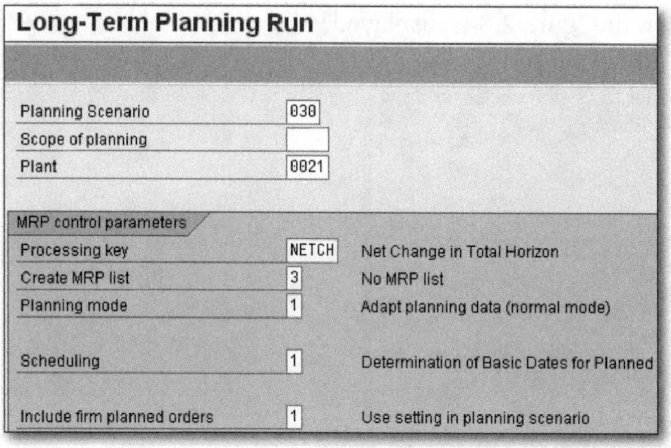

Figure 2.7 Long-Term Planning Run Initial Screen

Confirm the default settings and press Enter to carry out the planning run. The system calculates the dependant requirements of material 10000 in plant 0021 based on the BOM and routing.

In the following two sections we'll examine how to transfer these requirements to the purchasing information system and Cost Center Accounting.

2.3.3 Transfer Requirements to Purchasing Information System

Long-term MRP generates simulative planned orders, based on planned independent requirements. Simulative planned orders are not converted into purchase requisitions or production orders, and are for planning purposes only. Simulative data for external procurement can be transferred to the purchasing information system and evaluated for future purchasing requirements.

This information can be used as the basis for generating vendor requests for quotations (RFQs), negotiating raw material prices, and ensuring that purchasing info records are current. Updated purchasing info records can then be used in cost estimates as the basis for determining raw material purchase prices. You can transfer Long-Term Planning data to the purchasing information system with Transaction MS70 or by following the menu path LOGISTICS • PRODUCTION • PRODUCTION PLANNING • LONG-TERM PLANNING • EVALUATIONS • PURCHASING INFO SYSTEM • SET UP DATA. The screen shown in Figure 2.8 is displayed.

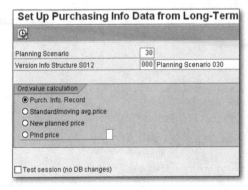

Figure 2.8 Set Up Purchasing Info Data from Long-Term Planning

The Version Info Structure S012 field allows you to determine the receiving version of the purchasing plan data. If you do not enter a version, the system uses the Planning Scenario as the planning version number. You can also choose how the purchase order value is calculated, in the Ord.value calculation section. Complete the selection screen and click the execute icon to run the transaction. Figure 2.9 shows an example of messages displayed after running Transaction MS70.

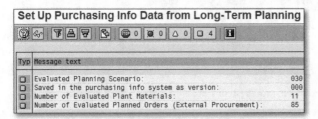

Figure 2.9 Messages Displayed After Sending Data to Purchasing Information System

The messages indicate the quantity of information transferred. You can also run a report on Long-Term Planning purchasing data with Transaction MCEC or by following the menu path LOGISTICS • PRODUCTION • PRODUCTION PLANNING • LONG-TERM PLANNING • EVALUATIONS • PURCHASING INFO SYSTEM • MATERIAL. The selection screen shown in Figure 2.10 is displayed.

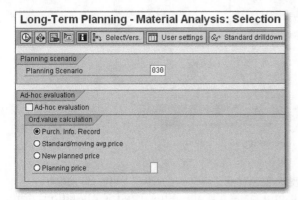

Figure 2.10 Purchasing Information System Selection Screen

The Planning Scenario field allows you to choose the Long-Term Planning scenario on which to base the analysis. You can also choose how the purchase order value is calculated, in the Ord.value calculation section. Complete the selection screen and click the execute icon. Figure 2.11 shows an example of the data displayed.

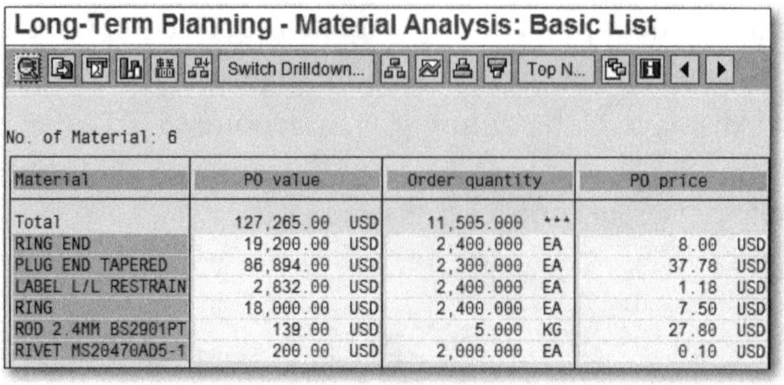

Material	PO value	Order quantity	PO price
Total	127,265.00 USD	11,505.000 ***	
RING END	19,200.00 USD	2,400.000 EA	8.00 USD
PLUG END TAPERED	86,894.00 USD	2,300.000 EA	37.78 USD
LABEL L/L RESTRAIN	2,832.00 USD	2,400.000 EA	1.18 USD
RING	18,000.00 USD	2,400.000 EA	7.50 USD
ROD 2.4MM BS2901PT	139.00 USD	5.000 KG	27.80 USD
RIVET MS20470AD5-1	200.00 USD	2,000.000 EA	0.10 USD

Figure 2.11 Purchasing Information System Data

This report provides information on future purchasing requirements. You can display purchasing requirements per period by clicking the time series (magnifying glass) icon shown in Figure 2.11. An example of the output screen is displayed in Figure 2.12.

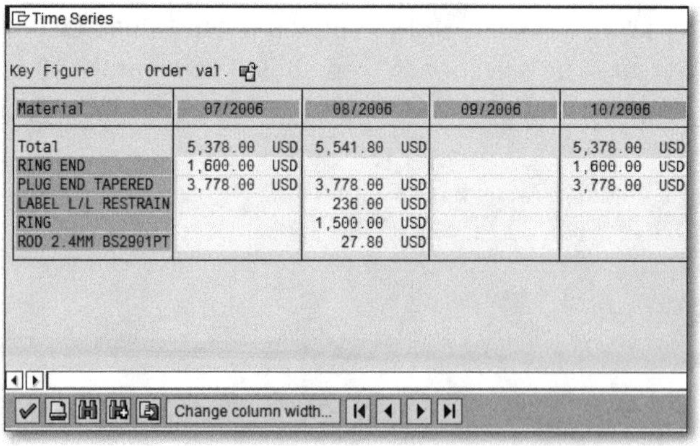

Material	07/2006	08/2006	09/2006	10/2006
Total	5,378.00 USD	5,541.80 USD		5,378.00 USD
RING END	1,600.00 USD			1,600.00 USD
PLUG END TAPERED	3,778.00 USD	3,778.00 USD		3,778.00 USD
LABEL L/L RESTRAIN		236.00 USD		
RING		1,500.00 USD		
ROD 2.4MM BS2901PT		27.80 USD		

Figure 2.12 Time Series of Purchasing Requirements

Click Order val. to toggle between purchase order value, quantity, and price. This provides useful data for obtaining vendor quotations for future requirements of purchased materials.

Activated planned independent requirements are also visible in operative MRP. In addition to data transferred to the purchasing information system, the purchasing department has visibility of activated planned independent requirements through planned orders generated by operative MRP and purchase requisitions converted from planned orders. These also can be the basis for updating purchasing info records.

2.3.4 Transfer Activity Quantities to Cost Center Accounting

In addition to ensuring that purchasing info records are up to date, Long-Term Planning activity quantities can be transferred to Cost Center Accounting. From the production plan for products, long-term MRP generates requirements for all lower-level components and work centers. The activity requirements are then transferred to corresponding cost centers with Transaction KSPP or via the menu path LOGISTICS • PRODUCTION • PRODUCTION PLANNING • LONG-TERM PLANNING • ENVIRONMENT • CO ACTIVITY REQUIREMENTS • TRANSFER TO COST CENTER. The screen shown in Figure 2.13 is displayed.

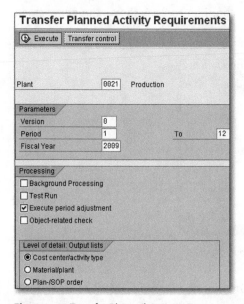

Figure 2.13 Transfer Planned Activity Requirements Selection Screen

This selection screen allows you to enter the parameters of the activity quantities to send to Cost Center Accounting. Because we are interested in activity quantities sent to cost centers per activity, we'll make the appropriate selection in the Level of detail: Output lists section. Complete the selection screen and click the Transfer control button. Figure 2.14 shows the next screen that is displayed.

Figure 2.14 Transfer Controls for Activity Requirements

Each line in Figure 2.14 corresponds to a controlling version. Versions are used to carry out scenario testing with different cost center plans, activity prices, and any other parameter in Cost Center Planning. You can create many versions, but normally only Version 0 contains both plan and actual data. To change transfer control settings, select a row and click the magnifying glass icon. Figure 2.15 shows the next screen that is displayed.

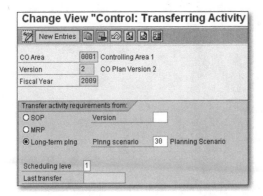

Figure 2.15 Transfer Control Definition Screen

You transfer SOP (Sales and Operations Planning), MRP or Long-term plng (Long-Term Planning) activity quantities to Cost Center Accounting by making the appropriate selection in the Transfer activity requirements from: section in the screen shown in Figure 2.15. Press the F3 key twice and click the Execute button shown in Figure 2.13 to start the transaction.

You can create only one transfer control per version. Figure 2.16 displays an example of the resulting list of activity requirements transferred to Cost Center Accounting.

Transfer Planned Activity Requirements

Cost Ctr	ActTyp	Activity scheduled	UM
1610	RUN	1,429.749	HR
1610	SET	108.104	HR
1620	RUN	1,167.609	HR
1620	SET	52.631	HR
1650	RUN	2,919.856	HR
1650	SET	62.202	HR
1660	RUN	1,064.603	HR
1660	SET	111.246	HR
1670	MAC	487.301	HR
1670	RUN	121.685	HR
1670	SET	15.8	HR
2100	RUN	346.201	HR
2100	SET	4.750	HR
125A	RUN	3.450	HR
173A	RUN	107.250	HR
* Total		8,002.437	HR

Figure 2.16 Transfer Planned Activity Requirements

Display activity quantities per period by double-clicking any scheduled activity quantity shown in the Activity scheduled column. Scheduled quantities transferred to Cost Center Accounting are displayed in the planned activity price entry screen, as we'll discuss in Section 2.4.2.

In Long-Term Planning we determined the component purchasing requirements and transferred them to the purchasing information system. We also determined the scheduled activity requirements and transferred them to Cost Center Accounting. The next step in Integrated Planning is to carry out cost element planning, and then, together with scheduled quantities transferred from Long-Term Planning, calculate the planned activity rate required by cost estimates to determine activity costs.

2.4   Cost Center Planning

Cost Center Planning meets two requirements for variance analysis:

▶ Cost element planning functions as a benchmark for comparison with actual costs as they occur. This analysis provides a measure of cost center manager performance.

> ▶ Dividing cost center planned and activity costs by the planned activity quantity provides an estimate of the planned activity rate, which is needed for cost estimates to determine activity costs.

Let's examine each of the above points in further detail in the following sections.

2.4.1 Cost Element Planning

Refer to Chapter 3 for more information on primary cost elements You enter the plan for primary costs by primary cost element, corresponding to a general ledger (G/L) expense account. Examples are planned payroll and depreciation costs against corresponding cost elements for each cost center.

Enter a primary cost plan for a cost center with Transaction KP06 by following the menu path ACCOUNTING • CONTROLLING • COST CENTER ACCOUNTING • PLANNING • COST AND ACTIVITY INPUTS • CHANGE. A selection screen is displayed, as shown in Figure 2.17.

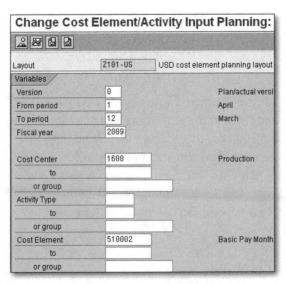

Figure 2.17 Cost Element Planning Selection Screen

You may see different fields, depending on the planning layout selected. You can scroll through available planning layouts with the left- and right-pointing arrow icons.

Any number of versions can be created, for which planning data can be entered. In this example, we will use Version 0. Actual costs post to Version 0, and this is the version compared with actual costs during variance analysis. Complete the selection screen and click the overview (mountain range and sun) icon to display the screen shown in Figure 2.18.

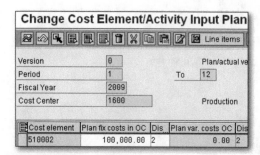

Figure 2.18 Cost Element Planning Screen for Cost Centers

This screen allows you to enter cost center plan fixed costs per cost element. These are activity-independent costs, because we did not enter an activity in the Activity Type field in the screen shown in Figure 2.17. To carry out primary cost planning, enter the plan cost in the Plan fix costs in OC (object currency) column. Click on the period screen (graph) icon to plan costs at an individual period level, if necessary.

If an activity type is entered in the selection screen shown in Figure 2.17, both fixed and variable costs can be planned in the screen shown in Figure 2.18.

Several reports are available to view planning data. One such report can be viewed with Transaction KSBL or via the menu path ACCOUNTING • CONTROLLING • COST CENTER ACCOUNTING • INFORMATION SYSTEM • REPORTS FOR COST CENTER ACCOUNTING • PLANNING REPORTS • COST CENTERS: PLANNING OVERVIEW. A selection screen is displayed, as shown in Figure 2.19.

This selection screen allows you to make entries in the Report parameters section to determine the values in the output screen. Complete the selection screen and click the Execute button to start the transaction. Figure 2.20 shows an example of the plan data displayed.

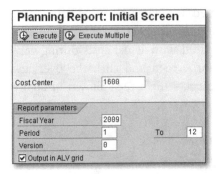

Figure 2.19 Cost Center Planning Report Selection Screen

Cost Centers: Planning Report		
Cost element/description	□	Value report curr.
500335 Indirect Prod Mats		5,000.00
506105 Cons Stores Safety		1,000.00
506109 Consumables - Misc		600.00
510002 Basic Pay Monthly		283,683.76
510004 Overtime at 1.5		4,792.12
541000 PR Tax Employer		24,174.68
541100 Workers Compensat...		4,989.02
546000 Health/Dental		56,104.44
547000 Life/Disability		5,048.20
625132 Accom. & Sub.		4,000.00
635243 Trade Publications		300.00
645101 Depr Land & Buildings		115.36
645120 Depr Plant Machinery		75,492.42
645130 Depr Furniture & Fix		6,422.48
645140 Depr Computers		362.70
660060 Education & Training		5,000.00
Primary Costs	▪	**477,085.18**
Activity-Independent Costs	▪ ▪	**477,085.18**
Debit	▪ ▪ ▪	**477,085.18**
Under/Over-Absorbed Overhead	▪ ▪ ▪ ▪	**477,085.18**

Figure 2.20 Cost Center Planning Overview Report

This screen displays a summary view of planned primary costs for cost center 1600. Let's examine how to calculate and enter activity rates.

2.4.2 Activity Price Planning

Determining the planned workload (activity quantities) of production cost centers for the next fiscal year is a best practice prerequisite for Cost Center Planning. Activity quantities are necessary to determine variable costs such as wages and energy. Planned activity quantities are determined from work center loads resulting from the production plan, which is in turn determined from the sales plan. You can transfer scheduled activity quantities from Sales and Operations Planning, MRP, or Long-Term Planning to Cost Center Planning. You then convert the scheduled activity quantities into planned activity quantities using plan reconciliation.

After cost element costs have been planned for the next fiscal year as discussed in the previous section, you can manually calculate and enter activity rates, or the system can automatically calculate them. Many companies calculate and enter planned activity rates manually for the first couple of years after system implementation. This allows them to fine-tune master data and plan costs.

You enter planned activity prices for a cost center with Transaction KP26 or by following the menu path ACCOUNTING • CONTROLLING • COST CENTER ACCOUNTING • PLANNING • ACTIVITY OUTPUT/PRICES • CHANGE. A selection screen is displayed, as shown in Figure 2.21.

Figure 2.21 Planned Activity Price Selection Screen

This selection screen allows you to enter the version, time period, cost center, and activity type to plan. Complete the selection screen and click the overview icon to display the screen shown in Figure 2.22.

In this screen you enter plan activity quantity, capacity quantity, and plan fixed and variable (Var) activity prices.

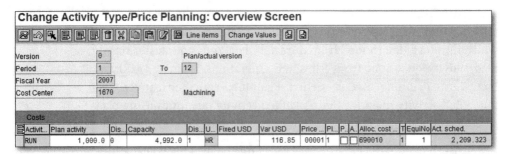

Figure 2.22 Planned Activity Price Entry Screen

Planned activity quantity, entered in the second column in Figure 2.22, is required to automatically calculate the planned activity price. Another, less well-known, benefit of entering the planned activity quantity is that it appears at the bottom of the standard cost center report S_ALR_87013611 – Cost Centers: Actual/Plan/Variance. You can then compare plan and actual activity quantities in the cost center report to analyze production and cost center variance.

Act. sched. (scheduled activity quantity), the last column in Figure 2.22 was previously transferred from Sales and Operations Planning, MRP, or Long-Term Planning, as we discussed in Section 2.3.4. This field cannot be adjusted manually. You can use it to overwrite the planned activity quantity, the second column in Figure 2.22, with Transaction KPSI or by following the menu path ACCOUNTING • CONTROLLING • COST CENTER ACCOUNTING • PLANNING • PLANNING AIDS • PLAN RECONCILIATION. A selection screen is displayed, as shown in Figure 2.23.

This selection screen allows you to enter the parameters to choose which cost centers and periods will be updated with the scheduled activity quantity from Long-Term Planning. Complete the selection screen and click the execute icon to start the transaction. Figure 2.24 shows an example of the data displayed.

The following points describe the columns in Figure 2.24:

▸ Pln actvty (planned activity) corresponds to the second column in Figure 2.22.

▸ New PlnAcv (new planned activity) corresponds to the last column in Figure 2.22.

▶ Actv diff. (activity difference) is the difference between the two previous columns in Figure 2.24.

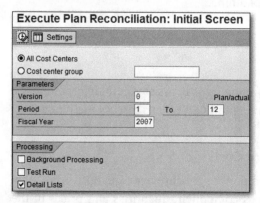

Figure 2.23 Execute Plan Reconciliation Screen

OTy	Object	AUn	Pln actvty	New PlnAcv	Actv diff.
ATY	1610/RUN	HR	4,000.0	6,657.820	2,657.820
ATY	1610/SET	HR	0.0	671.682	671.682
ATY	1620/RUN	HR	2,500.0	17,056.014	14,556.014
ATY	1620/SET	HR	0.0	1,161.867	1,161.867
ATY	1650/FAE	HR	0.0	1,817.960	1,817.960
ATY	1650/RUN	HR	11,000.0	57,352.511	46,352.511
ATY	1650/SET	HR	0.0	456.539	456.539
ATY	1660/FAE	HR	0.0	24.360	24.360
ATY	1660/RUN	HR	3,500.0	7,509.271	4,009.271
ATY	1660/SET	HR	0.0	936.768	936.768
ATY	1670/FAE	HR	0.0	62.4	62.4
ATY	1670/MAC	HR	2,500.0	13,085.993	10,585.993
ATY	1670/RUN	HR	1,000.0	2,209.323	1,209.323
ATY	1670/SET	HR	0.0	548.936	548.936
ATY	2100/RUN	HR	4,500.0	1,161.934	3,338.066-
ATY	2100/SET	HR	0.0	7.0	7.0
ATY	2500/RUN	HR	1,800.0	1,800.0	0.0
ATY	2600/RUN	HR	2,000.0	2,000.0	0.0

Figure 2.24 Plan Reconciliation List

When you execute plan reconciliation, the planned activity manually entered in the second column in Figure 2.22 is automatically overwritten with the scheduled activity from the last column in Figure 2.22.

Now that you've carried out cost element and activity type planning, you can automatically calculate the planned activity price with Transaction KSPI or by following the menu path ACCOUNTING • CONTROLLING • COST CENTER ACCOUNTING • PLANNING • ALLOCATIONS • PRICE CALCULATION. In the selection screen you enter the version, time frame, and cost centers and click the execute icon.

Now that we've completed Cost Center Planning, there are still some more steps to take in the Integrated Planning cycle. We'll discuss these in the next section on final planning.

2.5   Final Planning

You can take some more planning steps to assist you in determining the accuracy of your initial planning in CO-PA. Let's discuss these now.

2.5.1   Calculate Standard Costs

We've estimated future component procurement quantities in Long-Term Planning and can access component quantities and prices in the purchasing information system.

We've also estimated future activity quantities in Long-Term Planning, transferred this information to Cost Center Accounting, and calculated planned activity prices.

Refer to Chapter 10 for detailed information on standard cost estimates

This information, together with the necessary master data and configuration setup we'll discuss in following chapters, allows you to create standard cost estimates. These allow you to estimate projected procurement and manufacturing costs for components and finished goods and update inventory valuation based on these planned costs.

After you've created and released standard cost estimates, you can transfer this information to CO-PA for detailed margin analysis and reporting, as we'll discuss in the next section.

2.5.2   Transfer Standard Costs to CO-PA

You can transfer standard cost estimate cost component information to CO-PA using valuation functionality. Refer back to the planning layout in Figure 2.1 after calculating standard cost estimates and click the Valuate button to transfer the cost information. You can also display this data with standard CO-PA reports with Transaction KE30 or by following the menu path ACCOUNTING • CONTROLLING • PROFITABILITY ANALYSIS • INFORMATION SYSTEM • EXECUTE REPORT. You can choose an existing report or create your own to compare planned sales and cost information.

This concludes the Integrated Planning chapter, so let's review what we've covered.

2.6   Summary

In this chapter we discussed the Integrated Planning functionality and scenarios. First, we looked at creating a sales plan in CO-PA. We then considered either creating a sales plan directly in Sales and Operations Planning or transferring the plan from CO-PA. We converted the sales plan into a production plan that we transferred to Demand Planning as planned independent requirements.

We then ran Long-Term Planning and generated planned dependent requirements based on BOM and routing information. Purchasing requirements were analyzed in the purchasing information system. Work center loads were transferred to Cost Center Accounting.

Cost center activity quantities transferred from Long-Term Planning, together with cost element planning, allowed us to calculate planned activity prices. We then considered the final planning steps of creating standard cost estimates and using the valuation functionality in CO-PA for margin reporting on planned sales and cost information.

Now that we've considered Integrated Planning, we'll next examine controlling master data in Chapter 3, material master data in Chapter 4, and logistics master data in Chapter 5. This information is a prerequisite to creating standard cost estimates, which we'll discuss in detail in Chapter 10.

> **Note**
>
> The material presented in this chapter outlines some basic procedures and best practices for Profitability Analysis planning. More detailed information on this functionality can be found in the SAP PRESS book *Controlling-Profitability Analysis (CO-PA) with SAP*.

PART II
Product Cost Planning

Product Cost Planning is the second part we examine in this Product Cost Controlling book.

We looked first at Integrated Planning, which gathers initial planning information from other components such as Sales and Operations Planning, Long-Term Planning, and Material Requirements Planning. This planning information is usually generated from projected sales plans over the next one to three years or longer. This forecast sales information provides a basis for planning future purchasing and production requirements.

In this part we look at Product Cost Planning, which involves creating master data and configuration required to plan the cost of manufacturing products. This combined with the Integrated Planning data allows companies to project the total costs of manufacturing into future periods and years. It also allows both internal and external manufacturing capacity to be analyzed and assists with planning future capital expenditure requirements.

Controlling master data identifies the type of cost, and provides information for the responsible department, project, or person.

3 Controlling Master Data

Master data is information that stays relatively constant over long periods of time, such as cost elements and activity types.

Controlling master data provides information for the department, project, or person responsible for costs, and identifies the type of costs. Material master data provides all of the information required to manage a material, whereas logistics master data provides information on how materials are procured and manufactured.

Even though master data is relatively stable, companies that want to remain competitive in rapidly changing environments constantly assess whether it's more cost effective to manufacture assemblies in-house, procure externally, or outsource. Changing methods of procurement can produce large effects on variance calculation and require constant master data and purchasing information maintenance. This may also influence the frequency of price updates with standard cost estimates.

Rapidly changing environments

In this chapter we'll discuss Controlling master data relevant to Product Cost Controlling and how it influences cost estimates and reporting. In the next two chapters we'll look at material and logistics master data. The first Controlling master data item we'll analyze is the cost element.

3.1 Cost Element

All costs posted within Controlling (CO) are identified by cost elements that indicate the *type* of cost. These postings can be divided into two groups based on posting origin. Postings to CO from *external* business transactions are identified by primary cost elements. Business transactions *within* CO are identified by secondary cost elements. In the following sections we'll examine primary and secondary postings further.

3.1.1 Primary Postings

All costs within CO originate from postings identified by primary cost elements corresponding to general ledger (G/L) accounts in Financial Accounting (FI). During implementation you first create G/L expense accounts in FI, and then either automatically or manually create corresponding primary cost elements in CO. The existence of a primary cost element in CO results in all postings to the expense G/L account also posting in parallel to a cost object in CO. Typical cost objects are cost centers, internal orders, product cost collectors, and work breakdown structure (WBS) elements in Project System (PS). This process ensures that expenses in FI and primary costs in CO can be reconciled. An example of a primary expense account posting is shown in Figure 3.1.

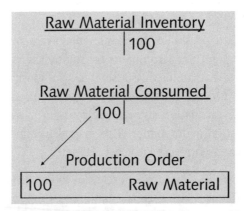

Figure 3.1 Goods Issue Debits to Production Order

Components with a value of 100 are issued from inventory to a production order. The raw material consumed G/L expense account receives a debit of 100, resulting in a production order debit of 100.

Now that we've discussed how primary cost postings occur, we'll examine how to maintain primary cost elements.

You create primary cost elements with Transaction KA01 or by following the menu path ACCOUNTING • CONTROLLING • COST CENTER ACCOUNTing • Master Data • Cost Element • Individual Processing • Create Primary. The selection screen shown in Figure 3.2 is displayed.

> **Note**
>
> You create secondary cost elements with Transaction KA07. We'll discuss secondary cost elements in detail in Section 3.1.2.

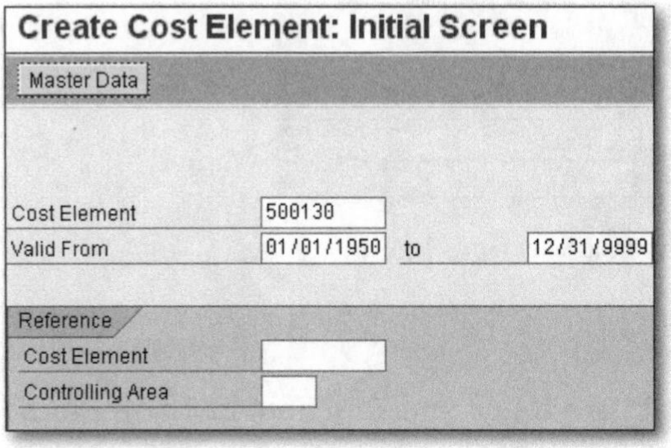

Create Cost Element: Initial Screen

Master Data

Cost Element	500130	
Valid From	01/01/1950 to	12/31/9999

Reference
Cost Element
Controlling Area

Figure 3.2 Create Primary Cost Element Initial Screen

A primary cost element must correspond to a G/L account. If you attempt to create a primary cost element without a corresponding G/L account, you'll receive an error message similar to the one shown in Figure 3.3.

Create the G/L account 500131 first

Figure 3.3 Primary Cost Element Error Message If There's No G/L Account

This message indicates that you need to create the G/L account before you can create the corresponding primary cost element.

After entering a primary cost element and valid from and to dates as shown in Figure 3.2, press Enter to display the screen shown in Figure 3.4.

Let's examine the first three fields in the Basic Data tab in detail. We'll discuss the remaining cost element fields in Section 3.1.2 on secondary postings.

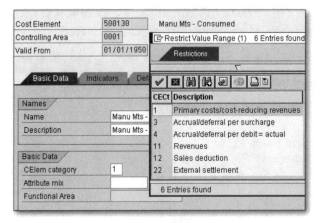

Figure 3.4 Primary Cost Element Basic Screen

Name and Description

The first fields you maintain are Name and Description. These can be changed at any time and appear in the description in reports containing cost elements such as cost center and product cost collector reports.

Cost Element Category

Right-click in the CElem category (cost element category) field and select Possible Entries to display the dialog box shown in Figure 3.4. This screen shows typical cost element category entries for *primary* cost elements. There is a different list of possible cost element types for *secondary* cost elements, as we'll see in Figure 3.6. The more commonly used primary cost element categories are described as follows:

- **Category 1**: These are created for primary expense G/L accounts.
- **Category 11**: These are created for revenue G/L accounts.
- **Category 12**: These are created for sales deduction accounts such as cost of sales and sales discounts and rebates.
- **Category 22**: These are created for external settlement. Usually, costs enter CO through postings to primary G/L accounts with corresponding primary cost elements. It's also possible to settle costs from CO back to G/L accounts in FI. You do this with category 22 cost elements.

The cost element category cannot be changed after either plan or actual transactional data exists for a cost element during the current fiscal year. The only option you have is to delete the cost element from the start of the next fiscal year with Transaction KA04, and re-create the same cost element from the start of the next fiscal year with the required cost element category.

The following case scenario provides a typical example of why you may need to change the cost element category.

Case Scenario

It's possible to create category 12 (sales deduction) cost elements for difference accounts such as purchase price difference and physical inventory adjustment described as follows:

▶ Purchase price difference postings occur when the purchase price is different from the standard price for a material.

▶ Physical inventory adjustment postings occur when adjustments are made to inventory quantities during a physical inventory count and reconciliation with inventory quantities in the system.

Some companies create these cost elements as category 12 because you don't need to determine or set up automatic account determination, that is, configure which cost centers are posted to automatically when expenses post to different accounts. Revenue and sales deduction postings don't require automatic account assignment to cost centers because they are not considered as expenses and usually post directly to profit centers. However, you lose the advantage of the excellent cost analysis capability with standard cost center reports.

Because it's not possible to change cost element categories during a fiscal year after transactional data has posted, the category 12 cost elements were deleted from the start of the next fiscal year with Transaction KA04, and re-created as category 1 from the start of next fiscal year. Automatic account assignment configuration (Transaction OKB9), which allows the system to automatically determine cost center postings, was also implemented at the same time. We'll discuss automatic account assignment in more detail in Section 3.1.5.

The field status group in the G/L account definition (Transaction FS00) was adjusted to allow entry of the cost center in the cost center field during postings to the G/L account. Field status groups control which fields are available during transactions. Because the cost center field was not required when the cost element was category 12, the cost center field was not available. The field status group was changed to allow the cost center field to be populated by automatic account assignment with Transaction OKB9.

Now that we've discussed primary postings, let's see how secondary postings occur.

3.1.2 Secondary Postings

You can move costs within CO independently of primary postings from FI. These are called secondary postings, and they occur, for example, when you confirm production order activities. In the example shown in Figure 3.5, the production order is debited and a cost center credited. The reason for secondary postings is to progressively move overhead costs from cost centers where primary expense postings occur through to manufacturing orders so each assembly and finished good can bear its share of overhead costs. To increase the rate of distribution of overhead to production cost centers and orders, you can either increase the planned activity rate or the standard activity quantity in production routings. We'll discuss production routings in Chapter 5. Figure 3.5 contains secondary cost postings that are typical when confirming a production order.

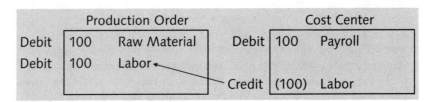

Figure 3.5 Production Cost Center Allocation during Confirmation

In this example payroll for the factory is expensed to the cost center with primary postings, and then progressively allocated to each production Order with secondary postings during labor activity confirmation.

Now that we've discussed the concept of how secondary postings allocate costs within Controlling, let's further examine cost element master data. We'll first look at the Basic Data tab.

3.1.3 Basic Data

You can view or change secondary cost elements with Transaction KA02 or by following the menu path ACCOUNTING • CONTROLLING • COST CENTER ACCOUNTING • MASTER DATA • COST ELEMENT • INDIVIDUAL PROCESSING • CHANGE. Type in the cost element you want to examine and press Enter to display the Cost Element Basic Screen, as shown in Figure 3.6.

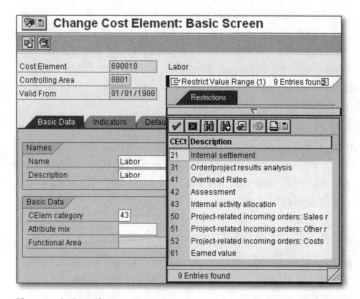

Figure 3.6 Cost Element Basic Screen

The Basic Data tab contains basic information and the cost element category, which we'll now discuss in detail.

Name and Description

These can be changed at any time and appear in the description in reports containing cost elements such as cost center and product cost collector reports.

> **Note**
>
> The commonly used standard Actual/Plan/Variance cost center report S_ALR_87013611 uses the text from the Description field in cost element master data, and can be changed at any time.

Cost Element Category

Right-click in the CElem category field and select Possible Entries to display the dialog box shown in Figure 3.6. This screen shows typical cost element category entries for *secondary* cost elements. You see a different list of cost element types for *primary* cost elements, as shown in Figure 3.4. The more common secondary cost element categories are described below:

▸ **Category 21**: These are created for Internal settlement, which involves moving costs between cost objects during the period-end settlement process. For example, you may settle costs from internal orders that represent short-term project costs to cost centers that represent long-term ongoing department costs.

▸ **Category 41**: These are created for Overhead Rates which involves using costing sheets to allocate costs from production cost centers to manufacturing orders or product cost collectors during period-end processing. A costing sheet summarizes the rules for allocating overhead from cost centers to cost estimates, product cost collectors and manufacturing orders.

▸ **Category 42**: These are created for Assessment which involves allocating costs from detailed overhead cost centers to more general overhead cost centers and then to production cost centers. Assessment is a Controlling period-end activity.

▸ **Category 43**: These are created for Internal activity allocation which involves allocating costs from production cost centers to manufacturing orders or product cost collectors during activity confirmation.

Now that we've discussed cost element categories, let's look at the next fields in the Basic Data tab.

Note

You can create secondary cost elements with any cost element number because they don't need to correspond with an existing G/L account number. You should always determine a numbering logic for secondary cost elements. For example, Assessment cost elements (category 42) should belong to a different number series than activity confirmation cost elements (category 43). You could, for instance, create a number series 942xxx for category 42 cost elements, and 943xxx for category 43 cost elements.

Using a numbering logic allows you to more easily identify the cost element type, and readily group cost elements together in a range if needed for cost element groups or for reporting. A list of typical secondary cost element categories is shown in Figure 3.6.

Attribute Mix

The Attribute mix field in Figure 3.6 can be used to enter a maximum number of eight attributes for reporting independently of the chart of accounts if required. Cost element attributes are defined with Transaction OKA6, and attribute mix is defined with Transaction OKA4.

Functional Area

This field is explained in detail in Section 3.2.2 when we discuss cost center master data.

Now that we've looked at the fields in the Basic Data tab, let's examine the fields in the remaining tabs of cost element master data.

3.1.4 Indicators

Select the Indicators tab in Figure 3.6 to display the screen shown in Figure 3.7.

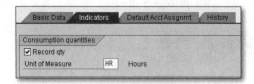

Figure 3.7 Cost Element Indicators

The fields in the Indicators tab are described as follows:

Record Quantity

Select the Record qty (record quantity) checkbox to define whether the system issues a message if either the quantity or quantity unit are not specified during postings. Although quantities are usually recorded during activity confirmation and inventory goods movements, it's also pos-

See Section 3.2.3 for discussion of the record quantity indicator in cost centers

sible to post costs manually in FI and CO with cost elements. This may be important if you're taking advantage of more advanced cost center reporting such as target cost analysis, which depends on quantities to analyze all cost center costs.

This indicator has no effect on planning or on the identification of quantities in reports. You should select this checkbox in the cost center master data as well, as discussed in Section 3.2.3, to record quantities for the combination of cost center and cost element. You must select this checkbox if you have an overhead that is dependent on the unit of measure posted with a cost element.

Unit of Measure

If you select the Record qty checkbox, you must also enter a Unit of Measure because quantity only has a meaning together with unit of measure.

Now that we've looked at the fields in the Indicators tab, let's examine the fields in the next tab.

3.1.5   Default Account Assignment

Select the Default Acct Assgnmt (default account assignment) tab in Figure 3.7 to display the screen shown in Figure 3.8.

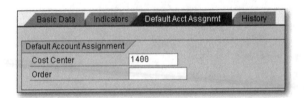

Figure 3.8 Cost Element Default Account Assignment

The fields in this tab allow you to enter default cost objects for a cost element.

Cost Center and Order

Enter a Cost Center, Order, or both in the screen shown in Figure 3.8 to maintain default account assignment for any postings identified by this cost element per controlling area. If you make an entry in both fields, the posting to the order will be *real*, and the posting to the cost center will be *statistical* or for reporting purposes only. This means the cost center will keep a record of the posting, but the costs won't be included in cost center total costs. If you enter either a Cost Center or Order in Figure 3.8, the posting will be real and included in the corresponding cost center or order total costs.

Cost elements are defined per controlling area

This method of setting up default account assignment is relatively easy because it requires only a master data change. However, this may not be suitable if two plants in the same controlling area require different cost centers assigned to the same cost element. In this case you'll need to assign cost objects with automatic account assignment configuration Transaction OKB9, which allows you to enter a default cost center per cost element for each plant.

We'll discuss automatic account assignment configuration in the section after next

A cost center entered in automatic account assignment takes priority over a cost center entered in cost element master data because it's more specific. Many plants can exist within a controlling area, whereas a cost element is defined for the entire controlling area. A posting identified by a cost element in a plant not defined in automatic account assignment will post to a cost center entered in cost element master data. If a cost center is not entered in the cost element master data or automatic account assignment, then either the cost center will need to be entered manually during the transaction or you will receive an error message until the cost center is entered or assigned.

Account assignment priority

Some transactions such as postings due to price differences occur automatically, and you don't get the opportunity to enter the cost object manually. In these cases you need to enter default account assignment either in the cost element master data or via automatic account assignment configuration. Let's examine each approach in more detail.

Collective Default Account Assignment

You can see a listing of all default account assignments in cost element master data with Transaction KA23 or by following the menu path ACCOUNTING • CONTROLLING • COST CENTER ACCOUNTING • MASTER DATA • COST ELEMENT • COLLECTIVE PROCESSING • DISPLAY. The screen shown in Figure 3.9 is displayed.

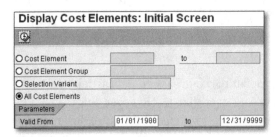

Figure 3.9 Display Cost Elements Collective Selection Screen

Cost element list If you're not sure which cost element to display, or would like to see a complete list, select All Cost Elements and then click the execute icon to display the screen shown in Figure 3.10.

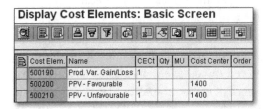

Figure 3.10 Cost Element List with Default Account Assignment

You can also see cost element categories in the CECt column The Cost Center and Order columns list default cost centers and orders. This list provides a quick check to see which cost elements have a default cost center or order entered in cost element master data.

Tip

It can be easier to keep track of default cost centers entered via *automatic* account assignment because they are maintained in one transaction and one screen. If you use this approach, the number of *default* cost centers entered in cost element master data should ideally be kept to a minimum.

If you decide to maintain default cost centers primarily in automatic account assignment, here are some steps to take:

▶ Monitor default cost centers listed in Figure 3.10 (Transaction KA23)

▶ Enter default cost centers in automatic account assignment (Transaction OKB9)

▶ Delete default cost center entries in cost element master data (Transaction KA02)

Only make default account assignment entries in cost elements when you need to make an account assignment quickly and don't have time to make the configuration change required for automatic account assignment.

Automatic Account Assignment

You maintain automatic account assignment entries in configuration with Transaction OKB9 or by following the IMG menu path CONTROL-LING • COST CENTER ACCOUNTING • ACTUAL POSTINGS • MANUAL ACTUAL POSTINGS • EDIT AUTOMATIC ACCOUNT ASSIGNMENT. The screen shown in Figure 3.11 is displayed.

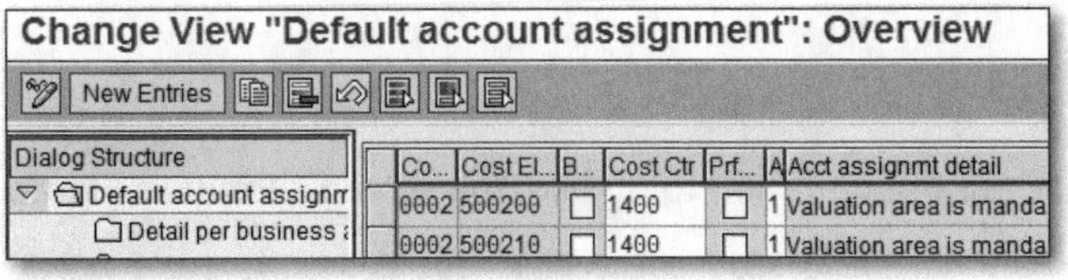

Figure 3.11 Automatic Account Assignment Configuration

Complete the following steps to proceed to a screen where you can assign a cost center per plant:

1. Type "1" in the A (account assignment detail) column.

2. Select the row of the required Cost El... (cost element).

3. Double-click Detail per business (detail per business area/valuation area).

4. Click the New Entries button.

The screen shown in Figure 3.12 is displayed.

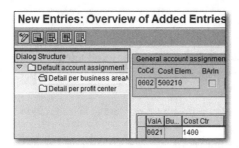

Figure 3.12 Default Cost Center per Plant Configuration

Valuation area is another term for plant

Complete the ValA (valuation area) and Cost Ctr (cost center) fields and save your work to make the cost center assignment. After you assign a cost center to a plant (valuation area), only the cost center field is changeable. You can add more plants and assign cost centers, or you can delete rows as required.

Now that we've looked at the fields in the default account assignment tab and discussed automatic account assignment let's examine the fields in the cost element History tab.

3.1.6 History

Select the History tab in Figure 3.8 to display the screen shown in Figure 3.13.

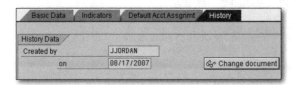

Figure 3.13 Cost Element History

The History tab contains creation and change information for a cost element.

History Data

This section allows you to determine which user created the cost element and when it was created.

Change Document

Click the Change document button to display a list of cost element fields changed since the master data record was created. Double-click a line to display details of changes made to each field.

All fields in the History tab are determined automatically and cannot be changed manually.

Now that we've examined the purpose of cost elements and how they are set up and maintained, let's look at cost centers.

3.2 Cost Center

Cost centers represent *where* costs occur, either by geographic location, area of responsibility, or both. They are grouped together in decision, control, and responsibility units in a hierarchical structure known as the standard hierarchy, which we'll now examine.

3.2.1 Standard Hierarchy

Because the standard hierarchy is a mandatory field in cost center master data, the standard hierarchy must be created and assigned to a controlling area before any cost centers can be created. This guarantees that the standard hierarchy contains all cost centers in a controlling area.

Each node of the standard hierarchy is a cost center group. This technique of creating a hierarchy by creating groups within groups is used in many other areas of the system, for example, in the bill of material. The standard hierarchy is really just a special cost center group that contains all cost centers. The system routinely breaks down what could otherwise be complicated structures into simple concepts such as master data groups.

The standard hierarchy contains all cost centers

You can view or change the standard hierarchy with Transaction OKEON or by following the menu path Accounting • Controlling • Cost Center Accounting • Master Data • Standard Hierarchy • Change. An example of a standard hierarchy is shown in Figure 3.14.

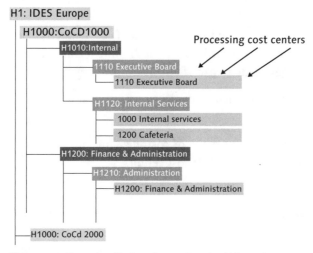

Figure 3.14 Example of a Cost Center Standard Hierarchy

Drag and drop You can drag and drop cost centers to reassign them to different nodes in the standard hierarchy. You can reassign cost centers by company code, business area, or profit center during a fiscal year if the following three conditions are met:

- The currency of the old company code is the same as the new company code.
- You post only plan data in the current fiscal year.
- The cost center is not assigned to a fixed asset, work center, or HR (human resources) master record.

As you maintain cost centers within the standard hierarchy, the cost center status changes, as shown in Figure 3.15.

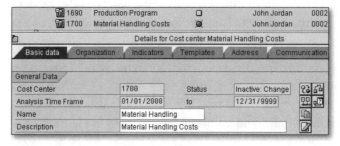

Figure 3.15 Cost Center Status in Standard Hierarchy

A cost center created or changed in the standard hierarchy transaction is initially assigned an inactive status and cannot receive or send costs. Cost centers with an inactive status can be deleted more quickly and easily while you initially set up and maintain the standard hierarchy because the system does not need to carry out checks for dependent entries.

To activate a cost center click on the green and red traffic light icon in the Basic data tab of the cost center during maintenance of the standard hierarchy as shown in Figure 3.15. Assignments are checked during activation, and once activated, the cost center can receive and send costs. Activated cost centers are indicated by a green traffic light icon in the activation status column in the standard hierarchy shown in the first line of Figure 3.15.

You can activate cost centers collectively with Transaction KEOA1 or by following the IMG menu path CONTROLLING • COST CENTER ACCOUNTING • MASTER DATA • COST CENTERS • ACTIVATE INACTIVE COST CENTERS.

You can delete inactive cost centers collectively with Transaction KEOD1 or by following the IMG menu path CONTROLLING • COST CENTER ACCOUNTING • MASTER DATA • COST CENTERS • DELETE INACTIVE COST CENTERS.

We'll discuss the remaining cost center master data fields in the following sections. Now that we've discussed the standard hierarchy, let's examine cost center master data. We'll first examine fields contained in the Basic Data tab.

3.2.2   Basic Data

You can view or change cost centers with Transaction KS02 or by following the menu path ACCOUNTING • CONTROLLING • COST CENTER ACCOUNTING • MASTER DATA • COST CENTER • INDIVIDUAL PROCESSING • CHANGE. Type in the cost center you want to maintain and press Enter to display the initial cost center screen shown in Figure 3.16.

We'll discuss each of the fields in this screen in detail in the following sections.

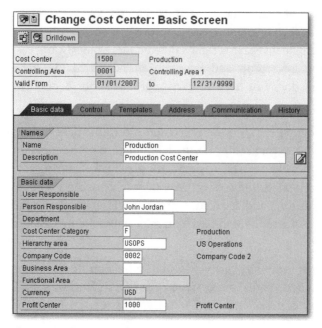

Figure 3.16 Cost Center Basic Screen

Name and Description

These fields appear in cost center and order reports and can be changed at any time. You can add long text to the Description field by clicking the pencil and paper icon.

> **Note**
>
> The commonly used standard Actual/Plan/Variance cost center report S_ALR_87013611 uses the text from the Name field in Figure 3.16.

User Responsible

This is an optional text field you can populate with the user responsible for maintaining cost center master data.

Person Responsible

This is a mandatory text field you should populate with the name of the person responsible for controlling cost center costs and analyzing the cost center planned and actual costs. This should be the name of a real person actually responsible for the costs, and not a high-level manager who receives cost center reports from lower-level managers who are responsible for explaining the costs.

Department

Department is an optional text field for reporting purposes only. For example, you can enter department names that are unique to your organization.

Cost Center Category

Cost Center Category identifies the type of activity a cost center performs, such as administration, production, or sales. You can also define your own additional cost center categories with configuration Transaction OKA2 or by following the IMG menu path CONTROLLING • COST CENTER ACCOUNTING • MASTER DATA • COST CENTERS • DEFINE COST CENTER CATEGORIES. Cost center categories allow you to restrict certain activity types for use with certain cost centers. For example, you can prevent production activities from posting incorrectly to administrative cost centers. We'll examine this further in Section 3.3 when we discuss activity types.

Hierarchy Area

Hierarchy area is a mandatory field that refers to the cost center location on the standard hierarchy. We discussed the standard hierarchy in detail in Section 3.2.1.

Company Code

You can assign a cost center to only one company code; it is a mandatory field. A company code is the smallest organizational unit in Financial Accounting for which a complete self-contained chart of accounts can be drawn up for external reporting purposes.

Business Area

You can create financial statements for business areas, and you can use these statements for various internal reporting purposes. The business area is an early SAP functionality that has been superseded by functional areas and profit centers, as discussed in the following sections.

Functional Area

Functional Area is part of cost of sales accounting that compares sales revenue with the manufacturing costs of an activity for a given accounting period. Expenses posted to the cost center are assigned to the functional area. Typical examples of functional area are listed below:

▶ R&D (research and development)

▶ G&A (general and administration)

▶ S&D (sales and distribution)

▶ COS (cost of sales)

Refer to OSS Note 85799 for more information on functional areas

Expenses and revenues that cannot be assigned to functional areas are reported in other profit and loss items sorted according to expense and revenue type. You can enter or change the functional area if no postings exist for this cost center.

You need to activate *cost of sales accounting for preparation* in order to enter values in the Functional Area field for G/L accounts and Controlling master data. You do this by following the IMG menu path FINANCIAL ACCOUNTING • FINANCIAL ACCOUNTING GLOBAL SETTINGS • COMPANY CODE • COST OF SALES ACCOUNTING • ACTIVATE COST OF SALES ACCOUNTING.

> **Note**
>
> Also review the slice-and-dice and other functionality available in Profitability Analysis reports based on market segment and functional areas in G/L accounts and Controlling master data. Reporting based on functional areas is required by U.S. GAAP (Generally Accepted Accounting Principles).

Currency

The cost center Currency field entry is determined automatically from the company code currency and cannot be changed in cost center master data. You assign company code currency during company code definition with Transaction OX02 or by following the IMG menu path ENTERPRISE STRUCTURE • DEFINITION • FINANCIAL ACCOUNTING • EDIT, COPY, DELETE, CHECK COMPANY CODE. Company code currency cannot be changed once transactional data exists in a productive company code.

Profit Center

A profit center receives postings made in parallel to a cost center and other master data such as orders. Profit Center Accounting is a separate ledger that enables reporting from a profit center responsibility point of view. You normally create profit centers in areas that generate revenue and have a responsible manager assigned. Operating results for a profit center can be analyzed using either the cost of sales approach or period accounting. The cost of sales approach may require maintenance of functional areas.

If Profit Center Accounting is active, you will receive a warning message if you do not specify a profit center, and all unassigned postings will go to a dummy profit center. You activate Profit Center Accounting during controlling area maintenance with configuration Transaction OKKP or by following the IMG menu path CONTROLLING • GENERAL CONTROLLING • ORGANIZATION • MAINTAIN CONTROLLING AREA.

Now that we've looked at the fields in the cost center Basic Data tab, let's examine the fields in the remaining tabs of the cost center master data.

3.2.3 Control

Select the Control tab in Figure 3.16 to display the screen shown in Figure 3.17.

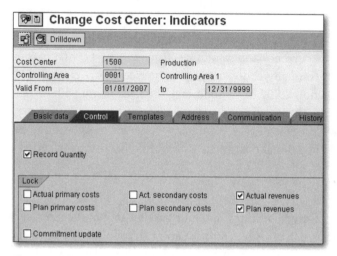

Figure 3.17 Cost Center Control Tab

The checkboxes in this screen are described below:

Record Quantity

Select the Record Quantity checkbox to define whether the system issues a message if you do not specify quantity or quantity unit during postings. Although quantities are usually recorded automatically during activity confirmation and inventory movements, it's also possible to post costs manually in FI and CO via cost elements and cost centers. This may be important if you are taking advantage of more advanced cost center reporting such as target cost analysis, which depends on quantities.

This checkbox has no effect on planning or on the identification of quantities in reports. You should also select this checkbox in the cost element to record quantities for the combination of cost center and cost element.

See Section 3.1.4 for a discussion of Record Quantity in cost element

Lock

Checkboxes in the Lock section in Figure 3.17 allow you to block postings of a certain type to a cost center. In the example shown in Figure 3.7, the cost center is blocked from receiving actual and plan revenues. These are typical default settings. Revenue can post statistically to the cost center if you deselect these indicators. You can report on statistical postings, but they are not included in the cost center total costs. Normally, revenues post directly to a profit center, whereas costs flow from postings to cost centers.

Example

A company structure changes and new cost centers are created and assigned in the standard hierarchy. To block all postings to previous cost centers, select all checkboxes in the Lock section of the Control tab.

Let's look at the fields in the Templates tab of a cost center.

3.2.4 Templates

Select the Templates tab in Figure 3.17 to display the screen shown in Figure 3.18.

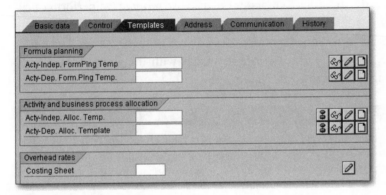

Figure 3.18 Cost Center Templates Tab

Templates provide you with flexibility when allocating overhead costs, and are part of the Activity-Based Costing component. Let's discuss the fields available in the Templates tab.

Formula Planning

Formula planning templates allow you to plan cost element and activity input values determined in many cost centers using a similar logic. For example, you may use the number of employees in a department as the basis for calculating personnel department planned costs. You can achieve this plan calculation with formulas in a template. You then evaluate the template with Transaction KPT6 or by following the menu path ACCOUNTING • CONTROLLING • COST CENTER ACCOUNTING • PLANNING • PLANNING AIDS • FORMULA PLANNING • COSTS AND STATISTICAL KEY FIGURES. The system displays the calculated plan values in a detailed list. You can display, edit, or create formula planning templates with the glasses, pencil, and new page icons shown in Figure 3.18.

Activity and Business Process Allocation

Functions and formulas

Activity and business process allocation templates allow you to allocate actual overhead costs between sender and receiver objects in a specific and dynamic way. Enter a template in either or both of these fields to assign this cost center as a receiver object. Templates use *functions* to access data that can be used as a basis to determine the allocation proportions dynamically. Templates can also use *formulas* to perform calculations on the data accessed by functions. The sending and receiving objects are determined by templates entered in these master data fields. You can display, edit, or create templates with the glasses, pencil, and new page icons shown in Figure 3.18.

> **Case Scenario**
>
> A dairy packaging facility handles large volumes of milk. The cost accountant determines that the most accurate way to allocate overhead costs to process orders is based on the volume of milk processed by a process order. A *function* within a template determines the volume from the Basic Data 1 view of the material master, and a *formula* uses this data to calculate the volume of milk processed by the order. The volume of milk is then used to calculate overhead costs allocated to process orders.

Overhead Rates

Read Chapter 6 for more information on costing sheets

Overhead Rates allow you to debit a cost center with overhead costs based on costing sheet configuration. You may be more familiar with debiting a manufacturing order or product cost collector with overhead costs via a costing sheet. You can debit a cost center with overhead costs in exactly the same way by entering the costing sheet in this cost center field.

3.2.5 Address and Communication

The Address tab contains street address text information for the cost center. These fields are for information purposes only and are not normally mandatory. It also contains a tax jurisdiction field that is used for determining tax rates in the USA.

The Communication tab contains telephone, fax, and other communication fields.

Entering cost center address and communication data is especially useful for large and global organizations. Now let's examine the History tab fields.

3.2.6 History

Select the History tab in Figure 3.18 to display the screen shown in Figure 3.19.

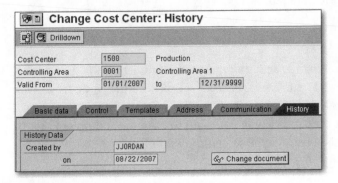

Figure 3.19 Cost Center History Tab

The History tab contains history and change information for a cost center.

History Data

This section allows you to determine which user created the cost center and when it was created.

Change Document

Click the Change document button to display a list of changed cost center fields. Double-click a line to display details of changes made to each field.

The entries in the fields in the History tab are determined automatically and cannot be manually changed.

Now that we've examined the purpose of cost centers and how the master data is set up and maintained, let's look at activity types.

3.3 Activity Type

Activity types describe activities provided by cost centers, and allow costs to be allocated to receiving objects such as manufacturing orders, product cost collectors, and other cost centers. We'll now examine the fields in the Basic Data tab.

3.3.1 Basic Data

You can view or change activity types with Transaction KL02 or by following the menu path ACCOUNTING • CONTROLLING • COST CENTER ACCOUNTING • MASTER DATA • ACTIVITY TYPE • INDIVIDUAL PROCESSING • CHANGE. Select the activity type you want to examine and press Enter to display the initial activity type screen shown in Figure 3.20.

The fields you maintain in the Basic data tab provide basic information together with control information about how the activity type can be used during confirmations and allocations. We'll discuss each field and checkbox in detail in the following sections.

Name and Description

These fields can be changed at any time and appear in the description in cost center and order reports. You can add long text to the description by clicking the pencil and paper icon (not shown in Figure 3.20).

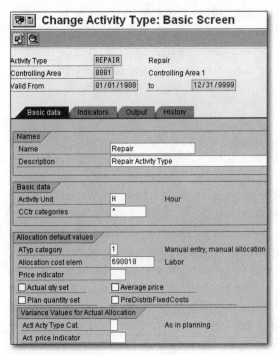

Figure 3.20 Activity Type Basic Screen

Activity Unit

The Activity Unit field in the Basic data section of Figure 3.20 is the unit that appears in the itemization in cost estimates and order costing. This can be different from the unit of measure recorded in work centers and operations in routings and manufacturing orders.

Refer to OSS Note 72442 for information on unit conversion

You cannot change the activity unit in the activity type master data if either plan or actual transactional data exists during the current fiscal year in any version. Even after you've deleted all activity type planning for all versions for the current fiscal year, you may still receive an error message due to dependent data. OSS Note 43230 recommends that you use report RKPLNC13 to delete control information stored in table CSSL after you've deleted all other activity type planning for all versions. You may then be able to change the activity unit in the activity type.

Cost Center Categories

You can restrict the use of the activity type to specific types of cost centers by making an entry in the CCtr categories (cost center categories) field. You can select any of the standard categories such as administration, production or sales, or you can define your own with configuration Transaction OKA2 or by following the IMG menu path CONTROLLING • COST CENTER ACCOUNTING • MASTER DATA • COST CENTERS • DEFINE COST CENTER CATEGORIES. Cost center categories allow you to, for example, prevent production activities from being incorrectly posted to administrative cost centers. You can enter multiple categories, up to a maximum of eight, or you can leave the assignment unrestricted by entering an asterisk (*). You can change the cost center category any time, even if transactional data exists during the current fiscal year.

Activity Type Category

The ATyp category (activity type category) determines whether and how an activity type is recorded and allocated. For example, for some activity types, you can allow certain activities to be allocated directly based on transactions, whereas others can be allocated automatically. Right-click in the ATyp category field and select Possible Entries to display the screen shown in Figure 3.21

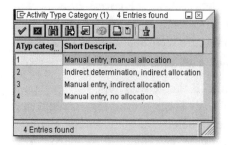

Figure 3.21 Activity Type Categories Possible Entries

Each activity type category is explained below:

▶ **Category 1: Manual entry, manual allocation**
With this category you manually plan activity quantities with activity input planning using Transaction KP26.

You manually allocate actual activity quantities based on business transactions such as activity confirmations. This is the category you normally use.

Direct allocation

▶ **Category 2: Indirect determination, indirect allocation and Category 3: Manual entry, indirect allocation**
These categories allow you to automatically plan and allocate *quantities*. This is similar to automatically allocating overhead *costs* to receiver cost centers with assessment and distribution cycles and segments. With these methods you carry out indirect activity allocation with Transaction KSCB, which allocates activity quantities and costs from sender to receiver cost centers based on tracing factors.

A tracing factor is a key for determining cost and quantity assignments

▶ **Category 4: Manual entry, no allocation**
With this category you manually plan activity quantities. You cannot specify receiver objects for this category, though you can calculate target costs.

The category you enter in the activity type is the default value for allocable activity type categories 1, 2, or 3 when planning activity prices and quantities with Transaction KP26. You can change this default value to a different allocable activity type category. You can only change nonallocable activity type category 4 to an allocable activity type category (or the other way round) if no dependent data exists.

Allocation Cost Element

The Allocation cost elem (allocation cost element) entry in Figure 3.20 determines the default value when you enter the planned activity price and quantity with Transaction KP26. You can overwrite the default cost element when planning for the first time. Once transactions occur, you cannot change this cost element.

Price Indicator and Actual Price Indicator

The Price indicator (planned price) and Act. price indicator (actual price) fields in Figure 3.20 indicate how the system automatically calculates the price of an activity for a cost center. If you do not set an actual price indicator, the system uses the planned price. Right-click in the Price indicator field and select Possible Entries to display the screen shown in Figure 3.22.

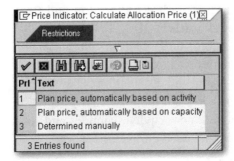

Figure 3.22 Price Indicator Possible Entries

When manually entering the planned activity price with Transaction KP26, you can also enter cost center planned activity and capacity quantities, which are used if the system automatically calculates planned activity rates.

▸ **Price indicator 1**: Activity price is calculated based on cost center planned activity quantity.

▸ **Price indicator 2**: Activity price is calculated based on cost center capacity. This setting usually leads to an under-absorption of the cost center because capacity is usually greater than planned activity quantity.

▸ **Price indicator 3**: This setting indicates that you plan the activity price manually and do not require automatic activity price calculation for this activity type.

The price indicator entered in the activity type defaults when you are planning activity prices and quantities with Transaction KP26. When you are planning for the first time this default value can be overwritten.

Actual Quantity Set

If this checkbox is selected, you must post a manual quantity in addition to the quantity with which the object is credited. You use this when the quantity leading to the credit of the object is to be determined indirectly, but the actual quantity from the sender view is already known.

Refer to OSS Note 760437 for more information on this checkbox

If the Actual qty set checkbox is set for the activity type with a direct activity allocation with Transaction KB21N, you have to manually post the actual activity quantity using Transaction KB51N.

Plan Quantity Set

If you select this checkbox, the corresponding checkbox will default as selected when planning activity prices and quantities with Transaction KP26, as shown in Figure 3.23.

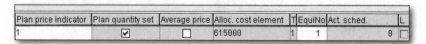

Plan price indicator	Plan quantity set	Average price	Alloc. cost element	T	EquiNo	Act. sched.		L
1	☑	☐	615000	1	1	0		☐

Figure 3.23 Plan Quantity Set Checkbox During Planning of Activity Price

Select this checkbox if you do not want to manually overwrite, during plan reconciliation, the planned activity quantity entered in the second column of Transaction KP26 (not shown in Figure 3.23) with the scheduled activity quantity automatically entered in the Act. sched. column of Transaction KP26. Scheduled activity quantities are transferred from Sales and Operations Planning, MRP, or Long-Term Planning with Transaction KSPP.

You can change the default setting for this checkbox in Transaction KP26 if you are planning for the first time.

Average Price

If you select this checkbox, the corresponding checkbox will default as selected when you are planning activity prices and quantities with Transaction KP26, as shown in Figure 3.24.

Plan price indicator	Plan quantity set	Average price	Alloc. cost element	T	EquiNo	Act. sched.	L
1	☐	☑	615000	1	1	0	☐

Figure 3.24 Average Price Checkbox During Planning of Activity Price

Select this checkbox if you want the automatically calculated activity price to remain constant for the entire fiscal year. You may decide to select this checkbox to keep the activity price constant for the fiscal year, which can make variance analysis easier. You can still manually change the price per period if necessary. You can change the default setting for this checkbox in Transaction KP26 if you are planning for the first time.

You can indicate that the activity price is to remain constant for the fiscal year either at the version level or the activity type or cost center:

▶ **Version**: In the Plan method field of the fiscal year dependant version, you can select average price.

▶ **Cost center or activity price**: If you have not defined an average activity price at the version level, you can define an average activity price for individual cost center or activity types.

You can change the default setting for this checkbox in Transaction KP26 if you are planning for the first time.

Predistribution of Fixed Costs

Select this checkbox if you want the activity type to be used in fixed cost predistribution. This is an advanced cost center functionality that requires a reconciled plan that calculates fixed and variable prices. It is important to do the planning as activity dependent for specific costs because this is the only way to calculate the variable portion of the price. A reconciled plan requires that you execute plan reconciliation, plan cost splitting, and plan price calculation.

The predistribution of fixed costs transaction distributes the planned fixed costs as actual fixed costs to the cost centers that planned the corresponding activity inputs. Predistribution of fixed costs avoids fixed-cost variances. This guarantees that planned fixed costs are covered regardless of the operating rate.

If the PreDistribFixedCosts checkbox is selected for an activity type, only the variable costs (variable prices multiplied by activity quantities) are debited to the receiver cost centers. Likewise, the sender cost center is credited only with its variable costs. You should not also set the Act. price indicator checkbox in the activity type because a predistribution of fixed costs contradicts an actual price calculation in the system.

> **Example**
>
> The predistribution of fixed costs is especially useful when you want to avoid fixed costs variances in service cost centers. Without predistribution of fixed costs, activity allocations with proportional service cost centers (especially operational fluctuations) can lead to incorrect over- or under-allocations of fixed costs.

Now that we've reviewed fields and settings in the activity type basic data screen, let's review the Indicators tab.

3.3.2 Indicators

Click the Indicators tab shown in Figure 3.20 to display the screen shown in Figure 3.25.

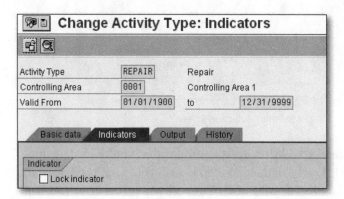

Figure 3.25 Activity Type Indicators Tab

The Lock indicator checkbox allows you to block against indirect activity allocation in plan and activity input planning. We discussed indirect activity allocation when looking at the activity type category in Section 3.3.1. Let's examine what is meant by *activity input planning*.

Input planning
Two types of input planning are available for cost centers:

- The most basic input planning that most companies use is primary cost planning for cost elements.
- A more advanced planning functionality is also available with planning Transaction KP06 or via the menu path ACCOUNTING • CONTROLLING • COST CENTER ACCOUNTING • PLANNING • COST AND ACTIVITY INPUTS • CHANGE. You will see a selection screen similar to the screen shown in Figure 3.26.

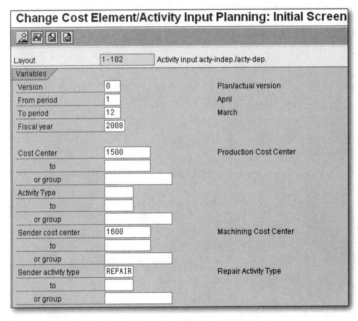

Figure 3.26 Activity Input Planning Selection Screen

Planner profile
To see this screen you'll first need to ensure that you're using planner profile SAPALL with Transaction KP04, and you may need to scroll across to Layout 1-102 using the right-pointing arrow icon in Figure 3.26. This layout allows you to plan quantities of a sender activity type from a sender cost center to a receiver cost center. The activity type Lock indicator checkbox shown in Figure 3.25 blocks against proceeding with this activity type entered in the Sender activity type field. If you attempt to proceed by clicking on the sun and two peaks icon, you'll encounter the message shown in Figure 3.27.

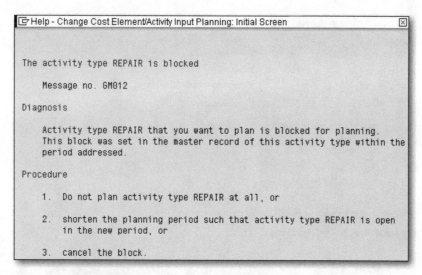

Figure 3.27 Blocked Activity Type Message

If you're using activity input planning, you'll normally set this indicator following plan reconciliation with Transaction KPSI. Plan reconciliation ensures that planned activity equals scheduled activity, and you activate the indicator to ensure that the planned quantity then remains unchanged.

Plan reconciliation

With the Lock indicator checkbox selected, you can still carry out actual postings, activity price changes, and planning other than activity input planning and indirect activity allocation in plan.

Now that we've reviewed the checkbox in the activity type indicators tab, let's review the Output tab.

3.3.3 Output

Select the Output tab in Figure 3.25 to display the screen shown in Figure 3.28.

The Output Unit is an alternative to the activity unit entered in the Basic Data tab. Select EDIT • ACTIVITY • OUTPUT from the menu bar when entering planned activity rates with Transaction KP26 to change between activity and output units.

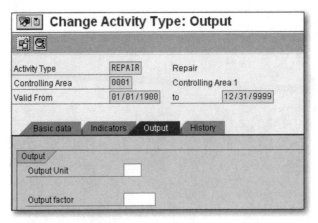

Figure 3.28 Activity Type Output Tab

> **Examples**
>
> One hour of activity type Machining produces 10 drills. The activity unit is Hours, and the alternative output unit is Pieces. You would specify an output factor of 10 in this case.
>
> It takes an average of 30 minutes to process a customer inquiry. The activity unit is Pieces, and the alternative output unit is Hours. The alternative output factor is 0.5.

The system can automatically derive the output from the scheduled activity using the alternative output unit and the alternative output factor.

You can also use the alternative output unit with direct internal activity allocation and when you create cycles for indirect internal activity allocation.

Now that we've reviewed the Output tab, let's look at the activity type History tab.

3.3.4   History

Click the History tab in Figure 3.28 to display the screen shown in Figure 3.29.

The History tab contains history and change information.

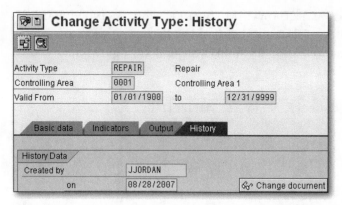

Figure 3.29 Activity Type History Tab

History Data

This section allows you to determine which user created the activity type and when it was created.

Change Document

Click the Change document button to display a list of changed activity type fields. Double-click a line to display details of changes made to each field. The entries in the fields in the History tab are determined automatically and cannot be changed manually.

Now that we've examined activity types and how they are set up and maintained, let's look at statistical key figures.

3.4   Statistical Key Figure

Statistical key figures define values describing cost centers, profit centers, and overhead orders such as number of employees or minutes of long-distance phone calls. You can use statistical key figures as the tracing factor for periodic transactions such as cost center distribution or assessment. You can post both planned and actual statistical key figures.

You can view or change statistical key figures with Transaction KK02 or by following the menu path ACCOUNTING • CONTROLLING • COST CENTER

ACCOUNTING • MASTER DATA • STATISTICAL KEY FIGURES • INDIVIDUAL PRO-CESSING • CHANGE. Select the statistical key figure you want to examine and press Enter to display the initial statistical key figure screen shown in Figure 3.30.

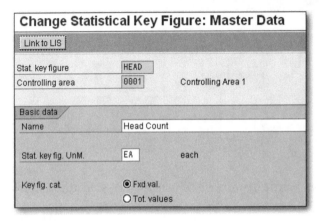

Figure 3.30 Statistical Key Figure Master Data

The first fields you maintain are Name and Stat. key fig. UnM. (statistical key figure unit of measure).

You define the statistical key figure category as a fixed or total value by selecting either Fxd val. or Tot. values.

Fixed value   The fixed value, such as Employees, is carried over from the period in which it is entered to all subsequent periods of the same fiscal year. You need to enter a new posting only when the value changes. The fiscal year total is an average of the period totals.

Total value   The total value, such as Long-Distance Calls, is not transferred to the following period but is entered each period. The fiscal year total is the sum of all the period values.

Now that we've examined the statistical key figure fields, let's review what we've covered in this Controlling master data chapter.

3.5   Summary

In this chapter we discussed Controlling master data relevant to Product Cost Controlling including cost elements, cost centers, activity types, and statistical key figures. We examined the master data fields and indicators and their roles in identifying, collecting, and allocating costing within the Controlling component.

Now that we've examined Controlling master data in this chapter, we'll look at material master data in Chapter 4 and logistics master data in Chapter 5.

A material master contains all of the information required to manage a material, including settings that cost estimates access to determine the cost to purchase or manufacture the material.

4   Material Master Data

Now that we've examined Controlling concepts and master data, let's look at material master data. The material master contains all of the information required to manage a material. Information is stored in views, each corresponding to a department or area of business responsibility. Views conveniently group information together for users in different departments, for example, sales and purchasing. The three views of particular interest for Product Cost Controlling are MRP, Costing, and Accounting. These views are plant specific, so plants can have different values for fields in these views. Material Requirements Planning (MRP) guarantees material availability by monitoring stocks and generating planned orders for procurement and production.

Cost estimates typically follow MRP settings when the cost to procure or manufacture a material is calculated. For example, the components MRP determines to be necessary to manufacture an assembly are also used by a cost estimate to calculate the material cost of the assembly. This is why this chapter examines the MRP as well as the costing and accounting sections of the material master.

Whereas most material master views contain some fields of interest to product costing, the MRP, Controlling, and Accounting views contain multiple fields that cost estimates access to determine the cost to purchase or manufacture the material. We'll now examine each of these views in detail, starting with the MRP view.

4.1 MRP 1 View

MRP guarantees
material avail-
ability

You can view or change material master views with Transaction MM02 or by following the menu path LOGISTICS • PRODUCTION • MASTER DATA • MATERIAL MASTER • MATERIAL • CHANGE • IMMEDIATELY. Select the MRP 1 tab to display the screen shown in Figure 4.1.

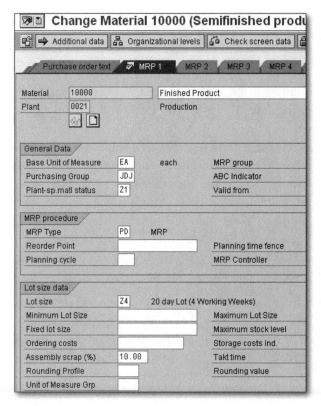

Figure 4.1 Material Master MRP 1 View

The fields most relevant to costing are located in the General Data and Lot size data sections. We'll consider each section in turn.

4.1.1 General Data

In the General Data section let's begin examining fields relevant to Product Cost Controlling.

Base Unit of Measure

Stocks of the material are managed in the base unit of measure. The system converts all quantities you enter in other units of measure (alternative units of measure) to the base unit of measure. You can use alternative units of measure, for example, during purchasing and sales.

Inventory is managed in the base unit of measure

> **Note**
>
> Enter alternative units of measure in the material master by clicking the Additional data button shown in Figure 4.1 and then selecting the Units of measure tab.

Plant-Specific Material Status

An entry in the Plant-sp.matl status (plant-specific material status) field determines if the material is costed. Plant-specific material status can also be used for purposes other than costing, such as to issue a warning or error message when a purchase or production order is created for discontinued materials. You can view the list of possible settings behind plant-specific material status with configuration Transaction OMS4 or by following the IMG menu path CONTROLLING • PRODUCT COST CONTROLLING • PRODUCT COST PLANNING • MATERIAL COST ESTIMATE WITH QUANTITY STRUCTURE • SETTINGS FOR QUANTITY STRUCTURE CONTROL • MATERIAL DATA • CHECK MATERIAL STATUS.

> **Note**
>
> You usually set a different plant-specific material status for discontinued and obsolete materials:
>
> ▸ Discontinued materials will be replaced by another material once the remaining inventory is consumed. You can allow a discontinued material to be costed, but you may want to issue a warning or error message when creating a purchase order. A discontinued parts section in the MRP 4 view allows you to enter the material number that the system can use in materials planning to replace the material to be discontinued once its warehouse stock is depleted.

> ▶ Obsolete materials are generally not intended for further use. This can arise, for example, if the material is out of date or has a design problem. Typically, in this situation you may decide to scrap or sell the remaining inventory. In the case of an obsolete material you can set the plant-specific material status to display either a warning or an error message during costing if the material is contained in the bill of material of an active assembly.

The plant-specific material status can also be used to restrict the use of new parts during different stages of product development.

Valid From

The Valid from field indicates the date from which the plant-specific material status is valid. For example, if a material is blocked from purchasing with the material status, no purchase orders can be created after the valid from date.

Now let's examine the fields most relevant to costing in the Lot size data section of the MRP 1 view.

4.1.2 Lot Size Data

Lot size is a quantity to produce or procure

MRP needs to determine proposed quantities and dates for manufacturing and purchase orders so a company can meet the needs of independent requirements such as customer sales orders. MRP uses information in the Lot size data fields of the MRP 1 view to calculate the quantity and date of proposed orders.

> **Case Scenario**
>
> A customer places an order for a quantity of 120 items, due for delivery one year from the date the sales order was placed. MRP needs to determine how many purchase orders to propose for components and manufacturing orders for assemblies, the quantity (lot size) for each, and the date each should be created. This depends on the quantity of components in stock and work center capacity and requirements generated by other sales orders. In this example, one manufacturing order for a quantity of 120 could be proposed sometime during the next year, or one order with a quantity of 10 could be proposed every month over the year.

Ordering Costs

Ordering costs are incurred independently of lot size for each purchase or production order over and above the purchase order price or production costs. Ordering costs are only used to calculate the lot size in an optimum lot-sizing procedure. This groups requirements from several periods to form a lot, in which an optimum cost ratio is determined between lot size–independent costs and storage costs. You must specify the ordering costs in the company code currency of the plant.

Assembly Scrap

A value entered in the Assembly scrap (%) field indicates the percentage output from manufacturing orders that does not meet required production quality standards. This number should be determined from your production statistics of scrap rates and updated prior to each costing run if the statistics change.

Assembly scrap increases MRP and costing assembly quantities

A *costing run* is a collective processing of cost estimates, which we'll discuss in detail in Chapter 10. The Assembly scrap (%) field does not appear in any other master data. The Net ID indicator on the bill of material (BOM) item Basic data tab can be used to ignore assembly scrap for a component. A BOM is a structured hierarchy of materials required to manufacture an assembly.

Now that we've discussed the fields and indicators relevant to Product Cost Controlling in the MRP 1 view, let's examine the MRP 2 view.

> **Note**
>
> Four MRP tabs are used to handle the MRP configuration: MRP 1, MRP 2, MRP 3, and MRP 4. If all of the MRP fields were on one tab, you would need to scroll to see them, so this was addressed by creating four tabs.

4.2 MRP 2 View

Select the MRP 2 tab in Figure 4.1 to display the screen shown in Figure 4.2.

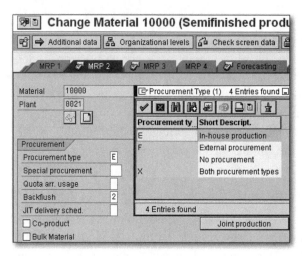

Figure 4.2 Material Master MRP 2 View

MRP guarantees material availability by monitoring stocks and requirements and generating planned orders for procurement and production. A cost estimate needs data on how the material is procured as the first step in determining the cost of the material, so let's take a look at procurement types.

Procurement Type

Procurement type indicates whether a material is produced in-house or procured externally

To display a list of possible entries for the Procurement type field, right-click in the field and select Possible Entries. A list of possible procurement types is displayed as shown in Figure 4.2. Let's discuss them now:

▶ **In-house production (E)**
An entry here means the system will search for production information such as a BOM and routing. A *routing* is a list of tasks containing standard activity times required to perform operations to build an assembly. We'll discuss BOMs and routings in more detail in Chapter 5.

▶ **External procurement (F)**
An entry here means the system will search for purchasing information, usually from a purchasing info record that contains purchasing information for a material from a vendor.

▶ **Both procurement types (X)**

An entry here means a planned order (proposed order) generated by MRP can be converted into either a production order or a purchase requisition. A cost estimate will be based on a BOM and routing if they are available; that is, the procurement type will behave as in-house production. You can make the cost estimate treat the material as though it's externally procured with an entry in the special procurement type field, as discussed in the next section.

Special Procurement Type

The Special procurement field found immediately below the Procurement type field as shown in Figure 4.2 more closely defines the procurement type. For example, it may indicate if the item is produced in another plant and transferred to the plant you are looking at. A cost estimate normally follows the MRP special procurement type when determining costs. However, an entry in the special procurement type for costing field in the Costing 1 view will be used by costing instead of the MRP setting.

Special procurement type more closely defines the procurement type

> **Note**
>
> The special procurement type can be used to override the procurement type if required. For example, if you enter a special procurement type that contains an external procurement type (F) in configuration Transaction OMD9, the material will behave as if it's externally procured, regardless of the procurement type setting.

Co-Product Checkbox

Select the Co-product checkbox if this material is a valuated product that is produced simultaneously with one or more other products. Selecting this checkbox allows you to assign the proportion of costs this material will receive in relation to other co-products within an apportionment structure. An apportionment structure defines how costs are distributed to co-products. The Co-product checkbox is also located in the Costing 1 view of the material master.

A co-product is produced at the same time as other products

Joint Production

Joint production involves the simultaneous production of many materials in a single production process. Clicking the Joint production button allows you to assign apportionment structures, which define how costs are distributed between co-products. You must first select the Co-product checkbox to assign the apportionment structures. The Joint production button is also located in the Costing 1 view of the material master.

Bulk Material Checkbox

Bulk materials are not relevant for individual costing in a cost estimate, and are instead expensed directly to a cost center

Select the Bulk Material checkbox if materials, such as washers or grease, are made available directly at a work center. Bulk materials are not relevant for costing in a cost estimate, and are instead expensed directly to a cost center. The cost can be included in the cost of sales as part of an overhead rate.

The Bulk Material checkbox can also be maintained in the BOM item. The indicator in the BOM item has higher priority (we'll examine BOM items in more detail in Chapter 5). If a material is always used as a bulk material, select the Bulk Material checkbox in the material master. If a material is only used as a bulk material in individual cases, select the checkbox in the BOM item.

Now that we've discussed the fields and indicators relevant to Product Cost Controlling in the MRP 2 view, let's examine the MRP 4 view.

> **Note**
>
> The MRP 3 view contains fields on configurable products which is a specialized topic that we'll discuss in Chapter 19.

4.3 MRP 4 View

Select the MRP 4 tab in Figure 4.2 to display the screen shown in Figure 4.3.

The MRP 4 view contains further BOM and production version information. A *production version* is a unique combination of BOM, routing, and production line. A production line is used in repetitive manufacturing, and typically consists of one or more work centers. Let's examine the fields of interest to Product Cost Controlling.

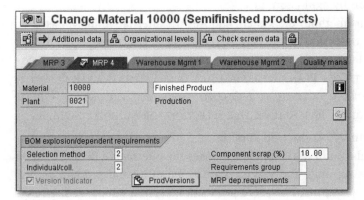

Figure 4.3 Material Master MRP 4 View

Selection Method

The Selection method field determines the selection of the alternative BOM when requirements are exploded by MRP and costing. To display a list of possible entries, left-click in the field and then right-click and select Possible Entries. A list of possible alternate BOM selection methods is displayed, as shown in Figure 4.4.

The selection method determines BOM selection by MRP and costing

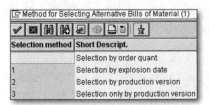

Figure 4.4 Possible Selection Methods for Alternative BOMs

The four possible BOM selection methods are described below:

▶ **Selection by order quant.**
With this method, the system chooses the alternative BOM based on a lot-size range that matches the order quantity, depending on the lot-size range and validity date range of the BOM. A cost estimate selects a BOM with a lot-size range that matches the costing lot size and

validity date. The costing lot size field is located in the Costing 1 view, and is discussed in more detail in Section 4.4 Costing 1 View.

▸ **Selection by explosion date**
With this method, the system chooses the alternative BOM based on validity dates you can display with configuration Transaction OPPP or via the IMG menu path CONTROLLING • PRODUCT COST CONTROLLING • PRODUCT COST PLANNING • MATERIAL COST ESTIMATE WITH QUANTITY STRUCTURE • SETTINGS FOR QUANTITY STRUCTURE CONTROL • BOM SELECTION • CHECK ALTERNATIVE SELECTION FOR MULTIPLE BOM.

▸ **Selection by production version**
With this method, the system chooses the alternative BOM based on the lot-size range and validity date range of a valid production version. A cost estimate selects a production version with a lot-size range that matches the costing lot size and validity date.

▸ **Selection only by production version**
With this method, the system chooses the alternative BOM defined in the valid production version, depending on the lot-size range and validity date range of the production version. If no production version is found, no manufacturing orders or cost estimates can be created. A cost estimate selects a production version with a lot-size range that matches the costing lot size and validity date.

Note

If the alternate BOM selection method is based on the production version and two valid production versions are available with matching lot size and validity date ranges, a cost estimate will automatically select the first production version. For example, if production versions 001 and 002 are both valid, a cost estimate will automatically select production version 001 to determine the quantity structure.

Now that we've discussed the alternate BOM Selection method field, let's examine the Individual/Coll. field, which determines if dependent requirements are considered individually or separately.

Dependent Requirements Indicator for Individual and Collective Requirements

To display a list of possible entries for the dependent requirements for the Individual/Coll. (individual and collective requirements) field, as shown in Figure 4.5, right-click in the field and select Possible Entries.

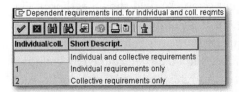

Figure 4.5 Dependent Requirements Indicator for Individual and Collective Requirements

This indicator determines whether the dependent (lower-level) requirements of an assembly can be grouped together (collective) or must be treated separately (individual). The three possible settings are discussed below:

> Dependent requirements indicator

- ▶ **Individual and collective requirements (blank)**
  This setting offers the most flexibility, and indicates that the component is planned the same way as the higher-level assembly.

- ▶ **Individual requirements only (1)**
  This setting means the material is specially manufactured or procured for a sales order. An individual requirement is created only if the higher-level material does not create a collective requirement.

- ▶ **Collective requirements only (2)**
  This setting means the material is produced or procured for various requirements and offers the advantage of economy of scale because you can group together requirements of higher-level assemblies for lower-level assemblies and components.

You can also maintain this indicator when customizing the BOM item basic data with Transaction OS17, which takes priority over the MRP 4 view setting.

You can ensure that the system uses the costing lot size of the highest-level material for lower-level materials with individual requirements with the Pass On Lot Size field on the Qty Struct. tab in the costing variant configuration transaction OKKN. We'll look at this indicator in more detail in Chapter 9.

Component Scrap

A value entered in the Component scrap (%) field shown earlier in Figure 4.3 indicates the percentage of this component quantity that does not meet required production quality standards before being inserted in the production process. This number should be determined by your production statistics of component scrap rates and updated prior to each costing run if the statistics change. The Component scrap (%) field can also be maintained in the BOM item. An entry in the Component scrap (%) field in the BOM item takes priority over an entry in the material master.

Version Indicator and Production Versions

The Version Indicator and ProdVersions (production versions) button are also located in the Costing 1 view, and are discussed in more detail in the next section, Section 4.4.

Now that we've discussed the fields and indicators relevant to Product Cost Controlling in the MRP 4 view, let's examine the Costing 1 view fields.

4.4   Costing 1 View

The Costing views are generally used by members of the Controlling or management reporting team. Select the Costing 1 tab to display the screen shown in Figure 4.6.

This screen is divided into two sections, General data and Quantity structure data. To make the discussion easier to follow, we'll consider the fields in each section individually. First, let's look at the fields in the General data section.

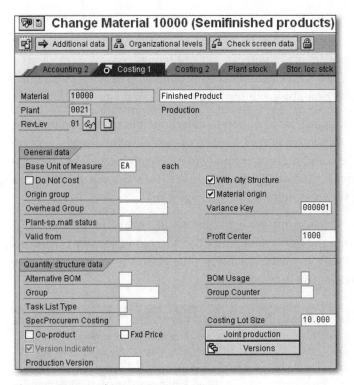

Figure 4.6 Material Master Costing 1 View

4.4.1   General Data

The General data section contains fields relating to costing, and cost estimates in general, that cannot be included in any of the more specific sections.

Do Not Cost

The Do Not Cost checkbox controls whether a cost estimate is created for the material. With the checkbox selected, the material is excluded from selection and BOM explosion in the costing run selection screen accessed with Transaction CK40N (we'll examine costing runs in more detail in Chapter 10). If the material is included as a component in another cost estimate, the valuation price is determined through the valuation variant, as discussed in Chapter 8.

The Do Not Cost checkbox controls if a cost estimate is created

Origin Group

An origin group separately identifies materials assigned to the same cost element

An *origin group* enables you to separately identify materials assigned to the same cost element so you can assign them to separate cost components. A *cost component* identifies costs of similar types, such as material, labor, and overhead, by grouping together cost elements.

The origin group can also be used to determine the calculation base for overhead. A *calculation base* is a group of cost elements to which overhead is applied, and is also a component of a costing sheet that summarizes the rules for allocating overhead. We'll discuss calculation bases and costing sheets in more detail in Chapter 6.

You can view origin group configuration settings with Transaction OKZ1 or by following the IMG menu path CONTROLLING • PRODUCT COST CONTROLLING • PRODUCT COST PLANNING • BASIC SETTINGS FOR MATERIAL COSTING • DEFINE ORIGIN GROUPS.

Case Scenario

In the pharmaceutical industry, the active pharmaceutical ingredient (API) is by far the highest-cost ingredient. If the same cost element is used for all ingredients, it's possible to identify the API as a separate cost component by creating an API origin group, populating all API material masters with the API origin group, and then creating an additional API cost component that includes the origin group with cost component structure configuration Transaction OKTZ. A cost component structure groups cost elements into cost components.

Overhead Group

An Overhead group allows you to apply different overhead percentages to individual or groups of materials. It's also possible to use the same overhead percentage rate across all materials in a plant, reducing the need for overhead groups. This minimizes the maintenance required for regularly updating rates associated with each overhead group.

Case Scenario

A company realized it was possible to assign different overhead percentage rates to individual materials within a plant, and created a separate overhead group for each family of materials.

This required setting up and maintaining a large overhead rate table with hundreds of entries in a costing sheet. Within a year the client realized that any potential gains from increased overhead accuracy were offset by the maintenance time required to calculate the percentages and update the costing sheet. Subsequently, the client changed to a simplified method of allocating overhead by using the same percentage across all materials within the plant.

Plant-Specific Material Status and Valid From

The Plant-sp. matl status (plant-specific material status) and Valid from fields are maintained in the MRP 1 view and were discussed in detail in Section 4.1.

With Quantity Structure Checkbox

You should select the With Qty Structure checkbox if you create cost estimates with quantity structure, that is, with BOMs and routings, or procure materials from other plants with a special procurement type.

The With Qty Structure checkbox allows more detailed reporting

If you create an individual cost estimate for a material with this checkbox deselected, the outcome depends on the transaction you're using to create the cost estimate, as follows:

- If you attempt to create an individual cost estimate with Transaction CK11N, the system will issue a warning message stating that the With Qty Structure checkbox is deselected. A cost estimate with quantity structure will still be created.

- If you attempt to create a cost estimate with costing run Transaction CK40N, the system will not consider the quantity structure, and will treat the material as a raw material without quantity structure. The system will search for a price as indicated by the valuation variant search strategy, typically a purchasing info record price or planned price entry in the Costing 2 view.

Tip

If you're not sure how this checkbox works, it's usually safest to leave it selected, or you may encounter unexpected costing run results as explained in the previous list.

One of the main uses of this checkbox is to save the system time searching for cost estimates without quantity structure (unit costing) when you are initially developing new or improved products and you don't yet have a BOM or routing created. *Unit costing* is a method of costing that does not use BOMs or routings. If you aren't using unit costing, deselecting the checkbox will actually slow the system down while searching for cost estimates without quantity structure that don't exist.

Tip

There's an advantage to leaving the With Qty Structure checkbox selected for raw materials: Many plants transfer raw materials from plant to plant using the special procurement type in the MRP 2 view as discussed in Section 4.2. A costing run considers this plant-to-plant transfer as part of a quantity structure and ignores the special procurement type for materials with the With Qty Structure checkbox deselected.

Next, let's look at the Material origin checkbox.

Material Origin

You should select the Material origin checkbox for all cost-critical components. This checkbox determines if the material number is displayed in detailed Controlling reports. This is one of the most important indicators for providing greater visibility of the causes of production variances. If you have already created material master records without the Material origin checkbox selected, you can use report RKHKMAT0 to select the checkbox automatically.

Variance Key

Variances are calculated only on manufacturing orders or product cost collectors containing a variance key. This key is defaulted from the Costing 1 view when manufacturing orders or product cost collectors are created. The variance key also determines if the value of scrap is subtracted from actual costs before production variances are determined.

Profit Center

A profit center receives postings made in parallel to master data such as cost centers and orders. Profit Center Accounting is a separate ledger that enables reporting from a profit center point of view. You normally create profit centers based on areas in a company that generate revenue with a responsible manager assigned. The Profit Center field is also displayed in the Sales, MRP, and Plant Data material master views.

If Profit Center Accounting is active, you will receive a warning message if you do not specify a profit center during a posting, and all unassigned postings will be made to a dummy profit center. You activate Profit Center Accounting with configuration Transaction OKKP, which maintains the controlling area.

4.4.2 Quantity Structure Data

Now that we've examined the fields in the General data section of the Costing 1 view, let's consider the fields in the Quantity structure data section, as shown in Figure 4.7.

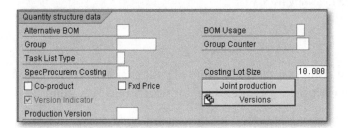

Figure 4.7 Quantity Structure Data Section

A *quantity structure* typically consists of a BOM and a routing. A cost estimate determines the quantity structure either from costing variant configuration, as discussed in Chapter 8, or from the production version, which is accessed by clicking the Versions button.

A quantity structure consists of a BOM and a routing

You usually do not need to make any entries in the screen shown in Figure 4.7, except for the mandatory Costing Lot Size field, which we'll examine later in this section. However, you can direct the cost estimate to use BOMs and routings independently of those determined automatically by MRP or costing configuration for individual materials by making entries in this screen. Let's examine each field in detail and look at case scenarios to show how these fields are used.

Alternative BOM

There can be multiple methods of manufacturing an assembly and many possible BOMs. The Alternative BOM field allows you to identify one BOM in a BOM group. A BOM group is a collection of BOMs for a product or number of similar products.

> **Example**
>
> Let's assume a production department sources a particular component from overseas, but in the near future the component will be sourced locally at a lower cost. For most of the following year the assembly will be manufactured with the cheaper local component, but the cost estimate would normally set the plan cost based on the present method of procurement (with the assembly with the more expensive overseas component) for the entire fiscal year. In this case, you can enter the alternative BOM containing the locally sourced component to ensure that the cost estimate incorporates this cheaper component for the following fiscal year.

BOM Usage

BOM usage determines a specific section of your company, such as production, engineering/design, or costing, for which a BOM is valid.

> **Case Scenario**
>
> You use the same material in the production and costing departments in your company. However, for each department you configure a separate BOM controlled by the BOM Usage field, as follows:
>
> ▶ The *production* BOM contains items that are relevant to production. These items are copied to the planned (proposed) order when MRP runs. Dependent items are generated, and the planned order is subsequently copied to the production order.
>
> ▶ The *costing* BOM contains items that are relevant when determining the material costs of a product. The costing BOM cannot be used for production.

You normally copy the costing BOM from the production BOM every year prior to the main costing run. If a BOM with usage of costing exists, cost estimates will typically refer to this instead of the production BOM. This means that changes in the production BOM during the year will only be reflected in costing after the costing BOM is copied from the production BOM.

It is not common to use costing BOMs because normally you want to see changes in production BOMs reflected in costing if new cost estimates are created during the year.

Group

A task list group identifies routings that have different operations (production steps) for one material. Just as you can create alternative BOMs to record different hierarchies of components to manufacture an assembly, you can maintain routings containing different production steps for an assembly. A task list group entered in this field is used by a cost estimate to determine activity costs for this material, independent of the task list group used by production.

Group Counter

A group counter identifies a unique routing within a task list group.

Example

Group counters can be used to identify different lot-size ranges. For example, a manufacturer can machine a work piece either on a conventional machine or on a numerically controlled (NC) machine. The NC machine has a longer setup time than the conventional machine, although machining costs are considerably less. Therefore, whether you use an NC machine will depend on the lot size. The different machines can be set up on different routings for the same material, depending on lot size. Another term for the different sequence of operations depending on lot size is *alternative sequence*.

Task List Type

Task list type classifies a task list according to its functionality. Left-click in the Task List Type field shown earlier in Figure 4.7, and then right-click and select Possible Entries to display the list shown in Figure 4.8.

Task list type classifies a task list

Type	Description
0	Standard Network
2	Master Recipe
3	Rough-cut Planning Profile
A	General maintenance task list
E	Equipment Task List
M	Reference Rate Routing
N	Routing
Q	Inspection Plan
R	Rate Routing
S	Reference Operation Set
T	Task List for Funct. Location

Figure 4.8 Task List Type Possible Entries

If you make an entry in this field, the system will search for an existing task list of this type, or a suitable production version containing a task list of this type, when creating a cost estimate. If a suitable task list or production version is found, it will be used for the cost estimate, independent of the production process. If a suitable task list or production version is not found, you will receive a warning message indicating that the material will be costed without reference to a routing or production version. The system will attempt to cost the material based on the valuation strategy contained in the costing variant, which we discuss in detail in Chapter 8.

> **Tip**
>
> Task list types 3, A, E, and T are not relevant to costing and will result in an error message if you attempt to enter them in this field.

Special Procurement Type for Costing

Cost estimates use the special procurement type for costing in preference to the MRP setting

An entry in the SpecProcurem Costing (special procurement type for costing) field shown earlier in Figure 4.7 will be used by costing, and an entry in the equivalent field in the MRP 2 view maintained by production will be ignored. The special procurement type for costing is used to more closely define the procurement type, which determines whether a material is produced in-house or procured externally.

Case Scenario

Let's assume that the procurement type is set to Both procurement types (X) in the MRP 2 view, and a BOM and routing are maintained so the material can be produced in-house as required. However, the cost estimate needs to be based on the price maintained in a purchasing info record, because the material is procured externally (purchased) in most cases. To handle this requirement, you can maintain a *special* procurement type with an external procurement type F setting in configuration Transaction OMD9 (maintain special procurement type). If you enter this special procurement type in the Costing 1 view, a cost estimate will first search for a purchasing info record price. Special procurement type 20 supplied with the standard SAP system contains procurement type F.

Costing Lot Size

The Costing Lot Size field determines the material quantity on which cost estimate calculations are based. This is a mandatory field because a cost estimate must base cost calculations on a quantity. When a standard cost estimate is created, it uses the costing lot size value in the Costing 1 view by default. You have an opportunity to manually change the costing lot size defaulted from the Costing 1 view when creating a single cost estimate with Transaction CK11N. You don't get this opportunity when creating cost estimates collectively with costing run Transaction CK40N.

Costing lot size controls the quantity on which cost estimates are based

The costing lot size should be set as close as possible to actual purchase and production quantities to reduce lot size variance. Unfavorable variances may result if a production order is created for a quantity less than the costing lot size. Setup time is needed to prepare equipment and machinery for production of assemblies, and it is generally the same, regardless of the quantity produced. Setup time spread over a smaller production quantity increases the unit cost. This also applies to externally procured items, because vendors usually quote higher unit prices for smaller quantities.

A *cost estimate* typically calculates the cost of components at the lowest level in an assembly based on the costing lot size in the Costing 1 view of each component material master. The costing results are progressively converted to the costing lot size of the materials of the next-highest level to finally calculate the material costs for the finished product.

It's possible to calculate the costs for all materials in a multi-level BOM using the costing lot size of the highest material, based on a setting on the Quantity Structure tab in the costing variant with configuration Transaction OKKN. This function is typically used in sales order costing, and is discussed in more detail in Chapter 19.

> **Tip**
>
> The costing lot size cannot be smaller than the price unit. Because costing is based on the costing lot size, this combination could result in rounding problems when determining a new price. You receive an error message if you attempt to enter this combination in the material master.

Co-Product Checkbox and Joint Production Button

We already examined details of the Co-product checkbox and Joint production button in the MRP 1 view in Section 4.1, so let's move on to the Fxd Price (fixed price co-product) checkbox.

Fixed Price Co-Product

A fixed price co-product has a preset price

Select the Fxd Price (fixed price co-product) checkbox shown earlier in Figure 4.7 if you do not want a co-product material to be costed using a joint production process. This indicates that a preset price is to be used for a co-product instead of determining the costs using an apportionment method. The price for a fixed price co-product is either taken from a cost estimate without quantity structure or from the material master. You can only select this checkbox if you have also set the co-product indicator for the material. Fixed price co-products are shown in a cost estimate itemization with category M with negative quantities and values, instead of the category A you typically see for normal co-products.

In the next section we'll examine production versions and how they are associated with a material.

Production Version

Click the Versions button shown earlier in Figure 4.7 to display a list of production versions, as shown in Figure 4.9.

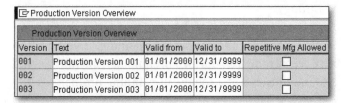

Figure 4.9 Production Version Overview

Production versions assigned to a material are listed in the Production Version Overview screen. You can assign many production versions to a material, and at least one production version must be assigned if you are using repetitive manufacturing or product cost collectors.

> You can assign many production versions to a material

Repetitive manufacturing eliminates the need for production or process orders in manufacturing environments with production lines and long production runs. It reduces the work involved in production control and simplifies confirmations and goods receipt postings. Select the Repetitive Mfg Allowed checkbox to allow a production version to be used in repetitive manufacturing.

Double-click Production Version 001 in Figure 4.9 to display the Production Version Details screen shown in Figure 4.10.

The Basic data section contains fields that allow you to lock the production version if required so it cannot be used, set the minimum and maximum lot size, and enter valid from and to dates.

In the Planning data section you can assign each production version to up to three work centers for different planning levels. Operations are carried out at a work center, which can represent, for example, machines, production lines, or employees. Your choices in this section are as follows:

▸ **Detailed planning**
Lets you determine which routing is used for materials requirements planning, product costing, and production orders.

▸ **Rate-based planning**
Lets you determine which rate routing is used in repetitive manufacturing.

▶ **Rough-Cut Planning**

Lets you determine in preliminary planning which rough-cut planning profile is used for sales and operations planning. If you want to create capacity requirements during preliminary planning, you should use a routing instead of a rough-cut planning profile.

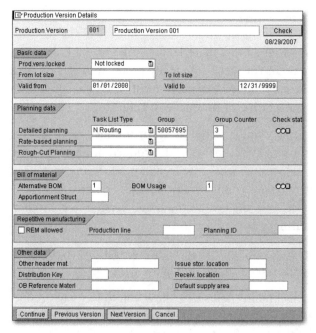

Figure 4.10 Production Version Details Screen

In the Bill of material section, you can do the following:

▶ Define an alternative BOM. There can be multiple methods of manufacturing an assembly, and many possible BOMs. The alternative BOM allows you to identify one BOM in a BOM group.

▶ Define the BOM usage that determines a specific section of your company, such as production, engineering/design, or costing, for which the BOM is valid.

▶ Enter an apportionment structure in the Apportionment Struct field. An apportionment structure defines how costs are distributed to co-products. The system uses the apportionment structure to create a settlement rule that distributes costs from an order header to the co-products. For each co-product, the system generates a further settlement rule that assigns the costs distributed to the order item to stock.

Now that we've discussed production versions, let's examine the last field in the Costing 1 view shown earlier in Figure 4.7, the Production Version field, which indicates the production version to be costed. A production version entered in this field is used by cost estimates rather than the production version used by the manufacturing process. If there is no entry in this field, costing will determine the production version automatically, provided you have configured the appropriate setting in the alternate BOM selection method screen in the MRP 4 view, as discussed earlier in Section 4.3.

Costing uses a production version entered in the Costing 1 view

Now that we've examined the fields in the Costing 1 view, let's look at the fields in the Costing 2 view.

4.5   Costing 2 View

Select the Costing 2 tab in Figure 4.6 to display the screen shown in Figure 4.11.

Figure 4.11 Material Master Costing 2 View

This screen is divided into three sections: Standard Cost Estimate, Planned prices, and Valuation Data. To make the discussion easier to follow, we'll consider the fields in each section individually. Let's first look at the Standard Cost Estimate section.

4.5.1 Standard Cost Estimate

Click the cost estimate buttons to quickly access cost estimates

You can click the Future, Current and Previous cost estimate buttons to display the corresponding cost estimates, if they exist. If a cost estimate exists, you'll notice an entry in the Period/Fiscal Year row under the corresponding cost estimate button. For example, in Figure 4.11, a current cost estimate exists that was released in period 10/fiscal year 2008. No future or previous cost estimate exists at this stage because there is no corresponding entry in the row under these buttons.

> **Tip**
>
> Many cost estimates can exist for a material. It can be difficult to locate the most recently released standard cost estimate using other methods if many cost estimates exist. The quickest way to display the current released standard cost estimate is via the Current cost estimate button in the Costing 2 view of the material master (Transaction MM03).

The cost estimate fields in the Standard Cost Estimate section are updated when a standard cost estimate is marked and released. When you first create and save a standard cost estimate, inventory valuation is not changed. The Future Planned price field is populated when a cost estimate is marked.

A *marked* cost estimate is a proposed standard price that has no effect on inventory valuation. You can create new standard cost estimates and mark them as many times as you like during a period, as long as a standard cost estimate has not been released during the period. This gives you an opportunity to make adjustments and corrections to cost estimates before they are released, at which time the inventory valuation is updated.

If no marked standard cost estimate exists, you can manually enter a price in the Future Planned price field in the standard SAP system. If you include this field in the material valuation strategy sequence in the costing variant as described in Chapter 8, a component cost estimate an take the value in this field when determining material valuation.

If you subsequently create and mark a standard cost estimate for this material, however, any manual entry in this field is overwritten with the results of the cost estimate and cannot be changed. To avoid manual entries being overwritten, many companies configure the component cost estimate to search first for a valid purchase info record price, and if unsuccessful, to then search for manual entries in the Planned price 1, Planned price 2, and Planned price 3 fields. We'll discuss this procedure in detail in Chapter 10.

The remaining fields in the Standard Cost Estimate section are handled as follows:

▶ The Current Planned price and Current Standard price fields are overwritten when you agree with the marked cost estimate proposed standard price and subsequently release the cost estimate. When a standard cost estimate is released, any change in inventory value posts as a financial document and is identified as resulting from a price difference.

▶ The Previous Planned price field is overwritten with the value of the previous released standard cost estimate a when marked cost estimate is released.

4.5.2 Planned Prices

We'll now examine the fields in the Planned prices section of the Costing 2 view, as shown in Figure 4.12.

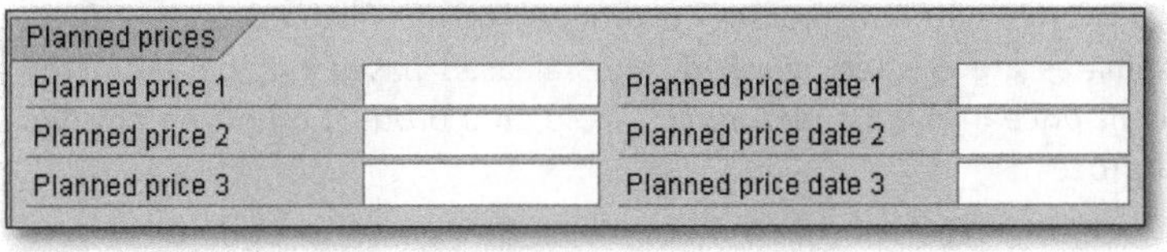

Planned prices		
Planned price 1	Planned price date 1	
Planned price 2	Planned price date 2	
Planned price 3	Planned price date 3	

Figure 4.12 Planned Prices Section

You can manually update the Planned price 1, 2, and 3 fields with estimated purchase prices

You can manually update the Planned price 1, 2, and 3 fields with estimated purchase prices. A standard cost estimate usually retrieves planned prices from these fields if no vendor quotations or purchasing info records exist for purchased items. This is useful when creating cost estimates before vendor quotations are received, early in the lifecycle of a new or modified product. Values entered in the three Planned price date fields indicate the date from which values entered in the three Planned price fields are valid.

Case Scenario

A manufacturer wants to retain a history of estimated purchase prices for new materials so it can gauge estimation accuracy over time. To do this, the manufacturer configures the costing variant so cost estimates search first for a purchasing info record price and then values in the Planned price 1, Planned price 2, and Planned price 3 fields in that sequence. (We'll discuss costing variant configuration in detail in Chapter 8.)

Early in the development of a new product, cost estimates are created to analyze cost viability. At this stage vendor quotations have not been received for new components, so a rough estimation of the purchase price is entered in the Planned price 2 field. A cost estimate searching for the component price first searches for a purchasing info record and then the Planned price 1 field before successfully locating a valid price in the Planned price 2 field. This iterative process allows product development to continuously develop the new product and accurately estimate its cost.

Product development progresses to the stage where production quantities need to be manufactured, though vendor quotations still have not been received for some components. This is a common scenario for many production companies, and is even more common when the product development phase is relatively short and dynamic. As companies become more competitive, they generally need to make new products available with a short and decreasing turnaround time.

Some time later, purchasing provides an estimated purchase price to accounting to enter in the Planned price 1 field, and a cost estimate now successfully locates this price without needing to proceed to the Planned price 2 field. Cost estimates are created, marked, and released based on the estimated component price in the Planned price 1 field, and production of the finished product proceeds.

When purchasing receives vendor quotations, they create or update the vendor purchasing info records directly.

When assembly standard cost estimates are created next, underlying component cost estimates are based on purchasing info record prices without any need to access the Planned price 1 or 2 fields in the Costing 2 view. Records of the purchase prices estimated by product development and purchasing are maintained in the material master Planned price fields for future reporting on component price estimation.

The key to the timely release of accurate standard cost estimates is coordination and communication between product development, production, purchasing and accounting. This can be achieved procedurally, that is, controlled manually by policies and procedures, which many successful companies achieve with a great deal of success.

The Workflow component can be useful in automating some of the communications required between users and departments when researching, developing, and manufacturing new products. For example, when product development indicates that a product is ready to progress from development to production by changing a status, an email can automatically notify purchasing that vendor quotations for components are required.

4.5.3 Valuation Data

Now that we've examined the fields in the Planned prices section, let's consider the Valuation Data section fields, as shown in Figure 4.13.

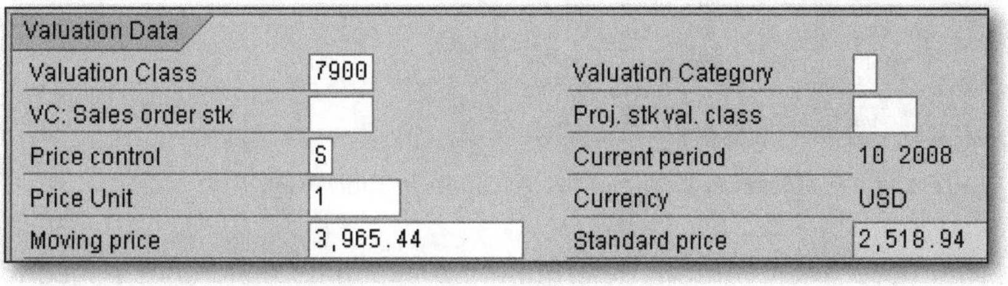

Valuation Data			
Valuation Class	7900	Valuation Category	
VC: Sales order stk		Proj. stk val. class	
Price control	S	Current period	10 2008
Price Unit	1	Currency	USD
Moving price	3,965.44	Standard price	2,518.94

Figure 4.13 Valuation Data Section

The Valuation Data section contains fields that define how a material is valuated, including Valuation Class, which determines the general ledger (G/L) accounts automatically determined during inventory movements, and Price control, which determines if inventory is valued by either standard or moving average price.

Valuation Class

The Valuation Class field in Figure 4.13 determines which G/L accounts are updated as a result of inventory movement or settlement. The Valuation Class field is plant- and material-type specific. A material type groups together materials with the same basic attributes such as raw materials, semi-finished products, or finished products. The G/L accounts to be updated are configured with Transaction OBYC, and stored in database table T030. The quickest way to determine the G/L accounts stored in table T030 is with the Data Browser via Transaction SE16N. Run the transaction, and in the selection screen enter your chart of accounts and valuation class to see a screen similar to that shown in Figure 4.14.

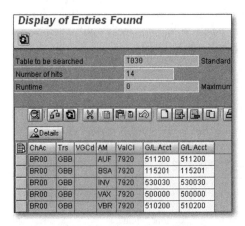

Figure 4.14 Data Browser Listing of G/L Accounts in Table T030

From this screen you can determine, for example, that goods issued to an order or cost center will post to G/L account (G/L Acct) 510200 because it appears on the same row as transaction (Trs) GBB and account modifier (AM) VBR. We'll examine account determination in more detail in Chapter 14. The screen in Figure 4.14 provides you with a quick overview of the G/L accounts configured for each valuation class (ValCl).

Valuation Class for Sales Order Stock and Project Stock

You only need to make entries in the VC:Sales order stk (valuation class for sales order stock) and Proj. stk val. class (valuation class for project stock) fields shown earlier in Figure 4.13 if you need to assign a different valuation class for these types of stock. This allows you to post inventory movements for these types of stock to specific G/L accounts. You do not normally need to assign separate valuation classes in these fields. (We'll discuss valuated sales order stock in more detail in Chapter 19.)

Valuation Category

The Valuation Category field shown earlier in Figure 4.13 determines which criteria are used to group partial stocks of a material to value them separately. The valuation category is part of the split valuation functionality. Normally, you will have only one price per material per plant. Split valuation allows you to valuate, for example, batches separately. Moving average price (V) is the only price control setting available if you activate split valuation and enter a valuation category. You assign valuation types to valuation categories and valuation categories to plants with configuration Transaction OMWC or by following the IMG menu path MATERIALS MANAGEMENT • VALUATION AND ACCOUNT ASSIGNMENT • SPLIT VALUATION • CONFIGURE SPLIT VALUATION.

Valuation category is part of the split valuation functionality

To create a material master subject to split valuation, you first need to create a *valuation header record* for the material. This is where the individual stocks of material are managed cumulatively. When creating the material for the first time, enter a value in the Valuation Category field, and leave the Valuation class field blank. When you save the material, the valuation header record is created.

To create a material master subject to split valuation, you first need to create a valuation header record for the material

To then create the material for a valuation type, create the material again with Transaction MM01. Because a valuation header record exists, you will be required to enter the valuation type for the valuation category. Repeat this step for every valuation type planned.

The Valuation Category field is also located in the Accounting 1 view.

> **Note**
>
> You should always investigate other options before implementing split valuation functionality, because of the extra data maintenance required, as you will have additional material master views to maintain for each valuation type.

In some special cases, split valuation is required, for example, when stocks of a material are kept in different companies or countries. In these cases, it may be necessary for group reporting purposes to determine and store the actual cost of manufacture in each separate company or country.

Price Control

Price control determines whether inventory is valuated at standard (S) or moving average (V) price

The Price control field determines whether inventory is valuated at standard (S) or moving average (V) price, as follows:

▸ If a material is assigned a standard price control (S), the value of the material is always calculated at this price. If goods or invoice receipts contain a price that differs from the standard price, the differences are posted to a price difference account. The variance is not taken into account in inventory valuation.

▸ If a material is assigned a moving average price control (V), the price is automatically adjusted if goods or invoice receipts are posted with a price that differs from the moving average price. The differences are posted to the stock account, and, as a result, the moving average price and the value of the stock change.

Tip

SAP recommends standard price control for assemblies and finished goods because this creates a level of price stability and does not allow errors or incorrect postings in manufacturing orders to flow through undetected to finished goods inventory valuation. This also allows you to analyze production efficiency via variance postings during finished goods receipt into inventory valued at standard prices. SAP also recommends moving average price control for purchased materials because this allows inventory valuation to automatically adjust for changing purchase prices.

Many European companies use the above inventory valuation strategy very successfully. American companies tend to take the more conservative approach of valuing all materials, including purchased materials, at standard prices. This strategy requires more maintenance because standard cost estimates are required for purchased materials, and purchase price difference (PPV) accounts need to be analyzed periodically. Although this strategy involves more work, it does allow you to measure purchasing efficiency by comparing actual with planned purchase prices.

Which valuation strategy is the best for any particular company depends mainly on the level of control required over the purchasing price maintenance process.

A third inventory valuation option is available if even more control and analysis options are required. The material ledger and actual costing can automatically calculate and post all differences from the lowest BOM levels to assemblies and finished goods. Implementation of this functionality requires significant analysis and testing, and it cannot easily be removed once in place. You need to be certain you require this level of control and analysis before proceeding. We'll discuss the material ledger in more detail in Section 4.7 when we look at the Accounting 1 view and in Chapter 19.

Current Period

The Current period field shown earlier in Figure 4.13 displays the current Materials Management (MM) period, which is set with Transaction MMPV or via the menu path LOGISTICS • MATERIALS MANAGEMENT • MATERIAL MASTER • OTHER • CLOSE PERIOD. This period is independent of the accounting period, which is maintained separately with Transaction OB52.

Quickly confirms the current Materials Management period

Material movements can only take place in the current and, if allowed, the previous MM periods. You have the option of closing the previous MM period with Transaction MMRV or following the menu path LOGISTICS • PRODUCTION • MASTER DATA • MATERIAL MASTER • OTHER • ALLOW POSTING TO PREVIOUS PERIOD. The option to post to the previous period is normally kept open for several days into the current period to allow period-end analysis to take place and for any correction postings to occur. The option to post to the previous period is then disabled so the data doesn't change after accounting and Controlling reports are run and saved for analysis by management.

Currency

The currency is determined by company code configuration and cannot be changed in the material master screen. The company code currency cannot be changed after postings occur. You can view more details of the company code currency with Transaction OB22.

Price Unit

The price unit is the number of units to which the price refers

The price unit is the number of units to which the price refers. You can increase the accuracy of the price by increasing the price unit. To determine the unit price, divide the price by the price unit.

You can change the price unit at any time with Transaction MM02. The prices are recalculated automatically to match the new price unit. The maximum price unit value you can enter is 10,000.

If you manually enter a price unit that is greater than the costing lot size, the costing lot size is automatically increased to the same value as the price unit. This is a requirement because a cost estimate is calculated based on the costing lot size, and there would be rounding issues if you then marked and released a standard cost estimate to the material master.

> **Tip**
>
> Let's say the price per unit of a material is $0.215. However, you can't enter this exact vaule as a price with a price unit of one because the material master price field will only accept a maximum of two values following the decimal point. You enter the exact price by entering a price of $2.15 with a price unit of 10, or a price of $21.50 with a price unit of 100.

Moving AveragePrice/Periodic Unit Price

The moving average price is updated with each valuated goods and invoice receipt

The system calculates the moving average price automatically by dividing the material value in the stock account by the quantity of all stocks in the plant concerned. It updates the price with each valuated goods and invoice receipt that has a different price from the current moving average price. If price control is set at moving average price (V), the price in this field determines inventory valuation. If price control is set at (S), the moving average price is statistical and for information only.

If the material ledger is activated with price determination control 3 (single/multilevel) for the material, the material's settlement control determines whether this price is the moving average price or the periodic unit price. Price determination control is discussed in Section 4.7.

Standard Price

The standard price is the result of releasing a material standard cost estimate, and remains constant for at least one period. Differences between the standard price and actual prices are posted to price difference G/L accounts.

Typically, companies keep the standard price constant for one year. Companies with rapidly changing prices may decide to release standard cost estimates more frequently, usually every three or six months. This makes variance analysis of the difference between the standard and actual costs easier, although stock valuation changes more frequently as a result.

Now that we've examined the costing fields, let's look at the fields in the Accounting Views.

4.6   Accounting 1 View

The Accounting views are commonly used by general and management accounting team members. Select the Accounting 1 tab (not shown) in Figure 4.11 to display the screen shown in Figure 4.15.

This screen is divided into two sections, General data, and Current valuation. To make the discussion easier to follow, we'll consider the fields in each section individually. Let's first look at the General data section.

4.6.1   General Data

The General data section contains fields relating to accounting in general that cannot be included in any of the more specific sections. Some fields appear in both the Costing and Accounting views. In this section, we'll only consider fields we haven't previously discussed in the Costing views.

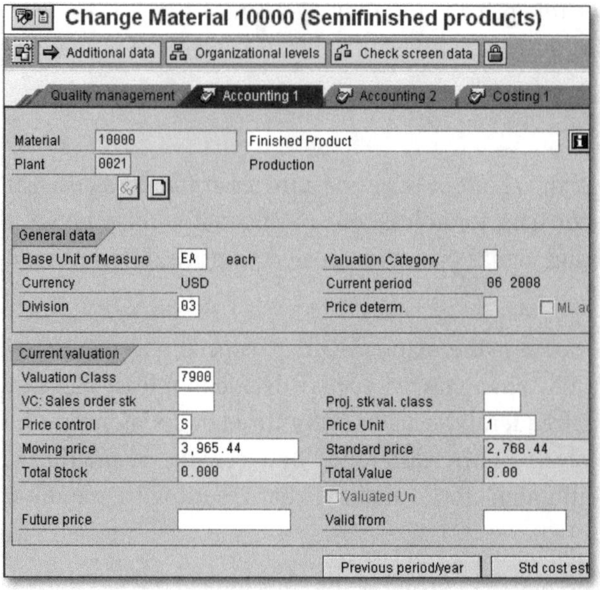

Figure 4.15 Material Master Accounting 1 View

Division

A division allows you to organize your sales structure around groups of similar products

A division allows you to group materials based on responsibility for sales or profits from saleable materials or services. A product or service is always assigned to just one division, which allows you to organize your sales structure around groups of similar products or product lines.

Example

If a sales organization sells food and nonfood products through both retail and wholesale distribution channels, each distribution channel could be further split into a food and nonfood division.

Price Determination

We'll examine price determination in detail in Section 4.7.

Material Ledger Activated

We'll examine the material ledger activated indicator in detail in Section 4.7.

Let's look at the fields in the Current valuation section of the screen shown in Figure 4.15.

4.6.2 Current Valuation

The Current valuation section contains fields that define how the material is valuated. We'll only consider fields not previously discussed in the Costing views.

Total Stock

The Total Stock field indicates the total quantity of all valuated stocks of the material in the Plant. This field provides a handy summary of the total stock of the material inventory without you needing to refer to inventory reports or transactions such as Transaction MMBE.

Total Value

Total value is the value of all valuated stocks of the material in the plant. This is determined by multiplying the total stock quantity by either the standard or moving average price, depending on the Price control field.

Future Price and Valid From

The Future price field provides you with two mechanisms to update the standard price of a material. Each is explained in detail in the following paragraphs.

You generally only use the first method of updating the standard price with the future price if you haven't implemented Product Cost Planning functionality and cannot create standard cost estimates to update standard prices. For example, you may have a very limited or small SAP system implementation, or you may have only implemented the Financial Accounting component (FI) and intend to implement the Controlling component (CO) at a later stage. This method of updating the standard price has limited functionality, but it still gives you some control over the price update because you need to run a separate transaction after entering a price in the future price field to update the standard price.

To release a future price to become the standard price, proceed as follows:

1. Enter the price you intend to become the new standard price for a material in the Future price field in the material master Accounting 1 view.

2. Enter a validity date in the Valid from field. The system will not update the standard price with the future price before this date.

3. Run Transaction OKME or follow the menu path LOGISTICS • MATERIALS MANAGEMENT • VALUATION • CHANGE IN MATERIAL PRICE • RELEASE PLANNED PRICES to display the RELEASE PLANNED PRICE CHANGES screen shown in Figure 4.16.

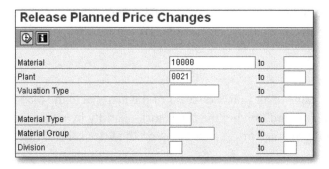

Figure 4.16 Release Planned Price Changes Screen

4. In this screen, you have many options for selecting a material or range of materials. Enter your data and click the execute icon to update the standard price in the selected material masters with the future price.

Upon successfully updating the standard price, the Future price and Valid from fields in Figure 4.15 are both blank and ready for entry of the next future price. The standard price will not be updated with this procedure if there are existing current or future standard cost estimates.

You can include the future price field in costing variant configuration

The second method for updating the standard price with the future price involves including the future price in the search strategy sequence in configuration of the costing variant with Transaction OKKN. (We'll discuss costing variant configuration in detail in Chapter 8.) This field can also provide you with an extra field in addition to the three Planned price fields in the Costing 2 view to plan prices. If the standard cost estimate successfully updates the standard price using the Future price field, the values in the Future price and Valid from fields remain until you overwrite them.

Now that we've discussed the Future price and Valid from fields, let's look at the Previous price and Last price change fields.

Previous Price and Last Price Change

If you display the material master with Transaction MM03, two extra fields appear just below the Future price and Valid from fields in the Accounting 1 view. These fields are not displayed when you enter the material master in change mode with Transaction MM02. These fields are Previous price and Last price change, as shown in Figure 4.17.

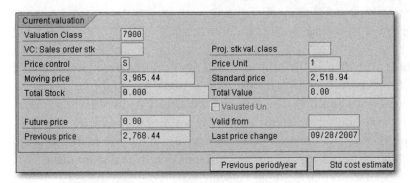

Figure 4.17 Display Previous Price and Last Price Change Fields

If you are using the Future price field to update the standard price without cost estimates, these fields are the only indication you have of the previous standard price and when it was released.

Now that we've examined the fields in the Current valuation section, let's look at the two buttons below this section, Previous period/year and Std cost estimate.

4.6.3 Previous Period/Year

Click the Previous period/year button in Figure 4.17 to display the screen shown in Figure 4.18.

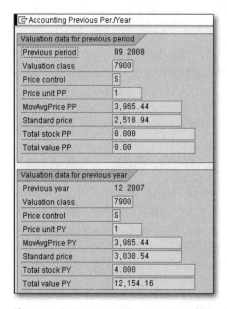

Figure 4.18 Accounting Previous Period/Year Screen

This screen displays fields from the Current valuation section populated with valuation data from the previous period (PP) and the last period in the previous year (PY). The values in this screen are useful when analyzing the reason for differences between postings to the current and previous period and previous year. These values allow you to decide if the difference in postings is due to a difference in the valuation data, or if you need to investigate other reasons.

4.6.4 Standard Cost Estimate

Click the Std cost estimate button in Figure 4.17 to display the screen shown in Figure 4.19.

This screen displays information from the Standard Cost Estimate section of the Costing 2 view. It saves time navigating to the Costing 2 view if you mainly work with the Accounting 1 view of the material master.

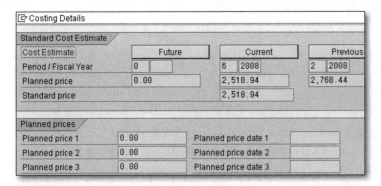

Figure 4.19 Accounting Standard Cost Estimate Screen

Let's consider fields available in the Accounting 1 view when the material ledger is activated.

4.7 Accounting 1 View – Material Ledger Activated

There are two reasons to activate the material ledger:

▶ The first reason to activate the material ledger is to carry material and inventory prices in multiple valuations and currencies. This is especially useful for global companies with inventories in more than one country and currency. The following is an example of two common valuation approaches (you can have up to three valuation approaches):

The Accounting 1 view contains additional fields when the material ledger is activated

  ▷ The first inventory valuation approach is based on legal valuation (includes transfer pricing) and company code currency (MXN for a Mexican subsidiary) for local reporting.

  ▷ The second inventory valuation approach is in group valuation (excludes transfer pricing) and group currency (USD for a U.S. global company) for group consolidated reporting.

Transfer pricing is the price charged for the transfer of a product from one business unit (company code or profit center) to another. The allowable amount to add to inventory transferred between business units is generally set by government tax departments. The resulting transfer price has tax benefits for the company. However, a global company needs a consolidated inventory report excluding transfer price to determine an accurate inventory valuation report based on actual external procurement and internal manufacturing costs.

▸ The second reason to activate the material ledger is to carry out actual costing. Actual costing valuates all goods movements within a period at the standard price (preliminary valuation). All price and exchange rate differences for the material are collected in the material ledger.

At the end of the period, an actual price is calculated for each material based on the actual costs of the period. This actual price is called the periodic unit price and can be used to revaluate the inventory for the period to be closed. You can use this actual price as the standard price for the next period. You also have the option of not revaluating inventory and posting to accrual accounts instead.

Actual costing determines what portion of the variance is to be debited to the next-highest level using material consumption. Variances are rolled up over multiple production levels to the finished product.

> **Note**
>
> It's possible to activate the material ledger and only record material ledger documents in one existing valuation approach of company code currency and legal valuation. You do not need to run period-end processing for the material ledger actual costing if you select a price determination setting of 2 as discussed in the following section.
>
> You can use this approach if you're not certain that you need the material ledger functionality when you initially implement your SAP system. Your system will simply store material ledger documents that can provide useful analysis information, and will simplify further implementation of the material ledger if you to decide to at a later stage.

General and management accountants as well as production and purchasing personnel may be interested in reviewing the material ledger data. When you activate the material ledger, additional information is available in the Accounting 1 view, as shown in Figure 4.20.

After you activate the material ledger, additional Period tabs are available in the Accounting 1 view. Each material-based transaction is recorded per period in the material ledger, allowing the material inventory to be valued in up to three different currencies or valuations. The material ledger is also the basis of actual costing, which allows you to roll up and allocate all material and production differences to assemblies and finished products at the end of each period.

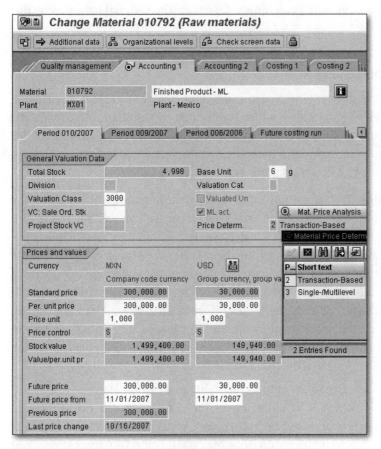

Figure 4.20 Accounting 1 View with Material Ledger Activated

Let's examine the fields in each of the sections of Figure 4.20, starting with the General Valuation Data section.

4.7.1 General Valuation Data

In the following sections, we'll examine the general valuation data fields we haven't previously discussed in the Costing views.

Material Ledger Activated

The ML act. (material ledger activated) checkbox is automatically se-lected when the material ledger is activated for the material. It is also grayed out, meaning you cannot deactivate the material ledger using this screen.

Price Determination

The Price determ. (price determination) field can only be used if the material ledger is active, which is indicated by automatic selection of the ML act. checkbox. To display a list of possible entries for the Price determ. field, right-click in the field and select Possible Entries. The two possible price determinations are displayed, as shown in Figure 4.20:

Select price deter-mination setting 2 for additional currencies or valuations

▶ **Setting 2:** Transaction-Based price determination functions in the same way as it does if the material ledger isn't active, but you're also able to store and display material ledger documents that include addi-tional currency and valuation data. This is the setting you use if you're interested in carrying standard (S) or moving average (V) prices in multiple currencies or valuations. Without the material ledger acti-vated, you can only record inventory-related transactions and data in one currency and legal valuation. This is also the setting the system automatically sets for all materials during production startup with the material ledger activated.

You can change the setting following production startup with Trans-action CKMM or by following the menu path ACCOUNTING • CONTROL-LING • PRODUCT COST CONTROLLING • ACTUAL COSTING/MATERIAL LED-GER • ENVIRONMENT • CHANGE MATERIAL PRICE DETERMINATION. You can also determine the material price determination proposed when creating new material masters following production startup with con-figuration Transaction OMX1 or by following the IMG menu path CONTROLLING • PRODUCT COST CONTROLLING • ACTUAL COSTING/MATE-RIAL LEDGER • ACTIVATE VALUATION AREAS FOR MATERIAL LEDGER.

Select price deter-mination setting 3 for actual costing

▶ **Setting 3:** Use this setting for Single-/Multilevel price determination to use the actual costing functionality of the material ledger. You can only use this option if the inventory price control is set at standard price (S). The preliminary valuation price (standard price) remains unchanged during a period. A periodic unit price is calculated when the period is closed for informational purposes and can also be used for material valuation of the closed period.

Material Price Analysis

Click the Mat. Price Analysis (material price analysis) button and change the view to price determination structure to display the screen shown in Figure 4.21.

Material price analysis button

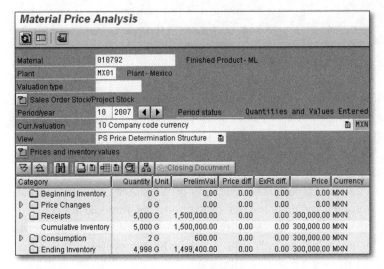

Figure 4.21 Material Price Analysis Screen

This screen can also be accessed with Transaction CKM3 or by following the menu path ACCOUNTING • CONTROLLING • PRODUCT COST CONTROLLING • ACTUAL COSTING/MATERIAL LEDGER • MATERIAL LEDGER • MATERIAL PRICE ANALYSIS. Here you can access all material transactions for a period. Transactions are grouped by category, which you can progressively expand to display all transaction documents within a category.

4.7.2   Prices and values

Now that we've discussed the fields in the General Valuation Data section of the Accounting 1 view, let's look at the fields in the Prices and values section, as shown in Figure 4.22.

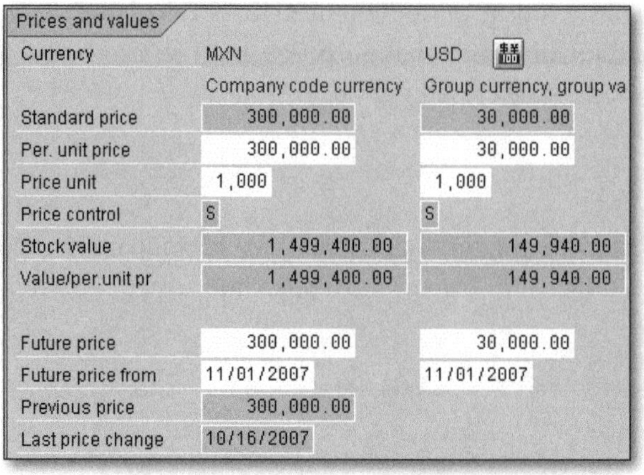

Figure 4.22 Prices and Values Section

The Prices and values section contains up to three columns, each representing the three possible currency or valuation approaches for inventory stored by the material ledger. The first column represents values stored in Company code currency and legal valuation. *Legal valuation* is based on transfer prices that include internal profits when products are transferred between company codes and profit centers. You use this valuation approach by default with or without the material ledger activated. The additional functionality supplied by activating the material ledger includes the periodic unit price, which represents the actual inventory price for a prior closed period.

The other two possible columns in this section represent extra valuation approaches available with the material ledger activated. In the example shown in Figure 4.22, the fields associated with an additional valuation approach of Group currency, group valuation are displayed in the second column. A global organization typically uses *group currency* in consolidated financial statements, and *group valuation* in management reports, which excludes internal profits when products are transferred between company codes and profit centers.

We'll now discuss the fields in this section that are different from the valuation fields already discussed in the current valuation section of the Accounting 1 view without the material ledger activated.

Periodic Unit Price

During a period, all transactions are carried out with the preliminary valuation price (standard price). The material ledger collects data for all activities that relate to the valuation of materials, and the preliminary valuation price stays constant during the period. You cannot change this price after data has been entered into the material ledger for the period.

The periodic unit price is calculated at the end of every period

The differences between the preliminary valuation price and actual price are recorded per material and posting, and each difference can be displayed during the period as soon as it is entered. The periodic unit price is determined once a period has ended. It reflects the actual costs of a material for the closed period. To determine the periodic unit price, the system uses the cumulative inventory (all goods received plus beginning inventory) and the cumulative difference (all differences between the standard price and the entered price for all goods received and the beginning inventory).

The periodic unit price represents the actual material costs for the closed period

Material price determination is the step that calculates the periodic unit price. The moving price field in the material master is updated with the calculated price for the closed period. The price control of the material remains set to standard price (S).

During the revaluation process, the system changes the price control for the material in the previous period from S to V. Thus, the periodic unit price (calculated during material price determination) becomes the valuation price for the previous period.

> **Note**
>
> You can only see the previous period price in the Accounting 1 view because this view contains material valuation per period when the material ledger is activated.

If you decide not to revalue your materials at period-end, the periodic unit price of the closed period is for information only, and price control stays as standard price.

You can use the periodic unit price for information only

The prices presented in each column are based on the currency or valuation of each valuation approach.

Stock Value

Stock value indicates the total of all valuated stocks of the material in the plant calculated with the standard price. The material ledger retains inventory values for each period that you can access by selecting the Period tabs.

Value Based on Periodic Unit Price

The stock value based on periodic unit price (Value/per.unit pr) field is calculated by multiplying the total stock quantity by the periodic unit price.

Future Price

You can enter a future price for each column corresponding to a different currency or valuation approach. The future price in the first column representing legal valuation in this example includes transfer pricing (internal profits). The future price in the second column representing group valuation excludes transfer pricing. You can create separate cost estimates for each valuation approach that access the future prices for purchased materials.

Future Price From

The system will not update the standard price with the future price before the date specified in the Future price from field.

Now that we've examined fields in the Accounting 1 view with the material ledger activated, let's consider fields in the Accounting 2 view.

4.8   Accounting 2 View

Select the Accounting 2 tab to display the screen shown in Figure 4.23.

The tax and commercial prices indicate the tax and commercial values. The distinction between these two valuations is not observed in the USA or in some European countries. You can use these fields many ways to determine alternate inventory valuations. In the following sections we'll follow two scenarios of how to populate the fields with information and how to then use information in the fields.

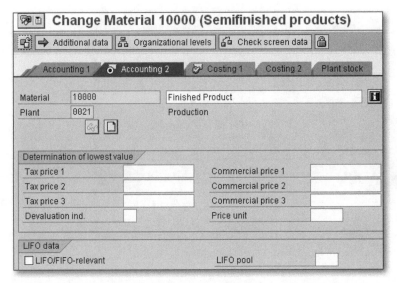

Figure 4.23 Material Master Accounting 2 View

4.8.1 Populate Tax and Commercial Price Fields

You can manually enter information in any of the Tax price and Commercial price fields, or they can be automatically populated. Many options are available for automatically populating these fields. Let's follow one scenario so you can see how the process works, and you can apply it to other possible inventory valuation scenarios as you like.

Market prices

Run Transaction MRN0 or follow the menu path LOGISTICS • MATERIALS MANAGEMENT • VALUATION • BALANCE SHEET VALUATION • DETERMINATION OF LOWEST VALUE • MARKET PRICES to display the screen shown in Figure 4.24.

This transaction allows you to retrieve prices from receipts, purchase orders, contracts, scheduling agreements, purchasing info records, or standard prices. You can compare these prices with existing prices such as the current material prices, and you can update any of the tax, commercial, or planned price fields in the Accounting and Costing views with the results. Let's analyze the fields and buttons in each section.

Figure 4.24 Determine Lowest Value: Market Prices

Restriction of Selection

The Restriction of Selection section allows you to select which materials determine market prices. Enter a material range, plant, or any other parameters to restrict the selection of materials.

Price Comparison

Select market prices

Click the Market Price button to display the screen shown in Figure 4.25

Figure 4.25 Overview Screen: Selecting Market Price Source

Selecting a checkbox on the Overview tab causes a corresponding tab to appear on this screen. For example, if the Standard prices checkbox was selected, the corresponding tab would appear after the Info Records tab. Each tab contains fields for selecting the appropriate data. Let's examine the POs (purchase orders) tab as an example. Select the POs tab to display the screen shown in Figure 4.26

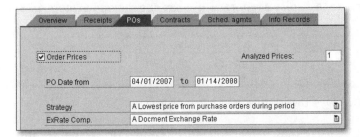

Figure 4.26 Purchase Orders: Selecting Market Price Source

This screen indicates that the lowest purchase order price during the current fiscal year beginning April 2007 will be chosen in this example. The Analyzed Prices field shows the number of purchase orders to be included in the calculation of the lowest price.

Now that we've selected market prices, we can compare them with existing prices. Click the Comparison Price button shown earlier in Figure 4.24 to display the screen shown in Figure 4.27.

Compare market prices

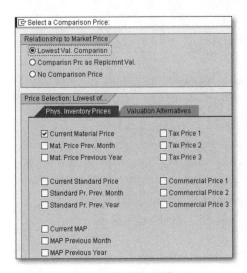

Figure 4.27 Comparison Price Selection

This screen allows you to select which prices you'd like to compare with the market price just retrieved from purchase orders in our example.

If you'd like to display a report without updating any material master fields, deselect Database Update, shown earlier in Figure 4.24, and click the execute icon to display a report such as the one shown in Figure 4.28.

Description	Comp.Price	New Price	Unit of Measure	Change	Suppl.	Itm	Price	Source	Rank	Purch.Doc.	Item	Date
LABEL IDENT WARNING	2.56	1.12	1	56.25-		1	1.12	Receipt Price	1	5000202250	1	12/21/2007
						2	1.12	PO Price	1	4500064035	2	09/18/2007
						3	2.56	Info Rec. Price	1	5300119020		

Figure 4.28 Determine Lowest Value Market Prices Report

This report displays the comparison price (Comp.Price column), proposed price (New Price column), source, and percentage change. After reviewing the report, you can either run the transaction again with changed parameters, or you can update the prices to fields in the material master as follows. Select Database Update as shown earlier in Figure 4.24 to display the screen shown in Figure 4.29.

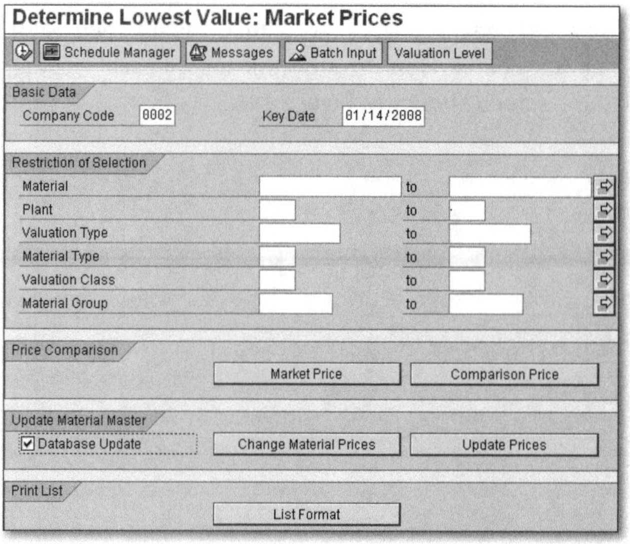

Figure 4.29 Determine Lowest Value Market Prices Database Update

Database update   When you select Database Update, two new buttons appear in the Update Material Master section. Let's look at the functionality of each one.

Click the Change Material Prices button to display the screen shown in Figure 4.30

Figure 4.30 Update Material Prices Button Screen

You will normally leave the default setting of No Update selected. You'll still be able to update the tax, commercial, and planned prices in the material master with this default setting. Only select Direct update if you're interested in updating the material standard price.

Direct update

> **Caution**
>
> Selecting Direct update and executing the transaction may result in updating the standard price, resulting in inventory revaluation. Always fully test this setting before using it in your production database.

Press Enter or click the green checkmark icon, and click the Update Prices button to display the screen shown in Figure 4.31.

In this screen select the material master fields to be updated with the results of the market price valuation. Select Reset to initialize the price in the material master field or to set the value to zero as required. Press Enter or click the execute icon, and then click the execute icon shown earlier in Figure 4.29.

You'll receive a report similar to the one shown in Figure 4.28, and the Tax price 1 field in the Accounting 1 view will be updated as shown in Figure 4.32.

> **Note**
>
> The Tax price 1 field was automatically updated by transaction MRN0.

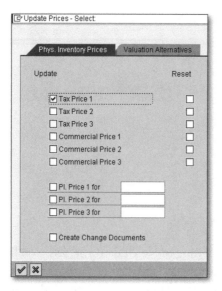

Figure 4.31 Update Prices Button Screen

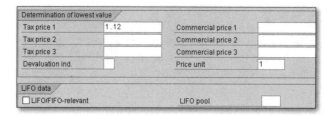

Figure 4.32 Accounting 1 View Tax Price 1 Field Updated

In this section we've followed an example of how to automatically update the tax and commercial prices. Now let's examine how to use these prices after they've been populated.

4.8.2 Using the Tax and Commercial Price Fields

U.S. and European companies usually don't have a requirement for a separate tax or commercial view of inventory. Once you have values populated in these fields, however, you can use them for whatever purpose you like. For example, you can create a report that accesses a price in one of these fields, multiply it by stock quantity, and generate an inventory valuation report based on any criteria. Or you can have a cost estimate access the price and base the standard price on it or populate another field with it.

We'll discuss costing variant configuration in detail in Chapter 8. However, here's a quick preview to demonstrate one of several available methods to use the tax and commercial price fields:

Costing variant configuration preview

1. Run Transaction OKKN or follow the IMG menu path CONTROLLING • PRODUCT COST CONTROLLING • PRODUCT COST PLANNING • MATERIAL COST ESTIMATE WITH QUANTITY STRUCTURE • DEFINE COSTING VARIANTS.

2. Double-click a costing variant.

3. Click the Valuation Variant button and left-click in any field in the Strategy sequence section to display the list of possible entries, as shown in Figure 4.33.

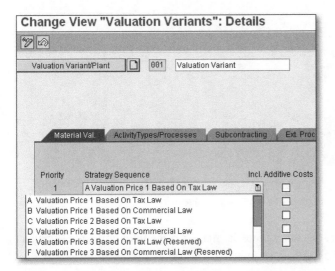

Figure 4.33 Valuation Variant Material Valuation Strategy Sequence

You can create a valuation variant that searches for the tax or commercial price fields. A cost estimate created with this valuation variant will retrieve a price entered in the corresponding field.

4. With this cost estimate you can then update any other price field with Transaction CK24 or by following the menu path ACCOUNTING • CONTROLLING • PRODUCT COST CONTROLLING • PRODUCT COST PLANNING • MATERIAL COSTING • PRICE UPDATE.

5. Click the OTHER PRICES button to display the screen shown in Figure 4.34.

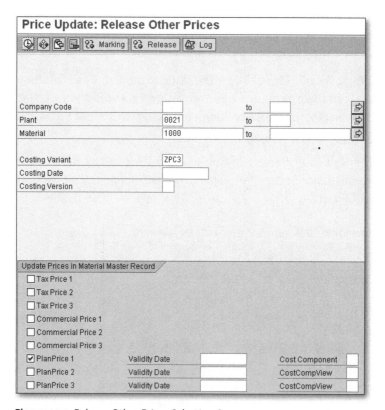

Figure 4.34 Release Other Prices Selection Screen

In this screen select any material master price field and click the execute icon to release the cost estimate price to the corresponding field.

This concludes the material master chapter, so let's review what we've covered.

4.9   Summary

In this chapter we discussed the material master fields relevant to Product Cost Controlling. We began with MRP fields, which cost estimates refer to when calculating the standard cost. We next examined the Costing material master views, including the Costing 1 and 2 views, which let you access all of the fields relevant to management accounting. Finally, we looked at the Accounting 1 and 2 views, which let you access all of the fields relevant to financial accounting.

Now that we've considered Controlling and material master data in Chapters 3 and 4, we'll examine logistics master data in Chapter 5.

Logistics master data provides information on how materials are procured.

5   Logistics Master Data

Now that we've examined Controlling master data in Chapter 3 and material master data in Chapter 4, we'll next look at logistics master data in this chapter. This data provides cost estimates with the quantity and price information needed to calculate the standard cost of a product. Bills of material provide component and assembly quantities, and routings provide activity quantities. Purchasing info records provide component prices that together with planned activity prices in Controlling provide cost estimates with price information. A purchasing info record stores all of the information relevant to the procurement of a material from a vendor. It contains the purchase price field, which the standard cost estimate usually searches for when determining purchase price.

Logistics master data contains quantity and price information for cost estimates

Let's examine logistics master data in detail starting with the bill of material.

5.1   Bill of Material

The bill of material (BOM) is a structured hierarchy of components necessary to build an assembly. BOMs, together with purchasing info records or vendor quotations, provide cost estimates with the information necessary to calculate material costs of products. An example of a BOM is shown in Figure 5.1.

A cost estimate created for the top-level finished good, P-100 in this example, selects materials at the lowest level in the BOM first. All materials with material type ROH (raw materials) are costed first, and then HALB (subassemblies), and finally FERT (finished goods). Material costs are rolled up from raw materials through subassemblies to the finished good.

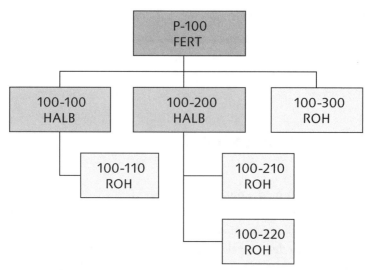

Figure 5.1 Example of a BOM

Each BOM item contains many fields and indicators relevant to Product Cost Controlling, which we'll now examine in detail. You can view or change BOMs with Transaction CS02 or menu path LOGISTICS • PRODUCTION • MASTER DATA • BILLS OF MATERIAL • BILL OF MATERIAL • MATERIAL BOM • CHANGE. The selection screen shown in Figure 5.2 is displayed.

Change material BOM: Initial Screen

Material			Plnt	Usage	AltBOM
	P-100			1	1
Material	P-100		1000	1	1
Plant	1000 Werk Hamburg	P-100	2300	1	1
BOM Usage	1 Production	P-100	3000	1	1
Alternative BOM					

Figure 5.2 Change Material BOM Initial Screen

Type in the material BOM, plant, BOM usage and alternative BOM you want to maintain. Right-click either the Plant or BOM Usage field and select Possible Entries to display the list shown in Figure 5.2. Select the combination of these fields for the BOM you want to maintain and press Enter to display the screen shown in Figure 5.3.

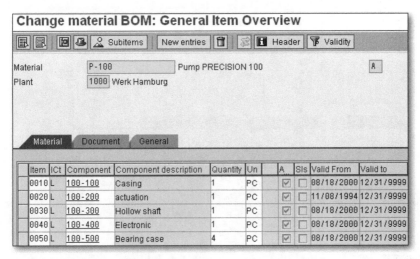

Figure 5.3 Change Material BOM General Item Overview

The General Item Overview screen displays a list of material BOM items required to manufacture the assembly. We'll now examine the fields in the Basic Data tab of an individual BOM item.

5.1.1 Basic Data

Double-click any BOM item in Figure 5.3 to display details as shown in Figure 5.4.

The fields you maintain in the Basic Data tab provide basic BOM item information together with item category, quantity and MRP data. We'll discuss the fields and checkboxes relevant to Product Costing Controlling in the following sections.

Item Number

The Item Number field shows the sequence of BOM components.

Component

The Component field shows the material number of each component.

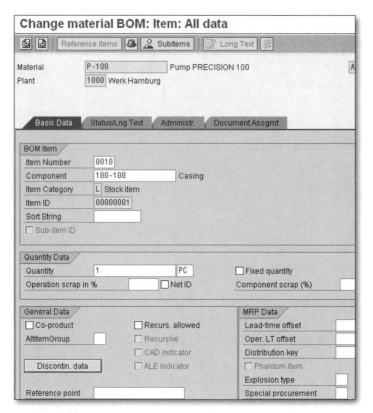

Figure 5.4 Change Material BOM Item

Item Category

The Item Category field groups BOM items into criteria such as stock, nonstock, document, or text items. Some item categories such as stock are usually relevant to costing, whereas others such as document or text items are not.

Fixed Quantity

This checkbox shows that the component quantity is always the same and is not in proportion to the assembly being produced or the order quantity. For text items the system automatically proposes this indicator.

Operation Scrap in %

Operation scrap entered in the BOM item ensures that the input quantity of valuable components inserted in an assembly is reduced. For a particular component, operation scrap allows you to enter a different scrap percentage, usually less than the assembly scrap percentage.

Net ID

The Net ID checkbox is selected to ignore assembly scrap, and must be selected if you enter operation scrap. Without this checkbox selected, assembly scrap entered in the upper-level assembly increases the quantities of all lower-level components, and is additive to a value entered in the Component scrap % field.

Component Scrap %

Component scrap can be defined as the percentage of component quantity that does not meet required production quality standards before being inserted in the production process. An entry in this field in the BOM item takes priority over an entry in the material master MRP 4 view.

Co-product

A co-product is a material that is a valuated product produced simultaneously with one or more other products. If you select this checkbox, you also normally enter a negative quantity. Selecting this checkbox allows you to assign the proportion of costs this material will receive in relation to other co-products within an apportionment structure. An apportionment structure defines how costs are distributed to co-products. You can only enter an item as a co-product if the material master MRP 2 view contains the material can be a *co-product* checkbox.

Now that we've looked at the relevant fields in the Basic Data tab, let's examine the fields in the remaining tabs of a BOM item.

5.1.2 Status/Long Text

Click the Status/Lng Text tab in Figure 5.4 to display the details shown in Figure 5.5.

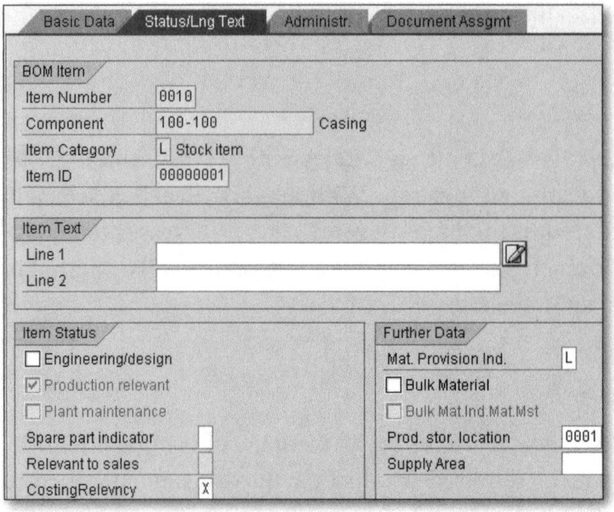

Figure 5.5 BOM Item Status Long Text

The fields you maintain in the Status/Lng Text tab allow you to enter text describing each BOM item and item status checkboxes that control the extent to which each item can be used in other processes.

Item Text

You can enter up to 40 characters in both the Line 1 and 2 fields. You can enter more characters by clicking the new page and pencil icon.

Now let's consider the relevant items in the Item Status section.

Production Relevant

Selecting this checkbox determines if the item is relevant to the production process. Items with this checkbox selected are copied to the planned order, and dependent items are calculated. These items are automatically copied to the production order when converted from the planned order.

This checkbox is not changeable due to the Product BOM Usage checkbox you selected in the initial screen.

Costing Relevancy

This checkbox determines whether the item is included in costing for the standard cost estimate and calculation of planned and actual costs for a manufacturing order. Deselecting the CostingRelevncy checkbox allows you to exclude the cost of some BOM items, for example, bulk materials. Bulk materials are expensed directly to a cost center, so the cost is already included in the cost estimate via overhead or activity rates.

> **Note**
>
> For *output materials*, that is, materials for which the co-product checkbox has been set in the material master and that have a negative BOM item, the CostingRelevncy checkbox has no effect on the BOM item.

Now let's consider the relevant checkboxes in the Further Data section.

Bulk Material

Bulk materials, for example, washers and grease are charged directly to a cost center and are not relevant for individual costing. The cost of these items is included in overhead cost components. The CostingRelevncy checkbox cannot be selected for a bulk material BOM item. If you attempt to select it, you will receive an error message because the cost of the item would be included in both the material and overhead cost components.

Bulk Material Indicator in the Material Master

The Bulk Mat.Ind.Mat.Mst checkbox shows whether a bulk material is defined in the material master MRP 2 view, which overrides the indicator in the BOM item. If a material is always used as a bulk material, select the checkbox in the material master. You cannot deselect the checkbox in the BOM item if the indicator is set in the material master.

Now that we've studied relevant fields and checkboxes in the Status Lng Text tab, let's look at the fields in the Administr. tab.

5.1.3 Administration

Click the Administr. (administration) tab in Figure 5.5 to show the details shown in Figure 5.6.

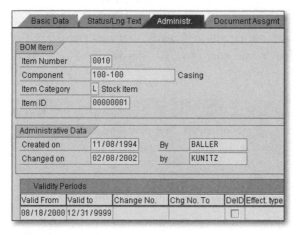

Figure 5.6 BOM Item Administration Data

These fields contain BOM item creation and change information and validity periods.

Created on and By

These two fields contain the BOM item creation date and who created it. This information can be useful if you need to contact the person who created the BOM item to get additional information.

Changed on and By

These two fields contain the BOM item change dates and who changed it. You can find more details of BOM item changes by selecting ENVIRONMENT • CHANGE DOCUMENTS from the menu bar when viewing a BOM item.

Validity Periods

When you create a standard cost estimate with Transaction CK11N, one of the selection screen fields is quantity structure date. This date determines which BOMs and BOM items are selected for the cost estimate based on validity periods shown in Figure 5.6.

Now let's examine the fields in the remaining tab of the BOM Item screen.

5.1.4 Document Assignment

Click the Document Assgmt tab in Figure 5.6 to display the screen shown in Figure 5.7.

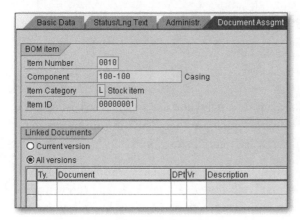

Figure 5.7 BOM Item Document Assignment

The Linked Documents section of this tab, allows you to attach different versions of documents, for example, design documents relevant to each BOM item.

Now that we've examined BOMs in detail, let's look at work centers. Material masters and BOMs provide cost estimates with material and assembly prices and quantities. To determine labor and activity standard quantities, we first need to consider work centers, and then routings, which are lists of work centers.

5.2 Work Center

Operations are performed at work centers that represent, for example, machines, production lines, or employees as shown in Figure 5.8.

Definition		Work Center
A work center is a physical location at which an operation is carried out.		
Example		
Any of the following could be a work center:		
• Individual work center	Lathe 17	
• Work center group	Turnery	
• Production line	Line 9	
• Individual employee	J. Jordan	
• Personnel group	Pool 19	

Figure 5.8 Examples of Work Centers

Work centers are defined within a plant and are assigned to cost centers. You first create work centers, which are then listed in routings to manufacture assemblies, as we will discuss in Section 5.3.2.

Each work center contains many fields and checkboxes relevant to Product Cost Controlling, which we'll now examine in detail. You can view or change work centers with Transaction CR02 or by following the menu path LOGISTICS • PRODUCTION • MASTER DATA • WORK CENTERS • WORK CENTER • CHANGE. The selection screen shown in Figure 5.9 is displayed.

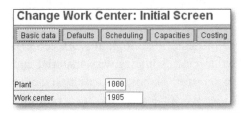

Figure 5.9 Work Center Initial Screen

Let's examine the fields in the Basic data tab of a work center.

5.2.1 Basic Data

Type in the plant and work center you want to maintain in Figure 5.9 and press Enter or click the Basic data button to display the screen shown in Figure 5.10

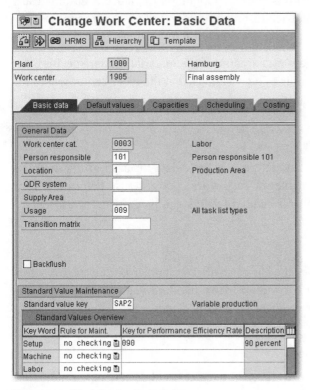

Figure 5.10 Work Center Basic Data

The relevant fields you maintain in the Basic data tab determine the work center application area and the standard value key, which we'll now discuss.

Work Center Category

You assign a work center category to an application area such as production, plant maintenance, or quality management. You configure screens and fields available for each work center category that are relevant to each application area.

Backflush

Backflushing automatically posts a goods issue for components after their actual physical issue for use in an order. Each material component in a BOM is allocated to an operation in the production order. The goods issue posting of backflushed components is carried out automatically during confirmation. Backflushing is used to reduce the amount of work in warehouse management, especially for low-value parts.

This checkbox is taken into account if the material master specifies that a material component is to be backflushed at the work center where the operation is carried out.

Standard Value Key

The standard value key determines basic data for each of the up to six standard values available for each work center. It also determines how many of the six available standard values can be used at a work center.

Key Word

The key word defines the basic use of each standard value such as setup, machine, and labor for the up to six standard values that can be confirmed with activity rates for each work center.

Rule for Maintenance

The Rule for Maint. (rule for maintenance) field determines whether it is possible, optional, or mandatory to enter a standard value in an operation of a routing.

Key for Performance Efficiency Rate

The performance efficiency rate key is the ratio between an individual's actual output and the planned average output. The performance efficiency from the work center is transferred to the operation and cannot be changed there. If you do not enter a performance efficiency rate key, the system assumes 100 % efficiency. The standard times used by capacity planning and costing are modified by the performance efficiency rate.

Description of the Performance Efficiency Rate Key

This is text that describes the performance efficiency rate key in more detail.

Note

Entering a performance efficiency rate key of less than 100 % increases both the planned and actual cost of using an activity. You may, for example, decide to use this key if you are uncertain of standard values when using an activity for the first time.

Many companies use an iterative process to increase the accuracy of standard values, which involves using a performance efficiency of 100 %. They compare planned with actual standard values and update the planned values as required prior to subsequent main costing runs. This technique is most effective if you record actual activity quantities during order or operation confirmation.

Now that we've studied relevant fields and indicators in the Basic data tab, let's look at the fields in the Default values tab.

5.2.2   Default Values

Click on the Default values tab shown in Figure 5.10 to display the screen shown in Figure 5.11.

The Default values tab contains data that defaults when you add an operation carried out at a work center in a routing. By entering default values, you reduce the effort necessary in editing operations in routings.

Control Key

The control key specifies how operation activities are performed and treated. Right-click in the Control key field and select Possible Entries to display the dialog box shown in Figure 5.12.

The Overview section contains a list of available control keys. You may need to scroll up or down to see the complete list. The Overview section also displays some fields and checkboxes for each control key.

To display more detailed control key information click Control key in the Overview section and then click the Detailed information button.

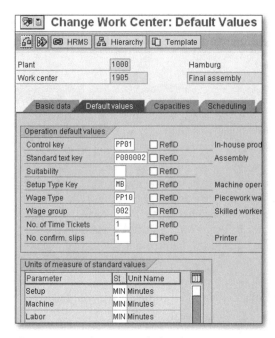

Figure 5.11 Work Center Default Values

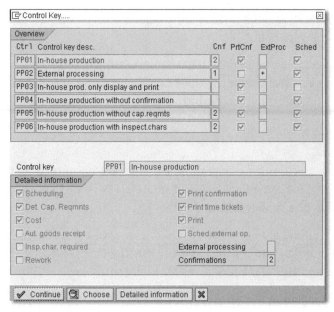

Figure 5.12 Control Key Detailed Information

Details of the checkboxes and fields relevant to Product Cost Controlling are listed below:

▶ **Cost**

The Cost checkbox in the Detailed information section of the Control Key screen determines if operations carried out at this work center can be included in planned (cost estimate) and actual (simultaneous) costing.

▶ **Auto Goods Receipt**

The Aut. goods receipt (auto goods receipt) checkbox determines if yield from this work center is automatically delivered into inventory during operation confirmation. If so, the manufacturing order automatically receives a credit based on the yield quantity times the standard price of the material.

▶ **Rework**

Operations carried out at work centers with the Rework checkbox selected in the Control Key screen are not taken into account when scheduling routings because you do not normally plan rework.

▶ **External Processing**

The control key determines if the operation is performed by in-house production or external processing. This in turn determines if the operation is costed by multiplying the standard value by the planned activity price or by referring to the external processing section of the routing operation details as described in Section 5.3. The following are possible entries in this field:

  ▷ Blank: Internally processed operation

  ▷ +: Externally processed operation

  ▷ X: Internally processed operation/external possible

▶ **Confirmations**

An entry in the Confirmations field determines if milestone confirmations are carried out at this operation, that is, if all operations up to the preceding milestone operation are confirmed during confirmation. It also can determine if confirmations are mandatory, not possible, or optional at this operation. The following are possible entries in this field:

- 1: Milestone confirmation (not PS/PM)
- 2: Confirmation required
- 3: Confirmation not possible
- Blank: Confirmation possible but not necessary

Now that we've examined the control key in detail, let's look at the other relevant fields in the Default values tab.

Control Key is Referenced

If you select any of the RefID (reference ID) checkboxes in the Default values tab shown in Figure 5.11, the values defaulted into the routing are not changeable.

> **Note**
>
> When you deselect the reference checkbox for a work center used in a routing, the default values from the work center are not copied to the routing. You must use the mass replacement function or replace these values manually in the routing.

Unit of Measure of Standard Values

The default standard value units of measure of the work center in Figure 5.11 determines the activity unit of measures when adding an operation to a routing.

Now let's look at the fields in the Capacities section of a work center.

5.2.3 Capacities

Capacity is the ability of a work center to perform a task. Click on the Capacities tab in Figure 5.11 to display the screen shown in Figure 5.13.

Let's discuss the relevant fields in the Capacities tab.

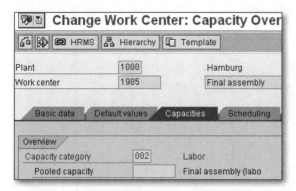

Figure 5.13 Work Center Capacity Overview

Capacity category

Capacities are differentiated according to capacity category. The capacity category enables you to differentiate between machine or labor capacity:

▸ Machine capacity is the availability of a machine based on planned and unplanned outages and maintenance requirements.

▸ Labor capacity is the number of workers who can operate a machine at the same time.

A capacity category can exist only once at each work center. However, capacities at different work centers can have the same capacity category.

To find out more information about a capacity category, click the Capacity button at the bottom of the Capacitates tab screen (not shown). The screen shown in Figure 5.14 is displayed.

The work center capacity header provides capacity information such as:

▸ Factory calendar ID, which defines work days and non–work days such as weekends and public holidays

▸ Start and finish times for shifts

▸ Lengths of breaks

Now that we've discussed capacity category, let's look at the next field in Figure 5.13.

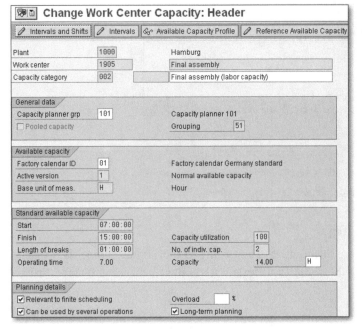

Figure 5.14 Work Center Capacity Header

Pooled Capacity

The Pooled capacity field shown in Figure 5.13 identifies an available capacity that can be used by several work centers.

Example

An example of a pooled capacity is a group of setup personnel who perform setups for many work centers.

If you do not enter a pooled capacity key when assigning capacity to the work center, the capacity is assigned only to that particular work center.

Note

With additional icons and buttons available at the bottom of the Capacities tab screen (not shown in Figure 5.13), you can perform additional functions as described below:

▶ Delete existing capacity categories

▶ Add additional capacity categories

- Display or change capacity header information
- Display details of formulas used to determine capacity requirements
- Test formulas with different quantities and standard values
- Set different formula constants
- Make settings for determining the actual capacity requirements

Work center capacity fields are normally set up and tested by production personnel with the additional functionality listed above.

The next section of a work center is Scheduling data.

5.2.4 Scheduling

Click on the Scheduling tab in Figure 5.13 to display the screen shown in Figure 5.15.

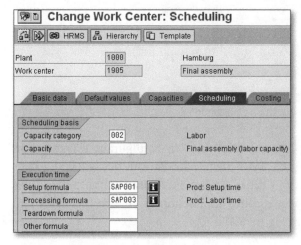

Figure 5.15 Work Center Scheduling

During scheduling the system calculates the start and finish dates of manufacturing orders or operations in an order.

Capacity Category

The capacity category specified in the Scheduling basis section is a capacity whose operating time you use for scheduling manufacturing orders.

See Section 5.2.3 for more information on capacity

Capacity

The Capacity field is for recording the name for which the capacity is created, changed, displayed, or used in the system.

Setup Formula

This is the formula used in scheduling to calculate the setup time of an operation. If you do not enter a formula, the system uses a scheduling setup time of zero. Click the information icon next to the Setup formula field to display details of the formula, as shown in Figure 5.16.

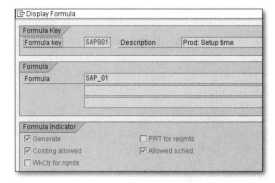

Figure 5.16 Work Center Execution Time Setup Formula

Define the formula key and formula with configuration Transaction OP54 or by following the IMG menu path PRODUCTION • BASIC DATA • WORK CENTER • COSTING • WORK CENTER FORMULAS • DEFINE FORMULAS FOR WORK CENTERS. You use this transaction to change the fields and indicators displayed in Figure 5.16.

You define formula parameters (SAP_01 in this example) entered in the Formula section with configuration Transaction OP51 or by following the IMG menu path PRODUCTION • BASIC DATA • WORK CENTER • COSTING • WORK CENTER FORMULAS • DEFINE FORMULA PARAMETERS FOR WORK CENTERS. Double-click parameter SAP_01 to display the parameters details screen shown in Figure 5.17.

The parameter definition for SAP_01 indicates that the setup time calculated by the formula in Figure 5.16 is equal to the standard value in the operation details of the routing, as we will discuss in Section 5.3.

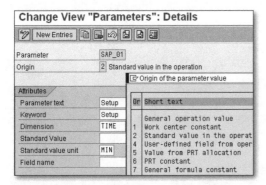

Figure 5.17 Formula Parameters for Work Centers

Right-click in the Origin field and click Possible Entries to display the list of possible Parameter value Origins as shown in Figure 5.17. It's possible to derive a parameter from different origins such as a user-defined field from the operation or from a constant.

> **Note**
>
> If you work in a process industry that manufactures the same product on a production line for several process orders sequentially, you will not incur setup time and costs for every process order. To manage this scenario, you can use functionality called production campaign, which you can access with Transaction PC02 or by following the menu path LOGISTICS • PRODUCTION – PROCESS • PRODUCTION CAMPAIGN.

Now that we've discussed the setup formula shown in Figure 5.15, let's examine the processing formula.

Processing Formula

This is the formula used in scheduling to calculate the processing time of an operation. If you do not enter a formula, the system uses a scheduling processing time of zero. Click the information icon next to the Processing formula field in Figure 5.15 to display details of the formula as shown in Figure 5.18.

You can figure out how the formula in Figure 5.18 works by determining the details of each of the formula parameters with the same method used to display Figure 5.17 using configuration Transaction OP51.

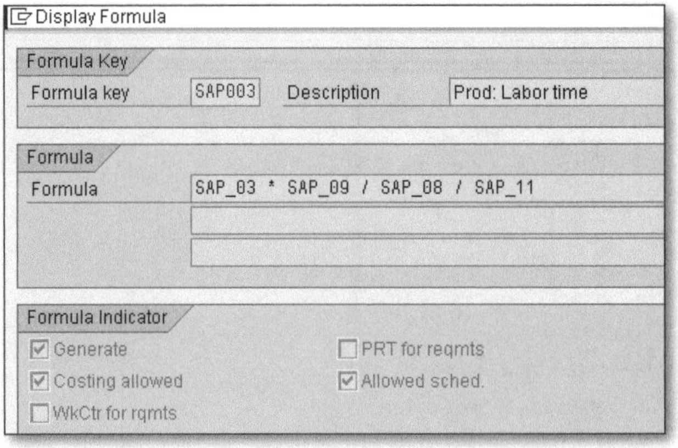

Figure 5.18 Work Center Execution Time Processing Formula

Note

Formula keys and parameters are normally set up by production personnel, and in most cases can be copied from SAP-supplied standard formulas. Accounting and Controlling personnel should understand how to analyze formulas in case there are any costing issues or messages, especially during initial implementation of an SAP system.

With the Costing allowed checkbox in the Formula Indicator section in Figure 5.18, you control whether the formula can be used to calculate costs.

Now let's consider the next field in the Execution time section of Figure 5.15.

Teardown Formula

Teardown time is the time needed to restore a work center to its normal state after operations have been processed. When you need to include a teardown formula in scheduling, you include the formula key in this field. Teardown time is similar in concept to setup time because they are both normally fixed independently of the production lot-size quantity. If you do not enter a formula, the system uses a teardown time of zero for scheduling.

Other Formula

In this field you can enter a formula for calculating the duration times of other types of internal processing in scheduling (for example, in networks, in process orders or in maintenance orders).

If you do not enter a formula, the system uses the duration you entered when maintaining an activity or operation in a network or maintenance order.

Now that we've looked at the Scheduling section of a work center, the next section to consider is Costing.

5.2.5 Costing

Click the Costing tab in Figure 5.15 to display the screen shown in Figure 5.19.

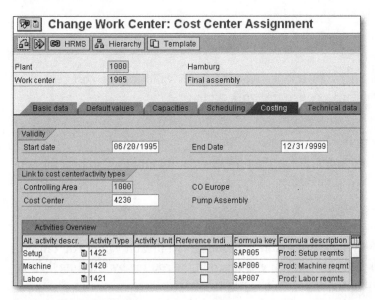

Figure 5.19 Work Center Cost Center Assignment

A Work Center uses resources from a Cost Center to cost the activities performed at the work center.

Start Date and End Date

For a validity period you must assign a work center to only one cost center.

Controlling Area and Cost Center

The cost center to which you assign the work center must exist for the validity period and belong to the same controlling area as the work center plant. You can assign several work centers in different plants to one cost center. The work centers must belong to the same company code as the cost center.

Alternative Activity Description

You use an alternative activity description (Alt. activity descr. field) if you are editing work centers and want to describe an activity on the Costing tab page.

Activity Type

You can assign an activity type, which is valid for the cost center, to every standard value in the work center.

Activity Unit

The activity unit is either the time or quantity unit used to post the consumed activity quantities.

Reference Indicator

The activity type appears in the routing as a default value. You can prevent this default from being changed in the routing by selecting the Reference Indi (reference indicator) checkbox.

Formula Key and Formula Description

The formula key refers to formulas used to determine:

▶ Execution time
▶ Capacity requirements

- Costs of an activity type
- Total quantity or usage value of a production resource or tool

> **Note**
>
> You can test and display details of formulas listed in the Costing tab screen with icons and buttons at the bottom of the screen (not shown) in a similar way as described in Section 5.2.3.

Now that we've looked at the fields in the Costing tab of a work center, let's discuss the functionality available in the Technical data section.

5.2.6 Technical Data

The fields in the Technical data tab of Figure 5.19 provide methods to determine and store data for standard values with CAPP (Computer Aided Process Planning) in a work center. Examples of such data are machine data, rounding categories, and additional value keys. You should assign to the work center at least one process with which the standard values should be calculated.

Now that we've examined BOMs and work centers in detail, let's look at routings. Material masters and BOMs provide cost estimates with material and assembly prices and quantities. Routings are lists of operations performed at work centers that allow you to determine labor and activity standard quantities,

5.3 Routing

A routing is a list of tasks containing standard activity times required to perform operations necessary to build an assembly. Routings, together with planned activity prices, provide the information necessary to calculate the labor and overhead costs of products for cost estimates. An example of a routing is shown in Figure 5.20.

A routing consists of one or more operations that process and assemble BOM items into subassemblies and final assemblies. Operations are performed at work centers, as we previously discussed in Section 5.2.

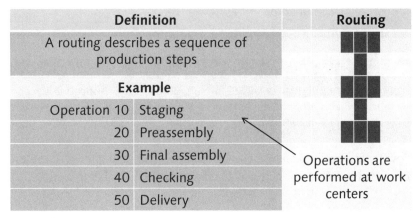

Definition	Routing
A routing describes a sequence of production steps	
Example	
Operation 10 Staging	
20 Preassembly	
30 Final assembly	Operations are performed at work centers
40 Checking	
50 Delivery	

Figure 5.20 Example of a Routing

Each routing contains many fields and indicators relevant to Product Cost Controlling, which we'll now examine in detail. First, we'll look at the routing header screen, which applies to the entire routing, then the operation overview screen, which lists all operations, and then the operation details screen, which displays details for each operation. You can view or change routings with Transaction CA02 or by following the menu path LOGISTICS • PRODUCTION • MASTER DATA • ROUTINGS • ROUTINGS • STANDARD ROUTINGS • CHANGE. The selection screen shown in Figure 5.21 is displayed.

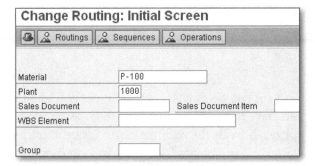

Figure 5.21 Change Routing Initial Screen

Let's examine the routing header screen.

5.3.1 Header

Type in the material and plant for the routing you want to maintain and click the header (hat) icon to display the screen shown in Figure 5.22.

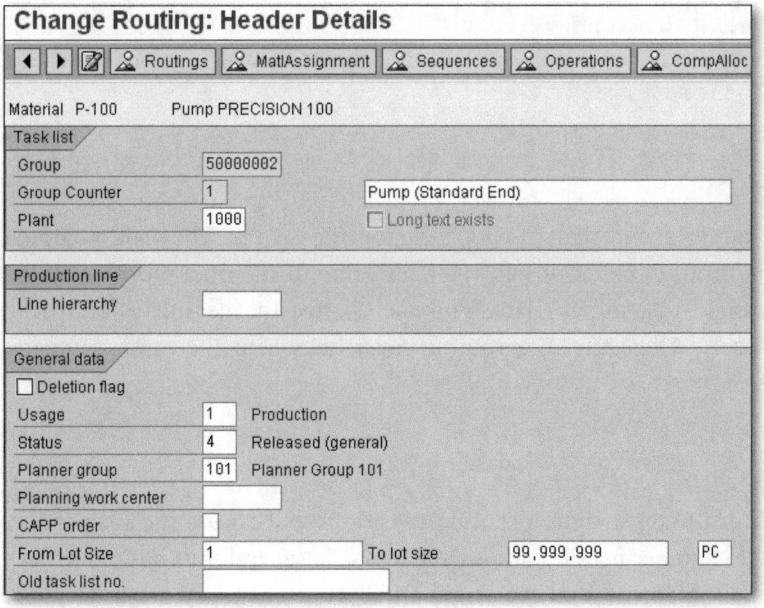

Change Routing: Header Details

| | Routings | MatlAssignment | Sequences | Operations | CompAlloc |

Material P-100   Pump PRECISION 100

Task list

Group	50000002	
Group Counter	1	Pump (Standard End)
Plant	1000	☐ Long text exists

Production line

| Line hierarchy | |

General data

☐ Deletion flag

Usage	1	Production
Status	4	Released (general)
Planner group	101	Planner Group 101
Planning work center		
CAPP order		
From Lot Size	1	To lot size	99,999,999	PC
Old task list no.		

Figure 5.22 Routing Header Details

We'll now discuss the relevant fields in the Routing Header Details screen.

Group

In the Task list section the Group field identifies routings that contain different production steps for the one material.

> **Example**
>
> You have an efficient method of manufacturing a material, but you must use a less efficient method at periods of high demand due to capacity requirements of in-house production. You can create a different task list group for each possible method of manufacture.

Group Counter

The group counter identifies a task list within a task list group. A task list group and group counter uniquely identify a task list.

> **Example**
>
> A group counter can be used to identify different lot-size ranges for manufacturing the same material.

Plant

This identifies the plant in which the routing is valid. The plant is copied to the routing operations as a default value. If the operations are to be performed in another plant, you can change the default value in the operation. All plants in a routing must belong to the same company code.

Usage

A task list usage assigns a routing to various work areas such as production or engineering. This allows you to create several routings to produce one plant material. You can assign a task list usage to a work order type.

> **Example**
>
> You can restrict routings of production usage to work orders of a type valid only for production. This avoids the possibility of routings in the development process being used in the production process.

The system uses the usage in a work order for automatic task list selection.

Status

You can use the Status field to indicate the processing status of a task list.

> **Example**
>
> You can indicate whether the task list is still in the creation or development phase, or if it has been released for production using the Status field.

Material Assignment

Click the MatlAssignment (material assignment) button or select ROUTING • MATERIAL ASSIGNMENT from the menu bar to display the screen shown in Figure 5.23.

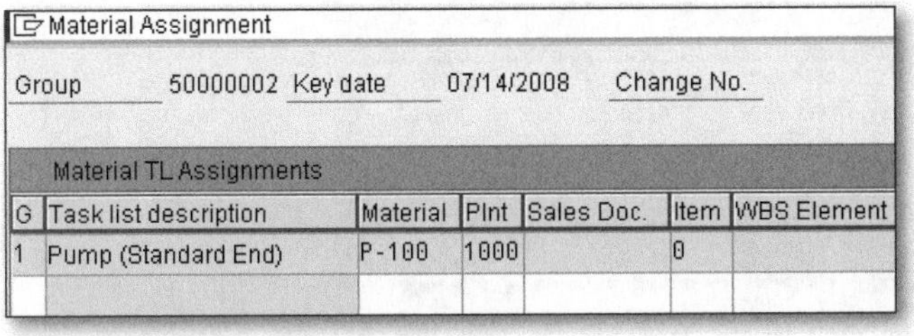
Material Assignment

Group 50000002 Key date 07/14/2008 Change No.

Material TL Assignments

G	Task list description	Material	Plnt	Sales Doc.	Item	WBS Element
1	Pump (Standard End)	P-100	1000		0	

Figure 5.23 Routing Material Assignment

You use this screen to determine which material is to be produced with a task list. On the basis of this assignment, the routing can be used for sales and operations planning, material requirements planning, creating production orders, and cost estimates for this material.

Note

The material produced by the routing determines the manufacturing order credit when the assembly is received into inventory. The credit is determined by multiplying the goods receipt quantity times the assembly standard price.

Now that we've examined relevant routing header fields, let's examine the Operations Overview screen.

5.3.2 Operation Overview

Click the Operations button in Figure 5.22 or select GOTO • OPERATION OVERVIEW from the menu bar to display the screen shown in Figure 5.24.

The Operation Overview screen displays a list of operations required to manufacture the assembly. Let's examine the fields in the Operation Details screen.

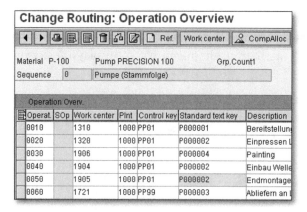

Figure 5.24 Routing Operation Overview

5.3.3 Operation Details

Double-click the 0030 row in the Operat. (operation) column to display the screen shown in Figure 5.25.

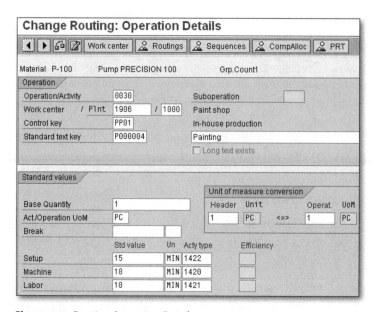

Figure 5.25 Routing Operation Details

The values you see in Figure 5.25 defaulted from work center 1906, except for the values in the rows in the Std value (Standard value) column. We've already discussed the relevant fields in the Operation section of Figure 5.25 while looking at work center default values in Section 5.2.2. Now let's examine the fields in the Standard values section of Figure 5.25.

Base Quantity

The standard values of the operation refer to the base quantity of the material to be produced. You can increase the accuracy of the standard values when required by increasing the base quantity. This is similar in concept to increasing the price unit to increase the accuracy of a standard or moving average price.

Activity/Operation Unit of Measure

The unit of measure (UoM) used in the operation for the material to be produced is valid for:

► Base quantity
► Minimum lot size
► Minimum send-ahead quantity when operations overlap

If the unit of measure in the header has already been maintained, this unit is used as the default value for the operation unit. You can change the unit of measure in the operation.

Standard Value

The standard value indicates how long it normally takes to perform each activity. The standard value multiplied by the planned activity rate of the activity type (Acty type field) provides planned labor and overhead costs. The calculation can be modified by a performance efficiency rate and formula. Labor costs are rolled up from subassemblies to the finished good.

Now that we've considered the Operations and Standard values sections in Figure 5.25, scroll down the Operation Details screen until you reach the General data section as shown in Figure 5.26.

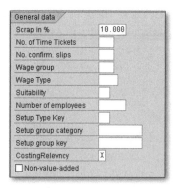

Figure 5.26 General Data Section of Operation Details

Let's discuss the relevant fields in the General data section of the operation details.

Operation Scrap

An entry in the Scrap in % (operation scrap percentage) field causes a decrease in quantity in the next operation because the quantity to be processed is reduced by the scrap quantity. The reduction of quantity is taken into account in scheduling and costing.

Costing Relevancy

For the standard cost estimate and the calculation of planned costs and actual costs for a work order, the CostingRelevncy checkbox determines whether the item is included in costing.

Example

Operation items are generally relevant for costing. You can indicate certain items such as documents and text items as not relevant for costing.

Non-Value-Added

You select the Non-value-added checkbox to flag an operation as not being part of the value-added chain. The system then takes the operations into account in the evaluations in the line balance or the reconciliation of the time capacity with the time requirements of a production line. For example, you can display the total non-value-added processing time.

Now that we've considered the General data section in Figure 5.26, scroll down the Operation Details screen until you reach the External processing section as shown in Figure 5.27.

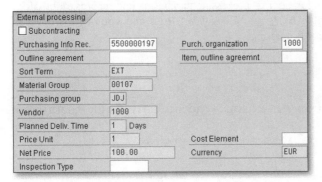

Figure 5.27 External Processing of Operation Details

This screen is where you enter information about operations that are performed at an external vendor workshop. The work center control key we discussed in Section 5.2.2, which defaults into the operation details screen as shown in Figure 5.25, determines if an operation is sent to a vendor for external processing. We'll examine the fields relevant to costing in the following sections.

Subcontracting

Selecting this checkbox specifies that this operation is subcontracted, and parts will be provided as necessary to an external vendor. A subcontracting purchase order is created for the external vendor.

Purchasing Info Record

You can create a purchasing info record for the external operation; this contains all necessary purchasing information such as vendor and price. If you enter the purchasing info record number in this field and press Enter, the relevant information defaults from the purchasing info record to the external processing section of the operation. This defaulted information is not changeable. If you need to change the information, you first have to delete the purchasing info record number.

> **Note**
>
> Purchasing info records for external processing operations are not associated with a material because you are purchasing a service or activity and not a material. To search for external processing purchasing info records, right-click in the field in Figure 5.27, select Possible Entries and scroll across to Info Records for External Processing.

Vendor

This is where you enter an external vendor to carry out the external processing.

Cost Element

You can enter a cost element to separately identify external processing costs in cost reports.

> **Note**
>
> The commonly used standard Actual/Plan/Variance cost center report S_ALR_87013611 identifies costs separately with external processing cost elements that you enter in the Cost Element field in Figure 5.27. You create primary external processing cost elements with Transaction KA01.

Price Unit

The price unit is the number of units to which the price refers. You can increase the accuracy of the price by increasing the price unit. To determine the unit price, divide the price by the price unit.

Net Price

This is where you enter the external processing costs payable to the vendor. You can only maintain the net price if you have not yet maintained the purchasing info record conditions. You must then maintain the price on the conditions screen. If the vendor's net price for the material has not been maintained in the purchasing info record, the net price of the last purchase order issued to the vendor is proposed when a new purchase order is created.

Component Allocation

Click the CompAlloc (component allocation) button shown in Figure 5.25 or select GOTO • COMP. ALLOC – GEN from the menu bar to display the screen shown in Figure 5.28.

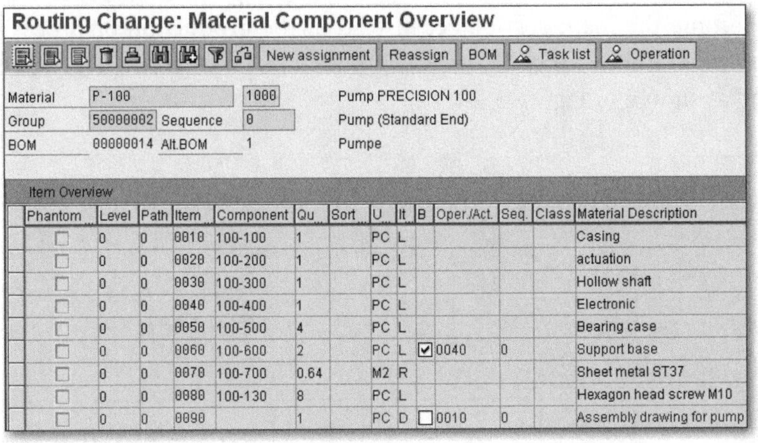

Phantom	Level	Path	Item	Component	Qu	Sort	U	It	B	Oper./Act.	Seq.	Class	Material Description
☐	0	0	0010	100-100	1		PC	L					Casing
☐	0	0	0020	100-200	1		PC	L					actuation
☐	0	0	0030	100-300	1		PC	L					Hollow shaft
☐	0	0	0040	100-400	1		PC	L					Electronic
☐	0	0	0050	100-500	4		PC	L					Bearing case
☐	0	0	0060	100-600	2		PC	L	☑	0040	0		Support base
☐	0	0	0070	100-700	0.64		M2	R					Sheet metal ST37
☐	0	0	0080	100-130	8		PC	L					Hexagon head screw M10
☐	0	0	0090		1		PC	D	☐	0010	0		Assembly drawing for pump

Figure 5.28 Material Component Overview

In this screen you assign material components from a BOM to individual operations in the routing in the Oper./Act. (operation/activity) column. Material components in a BOM that are not assigned to an operation in the routing are automatically assigned to the first operation when you create a manufacturing order.

You can assign material components from several BOMs or alternative BOMs to a routing. When you create a manufacturing order, you select the BOM and material components to be assigned in the manufacturing order.

Note

Components debit the manufacturing order when removed from inventory. The debit value is determined by multiplying the goods issue quantity times the component price.

Now that we've examined BOMs, work centers, and routings in detail, let's look at product cost collectors in the next section.

5.4 Product Cost Collector

A product cost collector collects actual costs during the production of an assembly. Product cost collectors are necessary for repetitive manufacturing and optional for order-related manufacturing. Product cost collectors become the main cost object instead of the production or process orders when linked for order-related production. Costs are analyzed per period as shown in Figure 5.29.

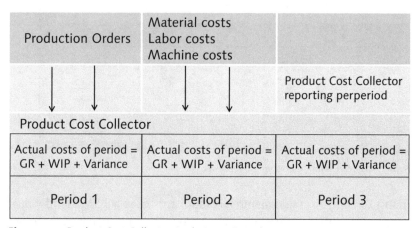

Figure 5.29 Product Cost Collector Analysis per Period

As you post activity confirmations and goods movements with reference to a production order, associated costs such as material, labor, and machine cost are assigned automatically to the product cost collector. You can display and analyze (product cost collector) costs such as target versus actual using standard information system reports such as KKBC_PKO.

All period-end Controlling functions are performed with reference to the product cost collector. The periodic actual costs can be divided into:

▸ Costs for products for which a goods receipt (GR) into inventory has been made in the period

▸ Costs for work in process (WIP). These are target costs for production quantities that have been confirmed for production operations, but for which no goods receipt (GR) has taken place.

▸ Variance calculated using the formula: variance = actual costs of period – GR – WIP.

Product cost collectors have been available since SAP R/3 Release 4.5 for use with production orders, as well as in repetitive manufacturing. Several advantages result from using product cost collectors:

▸ Period-end closing and information system performance is improved because there are fewer cost objects compared with Product Cost by Order. Costs for many manufacturing orders can be viewed collectively per period for a product cost collector.

▸ Variance analysis is carried out for a product instead of a manufacturing order. It's usually more relevant to know how efficiently different products are manufactured, rather than the efficiency of a particular manufacturing order.

▸ Product cost collectors enable you to collect costs at the product level independently of the production type. Regardless of whether the production environment is order-related production, process manufacturing, or repetitive manufacturing, you collect the production costs for the product on a product cost collector and analyze the costs in each period.

▸ If production orders remain open for multiple periods, variance reconciliation is easier using product collectors. For example, say the price of natural gas used in drying kilns increases unexpectedly one month. If the production order is finally delivered three months later, the production order variances in Controlling (CO) are posted in a later month compared with when the primary expenses occurred in Financial Accounting (FI). This makes reconciliation between CO and FI accounting difficult during any one period. With product cost collectors, WIP and variance are posted together during the month they both occur.

You can create, change, or view product cost collectors with Transaction KKF6N or by following the menu path ACCOUNTING • CONTROLLING • PRODUCT COST CONTROLLING • COST OBJECT CONTROLLING • PRODUCT

COST BY PERIOD • MASTER DATA • PRODUCT COST COLLECTOR • EDIT. A selection screen is displayed, as shown in Figure 5.30.

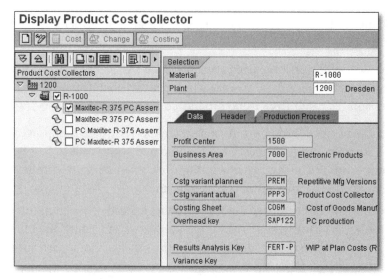

Figure 5.30 Display Product Cost Collector Data

A product cost collector contains all of the information needed to manufacture a product. This includes fields relevant to cost and variance analysis. To display these fields, proceed as follows:

1. Enter the relevant information in the Material and Plant fields.

2. Select the production version checkbox (yellow scroll) on the left.

3. Press Enter to display details of the product cost collector.

We'll now discuss each of the relevant fields, beginning with the Data tab.

5.4.1 Data

The Data tab contains the fields mainly related to costing.

Profit Center

A profit center receives postings made in parallel to master data such as cost centers and orders. Profit Center Accounting is a separate ledger that enables reporting from a profit center point of view. You normally create profit centers based on areas in a company that generate revenue with a responsible manager assigned. The Profit Center field is also displayed in the sales, MRP, and plant data material master views.

If Profit Center Accounting is active, you will receive a warning message if you do not specify a profit center during a posting, and all unassigned postings will be made to a dummy profit center. You activate Profit Center Accounting with configuration transaction OKKP, which maintains the controlling area.

Business Area

A business area is an organizational unit of Financial Accounting that represents a separate area of operations or responsibilities within an organization. You can create financial statements for business areas, and you can use these statements for internal reporting purposes.

> **Note**
>
> The use of profit centers for internal operations or responsibilities reporting is a more recent functionality and provides more flexibility for organizational changes than business area reporting. Profit center standard and alternate hierarchies, which are not available for business areas, also allow for more flexible reporting.

Costing Variant Planned

The costing variant determines how costs are calculated. The *planned* costing variant is used to determine the preliminary cost estimate, which, when compared with actual costs determined by the *actual* costing variant discussed in the next section, allow you to carry out production variance analysis.

Refer to Chapter 8 for more information on costing variants

You define the planned costing variant with configuration Transaction OKKN or by following the IMG menu path CONTROLLING • PRODUCT COST CONTROLLING • COST OBJECT CONTROLLING • PRODUCT COST BY PERIOD • PRODUCT COST COLLECTORS • CHECK COSTING VARIANTS FOR PRODUCT COST COLLECTORS • COSTING VARIANTS TO DETERMINE ACTIVITY QUANTITIES. The screen shown in Figure 5.31 is displayed.

Figure 5.31 Planned Costing Variant Overview Screen

A list of available planned costing variants is presented in the Costing Variant column. Double-click the standard SAP costing variant PREM and then click the valuation variant button to display the screen shown in Figure 5.32.

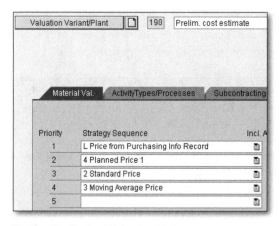

Figure 5.32 Planned Valuation Variant

Refer to Chapter 8 for more information on valuation variants

The planned valuation variant first searches for a component price from a purchasing info record price. Therefore, the preliminary cost estimate is based on the most recent vendor quotation, if available, for the material component.

The planned valuation variant also determines which costing sheet is used for preliminary costing.

Actual Costing Variant

This costing variant calculates actual costs by determining the following:

▶ What activity prices are used to evaluate confirmed internal activities

▶ Which costing sheet is proposed for calculating overhead costs in period-end closing

You define the actual costing variant with configuration Transaction OPL1 or by following the IMG menu path CONTROLLING • PRODUCT COST CONTROLLING • COST OBJECT CONTROLLING • PRODUCT COST BY PERIOD • PRODUCT COST COLLECTORS • CHECK COSTING VARIANTS FOR PRODUCT COST COLLECTORS • COSTING VARIANTS FOR VALUATION OF INTERNAL ACTIVITIES. The screen shown in Figure 5.33 is displayed.

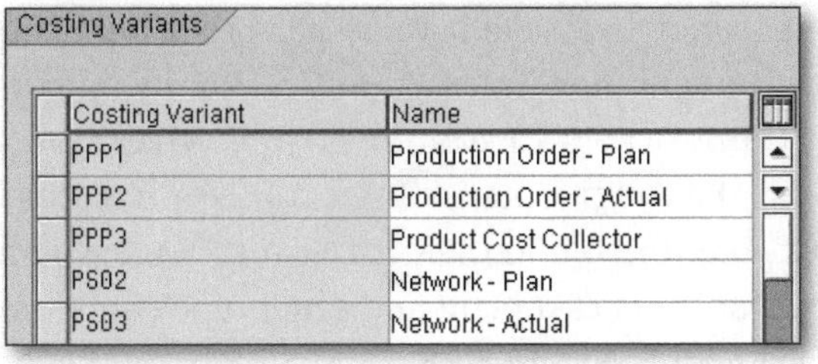

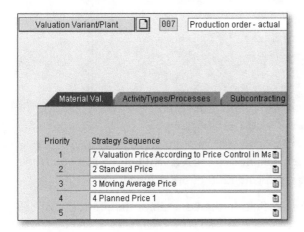

Figure 5.33 Actual Costing Variant Overview Screen

A list of available actual costing variants is presented in the Costing Variant column. Double-click the standard SAP costing variant PPP3 and then click the valuation variant button to display the screen shown in Figure 5.34.

Figure 5.34 Actual Valuation Variant

The actual valuation variant first searches for a material component valuation price according to the price control in the material master Costing 2 view. If you have the price control set to moving average price for your material components, this valuation variant will result in a more recent component price than that determined by the purchasing info record from the planned valuation variant.

Costing Sheet

Refer to Chapter 6 for more information on costing sheets

Costing sheet configuration contains the rules for allocating overhead. It is defaulted from the valuation variant that is stored in the costing variant. The costing variant is stored as a default value per order type and plant that you define with configuration Transaction OKZ3 or by following the IMG menu path CONTROLLING • PRODUCT COST CONTROLLING • COST OBJECT CONTROLLING • PRODUCT COST BY PERIOD • PRODUCT COST COLLECTORS • DEFINE COST-ACCOUNTING-RELEVANT DEFAULT VALUES FOR ORDER TYPES AND PLANTS. Double-click a plant and order type combination to display the screen shown in Figure 5.35.

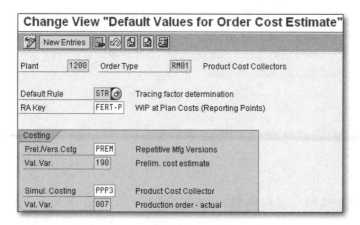

Figure 5.35 Default Values for Order Types and Plants

The values in this screen default into the relevant fields when you create product cost collectors for plant 1200 of order type RM01.

Now let's discuss the next field in the Data tab of the product cost collector in Figure 5.30.

Overhead Key

An overhead key is used to apply different overhead percentages to individual orders or groups of orders. You assign the overhead key in the overhead rate component of a costing sheet.

Results Analysis Key

Each product cost collector or order for which you want to create WIP must contain a results analysis key. The presence of a results analysis key means that the product cost collector or order is included in WIP calculation during period-end closing.

The results analysis key (RA Key) can be specified as a default value for each plant and order type as shown in Figure 5.35.

Variance Key

Variances are only calculated on manufacturing orders or product cost collectors containing a variance key. This key is defaulted from the Costing 1 view when manufacturing orders or product cost collectors are created. The variance key also determines if the value of scrap is subtracted from actual costs before variances are determined.

Now that we've discussed the fields in the Data tab of the product cost collector, let's examine the fields in the next tab.

5.4.2 Header

Select the Header tab in Figure 5.30 and then click the pencil and glasses icon to display the screen shown in Figure 5.36.

The Header section contains several fields relevant to product costing, which we'll now examine.

Description

The description defaults from the production version text when you create a product cost collector. You can change this description at any time.

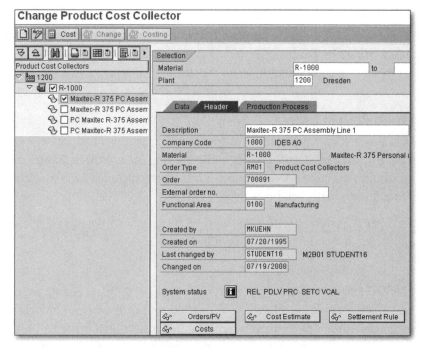

Figure 5.36 Product Cost Collector Header

This can sometimes be useful to clearly identify product cost collectors in information system reports.

Company Code

You initially define a product cost collector by plant, material, and production version. You assign a plant to a company code when initially setting up your organization with configuration Transaction OX18, so the company code is automatically determined from the plant and is not changeable.

Material

Because you can enter a range of materials in the Selection section of the screen in Figure 5.36, the material in the Header section represents the material selected in the left side of the screen.

Order Type

When you initially create a product cost collector by clicking the new page icon in Figure 5.36, the Order Type field is a mandatory, as shown in Figure 5.37.

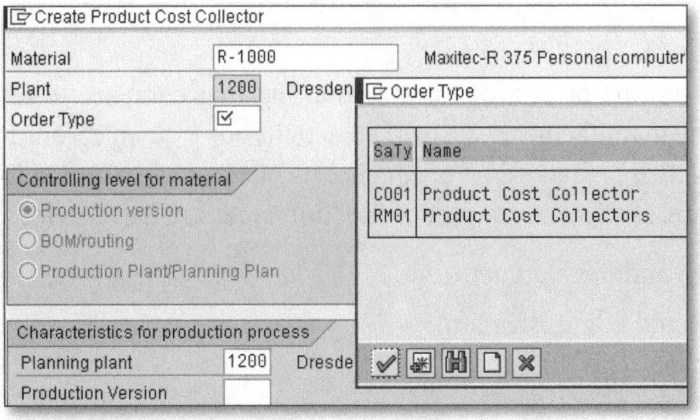

Figure 5.37 Create Product Cost Collector

Right-click in the Order Type field and select Possible Entries to display a list of possible product cost collector order types. Once you create a product cost collector, the order type is not changeable, as shown in Figure 5.36.

The order type differentiates orders according to parameters such as number range, costing variants, and settlement profile.

> **Note**
>
> The Controlling level for the material determines the characteristics for the production process that you must enter when creating a product cost collector. In Figure 5.37, the selected Controlling level of production version means you must enter the characteristic of production version when creating the product cost collector. You always use this Controlling level when you are using production versions or repetitive manufacturing.
>
> If a more detailed Controlling level has already been defined for the plant material, then that detailed Controlling level is used when a new product cost collector is created. Because a product cost collector has previously been created with the most detailed Controlling level of product version, this is the only available Controlling level in Figure 5.37.

External Order Number

You can enter any external number in this field to help identify your product cost collectors more easily. You can use this number as a selection criteria during collective processing.

Functional Area

Functional area is part of cost of sales accounting that compares sales revenue with the manufacturing costs of an activity for a given accounting period. Expenses posted to the product cost collector are assigned to the functional area. Typical examples of function areas are listed below:

▶ R&D (research and development)

▶ G&A (general and administration)

▶ S&D (sales and distribution)

▶ COS (cost of sales)

Refer to OSS Note 85799 for more information on functional areas Expenses and revenues that cannot be assigned to functional areas are reported in other profit and loss items sorted according to expense and revenue type. You can enter or change the functional area, provided no postings exist for this product cost collector.

Created and Changed

These four fields contain user and date information for the product cost collector creation and last change, and these fields are not changeable.

System Status

Click the information icon in Figure 5.36 to display detailed status as shown in Figure 5.38.

System status details inform you which processing steps have been carried out on the product cost collector. For example, period-end variances have been calculated if the VCAL checkbox is selected. System status determines which business processes are allowed at each stage of the product cost collector processing.

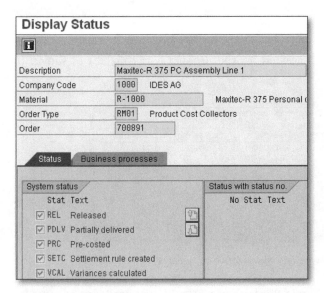

Figure 5.38 Display Status

Orders/PV

Clicking the Orders/PV (orders/production version) button in Figure 5.36 will produce either one of the following:

▶ A list of manufacturing orders linked to the product cost collector

▶ The production version if this is a repetitive manufacturing scenario

Displaying orders or production versions associated with a specific product cost collector can sometimes be quicker with this button than with Information System reports such as COOIS for production orders or COOISPI for process orders because you do not have to complete a selection screen.

Cost Estimate

Clicking the display Cost Estimate button will display a list of preliminary cost estimates created for the product cost collector as shown in Figure 5.39.

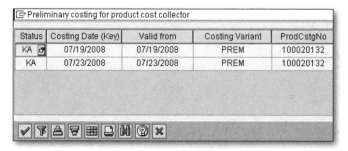

Figure 5.39 List of Available Preliminary Cost Estimates

Refer to Chapter 10 for more information on preliminary cost estimates

Double-click any line to display the corresponding preliminary cost estimate. You normally want to display the most recent preliminary cost estimate without errors based on the Status and Costing Date. Click a status and press the F4 key to display a list of possible entries and meanings.

To create an *individual* new preliminary cost estimate click the Cost button in Figure 5.36 after ensuring that the product cost collector is in change mode by clicking the glasses and pencil icon. This icon toggles between change and display mode for the product cost collector.

You can create preliminary cost estimates *collectively* with Transaction MF30 or by following the menu path ACCOUNTING • CONTROLLING • PRODUCT COST CONTROLLING • COST OBJECT CONTROLLING • PRODUCT COST BY PERIOD • PLANNING • PRELIMINARY COSTING FOR PRODUCT COST COLLECTORS.

Settlement Rule

Refer to Chapter 18 for more information on settlement rules

A settlement rule determines which portions of product cost collector costs are allocated to receivers. You generally settle a product cost collector to a material. The valuation class in the material master Costing 2 view then determines which general ledger (G/L) accounts are settled via automatic accounting assignment configuration Transaction OBYC or the IMG menu path Materials Management • Valuation and Account Assignment • Account Determination • Account Determination Without Wizard • Configure Automatic Postings.

Costs

Click the display Costs button to display a detailed report on cumulative costs for the product cost collector. Detailed reports provide cost element details by row and target, actual, and variance by column. The cost element rows can be grouped together by similar business transactions such as confirmations, goods issues, and goods receipts in the report. You can also access detailed reports in the Information System with Transaction KKBC_PKO.

Now that we've discussed the fields in the Header tab of the product cost collector, let's examine the fields in the next tab.

5.4.3 Production Process

Select the Production Process tab in Figure 5.36 to display the screen shown in Figure 5.40.

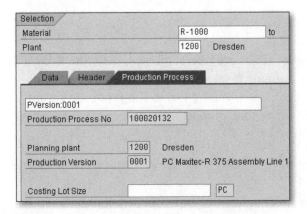

Figure 5.40 Product Cost Collector Production Process

From SAP R/3 release 4.5A on, product cost collectors are created with reference to a production process that describes the way a material is produced. The production process has characteristics whose values are unique to that production process. You specify which characteristics are updated for the production process via the Controlling level.

The Controlling level you select when you create a product cost collector determines the level at which the costs are collected:

- Production version
- BOM and routing combination
- Material and plant combination

Let's consider the fields in the Production Process tab.

Description

The name of a production process is created automatically from a combination of characteristic attributes that are defined by the Controlling level. You can manually change the description.

Production Process Number

This number is assigned automatically during the creation of the product cost collector and cannot be changed.

Planning Plant

This is the plant in which the goods receipt takes place for the manufactured material. If the planning plant and production plant are identical, you do not need to enter the planning plant. The production plant is copied automatically when the product cost collector is created as shown in Figure 5.37.

Production Version

A production version describes the types of production techniques that can be used for a material in a plant. It is a unique combination of BOM, routing, and production line. You enter the production version when you first create the product cost collector.

Costing Lot Size

The costing lot size determines the quantity on which the preliminary cost estimate calculations are based. If you leave this field blank, the costing lot size from the material master Costing 1 view is used during the cost estimate calculation.

If you enter a costing lot size in this field, you cannot change the value in this field after the product cost collector is saved. You can however change it with Transaction CK91N or by following the menu path ACCOUNTING • CONTROLLING • PRODUCT COST CONTROLLING • PRODUCT COST PLANNING • MATERIAL COSTING • MASTER DATA FOR MIXED COST ESTIMATE • EDIT PROCUREMENT ALTERNATIVES. Enter the material and plant and click the glasses and pencil icon to display the screen shown in Figure 5.41.

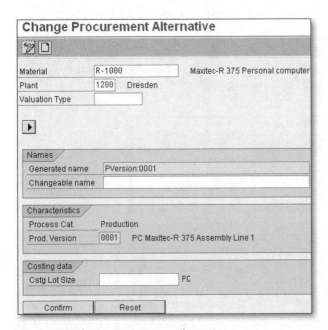

Figure 5.41 Change Procurement Alternative

Make an entry in the Cstg Lot Size (costing lot size) field and save the procurement alternative to change the costing lot size entry in the product cost collector.

Now that we've examined BOMs, work centers, routings, and product cost collectors in detail, let's look at purchasing info records in the next section.

5.5 Purchasing Info Record

A purchasing info record stores all of the information relevant to the procurement of a material from a vendor. It contains the purchase price field, which the standard cost estimate usually searches for when determining the purchase price. It's usually easiest to access a purchasing info record by selecting from a list that you can access with Transaction ME1M or by following the menu path LOGISTICS • MATERIALS MANAGEMENT • PURCHASING • MASTER DATA • INFO RECORD • LIST DISPLAYS • BY MATERIAL. The selection screen shown in Figure 5.42 is displayed.

> **Note**
>
> You can also list purchasing info records with other criteria such as by vendor with Transaction ME1L or material group with Transaction ME1W.

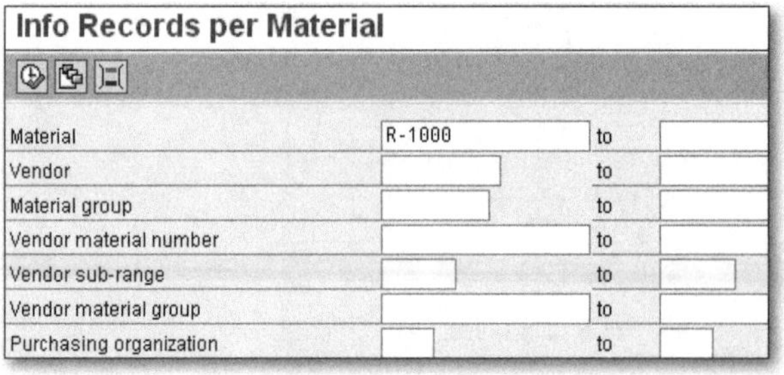

Info Records per Material

Material	R-1000	to	
Vendor		to	
Material group		to	
Vendor material number		to	
Vendor sub-range		to	
Vendor material group		to	
Purchasing organization		to	

Figure 5.42 Selection Screen for Listing Info Records per Material

Enter the selection criteria for the purchasing info records you want to display, such as Material, and click the execute icon to display a list of purchasing info records as shown in Figure 5.43.

Purchasing info records are listed by vendor in this screen. Purchasing info records are divided into several sections. The first section of an individual purchasing info record accessed from the list in Figure 5.43 is Purchasing Organization Data 1.

Purchasing Info Records for Material

🔍 ✏️ | Price Simulation | 🎞 Simulation

Material R-1000   Maxitec-R 375 Personal computer

Vendor Name		Info Rec. Rule	De
P.Org InfoCat Plnt P6p Plan Time	Minimum Qty Un Var	
Price Origin Net Price Currency Qty Un Document Item		QDp

```
  3021      MOBILE Inc.                    5300002676
☐ 3000  Standard    3000 001  5  Days            0  PC
   Condition    1,322.23      USD    1 PC  Net              12/31/9999
  8500      Supplies Group Pty Ltd         5300005346
☐ 8520  Standard          852  1  Days            1  PC
   Condition    1,000.00      AUD    1 PC  Net              12/31/9999
☐ 8530  Standard          853  1  Days            1  PC
   Condition    1,000.00      AUD    1 PC  Net              12/31/9999
☐ 8580  Standard          858  1  Days            1  PC
   Condition    1,000.00      AUD    1 PC  Net              12/31/9999
```

Figure 5.43 List of Purchasing Info Records for Materials

5.5.1 Purchasing Organization Data 1

Select a purchasing info record in Figure 5.43 and click on the pencil icon to display the screen shown in Figure 5.44.

Change Info Record: Purch. Organization Data 1

General Data | Conditions | Texts

Info Record	5300002676	
Vendor	3021	MOBILE Inc.
Material	R-1000	Maxitec-R 375 Personal computer
Material Group	012	Hardware
Purchasing Org.	3000	Plant 3800 Standard

Control

Pl. Deliv. Time	5 Days	Tol. Underdl.	%	☐ No MText
Purch. Group	001	Tol. Overdl.	%	☐ Ackn. Rqd
Standard Qty	100 PC	☐ Unlimited		Conf. Ctrl
Minimum Qty	PC	☐ GR-Bsd IV		Tax Code
Rem. Shelf Life	D	☐ No ERS		
Shippg Instr.				
		Procedure		
Max. Quantity	PC	Rndg Prof.		UoM Group

Conditions

Net Price	1,322.00 USD / 1 PC	Valid to	12/31/9999
Effective Price	1,322.00 USD / 1 PC	☐ No Cash Disc.	
Qty Conv.	1 PC <-> 1 PC	Cond. Grp	
Pr. Date Cat.	No Control		
Incoterms			

Figure 5.44 Purchasing Info Record Organization Data 1

This screen displays purchasing data relevant to a particular purchasing organization for a vendor and material combination. A purchasing organization procures materials and services, and negotiates conditions of purchase with vendors. Let's discuss the two price fields in detail.

Net Price

The net price is arrived at after taking all discounts and surcharges into account. You can either:

▶ Calculate and enter the net price manually

▶ Enter gross price, discount and surcharge conditions, as we will discuss in Section 5.5.2, and allow the system to calculate the net price

> **Note**
>
> You can only maintain the net price if you have not yet maintained the info record conditions, as we will discuss in Section 5.5.2. You must then maintain the price on the condition screen.

Effective Price

This is the end price after taking all conditions such as cash discounts and delivery costs into account. This price is determined automatically by the system.

5.5.2   Conditions

Purchasing conditions are similar in concept to sales conditions

Purchasing conditions allow you to record multiple vendor quotations for materials and services as well as discounts, surcharges, and other supplements in the system. Click the Conditions button in Figure 5.44 to display the screen shown in Figure 5.45.

Let's consider each section of the price conditions screen.

Variable Key

This section contains vendor, material, purchasing organization, and plant data. It also contains one of four possible purchasing info record categories listed below that you select when creating the info record:

- **Standard**

  Specifies that the info record is used only in connection with standard purchase orders.

- **Subcontracting**

  Specifies that the info record is used only in connection with subcontracting orders. In subcontracting you supply material parts to an external vendor where the complete assembly is manufactured.

- **Pipeline**

  Specifies that the info record is used for pipeline withdrawals. Pipeline materials such as oil or water flow directly into the production process. Stock quantities are not changed during withdrawal.

- **Consignment**

  Specifies that the info record is used for consignment withdrawals. Consignment is a form of business in which a vendor maintains a stock of materials at a customer site. The vendor retains ownership of the materials until they are withdrawn from consignment stores.

Now let's consider the next section of the Price Condition screen.

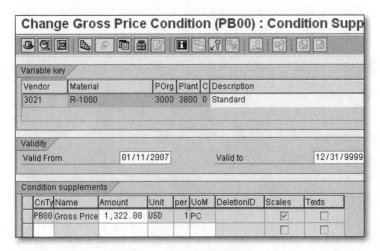

Figure 5.45 Purchasing Info Record Price Conditions

Validity

Refer to
Chapter 10 for
more information
on the cost
estimate
valuation date

Purchasing info record price condition validity dates allow you to keep a record of previous, present, and future quotation prices. A cost estimate will access a price condition with a validity period corresponding to the valuation date of the cost estimate.

Condition Supplements

The gross price of 1,322.00 USD is the vendor quotation excluding discounts or surcharges. You can enter discounts and surcharges if applicable as additional condition supplements in the lines following the gross price condition. The system will automatically take any supplements into account when calculating the net price as discussed previously in Section 5.5.1.

It is also possible to enter scales that represent vendor quotations that contain reduced prices for greater purchase quantities. In Figure 5.45 the checkbox in the Scales column is selected. This means that more than one vendor price has been entered based on the quantity ordered. To display details of the scales, double-click anywhere on the condition line. The screen shown in Figure 5.46 is displayed.

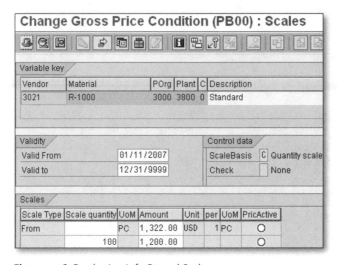

Figure 5.46 Purchasing Info Record Scales

The scale in Figure 5.46 indicates that the purchase price for a quantity between 1 and 99 is 1,322.00 USD, which is discounted to 1,200.00 USD for a quantity of 100 or more. A cost estimate determines which scale price to access based on the costing lot size. During a costing run, the cost estimate costing lot size is determined from the material master Costing 1 view.

> **Note**
>
> The costing lot size should be set as close as possible to normal purchase order quantities of components to minimize purchase price variance (PPV) postings because the standard cost estimate calculation is based on the costing lot size.

You can view details of changes to the purchasing info record price resulting from new vendor quotations by clicking the validity periods (calendar) icon.

This finishes the logistics master data chapter, so let's review what we've covered.

5.6   Summary

In this chapter, we discussed logistics master data in detail. We looked first at BOMs, which contain component and assembly quantities, and then at routings, which contain activity quantities. We considered work centers, where operations and activities are carried, and how they are listed in routings. We also looked at purchasing info records, which contain the purchase price field and other purchasing information.

Now that we've considered master data in this and the previous two chapters, we'll next examine costing configuration, beginning with the costing sheet in Chapter 6.

Costing sheet configuration determines how cost estimates calculate overhead costs.

6 Costing Sheets

In the previous three chapters we discussed Controlling, material, and logistics master data. This data provides cost estimates with the quantity and price information necessary to calculate the standard cost to procure or manufacture a material. In this chapter we discuss costing sheet configuration, which determines how cost estimates calculate overhead costs.

6.1 Overhead

In addition to material and labor costs, overhead costs usually need to be included as a component of the finished product standard price. Overhead costs may include costs such as building lease, insurance, and general office staff not directly involved in the production process. You can either increase the planned activity price to include overhead, or you can create separate overhead activity types. Advantages of this method of overhead allocation include real-time posting during activity confirmation, and no configuration requirement. A disadvantage of dedicated overhead activity types is the increased production data setup required in work centers and routings and possibly increased maintenance during activity confirmations.

Costing sheets offer more flexibility in allocating overhead across individual products or product groups. Also, less production data maintenance is required. Configuration is required, however, as explained in the following sections.

Refer to OSS Note 310768 for information on costing sheet maintenance

Let's inspect the configuration of a costing sheet to see how it works. To view the settings use configuration Transaction KZS2 or follow the IMG menu path CONTROLLING • PRODUCT COST CONTROLLING • PRODUCT COST PLANNING • BASIC SETTINGS FOR MATERIAL COSTING • OVERHEAD • DEFINE COSTING SHEETS. The screen shown in Figure 6.1 is displayed.

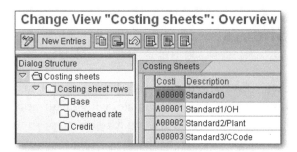

Figure 6.1 Costing Sheet Overview

Available costing sheets are listed on the right of this Overview screen. You can use existing costing sheets or copy one and create your own. Let's choose an example costing sheet and examine the components. Select the first costing sheet (A00000 in this example) and double-click Costing sheet rows on the left. The screen shown in Figure 6.2 is displayed.

Change View "Costing sheet rows": Overview

New Entries · Variable List · Row Numbering

Dialog Structure
- ▽ ☐ Costing sheets
  - ▽ ☐ Costing sheet rows
    - ☐ Base
    - ☐ Overhead rate
    - ☐ Credit

Procedure A00000 Standard · Check

Costing sheet rows

Row	Base	Overhea...	Description	Fro...	To Row	Credit
10	B000		Material			
20		C000	Material OH	10		E01
30			Material usage......			
40	B001		Labour			
45	B002		Salaries			
50		C001	Manufacturing OH	40	45	E02
60			Manufacturing costs...	40	50	
70			Cost of goods manufactured...			
80		C002	Administration OH			E03
90		C003	Sales OH	70		E04
100			Cost of goods sold...			

Figure 6.2 Costing Sheet Rows Overview

The three costing sheet components, Base, Overhead rate, and Credit, are listed on the left of the screen, and Costing sheet rows are displayed on the right.

When overhead is calculated during period-end processing (discussed in Part 3), the manufacturing order or product cost collector receives a debit, and a cost center receives a credit with the calculated overhead value. Let's examine each costing sheet component in detail.

6.2   Calculation Base

A base is a group of cost elements to which overhead is applied. Each cost element identifies unique cost types within a cost estimate, such as raw material or machining labor costs. These costs, identified by the base, are then multiplied by an overhead rate to determine the overhead value in the cost estimate.

To see how cost elements are entered in a base, select any row with an entry in the Base column in the screen shown in Figure 6.2, and double-click Base at the left of the screen. The screen shown in Figure 6.3 is displayed.

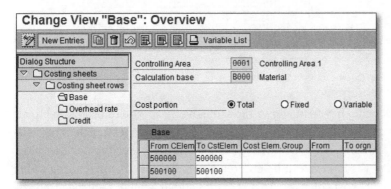

Figure 6.3 Calculation Base Overview

You can enter individual cost elements or ranges in the From CElem and To CstElem columns. You also have the option of entering a cost element group in the Cost Elem. Group column. You can subdivide within cost elements by entering origin groups in the To orgn column, and in the material master Costing 1 view. You can also divide the calculation base into fixed and variable costs if necessary by selecting the appropriate radio button. Now that we've discussed how bases work, let's examine the next cost sheet component, the overhead rate.

6.3 Overhead Rate

The overhead rate is a percentage factor applied to the value of the calculation base (group of cost elements). To see how percentage rates are entered in a calculation rate, select any row with an entry in the Overhea... (overhead) column shown in Figure 6.2 and double-click Overhead rate at the left of the screen. The screen shown in Figure 6.4 is displayed.

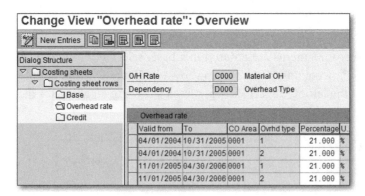

Figure 6.4 Overhead Rate Overview

The Dependency field allows the same overhead rate to be applied to all materials within a plant or company code. Other dependencies are available, allowing different rates to be applied per order type or overhead key. Overhead keys can be entered per individual manufacturing order or product cost collector. This provides a high level of control and flexibility, but also increases setup and maintenance requirements.

Refer to OSS Note 208474 for information on batch input of overhead rates

Overhead rates are date-dependant, allowing different rates to be entered per fiscal year or even fiscal period, if required. Before utilizing this functionality at its most detailed level, be sure the maintenance effort required is offset by any increased accuracy of overhead allocation.

You can also maintain percentage overhead rates with Transaction S_ALR_87008275 and quantity-based overhead rates with Transaction S_ALR_87008272 or by following the menu path ACCOUNTING • CONTROLLING • PRODUCT COST CONTROLLING • COST OBJECT CONTROLLING • PRODUCT COST BY PERIOD • PERIOD-END CLOSING • CURRENT SETTINGS.

> **Note**
>
> Refer to OSS Note 310768 for further information on current settings for costing sheets. Current settings allow you to perform some configuration transactions via the standard user menu path. Because you may need to update costing sheets routinely, you can allow users to easily make these changes.

Now that we've looked at bases and overhead rates, let's examine the final costing sheet component, the credit key.

6.4 Credit Key

You assign a credit key in the Credit column shown in Figure 6.2 to each row with an entry in the Overhea... (overhead rate) column. During overhead allocation, a manufacturing order or product cost collector is debited, and a cost center is credited. The credit key defines which cost center receives the credit. To display how a cost center is entered in a credit key, select any row with an entry in the Credit column shown in Figure 6.2, and double-click Credit at the left of the screen. The screen shown in Figure 6.5 is displayed.

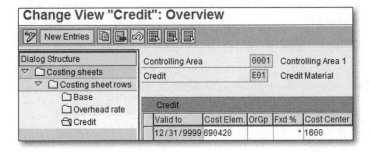

Figure 6.5 Credit Overview

A secondary cost element is a required entry in the Cost Elem. column. The secondary cost element identifies the *planned* overhead cost in the cost estimate and the *actual* overhead debit in manufacturing order and product cost collector cost reports. It also identifies the overhead credit to the cost center in cost center reports such as the standard Cost Centers: Actual/Plan/Variance report accessed with Transaction S_ALR_87013611.

This concludes the costing sheet chapter, so let's review what we've covered.

6.5   Summary

In this chapter we discussed how costing sheet configuration allows cost estimates to calculate overhead costs. We looked in detail at the three costing sheet components: the base, overhead rate, and credit.

Now that we've examined master data in previous chapters and costing sheets in this chapter, structures are in place for the cost estimate to determine material, labor, and overhead costs. The next step is to instruct the cost estimate on how to group costs together for the cost component view in the cost estimate. This complements the basic itemization view, or a simple listing of items in the cost estimate. The most common cost components are materials, labor, and overhead. We'll now examine cost components in further detail in Chapter 7.

Cost components group together similar costs such as material, labor, and overhead. You assign cost elements to cost components, and cost components to cost component views in the cost component structure.

7   Cost Components

In previous chapters we discussed Controlling, material, and logistics master data. This data provides cost estimates with the quantity and price information necessary to calculate the standard cost to manufacture or procure a material. In this chapter we'll discuss configuration of the cost component structure, which determines how costs are grouped to display summarized reporting for cost estimate information and cost estimate lists.

Cost components group together costs of a similar type by cost element. The most common examples of cost components are materials, labor, and overhead. A lot of functionality and flexibility is available when configuring the cost component structure. As usual, you should always choose the simplest possible cost component solution to achieve your required reporting level of detail. In this chapter we'll examine the reporting options available.

Cost component
structure

Let's start by clarifying the terminology.

7.1   Cost Component Terms

Many similar-sounding terms are related to cost components. Clearly defining the meaning of each term helps when setting up configuration and master data. Let's look at nine terms.

▶ **Cost component**

Cost elements
This identifies costs of similar types, such as material, labor, and overhead, by grouping together cost elements. You can use origin groups for detailed reporting at a lower level than cost elements. Cost elements and origin groups identify costs, whereas cost components bundle them together for summarized reporting. You can create up to 40 cost components.

▶ **Cost component split**

Cost components
This is the combination of cost components that makes up the total cost of a material. For example, if you need to view three cost components (material, labor, and overhead) for reporting requirements, then the combination of these three cost components represents the cost component split. Analysis of cost components over time or across a range of products can assist in Profitability Analysis. Cost components increasing over time may result in an effort to reduce material, labor, or overhead costs. Comparison of cost components across products can influence marketing decisions. A manufacturing company may decide to focus on products that require less labor and overhead, or may be interested in analyzing the results of efforts to reduce labor and overhead costs.

The cost component split for the cost of goods manufactured is the most commonly used cost component split. This provides a breakdown of the manufacturing costs of each assembly into cost components. This also provides a roll up of each cost component from lower to higher levels. For example, the cost of raw materials required for a subassembly roll up into the raw material cost component for a finished product. This provides a transparent view of the material, labor, and overhead costs of manufacture.

▶ **Primary cost component split**

Alternative view
This provides an alternative view of cost components in a cost estimate based on primary costs from Cost Center Accounting and activity-based costing. It allows analysis of changes to primary costs such as wages, energy, and depreciation primary costs by displaying each as a cost component. These primary costs would normally be divided between manufacturing cost components as activities are consumed

during manufacturing. Overhead that goes into the primary cost component split is still treated as secondary costs.

This functionality is only required if you have significant primary costs that you need to analyze separately from the manufacturing process. To set this up you need to create a primary cost component split in Cost Center Accounting and automatically calculate the activity price. You also need to define a transfer structure, as we will discuss in Section 7.2.7, and assign an auxiliary cost component structure to organizational units, as we will describe in Section 7.4.

▶ **Main cost component Split**

The main cost component split is the principal cost component split used by the standard cost estimate to update the standard price. The main cost component split can be a cost component split for the cost of goods manufactured or a primary cost component split.

You define the main cost component split when assigning cost component structures to organizational units, as we will discuss in Section 7.4.

▶ **Auxiliary cost component split**

This can be used in addition to the main cost component split for comparisons and analysis. You can use it to analyze costs in cost estimates and Profitability Analysis. When viewing a cost estimate with an auxiliary cost component structure activated, you can switch between the main and auxiliary cost component splits.

Additional view

You define an auxiliary cost component split when assigning cost component structures to organizational units, as we will discuss in Section 7.4.

▶ **Initial cost component split**

This is a cost component split for raw materials, containing separate cost components for procurement costs such as purchase price, freight charges, insurance contributions, and administrative costs.

Raw materials

With an additive cost estimate, you can enter a cost component split for these additional procurement costs for a specific material. These costs are added to the price from the material master if the valuation variant allows this.

▶ **Cost component structure**

You define which cost components make up a cost component split by assignment to a cost component structure. Within the cost component structure you assign cost elements and origin groups to cost components.

The cost component structure also allows you to define cost component views, assign cost component structures to company codes and plants, and create and assign cost component groups. We'll discuss how to set these up in detail in this chapter.

▶ **Cost component view**

Each cost component is assigned to a cost component view. When you display a cost estimate you choose a cost component view to filter the costs. In the simplest case, you assign all cost components in a cost component structure to one view, such as cost of goods sold. This would then be the only view available for displaying a cost estimate.

If you need to view manufacturing costs separately from sales and administration costs, you could, for example, define three cost component views. The cost of goods manufactured view contains all manufacturing cost components, excluding sales and administration cost components. The sales and administration view contains only sales and administration cost components, and filters out all manufacturing costs. The third view contains all cost components representing the total cost of goods sold. This is just one example; you can create as many cost component views as you require.

▶ **Cost Component Group**

Reporting

These allow you to display cost components as columns in standard cost estimate list reports. You can simply create a cost component group for each cost component, and assign each group to the corresponding cost component. The cost component groups become available to assign as columns in cost estimate list reports.

You can assign up to two cost component groups to each cost component. Whereas a cost accountant may be interested in analyzing each cost component, another user such as an operations manager may be interested in a more summarized view. You can create cost component groups that combine or subtotal cost components. For example you could create a total material cost component group that combines all of the material cost components into one group. We'll discuss this in more detail in Section 7.5.

Now that we've examined cost component terminology, let's see how to configure a cost component structure to streamline cost reporting.

7.2   Cost Components with Attributes

You can access cost component structure configuration settings with Transaction OKTZ or by following the IMG menu path CONTROLLING • PRODUCT COST CONTROLLING • PRODUCT COST PLANNING • BASIC SETTINGS FOR MATERIAL COSTING • DEFINE COST COMPONENT STRUCTURE. The screen shown in Figure 7.1 is displayed.

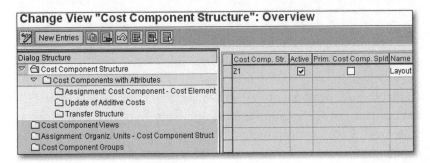

Figure 7.1 Cost Component Structure Overview

Available cost component structures (Cost Comp. Str. column) are listed on the right of this overview screen. Select the Prim. Cost Comp. Split checkbox to nominate a cost component structure as a primary cost component split. The Active checkbox must be selected (as shown) to create cost estimates or calculate activity prices with a cost component structure. You can use existing cost component structures or copy one and create your own. Let's choose cost component structure Z1 shown in Figure 7.1 and examine the components.

Overview

> **Note**
>
> You need to deselect the Active checkbox before you can save changes to a cost component structure.

After completing the changes, you need to return to this overview screen and reselect the Active checkbox, or you'll receive error messages when attempting to create cost estimates based on this cost component structure.

Select cost component structure Z1 and double-click Cost Components with Attributes to display the screen shown in Figure 7.2.

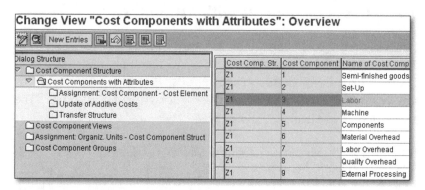

Figure 7.2 Cost Components with Attributes Overview

Cost components   Available cost components are listed on the right of this overview screen. You can use existing cost components or copy one and create your own. Each cost component structure can contain up to 40 cost components that contain variable costs, or up to 20 cost components that contain both fixed and variable costs.

Select a cost component and click the magnifying glass icon, or double-click the cost component, to display the screen shown in Figure 7.3.

Let's examine the fields in each section of this details screen, starting with the Control section.

7.2.1   Control

The Control section of the screen in Figure 7.3 is shown in Figure 7.4.

Let's examine the checkboxes in the Control section of this screen.

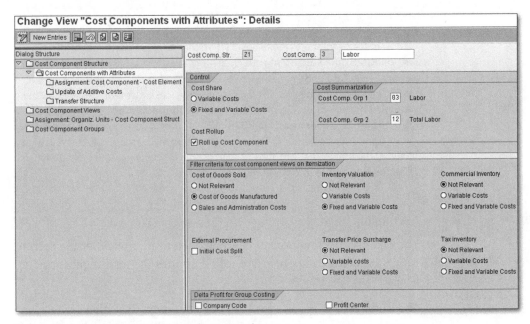

Figure 7.3 Cost Components with Attributes Details

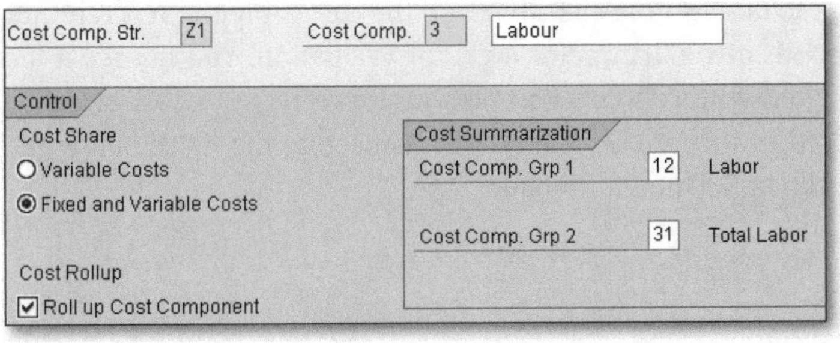

Figure 7.4 Control Section of Cost Component Details Screen

Cost Share

The Cost Share checkboxes control whether variable or fixed and variable costs are shown in separate columns in cost estimates. The most common setting is to select Fixed and Variable Costs, unless you don't want to work with fixed costs.

Now let's look at the next part of the Control section of Figure 7.4.

Fixed and variable costs

If you enter fixed and variable costs when planning activity prices with Transaction KP26, and you attempt to create a cost estimate based on a cost component structure with Variable Costs selected in Figure 7.4, you'll receive an error message stating the fixed costs for the cost element can be neither assigned nor rolled up. To proceed, you'll need to remove the planned activity fixed price with Transaction KP26, or select Fixed and Variable Costs in the cost component structure. The same situation will occur if you work with fixed and variable cost portions in the costing sheet calculation base. Refer to Chapter 6 for more information on costing sheets.

Cost Rollup

The Roll up Cost Component checkbox determines whether the costing results of a cost component are rolled up into the next-highest costing level.

There are restrictions on the use of this checkbox. Costs that are relevant to cost of goods manufactured or inventory valuation must be rolled up, and the checkbox must be selected. You'll receive an error message if you attempt to deselect the checkbox and the cost component is relevant to cost of goods manufactured or inventory valuation. You can see if the costs associated with this cost component are relevant to cost of goods manufactured or inventory valuation by inspecting the fields below the roll up checkbox, as shown in Figure 7.5.

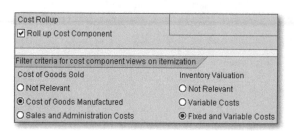

Figure 7.5 Inventory Valuation Fields Affecting Cost Rollup

If you attempt to deselect the Roll up Cost Component checkbox with Cost of Goods Manufactured selected as shown in Figure 7.5, you'll receive an error message. This guarantees that all costs of goods manufactured are rolled up.

If you attempt to deselect the Roll up Cost Component checkbox with inventory valuation relevant for either variable or fixed and variable costs, you'll also receive an error message. This guarantees that costs relevant to inventory valuation are rolled up. This control ensures that all manufacturing costs are rolled up by cost components for a standard cost estimates.

Inventory valuation

Now that we've looked at the checkboxes in the Control section, let's examine the Filter criteria for cost component views on itemization section.

7.2.2   Filter Criteria for Cost Component Views on Itemization

The fields in this section are shown in Figure 7.6.

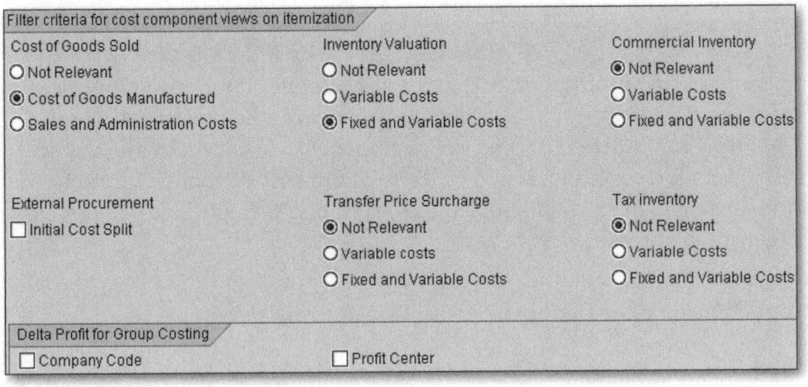

Figure 7.6 Filter Criteria for Cost Component Views on Itemization

The checkboxes in this screen allow you to associate a cost component and a cost component view. A cost component view allows you to filter costs displayed in a cost estimate. Let's examine each section of this screen in detail.

Filter criteria

Cost of Goods Sold

These checkboxes allow you to define the cost of goods sold for this cost component. The most common setting is to select Cost of Goods Manufactured.

You select Cost of Goods Manufactured and then create a cost component view with cost of goods manufactured selected in the filter. All cost components with Cost of Goods Manufactured selected are displayed in a cost estimate with this cost component view.

We'll look at the cost estimate display in more detail when we discuss the cost component view in Section 7.3.

Inventory Valuation

These indicators allow you to define which cost components are relevant for inventory valuation. The most common setting is to select Fixed and Variable Costs.

Sales and administration costs are typically not relevant for inventory valuation, and do not appear in a cost component view based on inventory valuation. You can create a second cost component view to display sales and administration costs and a third to display both cost of goods manufactured and sales and administration costs. This is just one example, and you can create many cost component views.

Now let's consider the next two sections of this screen.

Commercial and Tax Inventory

If you're interested in reporting on commercial and tax inventory values, select these fields as relevant.

Transfer Price Surcharge

The following case scenario presents a typical situation where you may use the Transfer Price Surcharge checkbox in Figure 7.6.

Some companies create additive cost estimates to represent legal profits when transferring materials between company codes and profit centers.

You associate these additive costs with the Transfer Price Surcharge checkbox, and then create cost component views that include or exclude cost components with this checkbox selected. This provides you with flexibility when viewing inventory valuation with and without markup due to transfer price.

Refer to Chapter 4 for more information on transfer price.

External Procurement

Select the Initial Cost Split checkbox in the External Procurement section in Figure 7.6 to assign a cost component to an initial cost split. You have the option to group together all externally procured materials and associated costs with the corresponding checkbox selected in a cost component view. You can create an additive cost estimate for all procurement costs such as purchase price, freight charges, insurance contributions, and administrative costs, and include these costs in the initial cost split. An additive cost estimate allows you to enter costs manually in a unit cost estimate that you can then associate with a standard cost estimate.

Additive cost estimate

Now that we've discussed the indicators in the filter criteria for cost components views on itemization section, let's discuss the fields in the Delta Profit for Group Costing section of the Cost Components with Attributes Details screen.

7.2.3   Delta Profit for Group Costing

You select the Delta Profit for Group Costing checkboxes to display internal profits between company codes and profit centers as a cost component. This will only occur if the material ledger is activated with multiple valuations. You can only select the checkbox for one cost component per cost component structure. Delta profits cannot be relevant for inventory valuation, and you cannot assign cost elements to cost components with either of these checkboxes selected.

Multiple valuations

Let's discuss the Cost Summarization section of the Cost Components with Attributes Details screen.

7.2.4   Cost Summarization

The Cost Summarization fields are displayed in Figure 7.7.

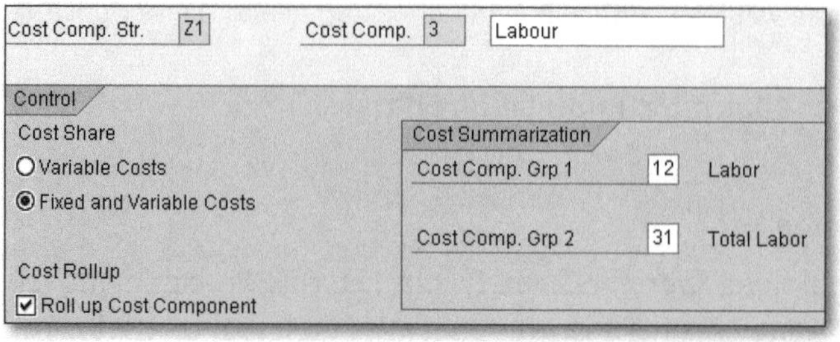

Figure 7.7 Cost Summarization Section

Refer to Section 7.5 for more information on cost component groups

Cost components are not available to add as columns in standard cost estimate list reports and costed multilevel bills of material (BOMs). If you create a cost component group for each cost component, however, and enter the cost component group in the Cost Comp. Grp 1 field of the corresponding cost component, you can then display the cost component groups as columns in standard cost estimate list reports. This report is important when comparing cost components quickly across products or a range of products. Many companies have a requirement for such a report, which can be set up with a standard configuration.

The addition of a second cost component group in the Cost Comp. Grp 2 field enables different levels of summarization. A cost accountant may need to carry out cost analysis of each cost component, such as three types of labor, across a range of products. An operations manager, on the other hand, may only be interested in analyzing total labor. In this case you can create summary cost component groups and assign them to the corresponding cost components.

> **Tip**
>
> When viewing cost component groups as columns in cost estimate list reports, you need to select EXTRAS • ACTIVATE COST COMP. GROUP 2 from the menu bar to view the summarized cost component values in the corresponding columns.

Now that we've discussed all of the fields in the Cost Components with Attributes Details screen, let's examine how you assign cost elements to cost components in the next section.

7.2.5 Assignment of Cost Elements to Cost Components

Let's take the Labor cost component as an example and examine the configuration. Select the Labor cost component (shown as selected) in Figure 7.2 and double-click Assignment: Cost Component – Cost Element. The screen shown in Figure 7.8 is displayed.

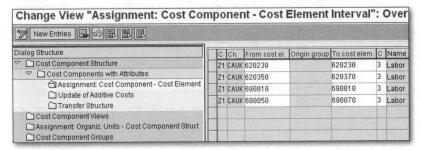

Figure 7.8 Cost Element Assignment Overview

Individual cost elements or cost element ranges are assigned to cost components in the From cost el. (from cost element) and To cost elem. (to cost element) columns.

For detailed reporting within cost elements, you can create an origin group and make an entry in the corresponding field in this screen. If you enter an origin group without entering cost elements, the cost component will include the cost of all materials with the origin group regardless of cost element.

> **Note**
>
> The From cost el., Origin group, and To cost elem. fields are not mandatory. If you leave these fields blank, all costs in the cost estimate not assigned to a cost component will be assigned to the cost component with a blank entry. You could make this a cost component for "other costs."

If you need to use origin groups when setting up component groups, you can create them with the following procedure.

> **Create Origin Group**
>
> You create origin groups with Transaction OKZ1 or by following the IMG menu path Controlling • Product Cost Controlling • Product Cost Planning • Basic Settings for Material Costing • Define Origin Groups. The origin group key is a four-digit alphanumeric field, so you can create many origin groups if necessary.

Costing 1 view   You can enter an origin group in the Origin Group column in Figure 7.8 immediately after you create it. You'll also need to enter the origin group in the Costing 1 view of all relevant material masters and create cost estimates for costs to appear in the cost component containing the origin group.

Now that we've discussed how to assign cost elements to cost components, let's examine how to assign cost elements for cost estimates without quantity structure.

7.2.6   Update of Additive Costs

Double-click Update of Additive Costs shown on the left in Figure 7.8 to display the screen shown in Figure 7.9.

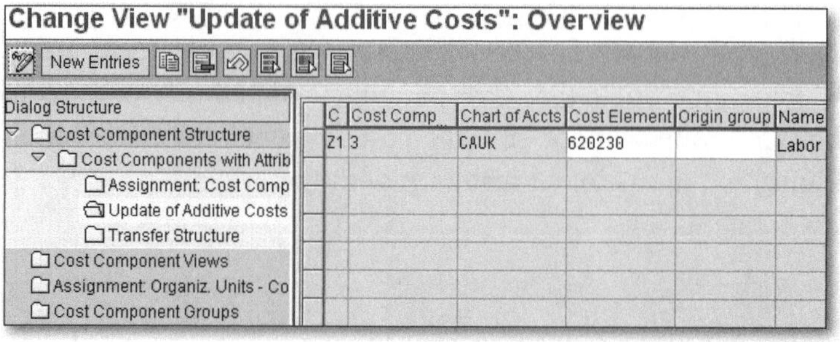

Figure 7.9 Update of Additive Costs Overview

In this screen you assign a cost element for additive costs and for a cost component in cost estimates without quantity structure, that is, without a BOM or routing. We'll discuss cost estimates without quantity structure in more detail in Chapter 12.

Next, we'll look at how to set up a transfer structure for the primary cost component split.

7.2.7   Transfer Structure

Double-click Transfer Structure on the left in Figure 7.9 to display the screen shown in Figure 7.10.

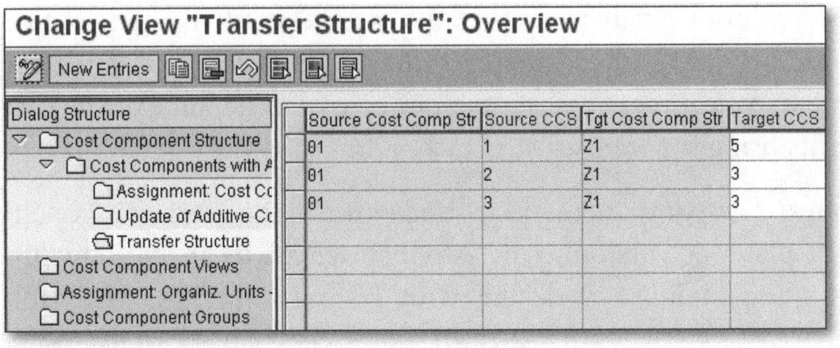

Change View "Transfer Structure": Overview			
Source Cost Comp Str	Source CCS	Tgt Cost Comp Str	Target CCS
01	1	Z1	5
01	2	Z1	3
01	3	Z1	3

Dialog Structure
▽ ☐ Cost Component Structure
  ▽ ☐ Cost Components with A
    ☐ Assignment: Cost Co
    ☐ Update of Additive Co
    ☐ Transfer Structure
  ☐ Cost Component Views
  ☐ Assignment: Organiz. Units -
  ☐ Cost Component Groups

Figure 7.10 Cost Component Transfer Structure Overview

A transfer structure transfers the costs from the cost components of one cost component structure to the cost components of another cost component structure. For example, you can specify a source cost component from the primary cost component split determined during activity price calculation to a target cost component assigned to the cost of goods manufactured cost component split.

Activity price calculation

Case Scenario

In Figure 7.10 source cost components from the primary cost component split (activity rate) map to the target cost of goods manufactured cost component split (production costs) as detailed by the following list with cost component descriptions:

▶ Source cost component 1 Materials maps to target 5 Components

▶ Source cost component 2 Wages maps to target 3 Labor

▶ Source cost component 3 Salaries maps to target 3 Labor

When you have a significant primary cost such as energy, you may decide to create an Energy cost component in both source and target cost component structures and map these on a one-to-one relationship. Generally, you will create more primary cost components than cost of goods manufactured cost components.

You can also create a component in both the source and target cost component structures for miscellaneous costs posted to the cost center.

Message

You must assign all components from the source cost component structure into the transfer structure, or you will receive an error message when attempting to activate the source cost component structure.

In addition to setting up a transfer structure, you need to calculate the activity price automatically to transfer the costs. The activity price can be divided into primary cost components during activity price calculation. The primary cost components are mapped to cost of manufacturing cost components using the transfer structure.

Planning version

You assign a cost component split, usually a primary cost component split, to the planning version so the activity price can be analyzed by primary cost components. You do this with Transaction OKEQ or by following the IMG menu path CONTROLLING • GENERAL CONTROLLING • ORGANIZATION • MAINTAIN VERSIONS. Select a version, double-click Settings for Each Fiscal Year, double-click a fiscal year, and then click the Price calculation tab to display the screen shown in Figure 7.11.

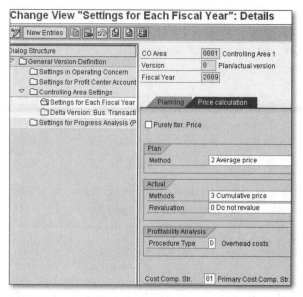

Figure 7.11 Assign Primary Cost Component Structure to Activity Price Calculation in Planning Version

You can assign a cost component structure in the Cost Comp. Str. field in Figure 7.11. This is not a mandatory field, and you do not have to assign a primary cost component split when automatically calculating the activity price. You need to enter a cost component split and then calculate the activity price to display a cost estimate with the primary cost component split. You also need to have defined a transfer structure and assigned an auxiliary cost component structure to organizational units, as we will discuss in Section 7.4.

Now that we've discussed cost components with attributes, let's examine the cost component view.

7.3   Cost Component View

Each cost component is assigned to a cost component view. When you display a cost estimate, you choose a cost component view that filters the cost components appearing in the cost estimate. In the simplest case, you assign all cost components in a cost component structure to one cost of goods manufactured or sold view, and this is the only view you use when displaying a cost estimate.

Filter cost components

Assigning a cost component to a cost component view is a two-step process. First, you enter filter criteria when defining the details of each cost component, as shown previously in Figure 7.3, and again in Figure 7.12.

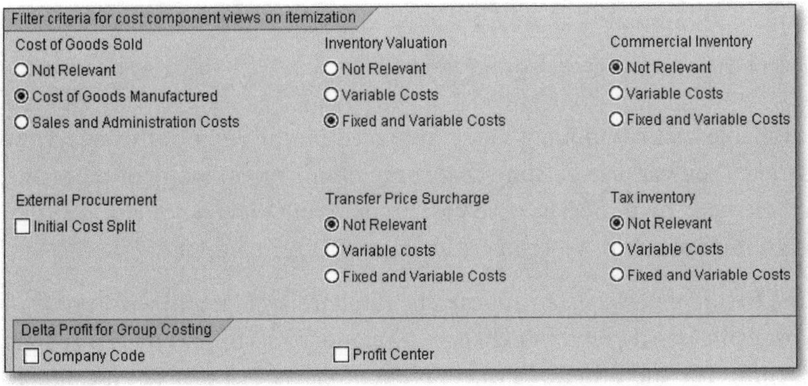

Figure 7.12 Cost Component Filter Criteria – Cost Component Views

Dependencies The filter criteria in a cost component view are based on the settings made in the screen. Certain relationships and conditions must be met when setting the filter criteria, as we discussed in Section 7.2. For example, all Cost of Goods Manufactured entries must also be relevant for inventory valuation.

The second step in assigning a cost component to a cost component view is to define each cost component view. To do this, double-click Cost Component Views in the cost component structure as shown in Figure 7.10 to display the screen shown in Figure 7.13.

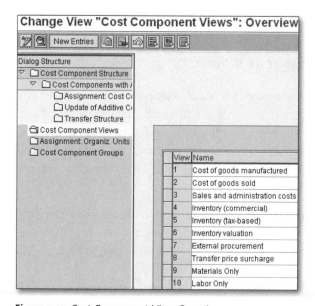

Figure 7.13 Cost Component View Overview

Available cost component views are listed on the right of this overview screen. You can use existing cost components or copy any of these and create your own. Because the cost component View key field is a two-digit numeric field, you can create up to 99 cost component views.

Standard system The first five views listed appear in a standard system and will appear in cost estimates if you don't change the standard settings. You can change the number and order of cost component views listed in a cost estimate by selecting SETTINGS • COST DISPLAY from the menu bar when displaying a cost estimate.

Let's look at the detail behind a cost component view. Double-click cost component view 1 in the overview screen to display the screen shown in Figure 7.14.

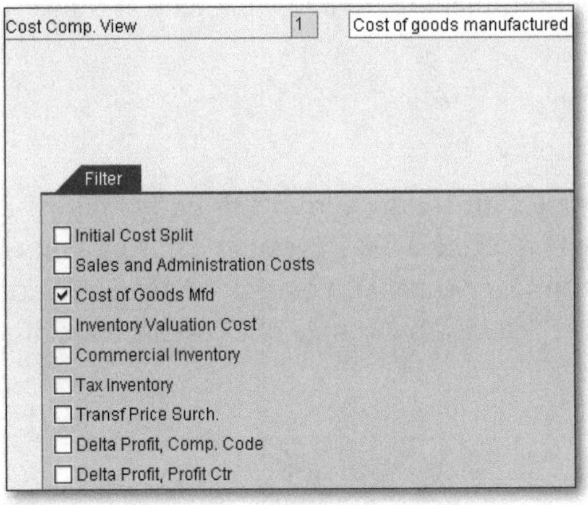

Figure 7.14 Cost Component View Details

The description of the cost component view normally corresponds to the cost components filtered.

Tip

Compare the filter criteria in the cost component details previously shown in Figure 7.12 with the filter list in the cost component view details shown in Figure 7.14. There are nine corresponding filter criteria on each screen, although it's not immediately obvious because they are not in the same order. For example:

- Cost of Goods Manufactured in Figure 7.12 has a corresponding entry as the third filter criteria (selected in this case) in Figure 7.14
- Sales and Administration Costs in Figure 7.12 has a corresponding entry as the second filter criteria in Figure 7.14
- Initial Cost Split in Figure 7.12 has a corresponding entry as the first filter criteria in Figure 7.14.

You can match all nine filter criteria in the same way.

You can easily create your own cost component views by matching the cost component and cost component view filter criteria. You may need to create your own cost component views in addition to the five supplied with the standard system. You have a lot of flexibility in setting up cost component views to meet your reporting requirements.

Now that we've examined how to define and set up cost component views, let's look at how you put them use. First, we'll look at the cost estimate display screen.

7.3.1 Cost Estimate Display

You can display a cost estimate with Transaction CK13N or by following the menu path ACCOUNTING • CONTROLLING • PRODUCT COST CONTROLLING • PRODUCT COST PLANNING • MATERIAL COSTING • COST ESTIMATE WITH QUANTITY STRUCTURE • DISPLAY. An example of a cost estimate display is shown in Figure 7.15.

Figure 7.15 Cost Estimate Displaying Cost Component Views

There are two ways to display details of the cost components included in each cost component view:

1. Double-click a cost component view listed.

2. Click Cost of goods manufactured to display a drop-down list of all cost component views, and then click a cost component.

You can adjust which cost components appear in a cost estimate by selecting SETTINGS • COST DISPLAY from the menu bar. The screen shown in Figure 7.16 is displayed.

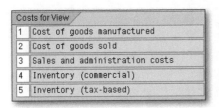

Figure 7.16 Costs to View in Cost Estimate

Entries you make in this screen determine the number and order of cost component views listed in the cost estimate display screen. If you leave a field blank, the cost component view will not appear in the cost estimate.

Now that we've examined how cost component views are used in cost estimates, let's look at how they are used when calculating overhead.

7.3.2 Overhead Calculation

Cost component views can be used in the calculation of overhead for semifinished goods in finished goods. In the costing type you can specify a cost component view as the calculation base for the calculation of overhead. You maintain a costing type with Transaction OKKI or by following the IMG menu path CONTROLLING • PRODUCT COST CONTROLLING • PRODUCT COST PLANNING • MATERIAL COST ESTIMATE WITH QUANTITY STRUCTURE • COSTING VARIANT: COMPONENTS • DEFINE COSTING TYPES. Double-click a costing type (01 in this example) and then select the Misc. tab to display the screen shown in Figure 7.17.

Refer to Chapter 8 for more information on costing types

Entering a cost component view as a calculation base allows you to determine overhead for semifinished goods on a calculation base independent of total cost estimate costs. Click on the blank Calculation Base field in Figure 7.17 to display a list of possible entries for the cost component view.

Calculation base

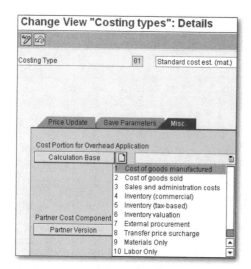

Figure 7.17 Cost Component View as Calculation Base for Overhead

Case Scenario

Semifinished products are entered in the cost estimate with costs including costs of goods manufactured, sales and distribution costs, and administration costs. You calculate material overhead on the basis of only costs of goods manufactured for the semifinished product by entering the corresponding cost component view as the calculation base.

Now let's look at how other components use cost component views.

7.3.3 Other Components

A variety of other components use cost component views as a method of categorizing costs, as described below:

▶ **Sales and Distribution**
The cost of goods sold cost component view determines which costs can be used as a basis for pricing to determine a net value for the sales order item.

▶ **Profitability Analysis**
The cost of goods sold cost component view determines which costs are compared to sales revenue to calculate the contribution margin for each product.

▶ **Materials Management**

The inventory valuation cost component view determines which costs go into the standard price of the material and the tax and commercial prices.

Now that we've looked at cost component views, let's examine how cost components are assigned to organizational units.

7.4   Organizational Units of Cost Components

The company code determines which cost component structure the standard cost estimate uses. This ensures that the same cost component structure is used for all plants and costing variants in a company code. If you use different cost component structures in different plants, the standard cost estimate in one plant cannot access the results of standard cost estimates in another plant. You cannot transfer costing data for materials transferred from one plant to another.

Company code

For other cost estimates, the cost component structure is determined through the combination of company code, plant, and costing variant.

To access assignment of organizational units, double-click Assignment: Organiz. Units as previously shown in Figure 7.13. The screen in Figure 7.18 is displayed.

Company	Plant	Costing Variant	Valid from	Cost Comp Str	Name	Cost Comp Str
0001	++++	++++	01/01/1900	Z1	Base Layout	01
0001	++++	PPC3	01/01/2000	MB	Current Costing	01
0002	++++	++++	01/01/1900	Z1	Base Layout	01
0002	++++	PPC3	01/01/2000	MB	Current Costing	01

Figure 7.18 Assignment of Organizational Units

In this screen you assign cost component structures to organizational units such as company code, plant, and costing variant. Some entries in this example employ masking. In the Plant column all four rows have the entry ++++. This is a shorthand method of assigning cost component structures to all plants. The same technique of masking can be employed in many other screens throughout the system.

Masking

Specific entries   Specific entries always take priority over masked entries, as discussed in the following example.

Example

In the Costing Variant column in Figure 7.18, rows with the specific PPC3 entry take priority over rows with masked entries in the same column. When a cost estimate is created for company codes 0001 and 0002 with costing variant PPC3, main cost component structure MB and auxiliary cost component structure 01 will be used. All other cost estimates for these plants will use main cost component structure Z1 and auxiliary cost component structure 01.

Now that we've discussed assignment of organizational structures in general, let's look first at assigning the main cost component structure and then at the auxiliary cost component structure.

7.4.1   Main Cost Component Structure

First column   The main cost component split is the principal cost component split used by a standard cost estimate to update the standard price. The main cost component split can be for cost of goods manufactured or a primary cost component split. You assign the main cost component structure in the first Cost Comp Str (cost component structure) column in Figure 7.18. If you widen the columns so you can see the entire text in the column headings as shown in Figure 7.19, you can see this more clearly.

Cost Comp Structure (Main CCS)	Name	Cost Comp Structure (Aux. CCS)
Z1	Base Layout	01
MB	Current Costing	01
Z1	Base Layout	01
MB	Current Costing	01

Figure 7.19 Main and Auxiliary Column Heading Text

You assign the main cost component structure in the first (Main CCS) column and the auxiliary cost component structure in the last (Aux. CCS) column. You don't have to assign an auxiliary cost component structure, but you do need to assign a main cost component structure to each row you define in this screen.

Now let's discuss the auxiliary cost component in more detail.

7.4.2   Auxiliary Cost Component Structure

The auxiliary cost component structure can be used in parallel to the main cost component split to allow comparisons and analysis. You can use it to analyze costs in cost estimates and Profitability Analysis. When viewing a cost estimate with an activated auxiliary cost component, you can switch between the main and auxiliary cost component splits.

Second column

You assign an auxiliary cost component structure to an organizational unit in the last column in Figure 7.19. Here are the additional steps needed to activate the auxiliary cost component structure:

1. Create an auxiliary cost component structure.
2. Create a transfer structure mapping the auxiliary cost components to the main cost components.
3. Assign the auxiliary cost component structure to organizational units (company code, plant, and costing variant).
4. Assign the auxiliary cost component structure to the plan version per fiscal year in the price calculation tab.
5. Automatically calculate the plan activity price.

You do not have to enter an auxiliary cost component structure. In most cases the cost of goods manufactured cost component structure alone provides sufficient cost component reporting. The auxiliary cost component structure is available if you need additional reporting on primary costs, especially in some European implementations.

Next let's look at a quick way to check assignment to organizational units.

7.4.3   Check Assignment to Organizational Units

You can check the assignment of cost component structures to organizational units by inspecting the costing variant. Let's take costing variant PPC1 as an example. Display costing variant PPC1 with Transaction OKKN, or click the costing variant in the Costing Data tab of a cost estimate. Select the Assignments tab and click the Cost Component Structure button to display the screen shown in Figure 7.20.

Costing variant

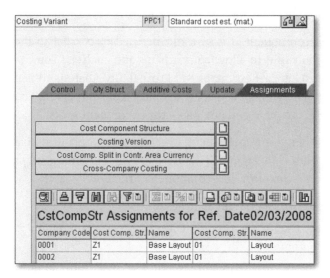

Figure 7.20 Cost Component Structure Assignments for Costing Variant

The main cost component structure assigned to company codes 0001 and 0002 is Z1, and the auxiliary cost component structure assigned is 01.

Plant You can also assign a cost component structure to a Plant. To add Plant as a column in Figure 7.20, click the down-pointing arrow to the right of the grid icon and select Change Layout to display the screen shown in Figure 7.21.

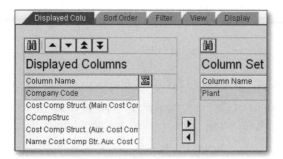

Figure 7.21 Change Layout to Include Plant Column

Double-click Plant to move it across to Displayed Columns and press Enter to display the screen shown in Figure 7.22.

> **Tip**
>
> Click the Save icon before pressing Enter to save this layout.

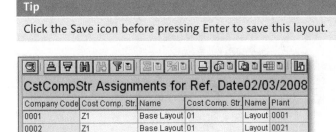

Figure 7.22 Cost Component Structure Assignments Including Plant

The cost component structure assignments for the costing variant now displays Plant.

Now that we've examined assignment of organizational units and cost component structures and how to check the assignment, let's look at cost component groups.

7.5 Cost Component Groups

You can include cost component groups as columns in cost estimate list reports and costed multilevel BOMs. A costed multilevel BOM is a hierarchical overview of the values of all items of a costed material according to the costed quantity structure (BOM and routing).

Reporting

You cannot include cost components as columns in these reports. You can, however, assign cost components to cost component groups that can be added to the reports. The procedure to do this is described in the following sections.

7.5.1 Create Cost Component Groups

To maintain cost component groups, double-click Cost Component Groups in Figure 7.13. The screen shown in Figure 7.23 is displayed.

Available cost component groups are listed on the right of this overview screen. You can use existing cost component groups or create your own. The Cost comp. grp (cost component group) key is a two-digit numeric field, so you can create up to 99 cost component groups.

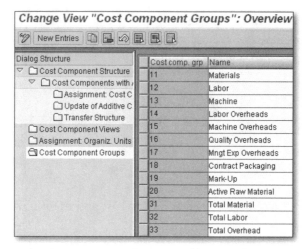

Figure 7.23 Cost Component Groups Overview

If you create all of your cost component groups with two digits, it's easier to follow the order of cost component groups listed. For example, cost component group 2 would be listed between cost component groups 19 and 20 on this screen, not between 1 and 3 as you would initially expect. You have spare numbering capacity because you can create up to 99 cost component groups, whereas there can only be a maximum of 40 cost components.

In Figure 7.23 cost component groups 11 to 20 correspond to unique individual cost components. Cost component groups 31, 32, and 33 correspond to groups of cost components.

Now that we've looked at how to create and number cost component groups, let's see how to assign them to cost components.

7.5.2 Assign Cost Component Groups to Cost Components

We discussed assigning cost component groups to cost components in Section 7.2.4. Let's quickly review how to make this assignment. Display cost component attribute details as shown in Figure 7.24.

In the Cost Summarization section you can assign two cost component groups to a cost component. You have flexibility in how to assign these groups. Let's discuss a case scenario of how you can assign each group.

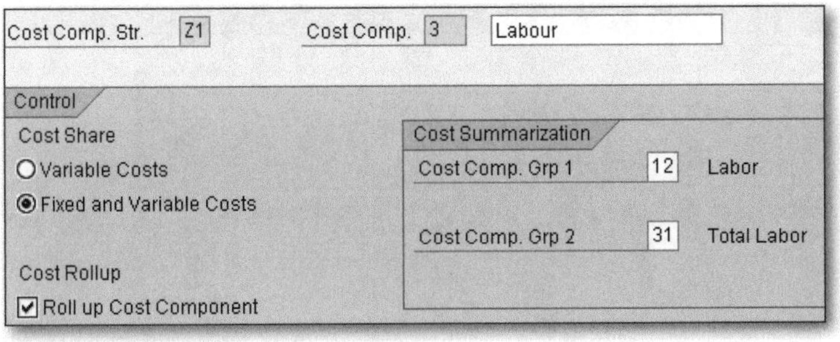

Figure 7.24 Cost Component Attribute Details – Cost Summarization

Case Scenario

A cost account required reporting on cost components in cost estimate lists and costed multilevel BOMs. One cost component group was created and assigned to each cost component in the Cost Comp. Grp 1 (cost component group 1) field shown in Figure 7.24.

The operations manager only required a more summarized cost component view. Three additional cost component views were created combining or sub-totaling cost components into total material, labor, and overhead. These summary cost component groups were assigned to corresponding cost components in the Cost Comp. Grp 2 (cost component group 2) field.

Now that we've discussed assigning cost component groups to cost components, let's see how you assign them as columns to reports.

7.5.3 Assign Cost Component Groups to Report Columns

Cost component groups are available to be added as columns in standard reports listing cost estimates, such as Transaction code S_P99_41000 111. Click on the change layout icon and move the required cost component columns on the right side of the screen to the left, as shown in Figure 7.25.

Change layout

The cost component groups become available as report columns and are listed in the Column set column in Figure 7.25. The cost component groups can be added to report columns by selecting them and clicking the left-pointing arrow icon. In this example Labor and Component Materials have been moved to the report Columns.

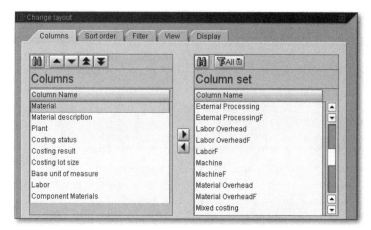

Figure 7.25 Add Cost Component Groups to Report Columns

Press Enter and the required cost components appear in the cost estimate list report as shown in Figure 7.26.

Analyze/Compare Material Cost Estimates

Material	Material description	Plant	Status	Costing result	Lot size	BUn	Labor	Component
MBCS...	STRAP ASSEMBLY	0021	FR	83.46	1.000	EA	26.92	3.98
MBCS...	STRAP ASSEMBLY	0021	FR	823.95	25.000	EA	671.89	99.50
MBCS...	MAIN ASSEMBLY	0021	FR	504.19	1.000	EA	144.76	2.35
MBCS...	MAIN ASSEMBLY	0021	FR	4,041.48	25.000	EA	3,625.39	58.75

Figure 7.26 Cost Component Groups Displayed as Columns

The Labor and Component Materials cost components now appear as columns in the cost estimate list report. Labor and Component materials cost components do not add up to the total cost shown in the Costing result column because the Overhead cost component is not included in this example. Simply use the same procedure to add other cost components as required.

You can use a similar technique to add cost component group columns to standard costed multilevel BOM reports. You can view these reports with Transactions CK86_99 and CK13N.

> **Tip**
>
> When viewing cost component groups as columns in cost estimate list reports, you need to select EXTRAS • ACTIVATE COST COMP. GROUP 2 from the menu bar to view the summarized cost component values in the corresponding columns.

There can be several active cost component structures in Transaction OKTZ (shown in Figure 7.1). You'll need to determine to which one you'll assign the newly created cost component groups. To do this, display a standard cost estimate with Transaction CK13N and click on the Costing Data tab to display the screen shown in Figure 7.27.

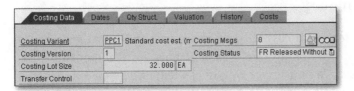

Figure 7.27 Standard Cost Estimate Costing Variant

Click the Costing Variant text to display the costing variant. Select the Assignments tab and then click the Cost Component Structure button to display the cost component structure assignment for each company code as shown in Figure 7.28.

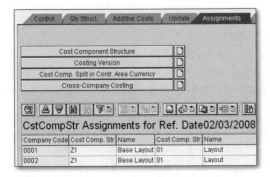

Figure 7.28 Costing Variant Cost Component Structure Assignments

The main cost component structure assigned to company codes 0001 and 0002 is Z1 Base Layout, and the auxiliary cost component structure assigned is 01 Layout. You'll only see the last two columns if you assigned an auxiliary cost component structure as discussed in Section 7.4.

In this example, if you're setting up cost component groups for company code 0002, you should deactivate Cost Comp. Str. (cost component structure) Z1, assign the cost component groups to the cost components, and then reactivate the cost component structure Z1.

Now that we've examined setting up cost component groups, that completes cost component structure configuration. Let's review what we've covered in this cost components chapter.

7.6   Summary

In this chapter we discussed cost components and how they relate to Product Cost Controlling. We looked at how cost components group together costs of a similar type by cost element. We defined cost component views and examined how to assign auxiliary cost component structures, transfer structures, and organizational units. We also looked at how to create and assign cost component groups.

Now that we've examined cost components in this chapter, we'll continue the preparation for creating cost estimates by examining costing variant configuration in Chapters 8 and 9.

A costing variant contains all of the control parameters and settings for creating cost estimates.

8   Costing Variant Components

Now that we've examined master data and cost components, let's look at the costing variant. Every cost estimate you create is based on a costing variant. The costing variant contains all of the control parameters and settings for costing such as selecting prices to access when costing materials, activities, and business processes.

Control parameters

A costing variant contains the following six control parameters:

- Costing type
- Valuation variant
- Date control
- Quantity structure control
- Transfer control (optional)
- Reference variant (optional)

We'll examine each of these components in detail in the following sections. First, let's look at the how the costing variant is set up and configured in general, and we'll then examine each component. In Chapter 9 we'll examine the costing variant tabs in detail.

8.1   Define Costing Variant

To access costing variant configuration settings, use Transaction OKKN or follow the IMG menu path CONTROLLING • PRODUCT COST CONTROLLING • PRODUCT COST PLANNING • MATERIAL COST ESTIMATE WITH QUANTITY STRUCTURE • DEFINE COSTING VARIANTS. The screen shown in Figure 8.1 is displayed.

A quantity structure typically contains a bill of material (BOM) and routing that cost estimates use to determine component and activity quantities.

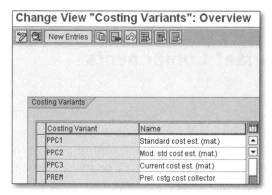

Figure 8.1 Costing Variants Overview Screen

Overview   Available costing variants are listed in the overview screen. The costing variants displayed are supplied with the standard system. You can either use the standard costing variants or create your own.

If you need settings different from the system-supplied costing variants, it's good practice to create your own costing variants beginning with the letters X, Y, or Z because these will not be overwritten during a system upgrade.

PPC1 is the system-supplied costing variant for standard cost estimates. You can create your own costing variant, for example, ZPC1, and make changes while referring back to system-supplied PPC1. You also know from the numbering logic that ZPC1 was copied from PPC1 settings.

If your changes involve settings in either the costing type or valuation variant components discussed in Sections 8.2 and 8.3, you should first copy the system-supplied components, and make the changes to your own costing variant components. You can then create your own costing variant that includes your own costing variant components.

If you copy a system-supplied costing variant you cannot change the costing type or valuation variant components. You must create your own costing variant and enter your own components. As soon as you create and save a new costing variant, the costing type and valuation variant are no longer changeable.

Select a costing variant in Figure 8.1, and click the magnifying glass icon or double-click a costing variant to display the screen shown in Figure 8.2.

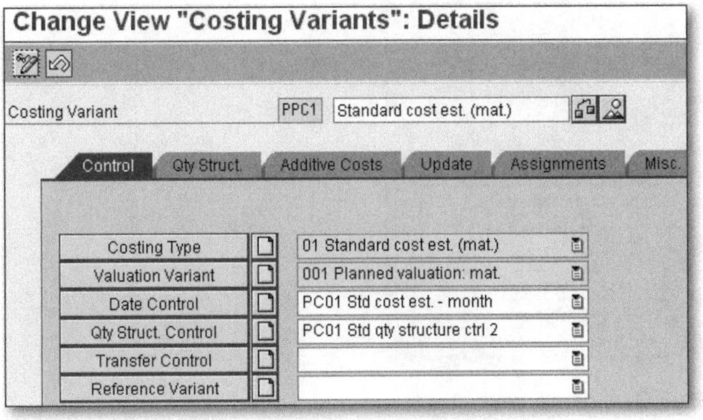

Figure 8.2 Costing Variants Details Control Tab

The Control tab lists the six costing variant control parameters. The Costing Type and Valuation Variant fields are not changeable because these make up the key structure of costing results rather than the costing variant.

Although it's technically possible to have two costing variants with the same costing type and valuation variant, this should be avoided to prevent data from being overwritten.

> **Tip**
>
> You can see an overview of all costing variant component settings by clicking the overview icon.

Let's examine each of the six components and then look at the remaining costing variant tabs in Chapter 9.

8.2   Costing Type

Click the Costing Type button in Figure 8.2 to display Costing Type 01 Standard cost est. (mat.). To display all costing types, click the new page icon next to the button. The screen shown in Figure 8.3 is displayed.

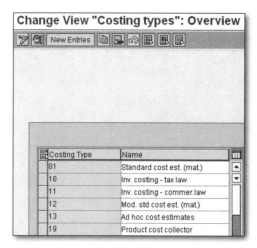

Figure 8.3 Costing Type Overview Screen

Available standard costing types are listed in the overview screen. You can either use the standard costing types or create your own.

Double-click a costing type to display the screen shown in Figure 8.4.

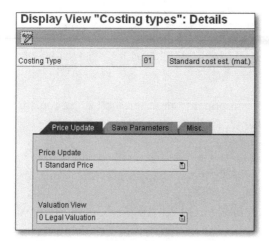

Figure 8.4 Costing Type Price Update Tab

Let's examine the fields in the Price Update tab, which is displayed when you initially view the costing type.

8.2.1 Price Update

The Price Update tab contains two fields, which we'll examine next.

Price Update

The Price Update field controls whether costing results can be written to the material master and which fields can be written to as shown in Figure 8.5.

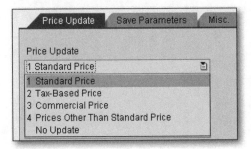

Figure 8.5 Price Update Tab Price Update Field

There can only be one costing type that updates the standard price for each valuation view. Inventory is usually valued based on legal valuation as shown in Figure 8.4. For the costing type that contains standard price in the Price Update field, this field is not changeable.

Because you normally assign each costing type to a unique costing variant, only one costing variant such as PPC1 can update the standard price. This allows you to control who can update the standard price by restricting access to the costing variant containing this costing type.

You can change the entry in the Price Update field for costing types that do not contain standard price in the Price Update field. This is because updating other material master fields such as Tax-Based and Commercial Price is not as critical because they do not directly affect inventory valuation.

Refer to Chapter 4 for more information on the planned price fields

You typically use the Prices Other Than Standard Prices entry to update the Planned Prices fields in the material master Costing 2 view.

> **Example**
>
> Product development needs to create cost estimates to determine the cost viability of proposed new and modified existing products. To allow the product development team the flexibility to create their own cost estimates, a costing variant containing a costing type with No Update in the Price Update field is created for their exclusive use. They can create as many cost estimates as they need to with their costing variant without any concern that they could potentially influence the standard price.

Now let's discuss the Valuation View field in the Price Update tab as shown in Figure 8.6.

Figure 8.6 Price Update Tab Valuation View Field

If you are working with one valuation, you'll only need to create a costing type for legal valuation. If you're working with parallel valuation, you'll create costing types for the valuations for which you need to create cost estimates. You activate parallel valuation per controlling area by assigning a valuation profile to the controlling area with Transaction 8KEM. When running reports with parallel valuation, you need to specify on which valuation view you need the report to be based. Let's discuss each of the possible valuation views:

▶ **Legal valuation**
This is the only valuation view you can have if you're not using parallel valuation. Currency is based on company code currency, and internal profits for transactions between internal trading partners are included.

▶ **Group valuation**

You typically base group consolidated reports on group valuation. Two aspects you should consider for group valuation are:

▸ Group currency

▸ Profit elimination between internal trading partners

All currencies must be converted into group currency, and internal profits between internal trading partners must be eliminated. Transfer pricing determines the markup representing internal profits added to materials transferred between internal trading partners.

▶ **Profit center valuation**

Business transactions between profit centers are reproduced for management approaches based on internal prices.

You typically create parallel valuation for a controlling area in conjunction with activating the material ledger. In Chapter 4 we discussed the extra columns available for each valuation view in the material master Accounting 1 view with the material ledger activated. Let's review the extra columns as shown in Figure 8.7.

Prices and values		
Currency	MXN	USD
	Company code currency	Group currency, group va
Standard price	300,000.00	30,000.00
Per. unit price	300,000.00	30,000.00
Price unit	1,000	1,000
Price control	S	S
Stock value	1,499,400.00	149,940.00
Value/per.unit pr	1,499,400.00	149,940.00
Future price	300,000.00	30,000.00
Future price from	11/01/2007	11/01/2007
Previous price	300,000.00	
Last price change	10/16/2007	

Figure 8.7 Accounting 1 View with Material Ledger Activated

The first column contains prices based on the legal valuation view. The standard price is updated by a standard cost estimate based on a costing variant with legal valuation in the Valuation View field of the costing type.

The second column contains a standard price based on the group valuation view. The standard price in this view is updated by a cost estimate based on a costing variant with group valuation in the Valuation View field of the costing type. In this case you'll typically retrieve a component group price from the Future price field in the group valuation column shown in Figure 8.7.

Now that we've discussed the fields in the Price Update tab, let's discuss the fields in the next tab.

8.2.2   Save Parameters

Click on the Save Parameters tab in Figure 8.6 to display the screen shown in Figure 8.8

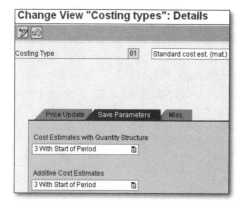

Figure 8.8 Costing Type Save Parameters Tab

Let's examine the fields in the Save Parameters tab.

Cost Estimates with Quantity Structure

This field determines which date is included in the key when a cost estimate with quantity structure is saved as shown in Figure 8.9.

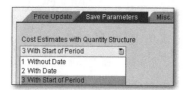

Figure 8.9 Save Parameters Tab Cost Estimates Date Field

Lets' discuss each of the three possible entries in this field:

► **With Start of Period**
The costing type used to create standard cost estimates must contain With Start of Period in this field. If you attempt to enter another option, you'll receive a message stating you can only save a standard cost estimate with the start of the period as the key date. Standard cost estimates are created for a minimum of a period, and a key field is the first day of the period.

► **With Date**
The start date of the cost estimate will be applied as the key date. Examples of when you use this entry are repetitive manufacturing and simulation cost estimates.

► **Without Date**
With this entry the cost estimate is not saved with a date as a key in the costing results. You use this entry for ad hoc cost estimates created on a one-off basis for reporting purposes only.

Now let's discuss the next field in the Save Parameters tab.

Additive Cost Estimates

This field determines which date is included in the key when an additive cost estimate is saved as shown in Figure 8.10.

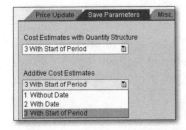

Figure 8.10 Save Parameters Tab Additive Cost Estimates Date Field

These entries are discussed in the previous points. If you don't intend to use additive cost estimates, you can enter Without Date in this field.

Now that we've discussed the fields in the Save Parameters tab, let's discuss the fields in the next tab.

8.2.3   Miscellaneous

Click the Misc. (miscellaneous) tab in Figure 8.10 to display the screen shown in Figure 8.11.

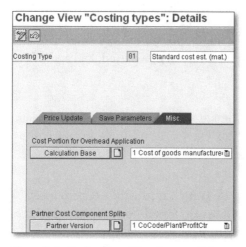

Figure 8.11 Costing Type Miscellaneous Tab

We'll examine the fields in this tab next.

Cost Portion for Overhead Application

Refer to Chapter 6 for more information on calculation base — Cost component views can be used as the calculation base in the calculation of overhead for semi-finished goods in finished goods. Cost component views filter cost components based on entries made in the cost components and cost component filters. To see a list of possible entries click on the field to display the screen shown in Figure 8.12.

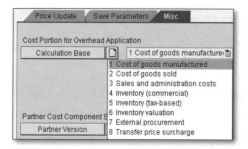

Figure 8.12 Miscellaneous Tab Cost Component Views

Entering a cost component view as a calculation base allows you to determine overhead for semi-finished goods on a calculation base independent of total cost estimate costs. Typically, you'll use a calculation base of cost of goods manufactured to calculate overhead for semi-finished goods. This means sales and distribution and administration costs are excluded from the calculation base. To view details of the cost component view shown in the field, click the Calculation Base button. To branch out to the cost component views configuration screen click the new page icon.

Refer to Chapter 7 for more information on cost component views

Now let's examine the next field in the costing type Misc. tab.

Partner Cost Component Splits

Click the Partner Version button in Figure 8.11 to view details as shown in Figure 8.13.

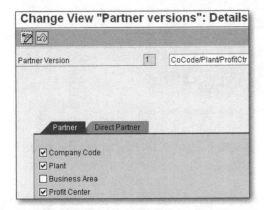

Figure 8.13 Partner Version Details

If you're using a group costing parallel valuation, you can specify a partner version of the costing type. (We discussed group costing and group cost estimates in Section 8.2.1.) A partner version is a key that uniquely defines a combination of partner and direct partner. A partner is a business unit involved in the value-added process, which can be assigned by making selections in Figure 8.13.

Parallel valuation

A direct partner transfers its product or service to another partner directly. A cost component split is generated for each partner by the group costing function, showing all value-added segments. If you do not want others to see the portion of the value added that the direct partner procured from the product or service when it is transferred to the receiving partner, it can be subsumed under the value added by the direct partner. The list of checkboxes available to select when you select the Direct Partner tab is the same as the list shown for the Partner tab in Figure 8.13.

When you create a cost estimate with a costing type with an assigned partner version, the Partner cost component splits button becomes available as shown in Figure 8.14.

Costing Data
Dates
Qty Struct.
Valuation
History
Costs
Costs Based On
1 Costing Lot Size
100
Cost Component View
Total Costs
Fixed Costs
Variable
Currency
Cost of goods manufactured 64,417.38 42,836.59 21,580.79 EUR
Cost of goods sold 64,417.38 42,836.59 21,580.79 EUR
Sales and administration costs 0.00 0.00 0.00 EUR
Inventory (commercial) 0.00 0.00 0.00 EUR
Inventory (tax-based) 0.00 0.00 0.00 EUR
1 Cost of goods manufactured
Partner

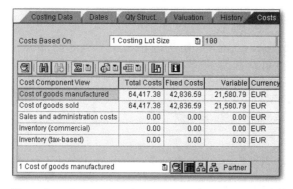

Figure 8.14 Partner Cost Component Splits Button Available

Click the Partner button shown in Figure 8.14 to display the screen shown in Figure 8.15.

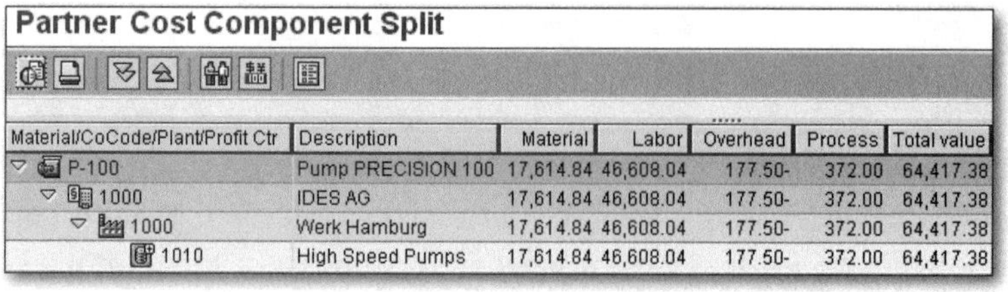

Partner Cost Component Split
Material/CoCode/Plant/Profit Ctr
Description
Material
Labor
Overhead
Process
Total value
P-100 Pump PRECISION 100 17,614.84 46,608.04 177.50- 372.00 64,417.38
1000 IDES AG 17,614.84 46,608.04 177.50- 372.00 64,417.38
1000 Werk Hamburg 17,614.84 46,608.04 177.50- 372.00 64,417.38
1010 High Speed Pumps 17,614.84 46,608.04 177.50- 372.00 64,417.38

Figure 8.15 Partner Cost Component Split

In this screen you can see the cost component split for the cost estimate shown in Figure 8.14. To view a partner cost component split, click the two person icon to display a list of partner views as shown in Figure 8.16.

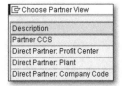

Figure 8.16 Choose Partner View Dialog Box

Double-click a partner view to display the associated costs.

Now that we've discussed fields contained in the costing type, let's look at the next costing variant component.

8.3   Valuation Variant

Click the Valuation Variant button in Figure 8.2 to display details of valuation variant 001. To display all valuation variants, click the new page icon next to the button to display the screen shown in Figure 8.17.

> **Note**
>
> You can also access valuation variants with Transaction OKK4 or by following the IMG menu path CONTROLLING • PRODUCT COST CONTROLLING • PRODUCT COST PLANNING • MATERIAL COST ESTIMATE WITH QUANTITY STRUCTURE • COSTING VARIANT: COMPONENTS • DEFINE VALUATION VARIANTS.

Available valuation variants are listed in this overview screen. You can either use a standard valuation variant or create your own. You can display more valuation variants supplied with the standard system by scrolling down this list. The valuation variant contains parameters required for the valuation of a cost estimate. Let's now discuss the details contained in a valuation variant.

8.3.1   Material Valuation

Double click a valuation variant to display the screen shown in Figure 8.18.

Let's examine the fields in the Material Val. (material valuation) tab, which is displayed when you initially view a valuation variant.

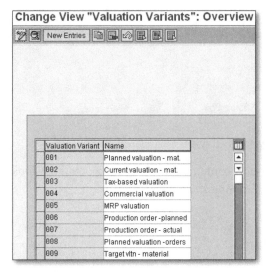

Figure 8.17 Valuation Variant Overview Screen

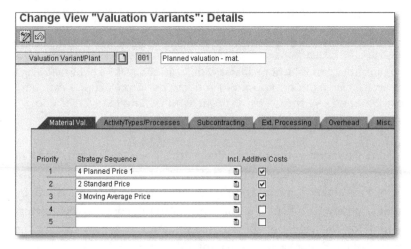

Figure 8.18 Valuation Variant Details Screen

Note

You can use different valuation strategies or different overhead rates in plants that belong to the same company code if necessary. Click the Valuation Variant/Plant button to assign a valuation variant to a plant. Otherwise, the same valuation variant applies to all your plants.

In material valuation you define the search sequence for prices for component materials. The Material Val. tab is divided into the Strategy Sequence and Additive Costs sections.

Strategy Sequence

The strategy sequence directs the system to search for entries in price fields in the material master, purchasing info record, and condition types. It continues to search the specified fields in a defined priority until a valid price is located. This price is taken as the component price, which is multiplied by the component quantity from the BOM to determine the material value, which is then rolled up to the highest-level material cost component. If the system is not successful in locating a price, an error message is issued.

A standard cost estimate cannot be released to update the standard price until all error messages are eliminated. After you eliminate the error messages, for example, by entering a valid purchasing info record price, the standard cost estimate can be created again and marked and released.

You can enter up to five strategies prioritized as shown in the Priority column in Figure 8.18.

Example

Enter the following strategy sequence in the Material Val. tab:
- ▶ 1. Planned price 1
- ▶ 2. Standard price
- ▶ 3. Moving average price

If the system finds a valid entry in the Planned price 1 field in the material master Costing 2 view, this is taken as the material price. If a value is not found in the Planned price 1 field, a price in the Standard price field is used. If there is no standard price, the moving average price is used.

A case scenario involving valuation strategies is presented in Chapter 4.

To display a list of possible entries in the valuation strategy fields, left click in a field. The screen shown in Figure 8.19 is displayed.

You'll need to scroll down this list to see all possible entries. Select a strategy to populate the field with your choice.

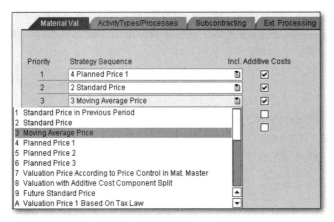

Figure 8.19 Material Valuation Strategy Possible Entries

The strategy sequence shown in Figure 8.19 may involve manually updating the Planned Price 1 field in the material master. You can also automatically update the Planned Price 1 field with cost estimates with a costing variant that retrieves prices from other fields. This is normally the valuation strategy you would use if purchasing does not maintain purchasing info records. A purchasing info record stores all of the information relevant to the procurement of a material from a vendor. This includes the latest purchase prices quoted by a vendor.

A more streamlined approach involves adding purchasing info records as part of the strategy sequence. Because purchasing info records are maintained by purchasing to store vendor quotation prices, there is no need to maintain entries in material master price fields.

> **Note**
>
> One of the many other advantages to purchasing by maintaining purchasing info records is that the latest valid vendor price defaults into the purchase price field when purchase requisition or purchase order is created.

Sub-Strategy Sequence with Purchasing Info Record Valuation

If you choose Price from Purchasing Info Record as a valuation strategy, additional fields become available in the Material Val. tab as shown in Figure 8.20.

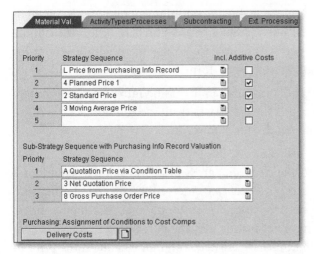

Figure 8.20 Sub-Strategy Sequence with Purchasing Info Record

Additional valuation strategies are required because multiple prices are available within purchasing info records. To display a list of possible entries in the purchasing info record valuation strategy fields, left click in a field. The screen shown in Figure 8.21 is displayed.

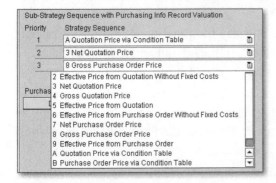

Figure 8.21 Purchasing Info Record Valuation Strategies

There are five types of purchasing prices you can choose from:

► **Gross price** (strategies 4 and 8)
This price does not take any discounts and surcharges into account. The system-supplied gross price condition is PB00. Conditions are stipulations agreed upon with vendors concerning prices, discounts,

and surcharges. You can maintain conditions in quotations, purchasing info records, outline agreements, and purchase orders. An outline agreement is a longer-term purchase arrangement with a vendor for the supply of materials or the performance of services.

If you enter the gross price in the purchasing info record, the system calculates the net and effective prices from the conditions if there are any entered in the purchasing info record.

▶ **Net price** (strategies 3 and 7)
This price is calculated from the gross price by taking discounts and surcharges into account. You can enter either the purchasing info record net price or gross price. You can only maintain the net price, however, if you have not maintained any purchasing info record conditions. Once conditions are created, you must maintain the price in the conditions screen that contains the gross price.

If the vendor's net price is not maintained in the purchasing info record, the net price of the last purchase order issued to the vendor is proposed when a new purchase order is created.

▶ **Effective price** (strategies 5 and 6)
This is the end price after taking all conditions including cash discounts and delivery costs into account. The price is determined automatically by the system. Display the purchasing info record or purchase order conditions to determine how the price was calculated.

▶ **Effective prices without fixed costs** (strategies 2 and 6)
The effective price is calculated from all of the conditions that are also contained in the assigned calculation schema, with the exception those with a condition type assigned to the Fixed amount calculation type. All tax conditions are excluded.

▶ **Price via condition table** (strategies A and B)
All general valid conditions and the conditions from the purchasing info record or the purchase order and scheduling agreement are included that are contained in the table that assigns condition types to origin groups. As of release 4.6A you can maintain this table using the Delivery Costs button, which we'll discuss further in the next section.

A scheduling agreement is a longer-term purchase arrangement with a vendor for the supply of materials or the performance of services.

These have a validity end date and predefined total purchase quantity or value. Specific dates or quantities for individual deliveries are not set. The two types of outline purchase agreements are contracts and scheduling agreements.

The prices discussed above can be retrieved from either the purchasing info record or last purchase order as discussed in the following points:

▸ **Purchasing info record prices** (strategies 2, 3, 4, 5, and A)
The net and effective quotation prices are maintained in the Purchasing Organization Data 1 data, and the gross quotation price and other conditions are maintained in the Conditions data of a purchasing info record.

▸ **Last purchase order prices** (strategies 6, 7, 8, 9, and B)
A record of the last purchase order is maintained by the system in the Purchasing Organization Data 2 data of a purchasing info record. You can access this screen by selecting GOTO • PURCH. ORG. DATA 2 from the menu bar when viewing a purchasing info record, or you can display the last purchase order directly by selecting ENVIRONMENT • LAST DOCUMENT. The last purchase order prices and conditions can be entered as valuation strategies in Figure 8.21.

> **Note**
>
> You can display the purchasing info record that a purchase order referenced by selecting ENVIRONMENT • INFO RECORD from the menu bar when viewing a purchase order. You can also display a list of purchasing info records for a material with Transaction ME1M, or for a vendor with Transaction ME1L. Double-click any purchasing info record in the lists to display further details.

We discussed purchasing info records in detail in Chapter 5.

Purchasing: Assignment of Conditions to Cost Components

Now that we've reviewed the strategy sequence sections of the Material Val. tab, let's discuss delivery costs as shown in Figure 8.22.

In this section you can assign purchasing info record condition types to origin groups. A condition type is a key that identifies a condition that can provide a detailed breakdown of material costs such as gross price, duty,

Refer to Chapter 7 for more information on cost components

freight, and insurance. This assignment provides a row in the cost estimate itemization under the same cost element for each assigned origin group. You can also assign the origin groups to separate cost components to provide more detailed reporting on material costs in cost estimates.

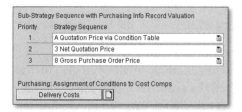

Figure 8.22 Delivery Costs Section of the Material Val. Tab

You assign condition types to origin groups by either clicking the Delivery Cost button, with Transaction OKYO, or by following the IMG menu path CONTROLLING • PRODUCT COST CONTROLLING • PRODUCT COST PLANNING • SELECTED FUNCTIONS IN MATERIAL COSTING • RAW MATERIAL COST ESTIMATE • ASSIGN CONDITION TYPES TO ORIGIN GROUPS. You'll see a screen similar to the one shown in Figure 8.23.

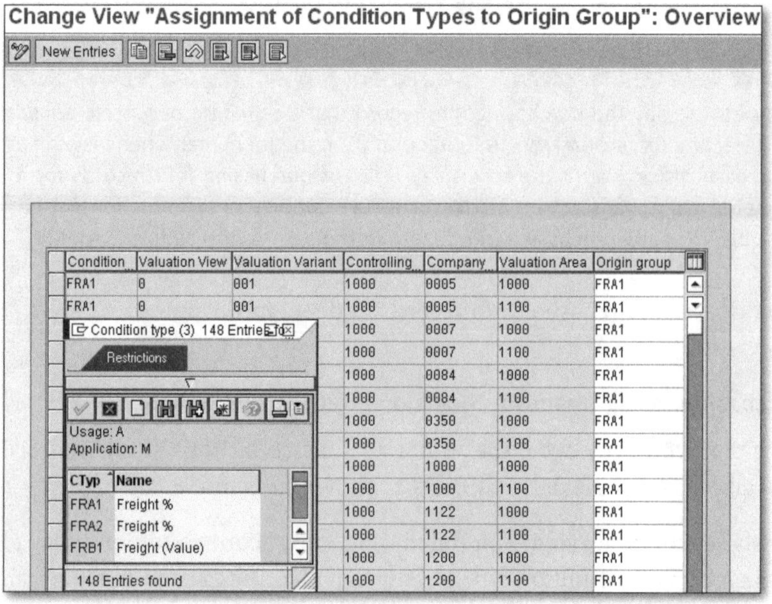

Figure 8.23 Assignment of Condition Types to Origin Group

Each condition type in the Condition... column is assigned to an origin group in the last column for each valuation area (plant) in a company code (Company... column). In this example freight condition type FRA1 is assigned to origin group FRA1 for plants 1000 and 1100 for multiple company codes. There are many condition types to choose from. At the top of the dialog box in Figure 8.23 there are 148 possible entries. Examples of condition types you may decide to assign to origin groups include duty, freight, and insurance. You can see these costs separately in the cost component split of a raw material cost estimate if you assign these origin groups to separate cost components. See Chapter 7 for more details on assigning origin groups to cost components.

> **Note**
>
> Assigning condition types to origin groups is only useful if purchasing assigns costs with condition types in purchasing info records and purchase orders. You should discuss and review the requirements of purchasing when considering using condition types in material costing.

Now that we've discussed assigning condition types to origin groups, let's examine how to include additive costs in automatic cost estimates.

Include Additive Costs

In the Material Val. tab you can select indicators that allow the inclusion of additive costs to raw material cost estimates depending on which valuation strategy is successful in locating a valid price, as shown in Figure 8.24.

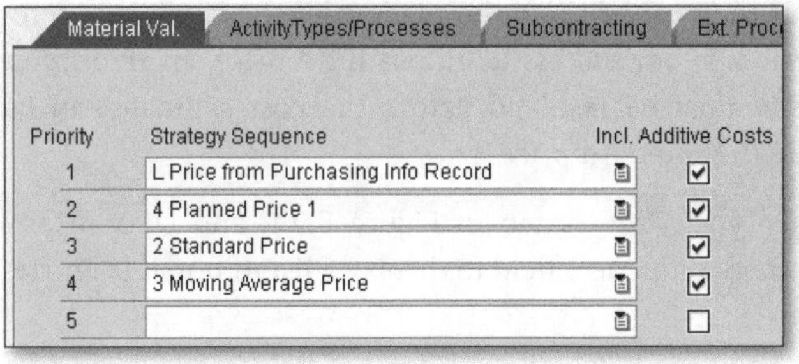

Material Val.	ActivityTypes/Processes	Subcontracting	Ext. Proc

Priority	Strategy Sequence		Incl. Additive Costs
1	L Price from Purchasing Info Record	🗎	☑
2	4 Planned Price 1	🗎	☑
3	2 Standard Price	🗎	☑
4	3 Moving Average Price	🗎	☑
5		🗎	☐

Figure 8.24 Include Additive Costs Indicators

Refer to
Chapter 12 for
more information
on unit cost
estimates
Additive costs allow you to enter costs manually in a unit cost estimate (spreadsheet in SAP) that can be added to an automatic cost estimate with quantity structure. By selecting a checkbox, you allow manual costs, if they exist, to be added to an automatic cost estimate depending on the successful valuation strategy. Let's follow a case scenario of when you may want to include additive costs in raw material cost estimates.

Case Scenario

A pharmaceutical company needs visibility of the price markup representing internal profits when a material is transferred between company codes in the USA. Additive costs are created representing the price markup, which is then included in the standard cost estimate.

Now that we've examined the fields and indicators in the Material Val. tab, let's move onto the next tab.

8.3.2 Activity Types and Processes

In activity types and processes you define the search sequence for internal activities and processes. The ActivityTypes/Processes tab is divided into the Strategy Sequence and Cost Center Accounting sections.

Strategy Sequence

The strategy sequence directs the system to search price fields in activity types and processes. It continues to search the specified fields in the priority you define until a valid price is located. This price is taken as the activity price, which is multiplied by the quantity to determine the activity value, which is then rolled up to the highest-level activity cost component. If the system is not successful in locating a price, an error message is issued that must be resolved before the cost estimate can be released to update the standard price.

Select the ActivityTypes/Process tab in Figure 8.24, and click in any Strategy Seq. (strategy sequence) field to display a list of possible entries as shown in Figure 8.25.

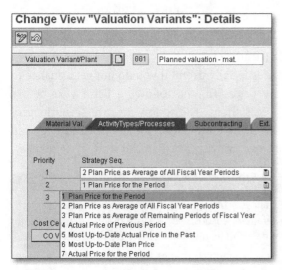

Figure 8.25 Activity Type Valuation Strategy Possible Entries

Select a strategy to populate the field with your choice. There are three types of activity prices to choose from:

▶ **Plan price** (strategies 1, 2, and 3)
Activity prices are planned per fiscal period. You have a choice of the Plan Price for the Period, Average of All Fiscal Year Periods, or Average of Remaining Periods.

An advantage of using an average plan price is that variance may be decreased during the year. The standard price is calculated using one activity price. If you base the cost estimate calculation on the plan activity price of one period, the activity price may vary in the remaining periods, resulting in a variance. To make variance analysis easier, one option is to base the cost estimate on an average plan price. You should then reduce the variance occurring due to activity type price variance. Some companies may need to analyze this variance, however, so it depends on your management reporting requirements. This also depends on how often you carry out main costing runs.

▶ **Actual price** (strategies 4 and 7)
You have a choice of using Actual Price for the Period or Actual Price of Previous Period. You calculate the actual price with Transaction KSII, which allocates all remaining cost center debits to manufactur-

ing orders or product cost collectors. This is useful if you carry out a main costing run every period.

▶ **Most up-to-date price** (strategies 5 and 6)
These two strategies are especially useful if you do not get a chance to update planned activity prices for the following fiscal year before activities attempt to access them. The following case scenario provides an example of how using the most up-to-date price strategy can be helpful when placed as a priority 2 or 3 in the strategy sequence.

Case Scenario

Manufacturing orders typically use costing variant PPP1 with valuation variant 006, which calculates order planned costs. This system-supplied valuation variant has Plan Price for the Period as the only activity type price strategy.

Production may need to create manufacturing orders for the next fiscal year before reaching the end of the current fiscal year. If you have not yet calculated and entered the plan activity rate for the next fiscal year, error messages will be generated when you attempt to calculate the manufacturing order plan costs.

However, if you include Most Up-to-Date Plan Price as a priority 2 strategy, the plan activity price for the current fiscal year will be successfully accessed even though there is no plan price in the period in the next fiscal year for which the manufacturing order is created.

Now that we've looked at activity type and processes strategy sequences, let's examine the next section of the ActivityType/Processes tab.

Cost Center Accounting

Version was previously known as plan version in earlier SAP R/3 versions

When entering plan activity rates with Transaction KP26, you enter a version in the selection screen. Version 0 is typically set up for both plan and actual costs, and this is the version you usually enter in the Cost Center Accounting section of the ActivityTypes/Processes tab as shown in Figure 8.26.

You can create over a thousand versions if necessary to configure alternate plan scenarios because the version key is a three-digit alphanumeric field. You typically carry out scenario analysis in other versions, and then copy the most likely scenario to version 0. Cost estimates are based on the activity type rates of version 0 if entered in the screen shown in Figure 8.26. Because version 0 also contains actual data, you can carry out variance analysis to explain the difference between planned and actual costs.

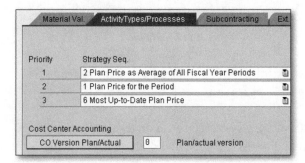

Figure 8.26 Activity Type CO Version Plan/Actual

You can see details of all versions by either clicking the CO Version Plan/Actual button shown in Figure 8.26, with Transaction OKEQ, or by following the IMG menu path CONTROLLING • GENERAL CONTROLLING • ORGANIZATION • MAINTAIN VERSIONS. You'll see a screen similar to the one shown in Figure 8.27.

General Version Definition

New Entries

Dialog Structure		General Version Overview					
▽ 🗁 General Version Definition		Version	Name	Plan	Actual	WIP/RA	Variance
🗀 Settings in Operating Concern		0	Plan/actual version	☑	☑	☑	☑
🗀 Settings for Profit Center Accounting		1	Plan version: change 1	☑	☐	☑	☑
▽ 🗀 Controlling Area Settings		2	Plan version 2	☑	☐	☑	☑
🗀 Settings for Each Fiscal Year		3	Plan version 3	☑	☐	☑	☐
🗀 Delta Version: Bus. Transactions		4	Plan version 4	☐	☐	☑	☐
🗀 Settings for Progress Analysis (Proje							

Figure 8.27 General Version Definition Screen

In the first row (version 0) of the General Version Overview section, both the Plan and Actual checkboxes are selected. Variance calculation will also be carried out in version 0. To see further details of version 0, select the first row and double-click Controlling Area Settings to see the screen shown in Figure 8.28.

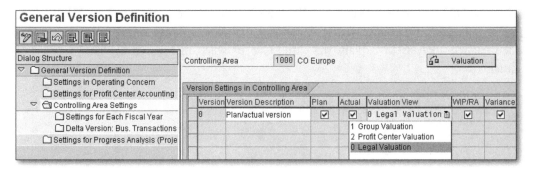

Figure 8.28 Controlling Area Settings Screen

Controlling area 1000 contains version 0 based on legal valuation. If you use parallel valuation and transfer prices, you define parallel actual versions in addition to the operational version 0 shown in Figure 8.28. Click the Valuation View field to see a list of possible entries as shown in Figure 8.28. If you are only using one valuation, you will see Legal Valuation in this field. If you are using multiple valuations, you can check the settings by clicking the Valuation button.

Select the first row and double-click Settings for Each Fiscal Year to display a list of fiscal years as shown in Figure 8.29.

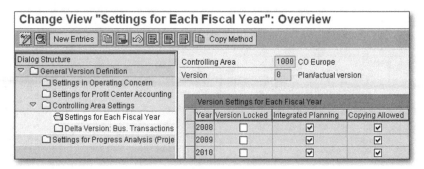

Figure 8.29 Settings for Each Fiscal Year

Double-click a row to display the detailed version settings for that fiscal year.

Now that we've looked at the ActivityType/Processes tab, let's examine the fields in the Subcontracting tab of the valuation variant.

8.3.3 Subcontracting

In subcontracting you supply material parts to an external vendor who manufactures the complete assembly. The vendor supplies a quotation that is entered in a purchasing info record.

Strategy Sequence

You can enter a strategy sequence for determining a subcontracting price by selecting the Subcontracting tab of the valuation variant as shown in Figure 8.30.

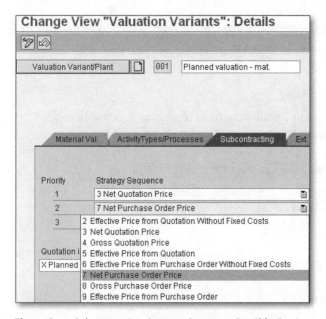

Figure 8.30 Subcontracting Strategy Sequence Possible Entries

In this screen you enter the sequence to search for prices in the purchasing info record and last purchase order. Click any field to display the list of possible entries as shown in Figure 8.30.

A special procurement type of subcontracting in the material master MRP 2 view of the assembly indicates to the system that this material is subject to subcontracting.

Refer to Section 8.3.1 for a previous detailed discussion on these prices

There are four categories of purchasing info records:

▶ Standard

▶ Subcontracting

▶ Pipeline

▶ Consignment

If the special procurement type indicates, for example, that this is a subcontract material, the cost estimate will only search for subcontracting category purchasing info records. Purchasing info records of other categories will not be considered.

Now that we've considered the Strategy Sequence section of the Subcontracting tab, let's look at the next section.

Quotation in Purchasing

Click the Quotation in Purchasing field to display a possible entries list as shown in Figure 8.31.

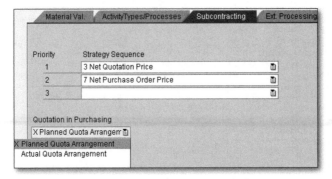

Figure 8.31 Quotation in Purchasing Possible Entries

Purchasing planned and actual quota arrangements are used to create a mixed price for materials that are manufactured with different external vendors with parts provided by the customer. You can specify whether the quota of the individual vendors entered in the source list for the material to be processed should be determined through the planned quota arrangement or the actual quota arrangement. The source list specifies allowed sources (purchasing info records) of a material for a plant within a validity period. If quota arrangements have been entered for multiple vendors for a subcontracting item, the system uses the vendor with the highest planned quota in this example.

Now let's look at the fields in the external processing tab of the valuation variant.

8.3.4 External Processing

Select the Ext. Processing tab in Figure 8.31 to display the screen shown in Figure 8.32.

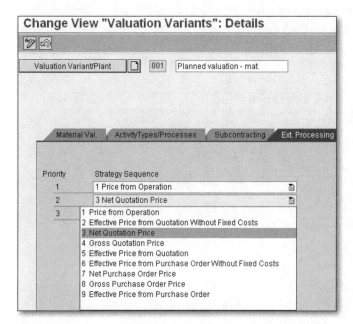

Figure 8.32 External Processing Strategy Sequence Possible Entries

We discussed purchasing info records and purchase order prices in Section 8.3.1. However, the first possible entry, Price from Operation, shown in Figure 8.32 has not been discussed yet. We first need to differentiate clearly between subcontracting and external processing:

▶ **Subcontracting**
  You send components to the external vendor and then receive the completed assembly from the vendor into inventory.

▶ **External Processing**
You can assign operations in a routing to an external vendor for processing. You send the unfinished assembly to the vendor. The operation, for example, degreasing, is carried out, and then the unfinished assembly is returned to you for further processing in the remaining operations in the routing.

Refer to Chapter 5 for a detailed discussion on external operations When an operation is processed externally, you maintain the data relevant to costing directly in the operation. You can access this data with Transaction CA02 or by following the menu path LOGISTICS • PRODUCTION • MASTER DATA • ROUTINGS • ROUTINGS • STANDARD ROUTINGS • CHANGE. Enter a routing with an external operation in the selection screen, click the Operations button, and double-click an operation with external processing (usually PP02 control key) to display the screen shown in Figure 8.33.

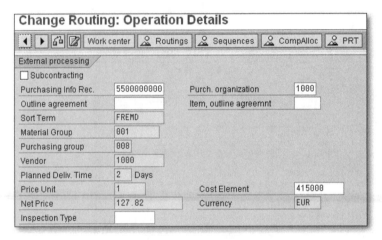

Figure 8.33 External Processing Section of Operation Details

You have two options for entering external processing price details:

▶ **Direct entry**
You can enter the price and associated information directly in the operation fields.

▶ **Purchasing info record**
You can store external processing cost information in a purchasing info record. When you enter the purchasing info record number and

press Enter, information is retrieved from the purchasing info record and automatically populated in the relevant fields of the operation. Information retrieved from the purchasing info record is not changeable in the operation. If you need to change the operation details fields, delete the purchasing info record number and press the Enter key. The information remains and all fields become changeable.

Select the Subcontracting checkbox in Figure 8.33 if you intend to send components with the unfinished assembly to the external vendor. A subcontracting category purchasing info record can only be used in this case, unless you enter the costing information directly in the operation fields.

Let's now look at the next valuation variant tab.

8.3.5 Overhead

Select the Overhead tab to the right of the Ext. Processing tab to display the screen shown in Figure 8.34.

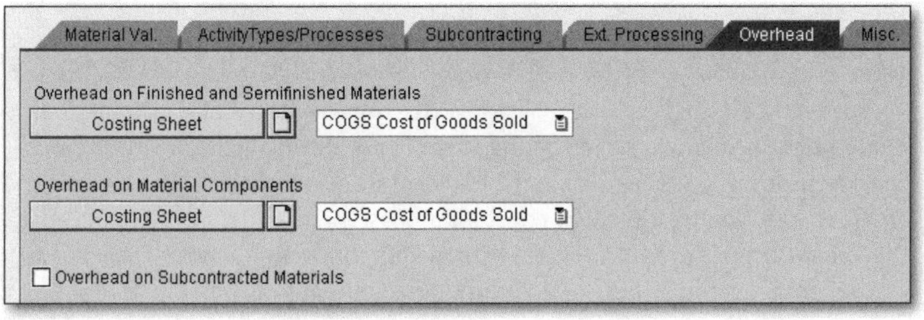

Figure 8.34 Valuation Variant Overhead Tab

Let's examine the three sections of the Overhead tab.

Overhead on Finished and Semifinished Materials

In this section you associate a costing sheet with the valuation variant for assemblies for the calculation of overhead. Let's now discuss this section:

▶ **Costing Sheet button**
Click this button to maintain the costing sheet shown in the field to the right of the button. Refer to Chapter 6 for details of how to maintain a costing sheet.

▶ **New page icon**
Click this icon to create a new costing sheet or to maintain details of another costing sheet.

▶ **Costing Sheet field**
Click this field to display a list of possible entries for costing sheets. The costing sheet entered in this field determines the calculation of overhead for finished and semifinished materials.

Now let's look at the next section in the Overhead tab.

Overhead on Material Components

You can calculate overhead on raw materials based on your entry in this section. The Costing Sheet button, new page icon, and Costing Sheet field work in exactly the same way as in the previous section.

> **Note**
>
> These overhead costs are usually for cost components that are non-stock-related because an overhead costing sheet is not normally used with the purchasing process. Overhead cannot be allocated when posting goods receipts and invoices. You would always post a purchase price variance (PPV) because the standard price would be greater than the goods and invoice receipt cost by the amount of overhead calculated in the standard cost estimate.
>
> With specific additional purchasing costs such as freight and duty, you can apply these as purchasing conditions that you can configure to post to specific general ledger accounts other than a PPV account.

Overhead on Subcontracted Materials

Select this checkbox if you want to apply overhead to subcontracted materials.

Let's now look at the last tab in the valuation variant.

8.3.6 Miscellaneous

Select the Misc. (miscellaneous) tab in Figure 8.34 to display the screen shown in Figure 8.35.

Figure 8.35 Costing Variant Miscellaneous Tab

With price factors you can control the extent to which a BOM item, operation, or suboperation in a routing is included in costing. In most cases you set the item as either fully relevant to costing (selected) or not relevant to costing (blank). These are system-defined price factors and are always available. First, let's look at how you set the Relevancy to Costing checkbox in a BOM item, and then we'll examine how you define price factors.

You maintain a BOM item with Transaction CS02 or by following the menu path LOGISTICS • PRODUCTION • MASTER DATA • BILLS OF MATERIAL • BILL OF MATERIAL • MATERIAL BOM • CHANGE. Double-click a BOM item and select the Status/Lng Text tab to display the screen shown in Figure 8.36.

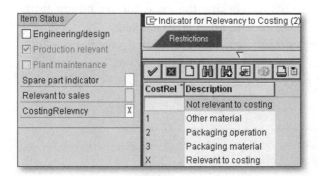

Figure 8.36 BOM Item Relevancy to Costing Indicator

Right-click the CostingRelevncy checkbox and select Possible Entries to display a list of possible choices as shown in Figure 8.36. The Not relevant to costing and Relevant to costing entries are system defined and always available. You can define your own indicators with Transaction OKK9 or by following the IMG menu path CONTROLLING • PRODUCT COST CONTROLLING • PRODUCT COST PLANNING • PRICE UPDATE • PARAMETERS FOR INVENTORY COST ESTIMATE • DEFINE RELEVANCY TO COSTING, as shown in Figure 8.37.

Costing Relevancy	Name
	Not relevant to costing
1	Other material
2	Packaging operation
3	Packaging material
X	Relevant to costing

Figure 8.37 Maintain Costing Relevancy Indicators

Costing Relevancy indicators 1, 2, and 3 are user defined in this example. The Costing Relevancy key is a one-character alphanumeric entry, allowing you to create up to 34 user-defined indicators.

Note

You cannot delete the system-supplied Costing Relevancy indicators.

After you've defined your own costing relevancy checkboxes, you can assign price factors by either clicking the Price Factors button in the Misc. tab of the valuation variant, using Transaction OKK7, or following the IMG menu path CONTROLLING • PRODUCT COST CONTROLLING • PRODUCT COST PLANNING • PRICE UPDATE • PARAMETERS FOR INVENTORY COST ESTIMATE • DEFINE PRICE FACTORS. The screen shown in Figure 8.38 is displayed.

Valuation Variant	Costing Relevancy	Fxd Prc. Factor	Var. Price Factor
+++	1	0.500	0.500
+++	2	0.250	0.250
+++	3	0.750	0.750
004	1	0.600	0.600

Figure 8.38 Factors for Relevancy to Costing Overview

In this screen you assign price factors to costing relevancy indicators to devalue items in an inventory cost estimate. You can assign factors separately for fixed and variable costs in the Fxd Prc. Factor (fixed price factor) and Var. Price Factor (variable price factor) columns.

The Valuation Variant entries of three plus signs (+++) indicate that the price factors are valid for all valuation variants that do not have specific entries. In this example valuation variant 004 and costing relevancy indicator 1 are assigned fixed and variable price factors of 0.600, whereas all other valuation variants are assigned a price factor of 0.500 for costing relevancy indicator 1.

Example

Packaging materials are allocated in part to sales and administration costs that may not be capitalized. In this case you can mark all of the BOM items, or the operations in a routing, directly related to packaging with a costing relevancy indicator you define for this purpose. This indicator together with the valuation variant determines the price factor used in an inventory cost estimate. An inventory cost estimate accesses the tax-based and commercial prices for purchased parts, and populates the same fields of the finished and semifinished products with the calculated value.

In this example if you assign costing relevancy indicator 3 to all packaging-related BOM items, these items will be devalued by a factor of 0.750 in an inventory cost estimate.

You can click a Costing Relevancy button (not shown) at the bottom of the screen in Figure 8.38 to maintain costing relevancy indicators shown in Figure 8.37.

Now that we've finished discussing the fields contained in the Valuation Variant, let's look at the next costing variant component.

8.4 Date Control

Date control determines which dates are proposed when a cost estimate is created and whether these dates can be changed by the user. You maintain date control either by clicking the Date Control button in the Control tab of a costing variant, with Transaction OKK6, or by following the IMG menu path CONTROLLING • PRODUCT COST CONTROLLING • PRODUCT COST

Refer to Chapter 10 for more information on cost estimates

Planning • Material Cost Estimate with Quantity Structure • Costing Variant: Components • Define Date Control. The screen shown in Figure 8.39 is displayed.

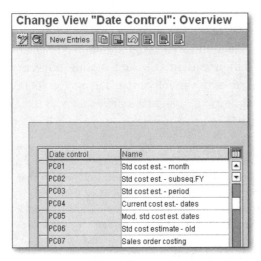

Figure 8.39 Date Control Overview Screen

The standard system contains predefined date controls. You can use these without making any changes. Select a date control and either click the pencil and glasses icon or double-click a date control to display the screen shown in Figure 8.40.

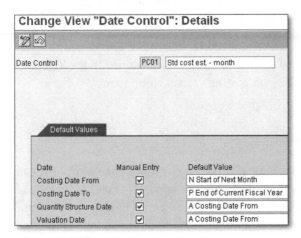

Figure 8.40 Date Control Details Screen

When you create a cost estimate, four dates corresponding to the dates assigned in the Default Values tab are proposed. If the Manual Entry checkbox is selected, the proposed dates can be changed by the user when creating a cost estimate. Let's examine the default value for each date.

8.4.1 Costing Date From

This field determines the validity start date of the cost estimate. The cost estimate cannot be marked and released or used to adjust inventory valuation until the start date has been reached. The start date can be changed to a previous date and the cost estimate created. However, a standard cost estimate cannot be saved, marked, or released with a start date in the past.

You generally create standard cost estimates for release at the start of the next month as shown in Figure 8.40. This provides you with an opportunity to correct problems indicated by cost estimate messages and to review the costs calculated during the current month and prior to the next month.

Modified standard cost estimates are based on the current quantity structure and planned prices, and are used for the costing of materials during the fiscal year to analyze cost developments. The system-supplied default Costing Date From for the modified standard cost estimate is today's date.

Current cost estimates are based on the current quantity structure and current prices, and are used for the costing of materials during the fiscal year to analyze development costs. The system-supplied default Costing Date From for the modified standard cost estimate is the start of the current month.

8.4.2 Costing Date To

This field determines the validity finish date of the cost estimate. Variance calculation requires a standard cost estimate that is valid for the entire fiscal year. This date is typically set to either the maximum possible date or the end of current fiscal year for a standard cost estimate.

The current and modified standard cost estimates default Costing Date To is usually set to the end of the current month.

8.4.3 Quantity Structure Date

This field determines which BOM and routing are selected for the cost estimate. Because these can change over time, it is useful to be able to select a particular BOM or routing by date.

You usually set the default date for standard cost estimates to be the same as the Costing Date From entry. The current cost estimate default date is usually set to today's date, and the modified standard cost estimate default date is usually set to the start of the current month.

8.4.4 Valuation Date

This field determines which material and activity prices are selected for the cost estimate. Purchasing info records can contain different vendor-quoted prices valid for different dates. Likewise, different activity prices can be planned per period within a fiscal year. It can be useful during product development, for instance, to hold the valuation date constant while changing the quantity structure date to isolate the cost effect of changing the structure of a BOM.

You usually set the default date for standard cost estimates to be the same as the Costing Date From entry. The current cost estimate default date is usually set to today's date, and the modified standard cost estimate default date is usually set to the start of the current month.

Now that we've examined the fields contained in the date control component, let's look at the next costing variant component.

8.5 Quantity Structure Control

Quantity structure control is used in cost estimates with quantity structure to specify how the system searches for valid alternative BOMs and routings in each plant. You can maintain quantity structure control either be clicking the Quantity Structure button in the Control tab of a costing variant, with Transaction OKK5, or by following the IMG menu path CONTROLLING • PRODUCT COST CONTROLLING • PRODUCT COST PLANNING • MATERIAL COST ESTIMATE WITH QUANTITY STRUCTURE • COSTING VARIANT: COMPONENTS • DEFINE QUANTITY STRUCTURE CONTROL. The screen shown in Figure 8.41 is displayed.

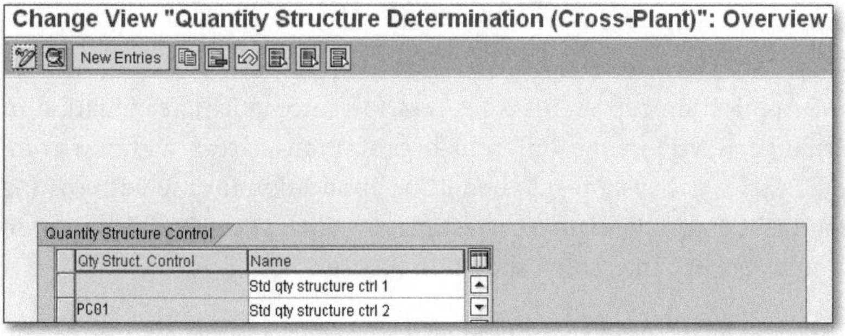

Figure 8.41 Quantity Structure Determination Overview

The standard system contains predefined quantity structure controls. You can use these without making any changes, or you can create your own. Select a quantity structure control and click the pencil and glasses icon, or double-click a quantity structure control (PC01 in this example) to display the screen shown in Figure 8.42.

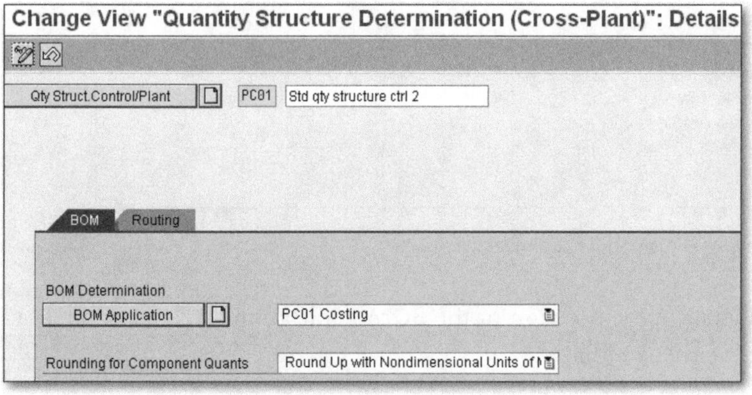

Figure 8.42 Quantity Structure Determination Details

Let's examine the details of how a BOM is selected by quantity structure control by examining the fields in the BOM tab.

8.5.1 BOM

BOM Application represents a process for automatic determination of alternative BOMs in the different organizational areas within a company. PC01 is the system-supplied BOM application for use with costing variant PPC1 for standard cost estimates. Click the BOM Application button to display the screen shown in Figure 8.43.

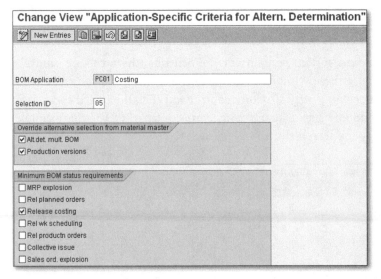

Figure 8.43 BOM Application Details

We'll analyze each section of the BOM application screen separately to make it easier to follow.

Selection ID

This key determines the order in which alternative BOMs are searched for based on BOM usage that identifies a specific section of your company such as production, engineering, or costing. You maintain details of selection ID with Transaction OPJI or by following the IMG menu path CONTROLLING • PRODUCT COST CONTROLLING • PRODUCT COST PLANNING • MATERIAL COST ESTIMATE WITH QUANTITY STRUCTURE • SETTINGS FOR QUANTITY STRUCTURE CONTROL • BOM SELECTION • CHECK BOM SELECTION. The screen shown in Figure 8.44 is displayed.

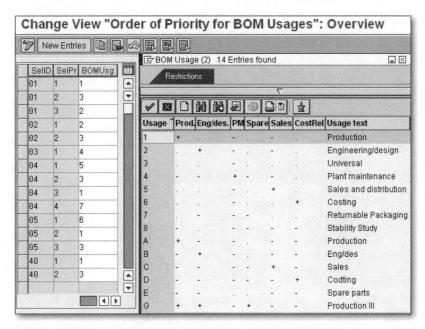

Figure 8.44 Selection ID Order of Priority for BOM Usages Overview

Let's examine SelID (selection ID) 05 because this is contained in BOM Application PC01, which is used by standard cost estimates with system-supplied settings. The SelPr (selection priority) column contains entries that assign the priority to the BOMUsg (BOM Usage) entries in the last column for each selection ID.

Click a BOMUsg field and press the F4 key to display a list of possible entries as shown in Figure 8.44. These settings relate to entries that can be made in BOM item status, which controls the areas of a company relevant to the BOM item. First, we'll discuss the meanings of the settings in the possible entries list and then see how this affects BOM item status:

▸ **Plus Sign (+)**
This BOM item status indicator must be selected.

▸ **Minus sign (-)**
This BOM item status indicator cannot be selected.

▸ **Period (.)**
This BOM item status indicator may be selected.

Access BOM item
status with Trans-
action CS02
Now let's see how the BOM usage of 1 for production affects the BOM item status indicators as shown in Figure 8.45.

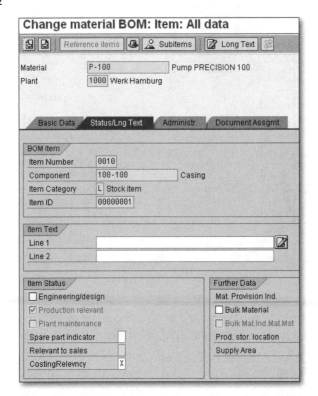

Figure 8.45 BOM Item Status Indicators for Production BOM

The Production relevant checkbox in the Item Status section is selected and cannot be changed for this BOM item. This corresponds to the plus sign in the BOM usage setting for production BOMs in Figure 8.44. BOM items with this indicator selected are copied to the planned order, and the system calculates dependent requirements for them. When the planned order is converted to a production order, the system automatically copies these items to the production order.

The Plant maintenance checkbox is not selected, and there is no entry in the Relevant to sales field. These checkbox and field settings cannot be changed. They correspond to the minus signs in the BOM usage setting for production BOMs in Figure 8.44. Items relevant to plant maintenance are used in maintenance BOM's. In sales order processing for variant products, you see items that are relevant to sales as order items for the header material.

The Engineering/design checkbox and the Spare part indicator and CostingRelevncy fields can be changed. This corresponds to the period signs in the BOM usage setting for Production BOMs in Figure 8.44. Engineering and design items are relevant to the area responsible for producing a functional design for production. The spare part indicator defines the item as a spare part. The CostingRelevncy field controls whether a BOM item, operation, or suboperation in the routing is included in costing.

Now that we've discussed how BOM usage controls BOM item status indicators, let's examine each of the three entries for selection ID 05 in Figure 8.44 to see how this controls BOM selection:

▶ **Selection ID 05, priority 1**
BOM usage 6 (costing) is assigned the first priority. Costing BOMs are usually copied from BOMs with a usage of production at the start of each fiscal year before the main costing run. You can make adjustments to costing BOMs that are not reflected in production BOMs. This is not generally recommended because standard cost estimates normally represent production costs.

▶ **Selection ID 05, priority 2**
BOM usage 1 (production) is assigned the second priority. If no costing BOM exists, a standard cost estimate will search for a production BOM.

▶ **Selection ID 05, priority 3**
BOM usage 3 (universal) is assigned the third priority. If there are no costing or production BOMs, standard cost estimates will search for a universal BOM.

Override Alternative Selection from Material Master

Now that we've discussed how selection ID automatically selects BOMs, let's discuss the next section of the BOM application screen (Figure 8.43) as shown in Figure 8.46.

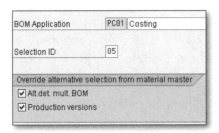

Figure 8.46 Override Alternative Selection from Material Master

In the material master MRP 4 view you can enter a method for selecting alternative BOMs, which we discussed in detail in Chapter 4. If you select the Alt.det. mult. BOM (alternative determination for multiple BOM) checkbox, the system will search for a specific alternative BOM for a certain date. You define alternative BOMs for a date with Transaction OPPP or by following the IMG menu path CONTROLLING • PRODUCT COST CONTROLLING • PRODUCT COST PLANNING • MATERIAL COST ESTIMATE WITH QUANTITY STRUCTURE • SETTINGS FOR QUANTITY STRUCTURE CONTROL • BOM SELECTION • CHECK ALTERNATIVE SELECTION FOR MULTIPLE BOM. The screen shown in Figure 8.47 is displayed.

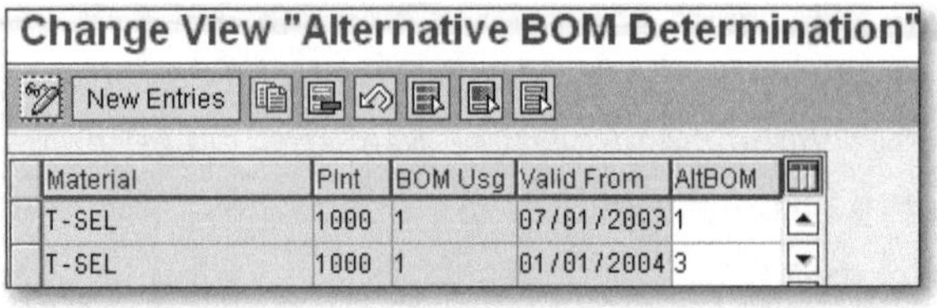

Change View "Alternative BOM Determination"

New Entries

Material	Plnt	BOM Usg	Valid From	AltBOM
T-SEL	1000	1	07/01/2003	1
T-SEL	1000	1	01/01/2004	3

Figure 8.47 Alternative BOM Determination Overview

You enter the date from when the alternative BOM is available. After this date a cost estimate will access this BOM, which overrides the method set for selecting alternative BOMs set in the material master MRP 4 field.

In the same section of the BOM application screen shown in Figure 8.46 is a Production versions checkbox. This checkbox shows that, when alternatives are selected automatically according to application, the production versions maintained in the material master record are used as selection criteria.

Minimum BOM Status Requirements

Now let's discuss the checkboxes in the remaining section of the BOM application screen shown in Figure 8.43, as displayed in Figure 8.48.

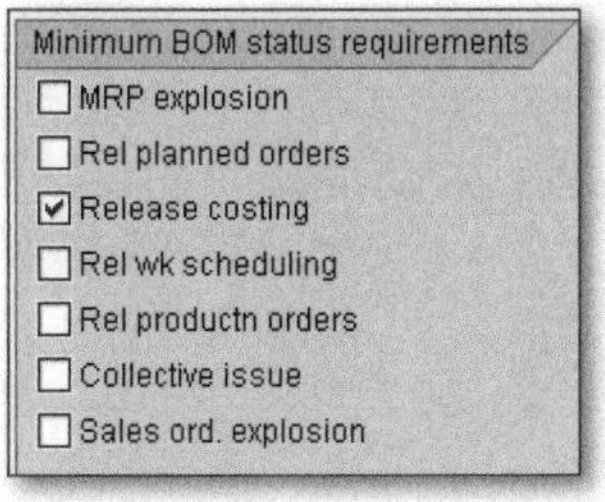

Figure 8.48 Minimum BOM Status Requirements Indicators

Before an alternative BOM is selected with the selection ID in the BOM application, it must meet minimum BOM status requirements. These requirements are shown by the selected checkboxes in Figure 8.48.

You can display a BOM status with Transaction CS02 or by following the menu path LOGISTICS • PRODUCTION • MASTER DATA • BILLS OF MATERIAL • BILL OF MATERIAL • MATERIAL BOM • CHANGE. Enter the BOM to review in the selection fields, press Enter, and then click the hat icon to display the BOM header as shown in Figure 8.49.

Click the BOM status field and then press the F4 key to display the list of possible entries for BOM status shown in Figure 8.49. The seven BOM status checkboxes and descriptions in Figure 8.48 correspond to the seven BOM status columns in Figure 8.49.

Because only BOM status 01 (active) has the Rel cstg (released to costing) checkbox selected in that column in Figure 8.49, only BOMs with this status will be selected by BOM application PC01.

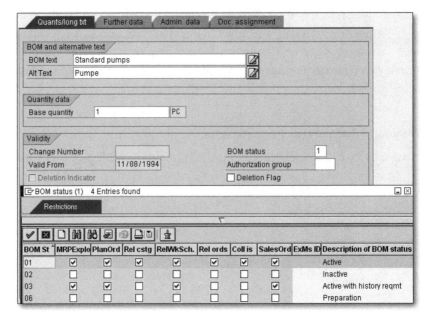

Figure 8.49 BOM Header Overview with BOM Status Possible Entries

Let's review both types of BOM status utilized by BOM applications:

▶ **BOM item status:** This applies to each BOM item. The BOM item status checkboxes and fields are controlled by BOM usage, which is used during BOM selection by selection ID.

▶ **BOM status at header level:** This applies to all BOM items. Checkboxes in the BOM application set minimum requirements for BOM status for selection of a BOM.

There is one remaining field we need to examine in the BOM tab of the Quantity Structure Determination screen shown in Figure 8.42.

Rounding for Component Quants

This field in the BOM tab is shown in Figure 8.50.

Rounding for component quants Click the field to display a list of possible entries as shown in Figure 8.50. When costing a material, this entry specifies whether the required quantity of a BOM component with a unit of measure that can only assume whole number values (such as "piece") is rounded up when the calculation of scrap-adjusted quantities produces a required quantity that is not a whole number.

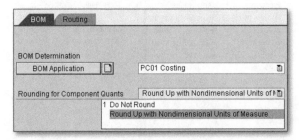

Figure 8.50 Rounding Indicator in Cost Estimate with Quantity Structure

Now that we've studied the fields in the BOM tab of the Quantity Structure Determination screen as shown in Figure 8.50, let's look at the fields in the Routing tab.

8.5.2 Routing

Select the Routing tab in Figure 8.50 to display the screen in Figure 8.51.

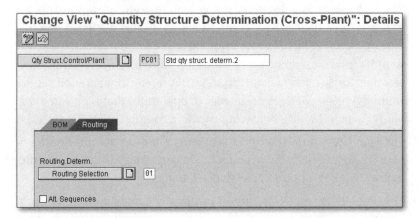

Figure 8.51 Routing Selection Details

Routing selection determines how routings are automatically selected by a cost estimate. Click on the Routing Selection button to display the details shown in Figure 8.52.

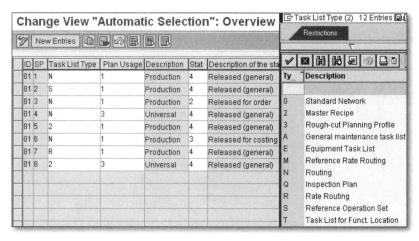

Figure 8.52 Routing Selection ID Details

Let's examine the details of the first row on the priority list to understand how a routing is automatically selected.

1. The ID column specifies the selection ID, 01 in this case.

2. The SP (selection priority) column specifies the sequence in which the system searches for each routing.

3. The Task List Type column entries specify the type of routing. Click a Task List Type field and press the F4 key to display the list of possible entries shown in Figure 8.52. From this list you can see that the selection ID first searches for N (routing) and, if unsuccessful, then searches for S (reference operation set). A reference operation set is a routing type that defines a sequence of operations that is repeated regularly, which simplifies entering data in a routing.

4. The Plan Usage and Description columns refer to a specific section of your company such as production, engineering, or plant maintenance. This concept is similar to BOM usage.

5. The Stat (status) and Description of the st columns indicate the processing status of a task list. You may assign a different status when the part is in research and development and when it's released for production.

Selection ID 01 will select a released production routing first if one is available when creating a standard cost estimate.

Now let's examine the Alt. Sequences (alternative sequences) checkbox in the Routing tab as shown in Figure 8.53.

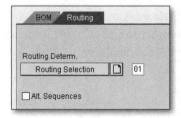

Figure 8.53 Alternative Sequences Transferred from Routing to Order

Select this checkbox to specify that alternative sequences can be transferred from the routing into the order. An alternative sequence is a sequence of operations that can be used as an alternative to a number of consecutive operations from the standard sequence. Alternative sequences are used, for example, if the production process differs according to lot size.

Now that we've looked at the quantity structure control component of the costing variant, let's examine transfer control.

8.6 Transfer Control

When a cost estimate is created for a finished good, cost estimates are first created for all of the lowest-level components and then progressively level by level up through the BOM hierarchy.

During a six-monthly or yearly costing run, you typically create new cost estimates for all components and assemblies. During the year if a new product contains all new components, a new standard price is needed for all components. However, some of the components may already exist and be shared with other existing products. Changing the existing standard price for these components could lead to a planned variance on production orders for existing products.

Transfer control allows the transfer of existing component and subassembly cost estimates to new product cost estimates. This is also known as partial costing.

293

You can maintain transfer control either by clicking the Transfer Control button in the Control tab of a costing variant, with Transaction OKKM, or by following the IMG menu path CONTROLLING • PRODUCT COST CONTROLLING • PRODUCT COST PLANNING • MATERIAL COST ESTIMATE WITH QUANTITY STRUCTURE • COSTING VARIANT: COMPONENTS • DEFINE TRANSFER CONTROL. The screen shown in Figure 8.54 is displayed.

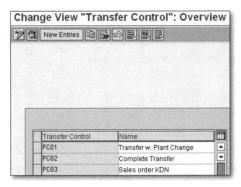

Figure 8.54 Transfer Control Overview

The standard system contains the predefined transfer controls displayed in Figure 8.54. You can use these or copy one and create your own. Let's examine transfer control PC02 as an example. Double-click PC02 to display the screen shown in Figure 8.55.

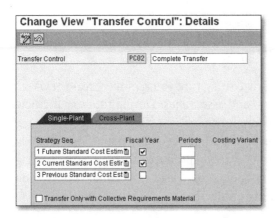

Figure 8.55 Single Plant Transfer Control Details

Let's discuss the fields and checkboxes in the Single-Plant tab first.

8.6.1   Single-Plant

This screen indicates that existing cost estimates for subassemblies and components within a plant are transferred to a new product cost estimate. This avoids recosting existing materials between main costing runs.

> **Note**
>
> Transfer control defined in the Single-Plant tab does not apply to materials transferred across plants using the special procurement key in the MRP 2 view. You define transfer control separately for materials transferred across plants in the Cross-Plant tab shown in Figure 8.55.

Strategy Sequence

The strategy sequence (Strategy Seq.) determines the order in which the system searches for existing cost estimates. If an existing cost estimate cannot be found that meets the requirements of any of the strategies, a new cost estimate is created. Click a strategy field to display a list of possible entries as shown in Figure 8.56.

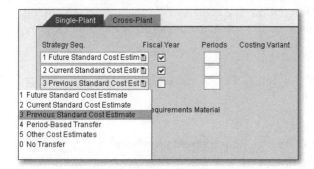

Figure 8.56 Transfer Control Strategy Sequence Possible Entries

If the Strategy Seq. field contains the current, previous, or future standard cost estimate, the system will only select a cost estimate with a start date within the current fiscal year or within specified periods.

Refer to the previous Section 8.4.1 for more information on cost estimate start date

Fiscal Year

If you select the Fiscal Year checkbox, the system will search for a cost estimate with a start date within the current fiscal year.

Periods

For current, previous, and other cost estimates, the Periods field refers to the number of periods in the past (that is, before the start date of the cost estimate).

For future cost estimates, the Periods field refers to the number of periods in the future (that is, after the start date of the cost estimate) and in the past (before the start date).

If you select Period-Based Transfer (period-based cost estimates), a Periods entry has no effect, because in this case the system searches for cost estimates that have exactly the same keys (that is, costing type, valuation variant, costing version, and, if applicable, period).

A Periods entry of zero means the current period. If you do not make any entries, the system interprets this as zero and searches for existing cost estimates in the current period only.

> **Note**
>
> If you enter Other Cost Estimates as a Strategy, two additional columns become available in Figure 8.56. The additional Costing Variant and Costing Version columns provide you with additional selection capability for selecting cost estimates.

Now let's examine the remaining checkbox in the Single-Plant tab shown in Figure 8.55.

Transfer Only With Collective Requirements Material

This checkbox is dependent on another setting made in the material master. We'll discuss this dependent setting first and then discuss this transfer control checkbox.

The dependant requirements checkbox for individual and collective requirements in the MRP 4 view of the material master determines whether the dependent (lower-level) requirements of an assembly can be grouped together (collective) or must be treated separately (individual):

- A collective requirements setting means the material is produced or procured for various requirements.

- An individual requirements setting means the material is specially manufactured or procured for a sales order.

If you select the Transfer Only with Collective Requirements Material checkbox in Figure 8.55, individual requirements materials especially for sales orders will be costed again even when a cost estimate already exists. This is particularly useful if your costs are very dependent on lot size.

Do not select this checkbox if existing costing data is also to be transferred for materials controlled by individual requirements. The system then searches for a cost estimate in the sequence of the specified strategies.

Now that we've investigated the fields and settings in the Single-Plant tab in Figure 8.55, let's look at the Cross-Plant tab.

8.6.2   Cross Plant

Select the Cross-Plant tab in Figure 8.55 to display the screen shown in Figure 8.57.

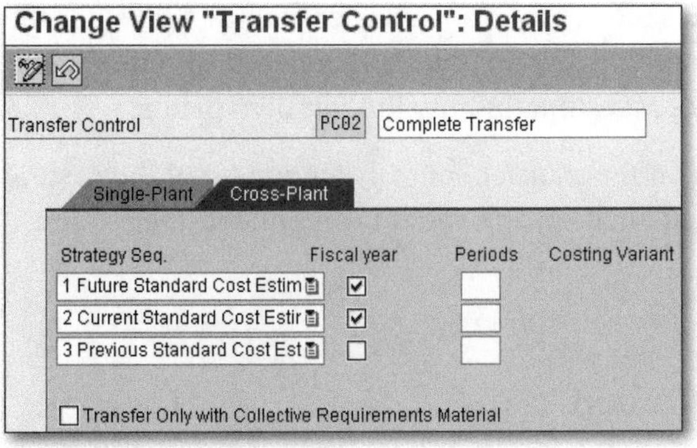

Figure 8.57 Cross Plant Transfer Control Details

The fields and checkboxes in this tab are the same as those in the Single-Plant tab, and they work in exactly the same way. Let's follow an example of how you can set up the checkboxes in these two tabs.

If your company has several plants, and an individual cost accountant is responsible for each plant, you may decide to use the SAP standard transfer control PC01. The Single-Plant tab settings are shown in Figure 8.58.

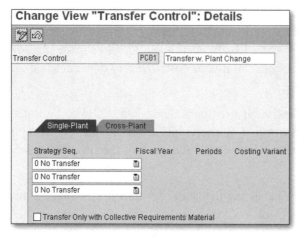

Figure 8.58 Single Plant Transfer Control PC01

Costing runs using transfer control PC01 will create and release new cost estimates within a single plant without using any existing cost estimates. The costing run, however, will use existing cost estimates from other plants if available because the cross-plant transfer control strategy is the same as shown in Figure 8.57. This strategy allows cost accountants to create and release new cost estimates only in their own plants.

Now that we've looked at the transfer control component of the costing variant, let's examine the final costing variant component, the reference variant.

8.7   Reference Variant

A reference variant is a costing variant component that allows you to create material cost estimates or costing runs based on the same quantity structure to improve system performance or make comparisons between cost estimates.

Whereas transfer control allows you to transfer an entire existing cost estimate, you can choose which parts of a reference variant to transfer, such as material components or internal activities.

You can maintain a reference variant either by clicking the Reference Variant button in the Control tab of a costing variant, with Transaction OKYC, or by following the IMG menu path CONTROLLING • PRODUCT COST CONTROLLING • PRODUCT COST PLANNING • MATERIAL COST ESTIMATE WITH QUANTITY STRUCTURE • COSTING VARIANT: COMPONENTS • DEFINE REFERENCE VARIANTS. The screen shown in Figure 8.59 is displayed.

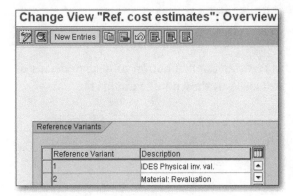

Figure 8.59 Reference Cost Estimate Overview

The overview screen displays a list of existing reference variants. You can use an existing variant or copy one and create your own. Double-click Reference Variant 2 in this example to display the details shown in Figure 8.60.

We'll discuss the details in the Cost Estimate Ref. tab first.

Cost Estimate Reference

Transfer control allows you to choose which cost estimate to use as a reference. Click the transfer control description to display a list of possible entries as shown in Figure 8.60.

You can either click the Transfer Control button to maintain the existing transfer control, or you can click the new page icon to create your own.

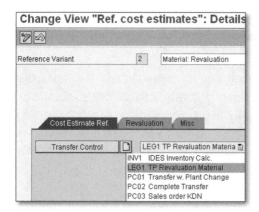

Figure 8.60 Reference Variant Cost Estimate

In this example, click the Transfer Control button to display details of the existing transfer control LEG1 as shown in Figure 8.61.

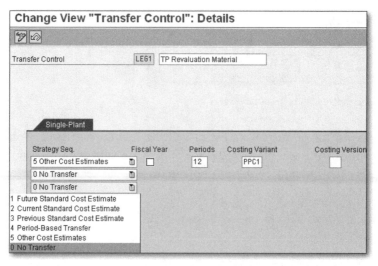

Figure 8.61 Reference Variant Transfer Control Details

See Section 8.6 for more information on transfer control You can only search for a reference cost estimate within the same plant because there is only the Single-Plant tab, and no Cross-Plant tab as in the transfer control component described in Section 8.6.2.

In the Strategy Seq. (strategy sequence) fields you determine the sequence in which the system searches for types of existing of cost estimates. Click a strategy sequence field to display a list of possible entries of cost estimate types.

In the subsequent columns you specify if the reference cost estimate must be:

▶ Valid within the current fiscal year

▶ Valid within a specified periods age

▶ Based on a certain costing variant

▶ Based on a certain costing version

Now let's examine the next tab of the reference variant.

Revaluation

Select the Revaluation tab in Figure 8.60 to display the screen shown in Figure 8.62.

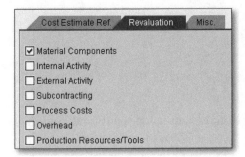

Figure 8.62 Reference Variant Revaluation Checkboxes

You select a checkbox in the Revaluation tab to specify whether an item should be revaluated when referencing a cost estimate. In the example shown in Figure 8.62, only the material components of a reference cost estimate will be revalued.

Now let's look at the final tab of the reference variant.

Miscellaneous

Click on the Misc. (miscellaneous) tab in Figure 8.62 to display the screen shown in Figure 8.63.

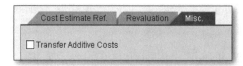

Figure 8.63 Reference Variant Transfer Additive Costs

You select this checkbox to specify that additive costs should be transferred when referencing a cost estimate.

Let's see an example of how you can use of a reference variant.

> **Example**
>
> You create a standard cost estimate and use it as a reference for an inventory cost estimate, changing only the value of the material components. With a reference variant, you use the quantity structure of the standard cost estimate when it calculates the inventory cost estimate without having to redetermine the quantity structure.

This concludes the costing variant components chapter, so let's review what we've covered.

8.8 Summary

In this chapter we discussed costing variant components and how they are used to create cost estimates. We looked at the definition of a costing variant and then examined each of the six components.

We first saw how the costing type determines if the cost estimate can update the material master. We then looked at how the valuation variant selects prices for the cost estimate. We examined how to use date control to set default dates when creating a cost estimate. Next, we looked at how quantity structure control determines which BOM and routing are selected for a cost estimate. Finally, we looked at how transfer control and the reference variant allow us to use existing cost estimates when creating new cost estimates.

Now that we've examined the six costing variant components in this chapter, we'll look at the costing variant tabs in Chapter 9.

A costing variant contains six tabs and six components for cost estimate configuration.

9 Costing Variant Tabs

We examined costing variant components in the previous chapter. In addition to the six costing variant components, there are six costing variant tabs containing configuration and settings:

- ▶ Control
- ▶ Quantity Structure
- ▶ Additive Costs
- ▶ Update
- ▶ Assignments
- ▶ Miscellaneous

We'll examine each of the tabs in detail in this chapter. First, let's look at the settings in the costing variant Control tab.

9.1 Control

You access costing variant configuration settings with Transaction OKKN or by following the IMG menu path CONTROLLING • PRODUCT COST CONTROLLING • PRODUCT COST PLANNING • MATERIAL COST ESTIMATE WITH QUANTITY STRUCTURE • DEFINE COSTING VARIANTS. Double-click SAP standard costing variant PPC1 to display the screen shown in Figure 9.1.

The Control tab lists the six costing variant control parameters that we discussed in detail in Chapter 8.

Costing variant components

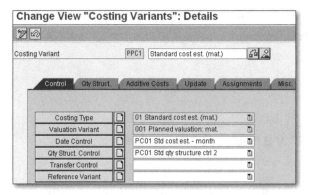

Figure 9.1 Costing Variant Details Control Tab

> **Tip**
>
> You can see an overview of all costing variant component settings by clicking on the overview (sun and two peaks) icon.

Let's now examine the settings in the quantity structure tab.

9.2   Quantity Structure

Select the Qty Struct. (quantity structure) tab to display the screen shown in Figure 9.2.

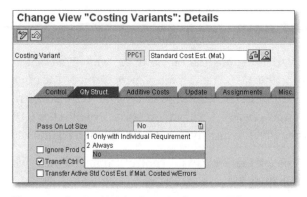

Figure 9.2 Costing Variant Quantity Structure Tab

First, let's examine how the Pass on Lot Size field works.

9.2.1 Pass On Lot Size

This field determines whether the costing lot size of all components is based on the costing lot size of the highest-level material. Click this field to display a list of possible entries as shown in Figure 9.2. Let's review the three possible options for this setting:

No – Do Not Pass on Lot Size

This setting indicates that materials further down the BOM are costed according to the lot size in the Costing 1 view of each component. This is the default setting for the PPC1 costing variant.

Costing lot size

> **Example**
>
> A finished product has a costing lot size of 10, whereas materials at the component (lower) level have a costing lot size of 100. A cost estimate for the finished product initially creates cost estimates for the lowest-level materials based on a costing lot size of 100.
>
> The cost estimate for the finished product is created based on a costing lot size of 10, and accesses the component cost estimate prices based on a costing lot size of 100 to determine material costs.

1 – Pass on Lot Size Only With Individual Requirements

In the MRP 4 material master view you can specify if a material is planned as an individual requirement, as we discussed in detail in Chapter 4. If this material is added to another material in a BOM, the cost estimate uses the lot size of the highest-level material.

> **Example**
>
> A component and finished product both have an individual requirements setting in the MRP 4 view. A cost estimate for the component uses the costing lot size of the finished product and ignores the costing lot size of the component material. The cost estimate is based on a costing variant with the Pass on Lot Size Only with Individual Requirements setting.

2 – Always Pass On Lot Size

With this setting all materials in a multilevel BOM are costed using the costing lot size of the finished product. This is the setting you normally

Sales order costing

use for sales order costing. When creating products for a specific customer requirement, components are procured just for this requirement. You do not necessarily get the purchasing benefits of pooling component requirements, so you need to be sure this is the setting you require.

> **Note**
>
> PPC4 is a system-supplied costing variant to create sales order cost estimates. This costing variant contains Pass on Lot Size Only with Individual Requirements selected by default. You can access this cost costing variant with Transaction OKY9 or by following the IMG menu path CONTROLLING • PRODUCT COST CONTROLLING • COST OBJECT CONTROLLING • PRODUCT COST BY SALES ORDER • PRELIMINARY COSTING AND ORDER BOM COSTING • PRODUCT COSTING FOR SALES ORDER ITEMS/ORDER BOMS • COSTING VARIANTS FOR PRODUCT COSTING • CHECK COSTING VARIANTS FOR PRODUCT COSTING.

Now that we've examined the Pass on Lot Size field in the quantity structure tab, let's look at the next checkbox.

9.2.2 Ignore Product Cost Estimate without Quantity Structure

This checkbox is shown in Figure 9.3.

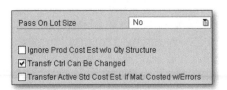

Figure 9.3 Quantity Structure Tab Checkboxes

Product development

The Ignore Prod Cost Est w/o Qty Structure (ignore product cost estimate without quantity structure) checkbox determines whether a cost estimate with quantity structure can access data that was produced by a cost estimate without quantity structure. Selecting this checkbox saves the system time unnecessarily searching for data produced by cost estimates without quantity structure. Many cost estimates without quantity structure may be created during new product development that do not need to be considered when creating standard cost estimates for existing products.

> **Note**
>
> Cost estimates without quantity structure are not based on a BOM and routing. Instead, you manually enter the components, activities, and overhead required to manufacture an assembly in a screen similar in appearance to a spreadsheet. This is also sometimes referred to as unit costing. Refer to Chapter 12 for more information on unit costing.
>
> You use this functionality during new product development, before a BOM and routing necessary for production are created. The unit cost estimate is useful for estimating the cost viability of a new product. You can easily compare the cost effectiveness of designs by substituting components and activities before prototyping or production occurs.
>
> You can also copy existing BOMs and routings into unit cost estimates and determine a new unit cost estimate based on proposed changes to an existing product design.

If you accept the default setting for the costing variant PPC1 and leave this checkbox deselected, standard cost estimates will search for all cost estimate data.

If you determine that you may benefit from selecting this checkbox, cost estimates ignore the with quantity structure checkbox setting in the Costing 1 view of all material masters.

Now let's review the next checkbox in the costing variant Qty Struct. tab.

9.2.3 Transfer Control Can Be Changed

This checkbox determines whether you have the option to change the transfer control parameter when creating a cost estimate. Transfer control requires a higher-level cost estimate to retrieve recently created standard cost estimates for lower-level materials. You can display the selection screen when creating an individual cost estimate with Transaction CK11N or by following the menu path Accounting • Controlling • Product Cost Controlling • Product Cost Planning • Material Costing • Cost Estimate with Quantity Structure • Create. The screen shown in Figure 9.4 is displayed.

The Transfer Control field entry can be changed because the Transfer Control Can Be Changed field in costing variant PPC1 is selected.

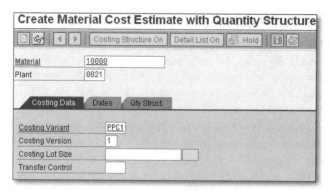

Figure 9.4 Transfer Control Field is Changeable

Let's see how the Transfer Control field appears when you use costing variant PPC2, as shown in Figure 9.5.

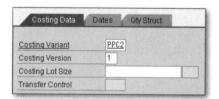

Figure 9.5 Transfer Control Field Not Changeable

Transfer control is discussed in detail in Chapter 8

Because the Transfer Control Can Be Changed checkbox is deselected for PPC2, you cannot change the default Transfer Control when creating a cost estimate. The default Transfer Control is set in the Control tab of the costing variant.

Case Scenario

A main costing run is carried out by a company yearly, and is used to update standard prices and inventory valuation. New standard cost estimates are required for every material during the main costing run. To help ensure that this requirement is met, a new costing variant, ZPC1, is copied from the standard PPC1, and the following settings are made:

- In the Qty Struct. tab the Transfer Control Can Be Changed checkbox shown in Figure 9.3 is deselected.
- In the Control tab the optional Transfer Control component field shown in Figure 9.1 is blank.

These settings ensure that when a main costing run is carried out with costing variant ZPC1, the Transfer Control field will be blank. This ensures that during a main costing run new standard cost estimates will be created for every material selected in the costing run.

When new products are created, standard cost estimates need to be created for the new products, new subassemblies, and components. If new products include subassemblies or components that already exist, the corresponding existing standard estimates are not to be overwritten. This scenario is achieved by ensuring that transfer control is included in standard cost estimates created for new products during the year.

A new costing variant, ZPC5, is copied from the standard PPC1, and the following settings are made:

- In the Qty Struct. tab the Transfer Control Can Be Changed checkbox shown in Figure 9.2 is deselected.
- In the Control tab the optional Transfer Control component field shown in Figure 9.1 is populated with a copy of standard transfer control ZC02 – Complete Transfer.

When standard cost estimates are created for new products and components with costing variant ZPC5 during the year, the transfer control field will be populated with ZC02. This ensures that existing standard cost estimates created during the main costing run with ZPC1 will remain in place for 12 months and not be overwritten during the year.

You can control which costing variant is allowed to be released with price update Transaction CK24. Click the Marking Allowance button to display a screen that allows you to enter an allowed costing variant per period and company code. You need to be able to mark a standard cost estimate before you can release it to update the material standard price. Add costing variant ZPC1 for the first period and ZPC5 for the remaining periods for each fiscal year, and you have successfully controlled the creation of standard cost estimates in line with company policy. You can restrict the number of people with access to Transaction CK24 and marking allowance with authorizations.

Now let's review the remaining indicator in the Qty Struct. tab.

9.2.4 Transfer Active Standard Cost Estimate if Material Costed with Errors

Cost estimate status

The status KF (costed with errors) of a cost estimate for a component or subassembly is normally passed up to the highest-level material. You select this checkbox to ensure that active standard cost estimates are used for any materials with errors, and costing continues up to the highest-level material without errors. If the system can't find an active standard cost estimate, it searches for a price in the material master in accordance with the valuation variant.

Case Scenario

You normally require the most recent vendor quoted prices contained in purchasing info records to be accessed by cost estimates during a costing run that updates standard prices and inventory valuation. If cost estimate errors occur for components without current purchasing info record prices, for example, you need these errors to be passed up to the highest-level materials. This ensures that the highest-level standard cost estimates cannot be marked and released to the standard price until the lower-level cost estimates are corrected.

You typically provide the list of materials that need purchasing info records updated with the latest vendor quotation prices to purchasing. After corrections are made, you carry out another costing run and continue eliminating errors until you're ready to mark and release the standard cost estimates.

To ensure that all lower-level standard cost estimate errors are corrected before a higher-level standard cost estimate can be released, you ensure that the checkbox in the Qty Struct. tab of costing variant ZPC1 is deselected. See the previous case scenario for the details of costing variant ZPC1.

For cost estimates that do not update standard prices and inventory valuation, it may be acceptable to use active standard cost estimates when errors are encountered. If you are developing new products by copying existing BOMs and routings and making proposed improvements or adjustments, you can create a new cost variant that has the indicator selected. This may shorten the product development process by not requiring cost estimates for products in development to be completely error free to obtain an estimated price.

We've now reviewed all of the fields and checkboxes in the Qty Struct. tab shown in Figure 9.2. There's another checkbox in this tab for sales order costing variants. Let's examine it before moving on to the next costing variant tab.

9.2.5 Transfer Cost Estimate of an Order BOM

You can access sales order costing variants with Transaction OKY9 or by following the IMG menu path Controlling • Product Cost Controlling • Cost Object Controlling • Product Cost by Sales Order • Preliminary Costing and Order BOM Costing • Product Costing for Sales Order Items/Order BOMs • Costing Variants for Product Costing • Check Costing Variants for Product Costing. Select the Qty Struct. tab to display the screen shown in Figure 9.6.

Sales order costing

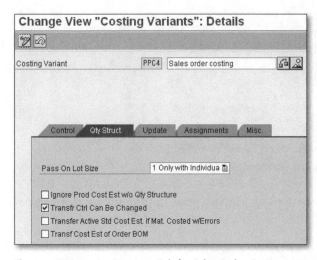

Figure 9.6 Quantity Structure Tab for Sales Order Costing Variants

The Tranf Cost Est of Order BOM (transfer cost estimate of order BOM) checkbox controls whether existing order BOM cost estimates should be transferred. An order BOM is a sales order BOM that is typically used in make-to-order and configurable product scenarios. These scenarios involve manufacturing products specifically for individual sales order line items. Customers specify certain required options for components and subassemblies for configurable products.

Make-to-order

The transfer of order BOM and cost estimates is recommended for complex make-to-order production. Transferring order BOM cost estimates improves system performance.

Now that we've discussed the fields and checkboxes in the costing variant Qty Struct. tab, let's move on the Additive Costs tab.

9.3   Additive Costs

Select the Additive Costs tab in Figure 9.2 to display the screen shown in Figure 9.7.

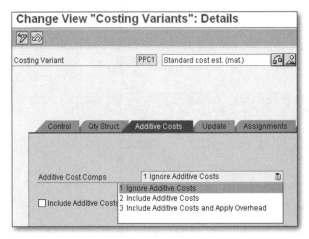

Figure 9.7 Costing Variant Additive Costs Tab

First let's examine how the Additive Cost Comps (additive cost components) field works.

9.3.1   Additive Cost Components

Manual costs   You can add costs manually to an additive cost estimate, which is similar in functionality to a spreadsheet. This field specifies whether cost estimates created with this costing variant can include manual costs in the form of an additive cost estimate. It also specifies if the additive costs are to be included when applying overhead. All three options are displayed in the list of possible entries shown in Figure 9.7. Let's examine each one in detail:

▶ **Ignore Additive Costs**
   You cannot manually add cost components with additive cost estimates for cost estimates created with this costing variant. Any existing additive cost estimates will be ignored. Choose this option if you need to ensure that cost estimates cannot be adjusted with manual costs.

▶ **Include Additive Costs**

You can include manual costs with additive cost estimates created with this costing variant. You can create and include additive costs for freight and handling charges, for example.

▶ **Include Additive Costs and Apply Overhead**

You can include additive costs and calculate overhead using these costs as part of the calculation base. This decision depends on how significant the additive costs are and on the method of overhead calculation.

9.3.2   Include Additive Costs with Stock Transfers

The next item to consider in the Additive Costs tab is shown in Figure 9.8.

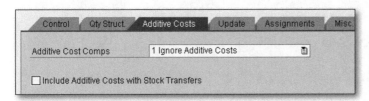

Figure 9.8 Costing Variant Additive Costs Tab

Selecting the Include Additive Costs with Stock Transfers checkbox allows you to include additive cost estimates for stock transfers between plants. This may be useful if you need to include transportation costs for stock transfers, for example.

The following special procurement types are taken into account by this checkbox:

▶ Transfer to another plant

▶ Production in another plant

The special procurement type signals to Material Requirements Planning (MRP) and cost estimates how materials are produced and transferred across plants. The standard price in the receiving plant includes the valuation calculated for the material in the issuing plant together with transportation costs in the additive cost estimate.

See Chapter 4 for more details on special procurement type

Now let's look at the next costing variant tab.

9.4   Update Tab

Select the Update tab in Figure 9.8 to display the screen shown in Figure 9.9.

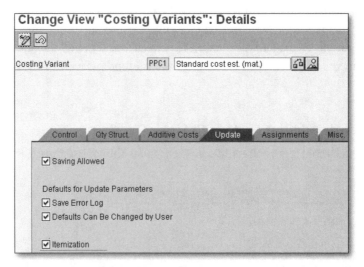

Figure 9.9 Costing Variant Update Tab

We'll examine the Saving Allowed checkbox in the Update tab first.

9.4.1   Saving Allowed

This checkbox determines whether you can save cost estimates created with this costing variant. If you intend to update prices in the material master, such as the standard price or planned prices in the Costing 2 view, you'll need to select this checkbox. You'll also need to select this checkbox if you intend to report on cost estimates or use the costing results in any of the following period-end activities:

▶ Variance calculation

▶ Work in process (WIP) calculation

▶ Result analysis

Let's consider the three checkboxes in the Defaults for Update Parameters section.

If you deselect the Saving Allowed checkbox, the remaining checkboxes in this tab automatically deselect. You need to be able to save the cost estimate in order to be able to save the error log and itemization. Itemization is a simple listing of a cost estimate's components and resources.

9.4.2 Save Error Log

When you create a cost estimate, an error log is created that contains messages that provide additional information on the cost estimate. It is good practice to analyze all cost estimate messages to ensure the integrity of the costing results. You can save a standard cost estimate status KF (costed with errors). This provides you with an opportunity to make necessary corrections before re-creating and saving the standard cost estimate.

Cost estimate integrity

You need to achieve a status KA (costed without errors) before you can mark and release a cost estimate resulting in an update of the standard price and inventory valuation.

You usually want to be able to save the error log so you can refer to messages and make corrections. There normally should be no storage capacity reasons preventing you from saving the error log. Selecting this checkbox is the most common setting.

This checkbox has no effect if you specify in the Parameters for Error Management field in the costing variant Misc. tab that the log containing the messages cannot be saved. We will discuss this setting further in Section 9.6.2.

Now let's consider the next checkbox in the Update tab.

9.4.3 Defaults Can Be Changed by User

When saving a cost estimate, you can specify whether the user has the opportunity to change the default settings for saving the message log and itemization. If you select the Defaults Can Be Changed by User checkbox, an Update Parameters dialog box will appear when you save the cost estimate, as shown in Figure 9.10.

Update parameters

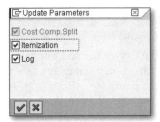

Figure 9.10 Update Parameters Dialog Box When Saving Cost Estimate

Let's discuss each checkbox in this dialog box.

Cost Component Split

The Cost Comp.Split (cost component split) checkbox is selected by default and cannot be changed. Cost components allow you to display costs in groups such as materials, labor, and overhead as discussed in detail in Chapter 7.

Itemization

Itemization provides cost details at an individual line item level of the resources necessary to manufacture a product. You normally want to retain itemization for review when analyzing costs.

Log

The log contains cost estimate messages that you may need to review to determine the integrity of cost estimates. It's normally good practice to retain cost estimate messages for review.

> **Typical Setting**
>
> We've just discussed that you'll typically want to save itemization and the message log because this is useful information that when analyzing costs and cost estimate integrity. You may decide it serves no purpose for the user to review the Update Parameters dialog box while saving every cost estimate. In this case you'll deselect Defaults Can Be Changed by User and select Save Error Log and Itemization in the costing variant Update tab.

Now let's review the final checkbox in the Update tab.

9.4.4 Itemization

A cost estimate creates an itemization list when calculating costs. You
have the choice in the costing variant of whether to save itemization
when the cost estimate is saved. Itemization is useful information when
analyzing and reviewing costs on a detailed level, whereas cost components provide summarized cost information.

Item level costs

Example
There are 20 components and subassemblies in a finished good BOM. All 20 items are listed separately in itemization. Likewise, all activity items from the routing and overhead items from the costing sheet are listed separately. A costing sheet contains the rules for allocating overhead from cost centers to cost estimates, product cost collectors, and manufacturing orders.
The cost component view summarizes costs based on cost element groups or ranges. Typical cost components are materials, labor, and overhead.

You normally save itemization information for analysis purposes. If you
only need summary information provided by the cost component view
and are not interested in more detailed item-level information, you may
decide not to save cost estimate itemization.

Now that we've reviewed the checkboxes in the costing variant Update
tab, let's move on to the next tab.

9.5 Assignments

Select the Assignments tab in Figure 9.9 to display the screen shown in
Figure 9.11.

You can check four assignments that influence cost estimates in the
Assignments tab. Let's look at each.

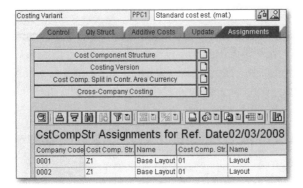

Figure 9.11 Costing Variant Assignments Tab

9.5.1 Cost Component Structure

Refer to Chapter 7 for more information on cost component structures

You can check the assignment of cost component structures to organizational units for this costing variant by clicking the Cost Component Structure button. In the example shown in Figure 9.11 the main cost component structure assigned to Company Codes 0001 and 0002 is Z1, and the auxiliary cost component structure assigned is 01.

For a listing of available cost component structures, or to create your own, click the new page icon next to the button.

9.5.2 Costing Version

Click the Costing Version button in Figure 9.11 to display the screen shown in Figure 9.12.

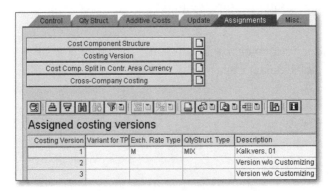

Figure 9.12 Costing Variant Costing Version Assignment

Costing versions enable you to create multiple cost estimates for the same material. Because the costing variant contains all parameters for costing, it can be time consuming to create new costing variants every time you want to make minor changes in the control parameters. The costing version enables you to simulate changes without having to create new costing variants. Let's examine the columns in Figure 9.12:

► **Variant for TP (transfer price determination)**
You can define settings for the selection of transfer prices in Customizing for Enterprise Controlling by following the IMG menu path ENTERPRISE CONTROLLING • PROFIT CENTER ACCOUNTING • TRANSFER PRICES. When you use costing versions, you can specify how these transfer variants are selected.

► **Exch. Rate Type (exchange rate type for currency translation)**
You can define settings for the selection of transfer prices in Customizing for Enterprise Controlling by following the IMG menu path ENTERPRISE CONTROLLING • PROFIT CENTER ACCOUNTING • TRANSFER PRICES. When you use costing versions, you can specify how these transfer variants are selected.

► **QtyStruct. Type (quantity structure type for mixed costing)**
Mixed cost estimates are created with reference to a costing version. You can create more than one mixed cost estimate for the same material with costing versions.

For a listing of available costing versions, either click the new page icon next to the button or use Transaction OKYD.

9.5.3   Cost Component Split in Controlling Area Currency

Click the Cost Comp. Split in Contr. Area Currency button in Figure 9.12 to display the screen shown in Figure 9.13.

You can specify that material cost estimate cost components are updated in the controlling area currency in an additional CCS (cost component split). This is in addition to the company code currency in the main CCS. This requires that the All currencies checkbox be selected for the controlling area with Transaction OKKP.

Refer to Chapter 7 for more information on cost component splits

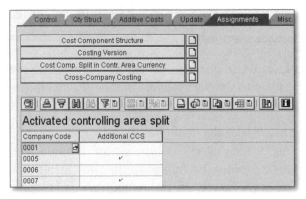

Figure 9.13 Costing Variant Controlling Area Currency Assignment

If the controlling area currency is not the same as the company code currency, the following are always updated:

- Cost component splits in company code currency
- Itemizations in both currencies (provided that the costing variant allows itemizations to be saved)

For a listing of additional cost component splits in controlling area currency, click the new page icon next to the button or use Transaction OKKP.

9.5.4 Cross-Company Costing

Click the Cross-Company Costing button in Figure 9.13 to display the screen shown in Figure 9.14.

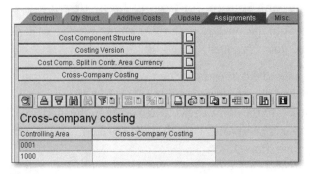

Figure 9.14 Costing Variant Cross-Company Costing

allows you to control whether additive costs can be included in the cost estimate. The Update tab allows you to determine if message logs can be saved and if the defaults can be changed by the user. The Assignments tab allows you to check organizational assignments of the costing variant, and the Misc. tab contains error management and message log settings.

Now that we've completed preparation for cost estimates with master data and basic configuration settings in previous chapters, we'll look at how to create cost estimates in Chapter 10.

You can allow cost estimates to access information in more than one company code. The system either re-costs the materials in plants that are assigned to the company code of the plant in which the cost estimate is created, or it transfers an existing cost estimate in accordance with transfer control parameters.

Refer to Chapter 8 for more information on transfer control

For materials in plants that are assigned to another company code, the Cost across company codes checkbox in Transaction OKYV or the IMG menu path CONTROLLING • PRODUCT COST CONTROLLING • PRODUCT COST PLANNING • SELECTED FUNCTIONS IN MATERIAL COSTING • ACTIVATE CROSS-COMPANY COSTING determines whether the materials are re-costed or whether the system uses an existing cost estimate in accordance with the valuation strategy.

For a listing of cross-company costing assignments, click the new page icon next to the button or use Transaction OKKP to create additional assignments.

Now that we've discussed the checkboxes in the costing variant Assignments tab, let's move on to the last tab.

9.6   Miscellaneous

Select the Misc. (miscellaneous) tab in Figure 9.14 to display the screen shown in Figure 9.15.

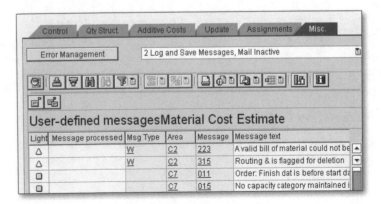

Figure 9.15 Costing Variant Miscellaneous Tab

This screen allows you to manage the processing of cost estimate messages. Let's first look at changing message types.

9.6.1 Error Management

Click the Error Management button to display a list of cost estimate messages. Change a message type by clicking a message row in the Msg Type column to display the list of possible entries shown in Figure 9.16.

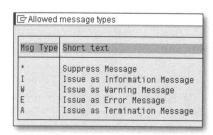

Figure 9.16 Allowed Message Types

Message type   A message type determines the importance of a message during the generation of a cost estimate. Double-click a message type to change its message type.

> **Example**
>
> The Message text column of the second message (message 315) listed in Figure 9.15 indicates that a routing is flagged for deletion. Because this is a warning message, a cost estimate containing this message could be released. To prevent any cost estimates with this message from being released, change the message type to an error.

Now that we've examined message types, let's look at the next field.

9.6.2 Parameters for Error Management

Click the field next to the Error Management button in Figure 9.15 to display a list of possible entries.

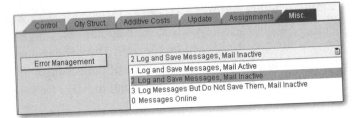

Figure 9.17 Parameters for Error Management

Let's examine each of the possible options:

▶ **0 Messages Online**
The messages are issued individually from the status bar. The log function is inactive in a cost estimate.

▶ **1 Log and Save Messages, Mail Active**
The messages are collected in a log, which can be saved. The messages can be sent to the person responsible for correcting the error.

▶ **2 Log and Save Messages, Mail Inactive**
The messages are collected in a log, which can be saved. The messages cannot be sent. This is the most common setting, allowing you to keep a record of all cost estimate messages you can refer to when analyzing the messages at a later date if necessary.

▶ **3 Log Messages But Do Not Save Them, Mail Inactive**
The messages are collected in a log, which can be processed online but not saved.

This concludes the costing variant tabs chapter, so let's review what we've covered.

9.7 Summary

In this chapter we discussed the information contained in costing variant tabs. We first considered the Control tab, which contains the six costing variant components discussed in Chapter 8. We then considered the Qty Struct. tab, which allows you to make settings on passing on the costing lot size and three checkboxes concerning the quantity structure and transfer control. Next we considered the Additive Costs tab, which

A cost estimate calculates the planned cost to manufacture a product or purchase a component.

10 Standard Cost Estimate

We completed preparations for creating cost estimates in previous chapters by updating activity and purchase prices and setting up master data and configuration.

Cost estimates provide a plan of how much it will cost to procure components and produce assemblies and finished goods. Standard cost estimates are typically created several weeks before the start of the next fiscal year. System messages are analyzed and corrective actions taken. For instance, missing purchasing info records or activity prices may need to be entered in the system.

After corrections are made and error messages eliminated, standard cost estimates are typically released on the first day of the fiscal year. Releasing standard cost estimates updates inventory valuation, and new material standard prices become the benchmark for all production and purchasing activities for the next 12 months.

Some companies with rapidly changing and developing products create and release standard cost estimates more frequently to keep pace with the changes. Otherwise, variances would become so large toward the end of the fiscal year that they would provide no assistance during variance analysis.

Standard costing allows you to keep production and procurement prices stable over at least one or more periods to allow you to analyze differences between the planned costs determined by cost estimates and actual prices.

Let's create a standard cost estimate, and then in the following sections we'll mark and release the cost estimate and mass-process cost estimates with a costing run.

10.1 Create Standard Cost Estimate

You create a standard cost estimate with Transaction CK11N or by following the menu path ACCOUNTING • CONTROLLING • PRODUCT COST CONTROLLING • PRODUCT COST PLANNING • MATERIAL COSTING • COST ESTIMATE WITH QUANTITY STRUCTURE • CREATE. A selection screen is displayed, as shown in Figure 10.1.

Figure 10.1 Create Standard Cost Estimate Screen

In this screen you enter the essential data necessary to create a cost estimate. The first two fields you need to complete are Material and Plant. We'll now review the data in each of the three tabs in Figure 10.1.

10.1.1 Costing Data

Let's review the fields in the Costing Data tab first.

Costing Variant

The Costing Variant field contains the configuration required for cost estimates to determine the planned prices. You can create an individual standard cost estimate with SAP standard costing variant PPC1. There is usually only one costing variant that can be used to update the standard price in the material master.

Costing Version

You can create different costing versions that can be useful for scenario analysis. You normally only allow costing version 1 cost estimates to be released to update inventory valuation.

Costing Lot Size

The costing lot size in the material master Costing 1 view determines the quantity on which cost estimate calculations are based. The costing lot size should be set as close as possible to actual purchase and production quantities to reduce lot size variance.

If you leave the Costing Lot Size field blank, the cost estimate retrieves the costing lot size from the corresponding field in the material master Costing 1 view.

Transfer Control

Transfer control is a costing variant component that requires a higher-level cost estimate to use recently created standard cost estimates for lower-level materials.

Refer to Chapter 9 for more information on transfer control

If you leave the Transfer Control field blank, a transfer control from the costing variant, if present, will default into this field. There is a configuration setting in the Qty Struct. tab of the costing variant to make this field not modifiable if required.

10.1.2 Dates

After completing the fields in the Costing Data tab, press Enter to display the screen shown in Figure 10.2.

Four default dates appear based on the date control component of the costing variant shown in Figure 10.1. You can either accept the default dates or change them if the date control component of the costing variant allows for this.

Figure 10.2 Create Standard Cost Estimate Dates Tab

Costing Date From

This field determines the validity start date of the cost estimate. The cost estimate cannot be marked and released, that is, used to adjust inventory valuation, until the start date has been reached. The start date can be changed to a previous date, and the cost estimate can be created. However, a standard cost estimate cannot be saved, marked, or released with a start date in the past.

Costing Date To

This field determines the validity finish date of the cost estimate. Variance calculation requires a standard cost estimate that is valid for the entire fiscal year. This date is typically set to the latest possible date.

Quantity Structure Date

This field determines which bill of material (BOM) and routing are selected for the cost estimate. Because these can change over time, it is particularly useful to be able to select a particular BOM or routing by date.

Valuation Date

This field determines which material and activity prices are selected for the cost estimate. Purchasing info records can contain different vendor-quoted prices for different dates.

Likewise, different activity prices can be planned per period. It can be useful to, for instance, hold the valuation date constant while changing the quantity structure date to isolate the cost effect of changing the structure of a BOM.

If you press Enter at this stage, the cost estimate will be created. Before creating the cost estimate, though, let's inspect the fields in the next tab.

10.1.3 Quantity Structure

Select the Qty Struct. (quantity structure) tab in Figure 10.2 to display the screen shown in Figure 10.3.

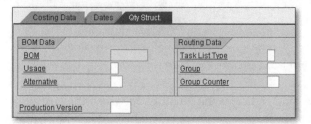

Figure 10.3 Create Standard Cost Estimate Quantity Structure Tab

If you do not make any changes to the fields in this screen, the standard cost estimate will be based on a BOM, routing, or production version entered in the Costing 1 view of the material master. If no entries are made in the quantity structure tab section of the Costing 1 view, the quantity structure will be determined by the quantity structure determination component of the costing variant as discussed in Chapter 8.

Refer to Chapter 4 for more information on material master settings

Press Enter to create the cost estimate, which is displayed in Figure 10.4.

A costed multilevel BOM is displayed at the left of the screen. Even though we initially created a cost estimate for material 10000 as shown in Figure 10.2, cost estimates are also created for all underlying components and subassemblies. Cost estimates are indicated by the cost estimate (calculator) icons in the costed BOM. Double-clicking any cost estimate in the multilevel costed BOM causes the information on the right of the screen to correspond to that individual cost estimate.

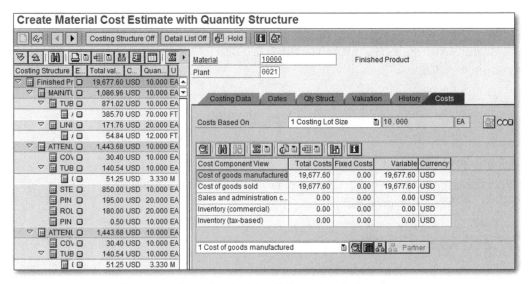

Figure 10.4 Create Standard Cost Estimate Results Screen

The Costs Based On field indicates the quantity on which the costs displayed are based. The costs are always calculated based on the costing lot size. The entry in the Costs Based On field defaults to the costing lot size. Purchasing or manufacturing in quantities that are different from the costing lot size can cause variances, because it is usually more efficient to purchase or manufacture items in larger quantities and less efficient to do so in smaller quantities.

To display costs based on a quantity of one (but still calculate them based on the costing lot size), click the Costing Lot Size text shown in Figure 10.4. The screen shown in Figure 10.5 is displayed.

Select 2 Price Unit and inspect the quantity displayed in the field to the right of the text. If the price unit is 1.000, the cost estimate costs displayed are now based on a quantity of one. Otherwise, click 3 User Entry and manually enter the quantity.

Now that we've created a standard cost estimate, the next steps are to mark and release the cost estimate. During the release step, inventory revaluation occurs if there is stock.

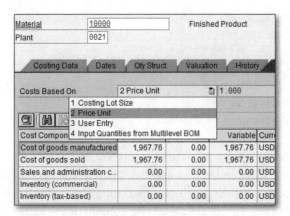

Figure 10.5 Change Cost Basis to Unit Entry

10.2 Mark and Release

After a standard cost estimate is saved without errors, it can be marked with Transaction CK24 or by following the menu path ACCOUNTING • CONTROLLING • PRODUCT COST CONTROLLING • PRODUCT COST PLANNING • MATERIAL COSTING • PRICE UPDATE. A selection screen is displayed, as shown in Figure 10.6.

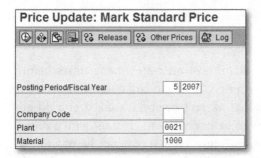

Figure 10.6 Mark Standard Cost Estimate Selection Screen

You mark and release cost estimates with this same selection screen. Mark a cost estimate by completing the Posting Period/Fiscal Year, Plant, and Material fields and then clicking the execute (clock) icon. The screen shown in Figure 10.7 is displayed.

331

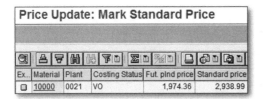

Figure 10.7 Mark Standard Cost Estimate Results Screen

A green traffic light icon, together with costing status VO, indicates that the standard cost estimate was successfully marked. There are no inventory revaluations or account postings during marking. The proposed standard price is copied to the Future Cost Estimate column of the material master Costing 2 view, as shown in Figure 10.8.

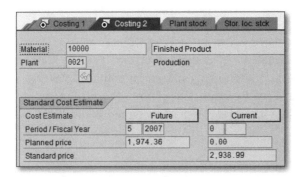

Figure 10.8 Marked Cost Estimate in Future Column

You can create and mark standard cost estimates many times before release. Within the same fiscal period, new standard cost estimates overwrite existing cost estimates that haven't been released. If you do not want a standard cost estimate to be overwritten, create it with a different costing version, as shown in Figure 10.1. It may not be possible to release cost estimates created with different costing versions, though. They are for reference only.

After you have successfully marked a cost estimate, check that the proposed standard price is correct. To release it, click the Release button shown in Figure 10.6, and then the execute icon. The screen shown in Figure 10.9 is displayed.

Price Update: Release Standard Price

Ex...	Material	Plant	Costing Status	Standard pri...	Price unit	Currency	Document Number
☐	10000	0021	FR	1,974.36	1	USD	3000009280

Figure 10.9 Release Standard Cost Estimate Results Screen

A green traffic light icon, together with costing status FR in the Costing Status column, indicates that the standard cost estimate was successfully released. You can display the price change document by clicking the underlined document number in the Document Number column. If there is valuated stock, inventory will be revalued, and a financial account posting will occur during release. The Future Standard price is moved to the Current Planned price and Standard price fields of the material master Costing 2 view, as shown in Figure 10.10.

> **Note**
>
> When a standard cost estimate is released, the previous standard cost estimate is moved to the Previous column to the right of the Current column (not shown in Figure 10.10).

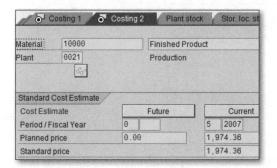

Figure 10.10 Released Cost Estimate in Current Column

Standard cost estimates can be released only once per fiscal period. As a rule, you should try to release cost estimates less frequently, for example, once every 12 months. This provides greater visibility to purchase price and production variances. Releasing cost estimates more frequently reduces variances, although inventory revaluation postings increase. Industries with rapidly moving purchase prices or short product development times may need to release cost estimates more frequently.

10.3   Costing Run

A costing run can create, mark, and release a large number of cost estimates, for example, all materials in a plant or company code. The costing run should be started well in advance of the required release date, because master data errors may need to be corrected, such as missing purchasing info record prices. Differences between proposed and existing standard prices may also need to be analyzed and approved before release.

Several steps are involved in processing a costing run. Let's follow the steps in detail, starting with creating a costing run. You can create a costing run with Transaction CK40N or by following the menu path ACCOUNTING • CONTROLLING • PRODUCT COST CONTROLLING • PRODUCT COST PLANNING • MATERIAL COSTING • COSTING RUN • EDIT COSTING RUN. A selection screen is displayed, as shown in Figure 10.11.

Figure 10.11 Edit Costing Run Initial Screen

In this screen enter an existing costing run name and press Enter to maintain the costing run. Click the pencil and glasses icon to toggle between edit and display modes for an existing costing run. Before editing an existing costing run, let's first follow an example of creating a new costing run.

10.3.1 Costing Data

To create a new costing run, click the create (new page) icon. The screen shown in Figure 10.12 is displayed.

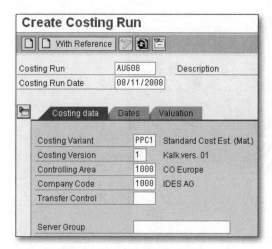

Figure 10.12 Create Costing Run Entry Screen

Enter the new costing run name, date, and description. Then fill out the required fields in the Costing data tab. You can use the entries shown in Figure 10.12 as an example. Then save your entries to display the screen shown in Figure 10.13.

> **Note**
>
> The Server Group field in Figure 10.12 allows you to process a costing run with several servers in parallel. This can reduce costing run processing time, which may be of benefit for costing runs involving many materials.

10.3.2 Dates

The Edit Costing Run screen allows you to carry out and record the results of all costing run steps in one screen. We'll begin by reviewing the information in the costing run tabs. We've already completed the fields in the Costing data tab, so now let's review the Dates tab.

335

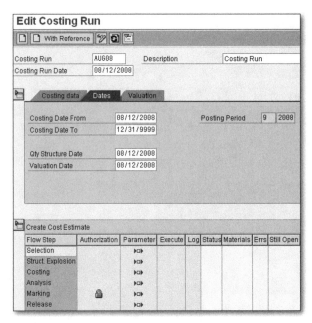

Figure 10.13 Edit Costing Run Dates Tab

Refer back to section 10.1.2 for more information on dates

The dates default from the dates component of the costing variant you entered in the Costing data tab. Depending on the costing variant configuration, you can change the default dates as necessary.

10.3.3 Valuation

Select the Valuation tab in Figure 10.13 to display valuation variant and costing sheet information derived from costing variant configuration. This information is for display only and is not modifiable. You do not need to click this tab to continue processing the cost estimate.

Now that we've discussed the information in the costing run tabs let's look at the Edit Cost Estimate section containing the six costing run steps.

10.3.4 Costing Run Steps

The costing run steps are listed in the Flow Step column of Figure 10.13. Let's examine each of the costing run steps.

Selection

To carry out the first costing run step, click the icon in the Parameter column of the Selection row. The screen shown in Figure 10.14 is displayed.

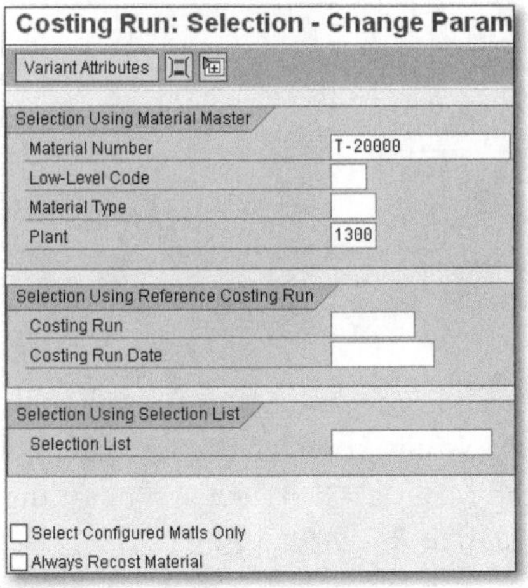

Costing Run: Selection - Change Param

Variant Attributes		

Selection Using Material Master

Material Number	T-20000
Low-Level Code	
Material Type	
Plant	1300

Selection Using Reference Costing Run

Costing Run	
Costing Run Date	

Selection Using Selection List

Selection List	

☐ Select Configured Matls Only
☐ Always Recost Material

Figure 10.14 Change Costing Run Selection Parameters

In the selection step you enter parameters to begin the process of selecting materials for inclusion in the costing run. Many options are available for using selection criteria. We'll follow a simple example to demonstrate how this step works. Fill in the Material Number and Plant fields, and save your entries. The screen shown in Figure 10.15 is displayed.

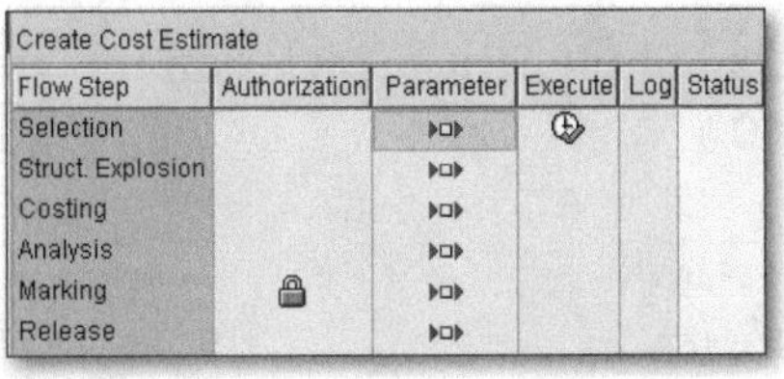

Create Cost Estimate

Flow Step	Authorization	Parameter	Execute	Log	Status
Selection		▶□▶	⊕		
Struct. Explosion		▶□▶			
Costing		▶□▶			
Analysis		▶□▶			
Marking	🔒	▶□▶			
Release		▶□▶			

Figure 10.15 Selection Step Parameters Saved

The icon in the Execute column of the Selection row indicates that selection parameters have been entered and saved. Click the execute icon to complete the selection step. The screen shown in Figure 10.16 is displayed.

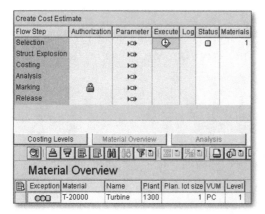

Figure 10.16 Selection Step Completed

The green traffic light icon in the Selection row and Status column indicates that the selection step was successfully completed. The materials selected in this step are shown in the Material Overview section of the screen. Now let's examine the next step in the costing run.

Structural Explosion

In the Struct. Explosion (structural explosion) step all materials contained at lower levels in BOMs selected in the selection step are selected. Click the icon in the Parameter column of the Struct. Explosion row to display the screen shown in Figure 10.17.

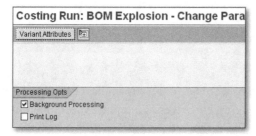

Figure 10.17 Costing Run Structural Explosion Parameters Step

You can select Background Processing to avoid overloading the system at busy times. Select Print Log to print messages created during the structural explosion step if required.

Save your settings, and click the green arrow icon and then the execute icon to display the screen shown in Figure 10.18.

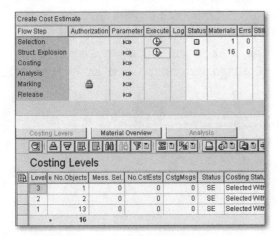

Figure 10.18 Structural Explosion Step Completed

The green traffic light icon in the Struct. Explosion row and Status column indicates that this step was successfully completed. The number of materials selected is shown in the Materials column. Now let's examine the next step in the costing run.

Costing

In the costing step of the costing run, cost estimates are created for all selected materials, starting with the lowest-level materials. Click the icon in the Parameter column of the Costing row to display the screen shown in Figure 10.19.

For large costing runs that generate many messages, you have two options to simplify the analysis process:

▶ **Cost estimates with errors only**
Because you cannot release cost estimates with errors, for large costing runs you can select this checkbox and make any necessary correc-

tions to eliminate errors only. You can then deselect the checkbox to create all cost estimates.

▶ **Log by costing level**

A costing run creates cost estimates at the lowest level of a BOM first and then progressively upward through the BOM structure to the highest-level assembly or finished good. If there are many messages, you can select this indicator to display and makes corrections where necessary as indicated by the lowest-level messages first. This will in turn reduce the number of messages and simplify analysis at higher levels. You can click the Costing Levels button to select the levels to display.

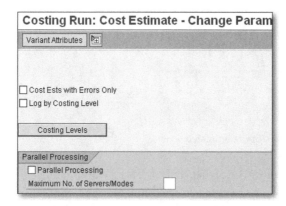

Figure 10.19 Costing Run Costing Parameters Step

For larger costing runs you can select Parallel Processing to reduce processing time by using more than one server.

Save your settings, and click the green arrow icon and then the execute icon to display the screen shown in Figure 10.20.

Click on the triangle icon in the Log column to display any messages generated during the costing step. Click the Material Overview button to display a list of cost estimates generated during the costing step.

> **Note**
>
> If any messages occur during the execute step of any costing run, a triangle icon will appear in the Log column. Click the icon to display the messages.

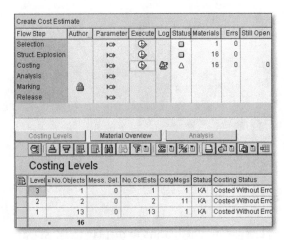

Figure 10.20 Costing Run Costing Step

Analysis

Click the icon in the Parameter column and Analysis row to display the selection screen shown in Figure 10.21.

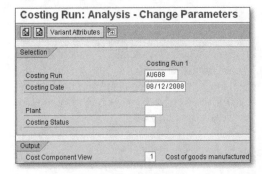

Figure 10.21 Costing Run Analysis Section Screen

The costing run you are presently working on defaults into the Costing Run and Costing Date fields. To display more selection fields click the plus sign icon to display the screen shown in Figure 10.22.

In the Output section you can select which material master price to compare with the standard cost estimate prices generated during the costing run. This together with inventory quantity allows you to determine the total change in inventory valuation when the costing run is released.

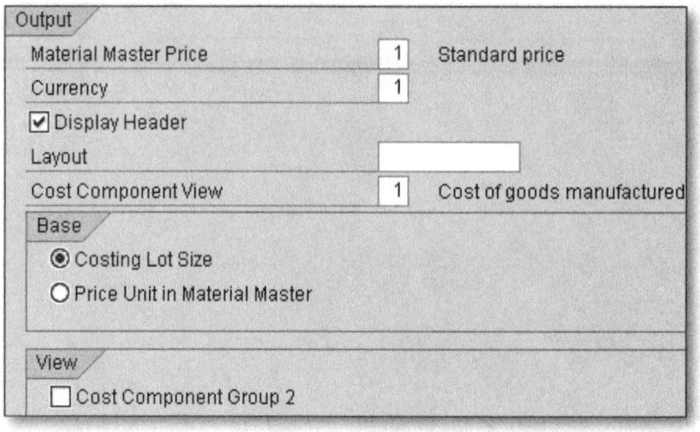

Figure 10.22 Analysis Step Extra Selections Screen

In the Base section you can choose in which units to display the cost estimate. You can change the default Costing Lot Size selection to Price in Material Master if necessary.

Refer to Chapter 7 for more information on cost component groups

In the View section you can select Cost Component Group 2 to display the cost report in this format as required

Save your selections, and click the green arrow icon and then the execute icon to display the screen shown in Figure 10.23.

> **Note**
>
> You can also analyze costing run results with Transaction S_P99_41000111 or by following the menu path ACCOUNTING • CONTROLLING • PRODUCT COST CONTROLLING • PRODUCT COST PLANNING • INFORMATION SYSTEM • OBJECT LIST • FOR MATERIAL • ANALYZE/COMPARE MATERIAL COST ESTIMATES.

Analyze/Compare Material Cost Estimates

Material	Material Description	Plant	Sta.	Costing Re	Lot Size	BUn
P-100	Pump PRECISION 100	1300	KA	593.32	100	PC
T-20000	Turbine	1300	KA	260,567.42	1	PC
T-20100	Turbine casing	1300	KA	51,129.20	1	PC
T-20200	Running gear	1300	KA	78,534.60	1	PC
T-20210	Turbine shaft	1300	KA	40,903.40	1	PC
T-20220	Guide blade	1300	KA	2,556.50	1	PC
T-20230	Rotating blade	1300	KA	2,147.40	1	PC
T-20300	Generator	1300	KA	76,693.80	1	PC

Figure 10.23 Analyze Material Cost Estimates

This screen displays a list of cost estimates generated during the costing step of the costing run. You can double-click any line to display the corresponding individual cost estimate details. You can display different columns in this screen by clicking the grid icon.

At this step you can carry out analysis to determine the total inventory revaluation if you proceed and mark and release the cost estimates in the costing run. You may decide to make adjustments and corrections to prices or quantities and rerun the previous costing run steps. Click the green arrow icon and then the Analysis button to display the screen shown in Figure 10.24.

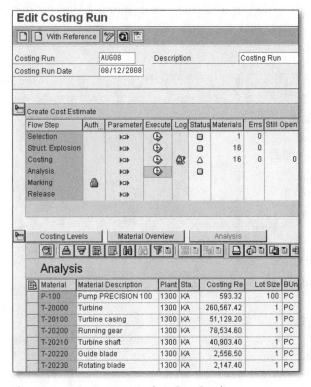

Figure 10.24 Costing Run Analysis Step Results

You can double-click any cost estimate in the Analysis section to display the individual cost estimate.

> **Note**
>
> There are many useful standard layouts for analyzing costing runs results and comparing existing and proposed inventory valuations. Click the grid icon to see a listing of standard layouts, or you can create and save your own layouts.

After you've created and analyzed the cost estimates created by the costing run, the next step is to mark them.

Mark

Refer to Section 10.2 for more information on mark and release

Before you can mark cost estimates, you must allow cost estimates to be marked in the period. To do this, click the lock icon in the Marking row in Figure 10.24 and then click a company code to display the screen shown in Figure 10.25.

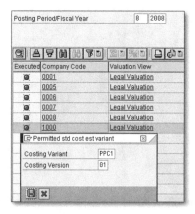

Figure 10.25 Allow Cost Estimate Marking Step

Click on a company code in this screen to choose a costing variant and costing version that can create cost estimates to be marked. Click the save icon and then the green arrow icon to return to the costing run screen. Click the Parameter icon in the Marking row in Figure 10.24 to display the screen shown in Figure 10.26.

Select the appropriate options for the costing run marking parameters, save your entries, and click the green arrow icon and then the execute icon to mark all of the cost estimates in the costing run. Click the green arrow icon to display the screen shown in Figure 10.27.

344

Processing Options
Test Run
With List Output
Parallel Processing
Background Processing

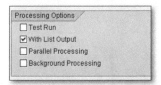

Figure 10.26 Costing Run Marking Parameters

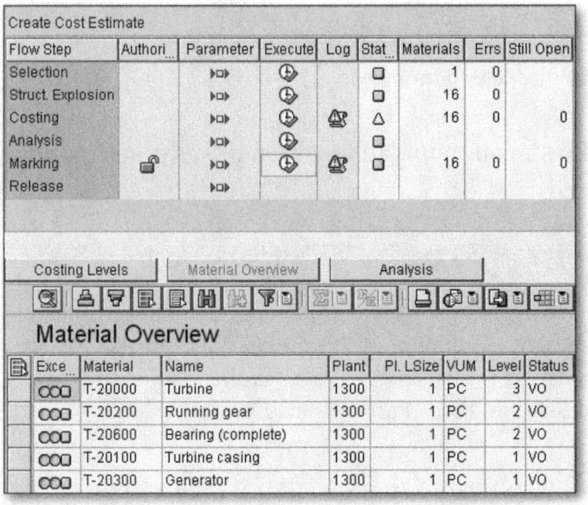

Create Cost Estimate
Flow Step | Authori... | Parameter | Execute | Log | Stat... | Materials | Errs | Still Open
Selection 1 0
Struct. Explosion 16 0
Costing 16 0 0
Analysis
Marking 16 0 0
Release
Costing Levels
Material Overview
Analysis
Material Overview
Exce... | Material | Name | Plant | Pl. LSize | VUM | Level | Status
T-20000 Turbine 1300 1 PC 3 VO
T-20200 Running gear 1300 1 PC 2 VO
T-20600 Bearing (complete) 1300 1 PC 2 VO
T-20100 Turbine casing 1300 1 PC 1 VO
T-20300 Generator 1300 1 PC 1 VO

Figure 10.27 Costing Run Marking Step Completed

The status VO indicates that the cost estimates were successfully marked without errors. You can double-click any line in the Material Overview section to display an individual cost estimate.

Release

The Release parameters screen is similar to the Mark screen, with the exception of the Other Prices button shown in Figure 10.28.

Refer back to Section 10.2 for more information on mark and release

Price Update: Release Standard Price
Other Prices

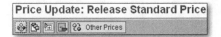

Figure 10.28 Release Step Other Prices Button

Click the Other Prices button to display the screen shown in Figure 10.29.

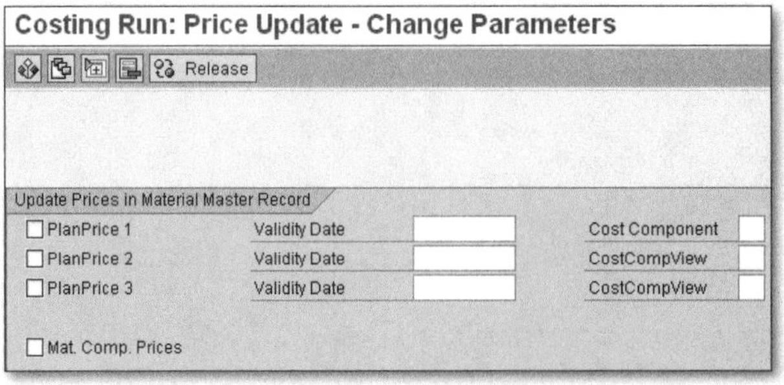

Figure 10.29 Release Other Prices Selection Screen

This selection screen allows you to update material prices other than the standard price if required.

Example

You may need to update the Plan Price 1 field in the material master Costing 2 view for purchased components if no purchasing info records are available. The standard cost estimate can then retrieve the Plan Price 1 price if the search for a purchasing info record price is unsuccessful.

Click the Release button to return to the selection screen shown in Figure 10.28, save your entries, and click the green arrow icon and then the execute icon to display the screen shown in Figure 10.30.

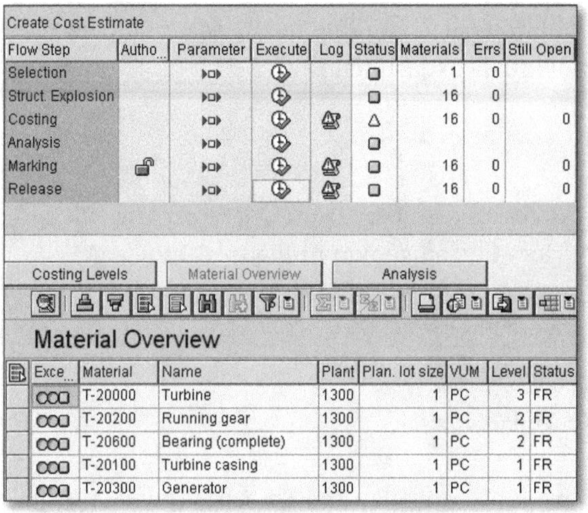

Figure 10.30 Costing Run Release Step Completed

The cost estimate status of FR indicates that the cost estimates have been successfully released and existing inventory revalued.

This concludes the standard cost estimate chapter, so let's review what we've covered.

10.4 Summary

In this chapter we discussed standard costing and how to create, mark, and release individual standard cost estimates. We also examined how to create costing runs that mass process standard cost estimates.

In the next chapter we'll examine preliminary cost estimates that do not revalue inventory but are used to determine production version and repetitive manufacturing costs.

A preliminary cost estimate calculates the planned costs for a manufacturing order or product cost collector.

11 Preliminary Cost Estimate

In Chapter 10 we discussed how to create standard cost estimates and update the material master standard price. It is also possible to create preliminary cost estimates based on manufacturing orders and production versions. A preliminary cost estimate for a product cost collector can calculate the costs for the production process or production version, which is a particular combination of a BOM and routing. Preliminary order cost estimates can be used to calculate planning variances and production variances.

Refer to Chapter 17 for more information on planning and production variances

> **Note**
>
> There can be a preliminary cost estimate for every order or production version, whereas there can only be one released standard cost estimate for each material.

Let's examine the steps involved in creating and analyzing a preliminary cost estimate.

11.1 Create Preliminary Cost Estimate

You create a preliminary cost estimate for a product cost collector with Transaction KKF6N or by following the menu path ACCOUNTING • CONTROLLING • PRODUCT COST CONTROLLING • COST OBJECT CONTROLLING • PRODUCT COST BY PERIOD • MASTER DATA • PRODUCT COST COLLECTOR • EDIT. The screen shown in Figure 11.1 is displayed.

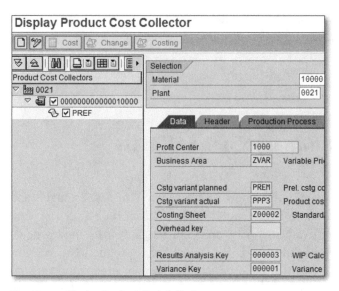

Figure 11.1 Display Product Cost Collector

Refer to Chapter 5 for more information on product cost collectors

You can create an individual preliminary cost estimate from this product collector screen. To create a preliminary cost estimate for a product cost collector, carry out the following steps:

1. Fill in the Material and Plant fields and press Enter.

2. Select the Production Version checkbox (PREF in this example) to display the details of the product cost collector.

3. Click the pencil and glasses icon to allow edits.

4. Click the Cost button to create the cost estimate.

5. Select the Header tab to display the Cost Estimate button.

The screen shown in Figure 11.2 is displayed.

Click the Cost Estimate button to display the most recent preliminary cost estimate, as shown in Figure 11.3.

> **Note**
>
> Click the Costs button to display a detailed cost report by cost element.

The preliminary cost estimate looks similar to the standard cost estimate we examined in Chapter 10. Two important differences, however, are the number of preliminary cost estimates possible per material and transfer control. We'll discuss these differences in the following subsections.

Figure 11.2 Product Cost Collector Header Tab

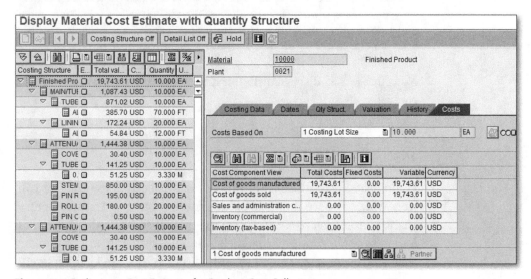

Figure 11.3 Preliminary Cost Estimate for Product Cost Collector

11.2   Production Process

Refer to Chapter 5 for more information on controlling levels

There can be only one standard cost estimate per material, whereas there can be many preliminary cost estimates. This is because preliminary cost estimates for product cost collectors are usually based on a production version controlling level. A production version is a unique combination of BOM, routing, and work center. Because there can be many different methods of manufacturing a material, there can be many production versions, and hence preliminary cost estimates.

Since release 4.5A on, product cost collectors are created with reference to a production process. A production process describes the way a material is produced, that is, which quantity structure is used. The quantity structure is taken from the production version, which is noted during the production process. The production process is determined by the following characteristics: material, production plant, and production version. One production process can be created for each production version.

> **Note**
>
> If you are using a product cost collector with the controlling level Production Plant/Planning Plant, you cannot create a preliminary cost estimate because the product cost collector does not have a quantity structure.

Now that we've discussed the product process, let's examine transfer control.

11.3   Transfer Control

Preliminary cost estimates for product cost collectors use transfer control, which is a component of the costing variant. Transfer control enables a top-level cost estimate to use previously created standard cost estimates for lower-level materials. The quickest way to create many standard cost estimates is with a costing run, as discussed in Chapter 10.

We'll examine transfer control in greater detail because it's important in order to create preliminary cost estimates for product cost collectors without errors. In the preliminary cost estimate shown in Figure 11.3, select the Costing Data tab to display the screen shown in Figure 11.4.

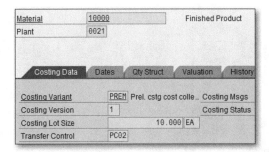

Figure 11.4 Preliminary Cost Estimate Costing Data Tab

The SAP standard costing variant for preliminary cost estimates is PREM, which contains transfer control PC02, as shown in Figure 11.4. Double-click the underlined text, PREM, in the Costing Variant field, to display the screen shown in Figure 11.5.

Refer to Chapter 8 for more information on costing variants

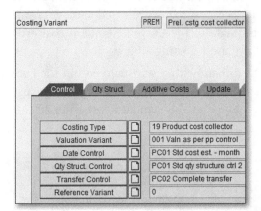

Figure 11.5 Costing Variant PREM Details Screen

This screen shows the components of costing variant PREM. Click the Transfer Control button to display the screen shown in Figure 11.6.

This screen shows the strategy sequence (Strategy Seq. section) that transfer control PC02 uses to search for existing cost estimates within a single plant. The three following points refer to each of the three search strategies shown in Figure 11.6.

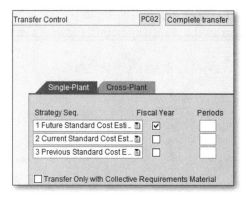

Figure 11.6 Transfer Control PC02 Details

1. A marked standard cost estimate with a start date within the current fiscal year, indicated by the selection in the Fiscal Year column. When a standard cost estimate is marked, it appears in the Future standard cost estimate column of the material master Costing 2 view.

2. A released standard cost estimate with a start date within the current fiscal period. When a standard cost estimate is released, it moves from the Future standard cost estimate to the Current standard cost estimate column of the material master Costing 2 view.

3. A previously released cost estimate with a start date within the current fiscal period. When a standard cost estimate is released, the cost estimate it replaces moves to the Previous standard cost estimate column in the material master Costing 2 view.

> **Tip**
>
> To provide a greater chance of a preliminary cost estimate successfully retrieving previously created standard cost estimates with transfer control, select the Fiscal Year checkbox for the second strategy sequence (Current Standard Cost Estimate) in Figure 11.6.

Preliminary cost estimates released in the same period that standard cost estimates are released for lower-level materials use the standard cost estimates. This is based on the second transfer control strategy sequence shown in Figure 11.6. To demonstrate this, in the cost estimate shown in Figure 11.3, double-click the second cost estimate on the left side of the screen, immediately below the highlighted Finished Product. The right side of the cost estimate screen now refers to the second cost estimate. Click the Costing Data tab to display the screen shown in Figure 11.7.

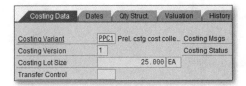

Figure 11.7 Lower-Level Cost Estimate Costing Data Tab

Notice that the lower-level cost estimate was previously created with costing variant PPC1, which indicates that this is a standard cost estimate. To find out when the standard cost estimate was created, select the History tab.

We've now created individual preliminary cost estimates and examined how they access existing standard cost estimates at lower levels in the BOM. Because preliminary cost estimates are normally used to valuate WIP and scrap during period-end processing in Product Cost by Period, you need to mass-create preliminary cost estimates immediately following a costing run. This ensures that the preliminary cost estimates will be current during the first period-end processing following the costing run. Let's examine how you do this in the next section.

11.4   Mass-Processing

You can create multiple preliminary cost estimates for product cost collectors with Transaction MF30 or by following the menu path ACCOUNTING • CONTROLLING • PRODUCT COST CONTROLLING • COST OBJECT CONTROLLING • PRODUCT COST BY PERIOD • PLANNING • PRELIMINARY COSTING FOR PRODUCT COST COLLECTORS. The screen shown in Figure 11.8 is displayed.

This selection screen allows you to enter a range or list of materials or production processes. To mass-create preliminary cost estimates, fill in the selection fields as required, and click the execute icon to run the transaction. The resulting screen displays a list of messages that should be analyzed. Errors should be resolved where necessary.

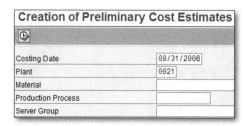

Figure 11.8 Preliminary Costing for Product Cost Collectors

11.5 Summary

In this chapter we examined the purpose of preliminary cost estimates and how they are created. We also discussed production processes and transfer control for product cost collectors. In Chapter 12 we'll look at unit cost estimates.

A unit cost estimate calculates the planned costs for materials without a bill of material or routing.

12 Unit Cost Estimate

When you first develop a new product or modify an existing product, there are several potential stages:

1. If you haven't yet developed any master data in the system, you can carry out initial cost planning by creating a base planning object, which we'll discuss in detail in Section 12.1.

2. When you've created the first material master, you can create a material cost estimate without quantity structure to manually plan costs for the new material. You can use the base planning cost estimate developed in step 1 above as a reference as required.

3. After you've created the necessary bills of materials (BOMs) and routings, you can create a material cost estimate with quantity structure.

We'll examine each of these product development stages starting with the base planning object.

12.1 Base Planning Object

You maintain a base planning object for a new product with Transaction KKE2 or by following the menu path ACCOUNTING • CONTROLLING • PRODUCT COST CONTROLLING • PRODUCT COST PLANNING • REFERENCE AND SIMULATION COSTING • CHANGE BASE PLANNING OBJECT. Enter a base planning object to maintain and press Enter to display the screen shown in Figure 12.1.

This screen displays preliminary master data information for the base planning object. We've examined in detail many of the fields in this screen in the previous two chapters on standard and preliminary cost estimates. After you've entered this basic information, you can create a basic structure and valuation in the Cost estimate section by clicking the calculator and pencil icon in Figure 12.1 to display the screen shown in Figure 12.2.

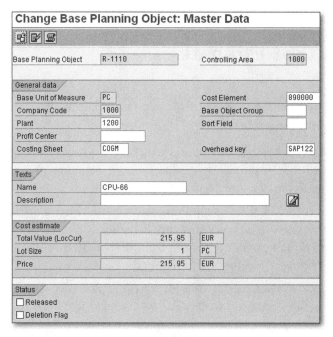

Figure 12.1 Change Base Planning Object

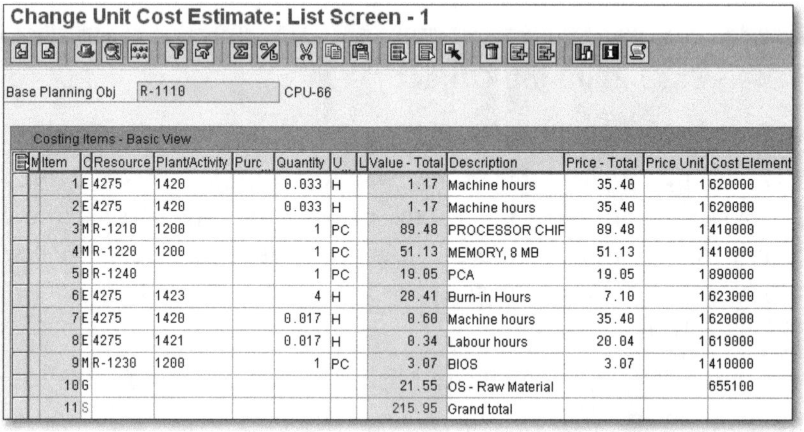

M	Item	C	Resource	Plant/Activity	Purc	Quantity	U	L	Value - Total	Description	Price - Total	Price Unit	Cost Element
	1	E	4275	1420		0.033	H		1.17	Machine hours	35.40	1	620000
	2	E	4275	1420		0.033	H		1.17	Machine hours	35.40	1	620000
	3	M	R-1210	1200		1	PC		89.48	PROCESSOR CHIF	89.48	1	410000
	4	M	R-1220	1200		1	PC		51.13	MEMORY, 8 MB	51.13	1	410000
	5	B	R-1240			1	PC		19.05	PCA	19.05	1	890000
	6	E	4275	1423		4	H		28.41	Burn-in Hours	7.10	1	623000
	7	E	4275	1420		0.017	H		0.60	Machine hours	35.40	1	620000
	8	E	4275	1421		0.017	H		0.34	Labour hours	20.04	1	619000
	9	M	R-1230	1200		1	PC		3.07	BIOS	3.07	1	410000
	10	G							21.55	OS - Raw Material			655100
	11	S							215.95	Grand total			

Figure 12.2 Unit Cost Estimate for Base Planning Object

This screen is in a spreadsheet format, and it's easy to make modifications and analyze the resulting changes in total value. Let's examine the relevant columns.

12.1.1 Item

You can modify existing items or add new items by clicking the green plus sign icon. You can easily explore the functionality of the other icons in this screen by clicking them.

12.1.2 Category

Right-click the C (item category) field and click Possible Entries to display the options shown in Figure 12.3.

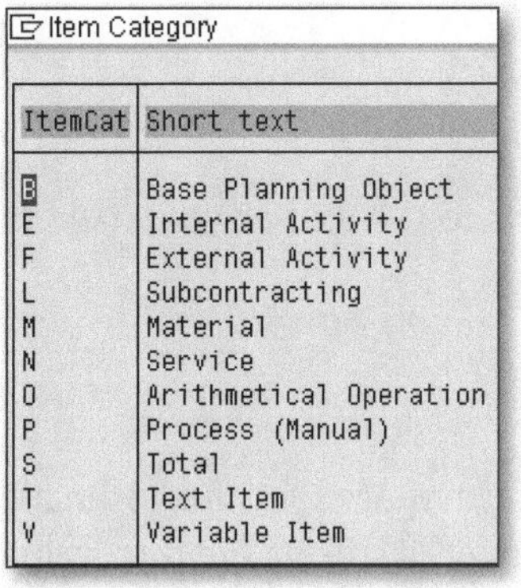

ItemCat	Short text
B	Base Planning Object
E	Internal Activity
F	External Activity
L	Subcontracting
M	Material
N	Service
O	Arithmetical Operation
P	Process (Manual)
S	Total
T	Text Item
V	Variable Item

Figure 12.3 Item Category Possible Entries

The item category you enter in this field influences the entries you can make in the following fields for each item. Let's look at some example item categories to see how they work:

▶ **B (base planning object)**
If you select this category, you must enter a previously created base planning object in the Resource column.

▶ **M (material)**
This category requires you to enter an existing material in the Resource column.

- ▶ **S (total)**

  For this category you leave the Resource column entry blank and instead enter a formula to, for example, total the value of previous items.

- ▶ **V (variable)**

  Use this category if you want to enter an item without any restriction, for example, to add some more value as a contingency.

12.1.3 Resource

The resource you enter in this field corresponds to the item category entered in the Category column. For example, if you enter item category M, you will be restricted to entering an existing material in the corresponding field in the Resource column. Some item categories such as V do not require an entry in the Resource column.

12.1.4 Plant/Activity

An entry you make in this field corresponds to the entries you made in the Item Category and Resource columns.

12.1.5 Quantity

This entry refers to the quantity of resources required for this estimate. You can easily change quantities and see how this affects the total value of the base planning object.

12.1.6 Value – Total

The total value for each item is calculated by multiplying the quantity by the entry in the Price – Total column. You should be aware of the value in the Price Unit column when considering base planning object prices. Divide the Price – Total entry by the Price Unit entry to calculate the unit cost. You increase the price unit to increase the accuracy of the price.

12.1.7 Cost Element

The cost element identifies the type of cost in cost reports. You can see standard base planning object detailed reports by following the menu path ACCOUNTING • CONTROLLING • PRODUCT COST CONTROLLING • PRODUCT COST PLANNING • INFORMATION SYSTEM • DETAILED REPORTS • FOR BASE PLANNING OBJECT.

Now that we've examined base planning objects, let's look at the next product development phase.

12.2 Material Cost Estimate Without Quantity Structure

After you've carried out initial research on the cost of items in new products with base planning objects, you may decide to create a material master to continue the development process. You may also take an existing material, copy the existing quantity structure, and manually make adjustments to carry out cost analysis.

You create a material cost estimate without quantity structure for a new or modified product with Transaction KKPAN or by following the menu path ACCOUNTING • CONTROLLING • PRODUCT COST CONTROLLING • PRODUCT COST PLANNING • MATERIAL COSTING • COST ESTIMATE WITHOUT QUANTITY STRUCTURE • CREATE. Enter a material and press Enter to display the screen shown in Figure 12.4.

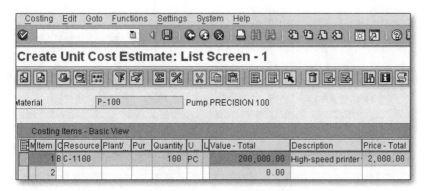

Figure 12.4 Create Cost Estimate Without Quantity Structure

This screen is similar to the unit cost estimate screen shown in Figure 12.2. Let's follow an example of how to copy existing structures and master data into a unit cost estimate. A base planning object R-1000 with a quantity of 100 has been entered and Item 1 selected. Now select FUNCTIONS • EXPLODE BASE PLANNING OBJECT... from the menu bar to display the dialogue box shown in Figure 12.5.

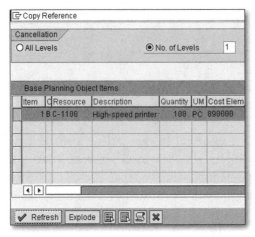

Figure 12.5 Copy Base Planning Object with Reference

In this example we'll explode the existing base planning object by selecting No. of Levels and entering 1, and then selecting the base planning object item and clicking the Explode button. The screen in Figure 12.6 is displayed.

Create Unit Cost Estimate: List Screen - 1

| Material | P-100 | | | Pump PRECISION 100 | | | | | |

Costing Items - Basic View

M	Item	C	Resource	Plant/	Pur.	Quantity	U.	L	Value - Total	Description	Price - Total
	1	M	C-1100	3200		100	PC		160,000.00	High Speed Printer	1,600.00
	2	M	R-1220	3200		100	PC		10,000.00	MEMORY, 8 MB	100.00
	3	E	4275	1421		50	H		5,000.00	Labor Hours	100.00
	4	V				100.000			2,000.00	External quality check	20.00

Figure 12.6 Base Planning Object Copied to Unit Cost Estimate

You can copy existing quantity structures, or modify, add, or delete existing individual items to a unit cost estimate.

> **Note**
>
> You can use drag-and-drop functionality when developing a base planning object and unit cost estimate with Transaction CKUC or by following the menu path ACCOUNTING • CONTROLLING • PRODUCT COST CONTROLLING • PRODUCT COST PLANNING • REFERENCE AND SIMULATION COSTING • CKUC – EDIT BASE PLANNING OBJECT – MULTILEVEL.

When you've developed a unit cost estimate and are ready to progress to the production phase, you can develop BOMs and routings and create cost estimates with quantity structure and standard cost estimates, as discussed in Chapter 10.

12.3   Summary

In this chapter we discussed basic aspects of the product development process including base planning objects, unit cost estimates, and cost estimates without quantity structure.

Additional advanced functionality for developing new and modifying existing products is available in the Product Cost Planning section of the standard menu path. The topics covered in this chapter provide a useful introduction to the basic functionality, which will assist in determining how the advanced functionality works.

PART III
Cost Object Controlling

Cost Object Controlling is the third part we examine in this book on the subject of Product Cost Controlling.

First, we looked at Integrated Planning, which gathers initial planning information from other components such as Sales and Operations Planning, Long-Term Planning, and Material Requirements Planning. This planning information is typically generated from projected sales plans over the next one to three years or longer. This forecast sales information provides a basis for planning future overall purchasing and production requirements.

Second, we looked at Product Cost Planning, which involves creating the master data and configuration required to plan the cost of manufacturing products. This combined with the Integrated Planning data allows companies to project the total costs of manufacturing into future periods and years. It also allows both internal and external manufacturing capacity to be analyzed and assist with planning future capital expenditure requirements.

Third, in this part we look at collecting and analyzing plan and actual costs on individual cost objects such as manufacturing orders and product cost collectors with the following three items:

▶ In preliminary costing we determine plan costs for each cost object.

▶ In simultaneous costing we collect actual purchasing and manufacturing costs for each cost object.

▶ In period-end processing we calculate overhead and work in process, and analyze the cause of variances between planned and actual costs.

There are many different possible manufacturing environments such as Product Cost by Period, Order, Sales Order, Engineer to Order, and

Intangible Goods and Services. In this part we'll focus on the most common environments of Product Cost by Period and Order. Using the principles and techniques of these common environments can help you determine how processes in the other more specialized environments work.

Preliminary costing refers to the process of assigning planned costs, both debits and credits, to cost objects such as manufacturing orders.

13 Preliminary Costing

In previous chapters we:

▶ Carried out initial planning with integrated planning options available

▶ Set up Controlling, material, and logistics master data

▶ Configured costing sheets, cost components, and costing variants

▶ Created standard cost estimates to plan the cost of manufacture of products

In this chapter we'll explore the first step in Cost Object Controlling, which involves preliminary costing for manufacturing orders.

Preliminary costing allows us to determine the planned costs of a product cost collector or manufacturing order. We discussed preliminary costing and cost estimates for product cost collectors in detail in Chapter 11.

To recap, in preliminary costing, the bill of material (BOM) components and routing activities are valuated using the valuation variant specified in the costing variant. The costing variant is determined by the order type, which is a required field when creating an order. The system calculates overhead expenses using the costing sheet if specified in the valuation variant.

Order type

In Chapter 11 we discussed how to display, change, or create a preliminary cost estimate for a product cost collector with Transaction KKF6N. Let's now look at how to access a preliminary cost estimate for a production order. First, we'll select a production order from a list and then display the preliminary costs.

13.1 Production Order Control

You can display a list of production orders with Transaction COOIS or by following the menu path LOGISTICS • PRODUCTION • SHOP FLOOR CONTROL • INFORMATION SYSTEM • ORDER INFORMATION SYSTEM. The screen shown in Figure 13.1 is displayed.

> **Note**
>
> You can display a list of process orders with Transaction COOISPI or by following the menu path LOGISTICS • PRODUCTION – PROCESS • PROCESS ORDER • REPORTING • ORDER INFORMATION SYSTEM • PROCESS ORDER INFORMATION SYSTEM.

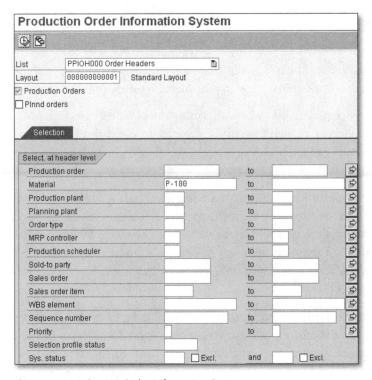

Figure 13.1 Production Order Information System

Many selection fields are available to display a list of production orders. Let's follow an example by entering "P-100" in the Material field and clicking the execute icon. The screen in Figure 13.2 is displayed.

Order Info System - Order Headers

Order	Material	Icon	Order Type	MRP ctrl	ProdSched.	Plant	Target qty	Unit	Bsc start	Basic fin. date
60003325	P-100		PP01	101	101	1000	10	PC	07/29/2008	08/06/2008
60003326			PP01	001		3000	10	PC	08/01/2008	08/11/2008
60003345			PP01	001			10	PC	08/04/2008	08/12/2008
60003346			PP01	001			10	PC		08/12/2008

Figure 13.2 Production Order List

This is a list of production orders created for material P-100. Select the first line, click the pencil icon to change the production order, and select the Control data tab to show the screen displayed in Figure 13.3.

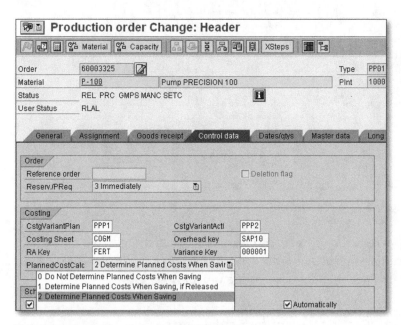

Figure 13.3 Production Order Control Data Tab

This screen displays production order fields relevant to costing of the order. Let's discuss the fields in the Costing section of the production order Control data tab.

13.1.1 Costing Variant for Planned Costs

Refer to Chapters 8 and 9 for more information on costing variants

The CstgVariantPlan (costing variant plan) field specifies which costing variant is used to determine production order plan costs. The order type determines the default costing variant, which in turn determines the valuation variant. You can maintain the default values for order types with Transaction OKZ3 or by following the IMG menu path CONTROLLING • PRODUCT COST CONTROLLING • COST OBJECT CONTROLLING • PRODUCT COST BY ORDER • MANUFACTURING ORDERS • DEFINE COST-ACCOUNTING-RELEVANT DEFAULT VALUES FOR ORDER TYPES AND PLANTS. Double-click a plant and order type combination to display the screen shown in Figure 13.4.

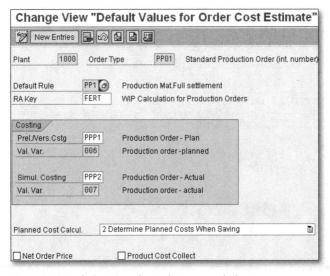

Figure 13.4 Default Values for Order Type and Plant

This screen allows you to display and maintain default values for a combination of plant and order type. In this example the default value for the production order plan costing variant is PPP1.

13.1.2 Costing Variant for Actual Costs

The CstgVariantActl (costing variant actual) field in Figure 13.3 specifies which costing variant is used to determine production order actual costs. The order type determines the default costing variant, which in turn determines the valuation variant as shown in Figure 13.4.

13.1.3 Costing Sheet

A costing sheet determines the allocation of overhead costs from cost centers to manufacturing orders. The costing sheet in Figure 13.3 defaults from the valuation variant, which in turn is determined by the costing variant. You can store the costing variant as a default value per order type and plant as shown in Figure 13.4.

Refer to Chapter 6 for more information on costing sheets

13.1.4 Overhead Key

An overhead key allows you to assign specific overhead rates to individual orders or groups of orders. This functionality gives you flexibility in assigning overhead rates to orders. However, more overhead keys may mean greater time required for frequent calculation and maintenance of overhead rates. Refer to Chapter 6 for more information on overhead key maintenance.

13.1.5 Results Analysis Key

The results analysis key (RA Key field) is used to determine period-end work in process (WIP) calculation. WIP is only calculated on orders with an entry in this field.

13.1.6 Variance Key

Variances are calculated at period-end on manufacturing orders or product cost collectors containing a variance key. This key is defaulted from the Costing 1 view when manufacturing orders or product cost collectors are created. The variance key also determines if the value of scrap is subtracted from actual costs before variances are determined.

13.1.7 Determine Plan Costs

This field determines when the manufacturing order plan costs are saved. Click the field to display the three possible entries as shown in Figure 13.3:

- **0: Do Not Determine Planned Costs When Saving**
  If you specify that no planned costs are calculated when saving the

manufacturing order, you can calculate planned costs at any time of the order by selecting GOTO • COSTS • ANALYSIS from the production order menu bar. You can choose this option to reduce the time required when saving many manufacturing orders.

▶ **1: Determine Planned Costs When Saving, if Released**
A manufacturing order status of Released indicates that you can post actual costs to the order. If you create manufacturing orders well in advance of releasing them, you can consider selecting this option to save time when initially saving many manufacturing orders.

▶ **2: Determine Planned Costs When Saving**
This is the most common setting. It indicates that planned costs are calculated when the manufacturing order is initially created and saved. This allows you to correct any costing errors earlier than the other two options.

The option of when to determine plan costs defaults from the order type and plant with Transaction OKZ3 as shown in Figure 13.4. With the Planned Cost Calcul. field entry, you can maintain the default value for saving manufacturing order plan costs.

Now that we've discussed how and when planned production order costs are calculated, let's look at how to display the planned costs.

13.2   Display Planned Costs

To display production order planned costs, select GOTO • COSTS • ANALYSIS from the production order menu bar. The screen shown in Figure 13.5 is displayed.

The production order planned costs are displayed in the Total plan column. Let's examine each section in the Transaction column of this report:

▶ **Goods Issues**
When the production order is created, the BOM is copied to the production order. The planned goods issues to the production order are determined from the BOM and displayed as a plant and material combination in the Origin column.

Transaction	Origin	Origin (Text)	¤ Total plan	¤ Ttl actual	¤ Variance	P/A var(%)
Goods Issues	1000/100-600	Support base	813.40	0.00	813.40-	100.00-
	1000/100-130	Hexagon head screw M10	40.00	0.00	40.00-	100.00-
	1000/100-700	Sheet metal ST37	14.53	14.55	0.02	0.14
	1000/100-400	Electronic	354.20	354.20	0.00	
	1000/100-500	Bearing case	412.80	412.80	0.00	
	1000/100-100	Casing	1,137.60	1,137.60	0.00	
	1000/100-300	Hollow shaft	2,039.30	2,039.30	0.00	
	1000/100-200	actuation	574.80	574.80	0.00	
Goods Issues			¤ 5,386.63	¤ 4,533.25	¤ 853.38-	
Confirmations	4220/1421	Pump Production / Wage H	29.16	0.00	29.16-	100.00-
	4230/1421	Pump Assembly / Wage Ho	458.40	0.00	458.40-	100.00-
	4280/1421	Quality Control / Wage Houi	24.99	0.00	24.99-	100.00-
	4220/1420	Pump Production / Machine	24.99	0.00	24.99-	100.00-
	4230/1420	Pump Assembly / Machine	83.35	0.00	83.35-	100.00-
	4220/1422	Pump Production / Setup H	2.10	0.00	2.10-	100.00-
	4230/1422	Pump Assembly / Setup Ho	18.78	0.00	18.78-	100.00-
Confirmations			¤ 641.77	¤ 0.00	¤ 641.77-	
Overhead	4130	Warehouse	86.79	0.00	86.79-	100.00-
Overhead			¤ 86.79	¤ 0.00	¤ 86.79-	
Goods Receipt	1000/P-100	Pump PRECISION 100	4,801.40-	0.00	4,801.40	100.00-
Goods Receipt			¤ 4,801.40-	¤ 0.00	¤ 4,801.40	
			¤ ¤ 1,313.79	¤ ¤ 4,533.25	¤ ¤ 3,219.46	

Figure 13.5 Production Order Planned Costs

► **Confirmations**

When the production order is created, the routing is copied to the production order. The planned activity confirmations are determined from the operations in the routing and displayed as a cost center and activity combination in the Origin column.

► **Overhead**

This is determined by the costing sheet in the production order Control tab as displayed in Figure 13.3. A costing sheet determines the allocation of overhead costs from cost centers to manufacturing orders. (You can read more about costing sheets in Chapter 6.) The cost center that receives the credit is shown in the Origin column.

► **Goods Receipt**

You are typically required to enter a material when a production order is created. The production order contains all of the information necessary to manufacture the material. When you place the manufactured material into inventory, the production order receives a credit based on the standard price of the plant and material shown in the Origin column of Figure 13.5.

> **Note**
>
> Notice that a production order preliminary cost estimate is single level, whereas a product cost collector preliminary cost as previously discussed in Chapter 11 estimate is multilevel.
>
> To see a multilevel cost estimate for the material being produced, go to the material master Costing 2 view and click the Current Cost Estimate button. The costed multilevel BOM is displayed in the costing structure section at the left of the screen.

See OSS Note 552486 for more information on preliminary costing

You can display different views of production order planned costs by selecting GOTO • COSTS • ITEMIZATION, GOTO • COSTS • COST COMP. STRUCTURE AND GOTO • COSTS • BALANCE from the production order menu bar.

13.3 Summary

In this chapter we looked at preliminary costing for manufacturing orders. We examined relevant fields in the production order Costing tab and how to display a preliminary cost estimate. In Chapter 14 we'll look at simultaneous costing, which involves actual postings that occur during a period. Then in Chapter 15 we'll examine postings and processes that occur at period-end.

NATION • ACCOUNT DETERMINATION WITHOUT WIZARD • CONFIGURE AUTOMATIC POSTINGS. The menu path is displayed in Figure 14.4.

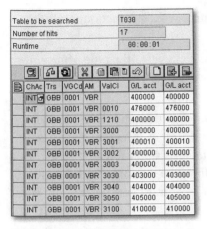

Table to be searched	T030
Number of hits	17
Runtime	00:00:01

ChAc	Trs	VGCd	AM	ValCl	G/L acct	G/L acct
INT	GBB	0001	VBR		400000	400000
INT	GBB	0001	VBR	0010	476000	476000
INT	GBB	0001	VBR	1210	400000	400000
INT	GBB	0001	VBR	3000	400000	400000
INT	GBB	0001	VBR	3001	400010	400010
INT	GBB	0001	VBR	3002	400000	400000
INT	GBB	0001	VBR	3003	400000	400000
INT	GBB	0001	VBR	3030	403000	403000
INT	GBB	0001	VBR	3040	404000	404000
INT	GBB	0001	VBR	3050	405000	405000
INT	GBB	0001	VBR	3100	410000	410000

Figure 14.3 Table T030 Entries

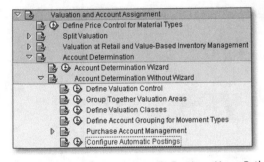

Figure 14.4 Configure Automatic Postings Menu Path

Click the paper and glasses icon to the left of Configure Automatic Postings to display excellent standard documentation on setting up automatic postings to G/L accounts. Click the execute icon to display the screen shown in Figure 14.5.

Figure 14.5 Automatic Account Assignment Initial Screen

Simultaneous costing refers to the process of assigning actual costs, both debits and credits, to cost objects such as manufacturing orders.

14 Simultaneous Costing

In Chapter 13 we discussed the calculation of planned costs during preliminary costing. In this chapter we'll discuss the process of posting actual costs to cost objects such as manufacturing orders and product cost collectors. In the following chapters we'll discuss period-end processing, which involves comparing planned and actual costs.

Actual costs debit or credit a product cost collector or manufacturing order during goods movements and activity confirmations during a period. We'll review each of these actual costs in this chapter.

14.1 Goods Movements

Goods movements to and from production orders result in debit or credit entries. Let's examine each in turn.

14.1.1 Debits

When goods are issued from inventory, a general ledger (G/L) balance sheet account is credited, and a profit and loss consumption account automatically debited. A primary cost element with the same number as the inventory consumption account ensures that a parallel posting in Controlling occurs at the same time. Because components are issued to a production order, the system automatically chooses the production order or product cost collector as the cost object. The debit value is calculated by multiplying the standard price by the component quantity issued from inventory. Figure 14.1 shows an example of account post-

> Refer to Chapter 3 for more information on cost elements

ings when components with a value of 100 are issued from inventory to a production order.

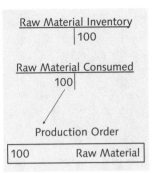

Raw Material Inventory
| 100

Raw Material Consumed
100 |

Production Order

| 100 | Raw Material |

Figure 14.1 Goods Issue Debits Production Order

You don't need to manually enter G/L accounts during goods issues to a production order because these accounts are entered in a table during initial implementation of the system. You can display the contents of this table with Transaction SE16N or by following the menu path TOOLS • ABAP WORKBENCH • OVERVIEW • DATA BROWSER. Enter the table name "T030" and press Enter to display the screen shown in Figure 14.2.

> **Note**
>
> If you use Transaction SE16 instead of SE16N, you may need to select SET-TINGS • USER PARAMETERS from the menu bar and select Field Label instead of Field name. This ensures that text instead of technical field names is displayed.

You can restrict the table entries displayed on the following results screen by making entries in the Selection Criteria section of Figure 14.2. To display accounts posted to during goods issues to production orders, make the following entries:

- **Chart of Accounts**
  There can only be one chart of accounts per controlling area. You typically restrict your selection by entering a chart of accounts.

- **Transaction**
  To display entries relevant to inventory movements, use Transaction GBB.

- **Valuation Grouping Code**
  You can assign company codes to different grouping codes if automatic account determination is to run differently for different company codes. You make this assignment with Transaction OMWD.

- **Account Modifier**
  You can make an entry in this field to indicate the type of inventory movement. VBR relates to goods issues to production orders.

- **Valuation Class**
  In the material master Costing 2 view, you assign a valuation class to each material. You normally assign different valuation classes to different material types such as raw materials and finished goods. This allows you to analyze inventory financial postings to different G/L accounts in detail. Refer to Chapter 4 for more information on valuation class.

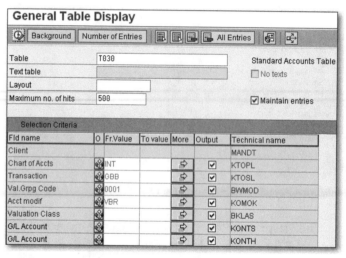

Figure 14.2 Table T030 Selection Screen

After you've made entries in the Selection Criteria field, click the execute icon to display the screen shown in Figure 14.3.

This screen displays the G/L accounts debited or credited during goods issues to production orders. You can find out more information on entries in table T030 by following the IMG menu path MATERIALS MANAGEMENT • VALUATION AND ACCOUNT ASSIGNMENT • ACCOUNT DETERMI-

The Simulation and G/L Accounts buttons allow you to analyze G/L accounts set up for automatic postings. To configure automatic postings to G/L accounts, click the Account Assignment button, double-click Transaction GBB, and enter the chart of accounts to display the screen shown in Figure 14.6.

Maintain FI Configuration: Automatic Posting

| ◀ | ▶ | ☐ | ☐ | ☐ | Posting Key | ☒ Procedures | Rules |

| Chart of Accounts | INT | Chart of accounts - international |
| Transaction | GBB | Offsetting entry for inventory posting |

Account assignment

Valuation	General m	Valuation c	Debit	Credit
0001	VBR		400000	400000
0001	VBR	0010	476000	476000
0001	VBR	1210	400000	400000
0001	VBR	3000	400000	400000
0001	VBR	3001	400010	400010
0001	VBR	3002	400000	400000
0001	VBR	3003	400000	400000
0001	VBR	3030	403000	403000
0001	VBR	3040	404000	404000
0001	VBR	3050	405000	405000
0001	VBR	3100	410000	410000

Figure 14.6 Configure Automatic Account Assignment

These configuration settings correspond to the table T030 entries shown in Figure 14.3. You can change these G/L accounts at any time, but for consistent reporting you may decide to restrict any changes to the beginning of a fiscal year, for example.

Now that we've examined debit postings during goods movements, let's look at credit postings.

14.1.2 Credits

As finished goods are delivered from a production order into inventory, an inventory balance sheet account is debited, and a profit and loss production output account is credited. Because a primary cost element corresponds to the production output account, a controlling cost object is also credited. The finished goods are delivered from a production order, so the system automatically chooses the production order or product cost collector to receive the primary credit. The credit value is calculated by multiplying the standard price by the finished goods quantity delivered to inventory. Figure 14.7 shows an example of a production order cost report with a primary credit of 250 for delivery to inventory.

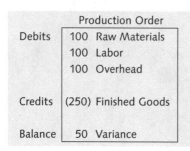

Figure 14.7 Production Order Delivery Credits

The G/L account posted to during delivery of finished goods from the production order into inventory is determined by a table T030 entry as discussed previously in Section 14.1.1.

Total variance is the production order balance, or the difference between total debits and credits. Variance calculation at period-end divides the variance into categories, based on the source of the variance. This assists in determining corrective action during variance analysis.

We'll discuss period-end variance processing further in Chapter 17

At period-end, the production order receives a secondary credit equal to the variance during settlement, resulting in a zero balance. This results in total product cost collector and manufacturing order costs posting to Financial Accounting and Profitability Analysis.

> **Note**
>
> The production order can also receive credits for other reasons such as return of components to inventory.

Refer to Chapter 3 for more information on cost elements

G/L postings to production orders due to goods movements result in postings within Controlling. This means there is always a financial G/L account corresponding to the primary cost element identifying the debits or credits to the production order. Primary cost elements ensure that there is always a parallel posting in Controlling in addition to the usual two-sided entry in Financial Accounting. This allows detailed analysis of all expenses within Controlling.

In addition to primary postings to production orders corresponding to goods movements, secondary postings occur during activity confirmations, which we'll now discuss in detail.

14.2   Confirmations

Activity confirmations normally involve secondary postings within Controlling. In the following sections we'll analyze these postings in detail, and then follow an example of posting an activity confirmation.

14.2.1   Secondary Postings

When production order activities are confirmed during a period, the production order or product cost collector is debited, and a cost center is credited. There are no corresponding postings to financial G/L expense accounts during activity confirmation. The postings are identified with secondary cost elements that exist only within Controlling.

A production cost center receives debits due to primary costs such as payroll and electricity during a period. Many products can be manufactured at a work center, with labor and facilities paid for by the cost center. Confirmation of labor and overhead activities allocates these primary costs across many products. Figure 14.8 shows an overview of labor allocation postings from a cost center to a production order.

A labor value of 100 is allocated from a production cost center to a production order in step 3 in Figure 14.8. This occurs during activity confirmation within a period.

> **Note**
>
> At least three methods are available to allocate overhead from cost centers to production orders or product cost collectors:
>
> ▶ You can increase the labor activity rate to include overhead.
> ▶ You can create a separate overhead activity type and allocate overhead in addition to labor during activity confirmation. An advantage of this method is that you can separately identify labor and overhead postings.

▶ You can distribute overhead costs at period-end during overhead calculation using costing sheets. (Refer to Chapter 6 for more information on costing sheets.)

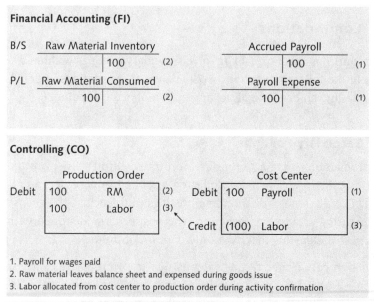

1. Payroll for wages paid
2. Raw material leaves balance sheet and expensed during goods issue
3. Labor allocated from cost center to production order during activity confirmation

Figure 14.8 Secondary Cost Allocation During Activity Confirmation

Now that we've discussed how secondary postings occur during activity confirmations, let's follow an example of these postings by first creating a production order and then carrying out an activity confirmation.

14.2.2 Create Production Order

You create a production order with Transaction CO01 or by following the menu path LOGISTICS • PRODUCTION • PRODUCTION CONTROL • ORDER • CREATE • WITH MATERIAL. A selection screen is displayed, as shown in Figure 14.9.

Note

You can also create production orders without reference to a material with Transaction CO07. This allows you to create, for example, repair or rework orders.

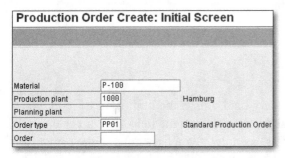

Figure 14.9 Create Production Order

Production orders are usually created based on a material. All relevant master data such as BOMs and routings are copied to the production order as you create it. Fill in the relevant fields in Figure 14.9 and press Enter to display the screen shown in Figure 14.10.

Figure 14.10 Create Production Order Header Screen

We'll now discuss each of the relevant fields you enter in this screen.

Total Quantity

This is the total quantity including scrap to be produced by this order.

Base Unit of Measure

To the right of the Total Qty field, this is the unit of measure in which inventory is managed, and it defaults into the field. You can change this unit of measure (PC in this example) if you have entered the conversion factor in the Additional data section of the material master.

Scrap Portion

This is the plan assembly scrap that defaults from the material master MRP 1 view. The system increases the order quantity by the assembly scrap percentage. This field is not mandatory.

Basic Finish and Start Dates

The dates you enter in these fields are dependent on the entry you make in the following Type field in the Scheduling section. Here are two examples:

▸ If you enter 2 Backwards, you must enter the finish date, and the system will automatically calculate the start date.

▸ If you enter 1 Forwards, you must enter the start date, and the system will automatically calculate the finish date.

You can manually change the basic dates the system automatically calculates.

Scheduling Type

This field specifies the scheduling type for detailed scheduling, for example forward or backward. Click the Type field to display the possible entries as shown in Figure 14.10. With production-rate and rough-cut scheduling, backward scheduling is always used.

Release

Once you've completed the previous fields you'll need to carry out the release step before you can collect any costs on the production order. You release the production order by clicking the green flag icon at the top of the screen.

Operation Overview

To review the operations copied from the routing to the production order, click the three vertical squares icon shown in Figure 14.10 to display the screen shown in Figure 14.11.

Production Order Create: Operation Overview

Order	%00000000001						Type	PP01
Material	P-100	Pump PRECISION 100					Plant	1000
Sequence	0	0 Standar☑ Pumpe (Stammfolge)						

OperationOverview

Op.	SOp	Start	Start	Work Ce	Plant	Co	StdText	Operation short text	T	SysSta
0010		08/27/2008	09:50:07	1310	1000	PP01	P000001	Bereitstellung gemäß Kor	☐	REL
0020		08/27/2008	11:44:24	1320	1000	PP01	P000002	Einpressen Laufrad in Ge	☐	REL
0030		08/28/2008	08:41:33	1906	1000	PP01	P000004	Painting	☐	REL
0040		08/28/2008	10:57:59	1904	1000	PP01	P000002	Einbau Welle in Gehäuse	☐	REL
0050		08/28/2008	12:03:34	1905	1000	PP01	P000002	Endmontage Pumpe	☐	REL
0060		08/28/2008	14:02:51	1721	1000	PP99	P000003	Abliefern an Lager	☐	REL

Figure 14.11 Production Order Operation Overview

You can review and change the operations as necessary. Any changes you make may result in a variance during period-end processing because the standard price is based on the operations copied from the routing.

Components Overview

To review the components copied from the BOM to the production order, click on the hierarchy icon shown in Figure 14.11. The screen shown in Figure 14.12 is displayed.

You can review and change the components as necessary. Any changes you make may result in a variance during period-end processing because the standard price is based on the components copied from the BOM.

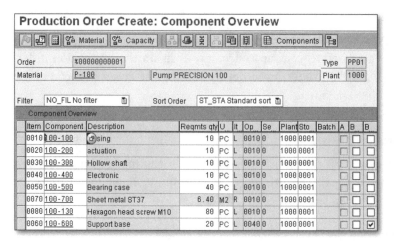

Figure 14.12 Production Order Component Overview

Now that we've discussed how to create and release a production order, let's look at how to post costs.

14.2.3 Confirm Activities

During activity confirmation, the activity quantity performed is entered in the system. The actual activity quantity is multiplied by the planned activity price to calculate the activity value. The production order is debited, and the production cost center is credited with the calculated value.

It is common practice to generate goods issues automatically during activity confirmation. This is known as backflushing. You can also make logistics settings to generate automatic goods receipts during activity confirmation. Backflushing and automatic goods receipts are routinely used because less manual entry of inventory transactions is required. Because all components required to make the assembly are listed in the BOM, it's relatively simple to transfer this information to the production order and issue the components automatically from inventory during activity confirmation. You can also carry out automatic goods receipt during final confirmation because the system already has all of the information required.

You confirm activities per operation with Transaction CO11N (time ticket) or CO19 (time event) or by following the menu path LOGISTICS •

PRODUCTION • SHOP FLOOR CONTROL • CONFIRMATION • ENTER • FOR OPER-
ATION. A selection screen is displayed, for a time ticket confirmation in
this example, as shown in Figure 14.13.

Enter time ticket for production order			
Goods movements	Actual Data		
Confirmation	98898		
Order	60003325	Material	P-100	Pump PRECISION 100
Oper./activity	0010	Sequence	0	Bereitstellung gemäß Kommissionierliste
Sub-operation			
Capacity cat.		Split	
Work center	1310	Plant	1000	Pre-Assembly I

Confirm.type	Partial confirmation	☐ Clear open reservations
Quantities		
	To confirm	Unit
Yield	0	PC
Scrap		
Rework		
Reason for Var.		
Activities		
	To confirm	Unit N
Setup		H ☐
Machine		H ☐
Labor	1.667	H ☐

Figure 14.13 Enter Time Ticket Activity Confirmation

You carry out a time ticket confirmation per operation, so you need to
enter the production order and operation number. After you enter this
data, press Enter to default expected activity and component quantities
into the relevant fields. If you manually change the default quantities,
you will introduce a variance during period-end processing, because the
default quantities were used to calculate the standard price of the assembly.

If this is the final operation and automatic goods receipt is activated, a
goods receipt will occur while saving the confirmation, based on the
yield quantity. Activity quantities are entered in the relevant activity
field at the bottom of the screen.

In the screen shown in Figure 14.13, click the Goods movements button
before saving the confirmation to display plan component goods issues
quantities. The components and quantities are automatically copied to
the confirmation from the production order.

Now that we've examined how simultaneous costs are posted, let's look at how to report on actual costs during a period. During variance analysis, you may need to analyze actual costs posted to a production order or product cost collector because actual costs are greater than expected.

14.3   Report Costs

You can report on actual costs posted during a period by displaying a detailed analysis of a product cost collector with Transaction KKBC_PKO or by following the menu path ACCOUNTING • CONTROLLING • PRODUCT COST CONTROLLING • COST OBJECT CONTROLLING • PRODUCT COST BY PERIOD • INFORMATION SYSTEM • REPORTS FOR PRODUCT COST BY PERIOD • DETAILED REPORTS • FOR PRODUCT COST COLLECTORS. A selection screen is displayed, as shown in Figure 14.14. Use Transaction KKBC_ORD for production and process orders.

Figure 14.14 Analyze Product Cost Collector Screen

Enter the relevant material, plant, and production process. You can display the information for all periods by selecting Cumulated, or restrict by period by selecting Limited. Click the execute icon to display the screen shown in Figure 14.15.

You can double-click any line to display actual posting line item details. Double-clicking actual Goods Issues and Goods Receipts displays material documents generated during the goods movements. Double-clicking actual activity Confirmations displays a list of confirmations. You can continue drilling down (double-clicking) on any line in the screen shown in Figure 14.15 to the original source document generated during the original transaction.

BusTran.	Origin	≈	Total tgt	≈	Ttl actual	≈	Variance	Crcy
Goods Issues	0021/MB...		12,057.49		11,940.48		117.01-	USD
	0021/MB...		12,022.64		11,904.04		118.60-	USD
Confirmations	1400/RUN		2.36		180.00		177.64	USD
	1610/RUN		745.48		1,243.79		498.31	USD
	1660/RUN		0.00		131.33		131.33	USD
	1680/RUN		286.03		134.58		151.45-	USD
	1700/RUN		0.00		0.00		0.00	USD
	1610/SET		0.00		23.85		23.85	USD
Debit		▪	**25,114.00**	▪	**25,558.07**	▪	**444.07**	**USD**
Goods Receipt	0021/MB...		25,114.01-		25,114.18-		0.17-	USD
Delivery		▪	**25,114.01-**	▪	**25,114.18-**	▪	**0.17-**	**USD**
Settlement			0.00		443.89-		443.89-	USD
Settlement		▪	**0.00**	▪	**443.89-**	▪	**443.89-**	**USD**
		▪ ▪	0.01-	▪ ▪	0.00	▪ ▪	0.01	USD

Figure 14.15 Analyze Product Cost Collector Results Screen

14.4 Summary

In this chapter we looked at simultaneous costing involving goods movements and confirmations that generate postings during a period. We discussed how goods movements generate primary postings and how activity confirmations generate secondary postings in Controlling. In Chapter 15 we'll look at period-end postings, beginning with overhead calculation.

Overhead calculation refers to the allocation of overhead from cost centers to manufacturing orders or product cost collectors.

15 Overhead

In previous chapters we created master data, configuration, and standard cost estimates, and carried out preliminary and simultaneous costing. We're now ready to carry out period-end processing, which includes the following processing steps:

- Overhead
- Work in process
- Variance calculation
- Settlement

Although other more advanced and specialized transactions are possible during period-end processing, the four explained in this and the following chapters are the most common. If you use other period-end processes, you can apply the principles you learn in this section to those processes. We'll look first at overhead configuration and then at the period-end process.

15.1 Configuration

During a fiscal period, primary (external) costs, such as payroll and electricity are debited to cost centers. Some of these costs may be included as part of the planned activity rate and allocated to products from production cost centers during activity confirmations, as discussed in Chapter 14.

Refer to Chapter 6 for more information on costing sheets Another method to allocate overhead costs to products is period-end overhead calculation. Overhead calculation offers flexible allocation across products through costing sheet configuration, as discussed in Chapter 6. Allocating overhead with costing sheets requires an additional period-end activity, although this is a straightforward procedure.

15.2 Overhead Period-End Processing

You run period-end overhead calculation with Transactions CO42 (individual) and CO43 (collective) or by following the menu path ACCOUNTING • CONTROLLING • PRODUCT COST CONTROLLING • COST OBJECT CONTROLLING • PRODUCT COST BY PERIOD • PERIOD-END CLOSING • SINGLE FUNCTIONS: PRODUCT COST COLLECTOR • OVERHEAD. A selection screen is displayed, as shown in Figure 15.1.

> **Note**
>
> You can carry out overhead calculation for production and process orders with Transactions KGI2 (individual) and CO43 (collective).

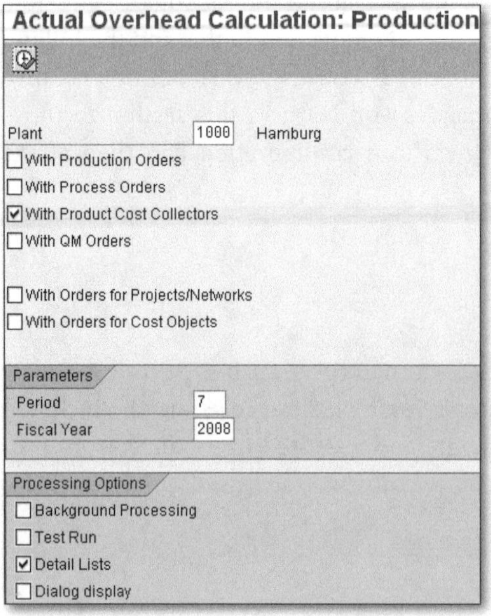

Figure 15.1 Actual Overhead Calculation Selection Screen

In this example we'll calculate overhead only for product cost collectors by selecting the With Product Cost Collectors checkbox. You can also select other objects depending on period-end processing time and the number of messages that require analysis following overhead calculation.

Select the Dialog display checkbox if you require more detailed information when analyzing the overhead calculation and messages. You normally only need this level of detail when initially calculating overhead following system implementation. It is most useful when analyzing overhead calculation for a single production order or product cost collector.

Complete the selection screen and click the execute icon to display the screen shown in Figure 15.2.

Actual Overhead Calculation: Production/Process		

Selection		
Selection Parameters	Value	Name
Plant	1000	Hamburg
With Product Cost Collectors	X	
Period	007	
Fiscal Year	2008	
Controlling Area	2000	CO N. America
Currency	USD	American Dollar
Exchange Rate Type	M	Standard translation at average rate

Figure 15.2 Actual Overhead Calculation Basic List

This screen provides basic information on the parameters entered in the previous selection screen such as period and fiscal year. Click the right-pointing arrow icon to proceed to a detailed overhead list (if you selected the Detail Lists checkbox in Figure 15.1) as shown in Figure 15.3.

Let's review each column:

► The Senders column shows the cost center credited.

► The Receivers column shows the product cost collector or manufacturing order debited.

▶ The Debit cost column shows the secondary cost element identifying the type of overhead cost. These cost elements appear on cost center and product cost collector reports.

▶ The ValueCOCur column shows the overhead value allocated in controlling area currency. By selecting SETTINGS • LAYOUT • CURRENT form the menu bar you can display additional columns, such as overhead value in object (company code) currency.

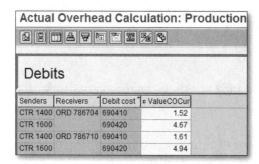

Figure 15.3 Actual Overhead Calculation Details

This concludes the overhead chapter, so let's review what we've covered.

15.3 Summary

In this chapter we calculated and allocated actual overhead. The next period-end processing step we'll examine, in Chapter 16, is to calculate work in process.

Work in process represents production costs of incomplete assemblies moved temporarily to work in process general ledger accounts at period-end.

16   Work in Process

In Chapter 15 we looked at the configuration and period-end processing of overhead calculation. In this chapter we'll analyze configuration settings and period-end processing of work in process (WIP) costs.

Production costs associated with manufacturing orders are temporarily tracked on the profit and loss financial statement. Components removed from inventory to a manufacturing order are expensed and removed from the financial balance sheet. Production costs are returned to the balance sheet when assemblies and finished goods are delivered to inventory from the manufacturing order.

WIP represents production costs of incomplete assemblies at period-end. In order for balance sheet accounts to accurately reflect company assets at period-end, WIP costs are moved temporarily to WIP balance sheet and profit and loss accounts. WIP postings are canceled during period-end processing following delivery of associated assemblies or finished products to inventory.

The two types of WIP valuations are:

▶ **Target**
WIP at target is valuated based on a cost estimate.

▶ **Actual**
WIP at actual is valuated based on actual debits and credits to a manufacturing order or product cost collector.

We'll now discuss WIP configuration and then WIP period-end processing.

16.1 WIP Configuration

WIP configuration for Product Cost by Period and Product Cost by Order are similar. Let's look at configuration for Product Cost by Period and highlight the differences along the way.

WIP configuration for reporting and posting is basically a mapping exercise as follows:

▶ Create results analysis keys and versions.

▶ Create line IDs and map to source cost elements.

▶ Map line IDs to WIP or Results Analysis cost elements (type 31) for reporting.

▶ Create posting rules for settling WIP to financial accounting.

Let's analyze each configuration step in the following sections.

16.1.1 Define Results Analysis Keys

You define results analysis keys with Transaction OKG1 or by following the IMG menu path CONTROLLING • PRODUCT COST CONTROLLING • COST OBJECT CONTROLLING • PRODUCT COST BY PERIOD • PERIOD-END CLOSING • WORK IN PROCESS • DEFINE RESULTS ANALYSIS KEYS. The screen shown in Figure 16.1 is displayed.

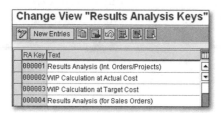

Figure 16.1 Define Results Analysis Keys

This overview screen displays a list of available results analysis keys. You can use an existing key or copy one and create your own. Each manufacturing order to be included in WIP period-end processing must contain a results analysis key in the Control tab. Product cost collectors must contain the results analysis key in the Data tab to be considered during WIP processing.

Refer to Chapter 14 for more information on the manufacturing order Control tab

The results analysis key can be specified as a default value for each order type and plant combination with Transaction OKZ3. It is then added by default when an order is created.

16.1.2 Define Results Analysis Versions

You define results analysis versions with Transaction OKG9 or by following the menu path Controlling • Product Cost Controlling • Cost Object Controlling • Product Cost by Period • Period-End Closing • Work in Process • Define Results Analysis Versions. The screen shown in Figure 16.2 is displayed.

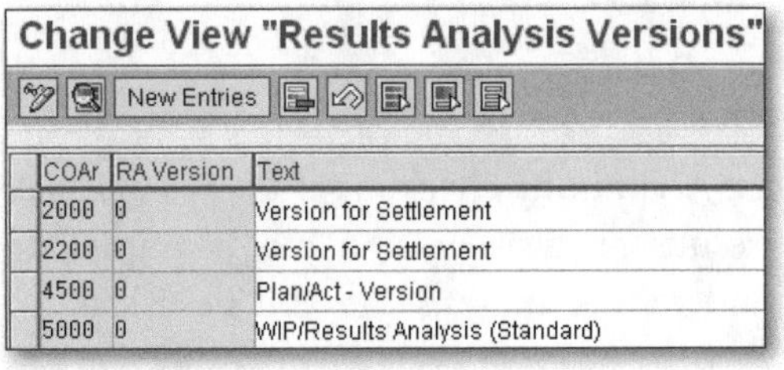

Change View "Results Analysis Versions"

New Entries

COAr	RA Version	Text
2000	0	Version for Settlement
2200	0	Version for Settlement
4500	0	Plan/Act - Version
5000	0	WIP/Results Analysis (Standard)

Figure 16.2 Define Results Analysis Versions

Results analysis versions allow you to define different methods of WIP calculation. For a simple WIP calculation you generally capitalize all WIP costs. In advanced results analysis functionality, you can define different amounts of WIP capitalization. Double-click a results analysis version in the RA Version column to display the details screen shown in Figure 16.3.

This screen allows you to define both simplified and expert settings for an RA version. Let's analyze each of the checkboxes in this screen.

Version Relevant to Settlement

The Version Relevant to Settlement checkbox is selected by default for results analysis version 0. A results analysis version is considered to be relevant to settlement if the results analysis data of that results analysis version is to be settled according to the settlement rule specified in the object to be settled.

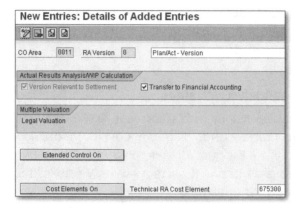

Figure 16.3 Results Analysis Version Details Screen

Transfer to Financial Accounting

Select the Transfer to Financial Accounting checkbox if the results analysis data saved under this results analysis version can be settled to Financial Accounting. WIP and results analysis can still be calculated without this selected.

Technical RA Cost Element

The Technical RA Cost Element for results analysis data is only for internal purposes, so you don't need to create a separate cost element for each section of advanced results analysis data. You only need one technical results analysis cost element. Enter a technical results analysis cost element of cost element category 31 (order/project results analysis).

Extended Control On and Cost Elements On

For more advanced results analysis and WIP calculations, click the Extended Control On and Cost Elements On buttons. More fields are revealed as displayed in Figure 16.4.

You can find more information on these additional fields by following the IMG menu path CONTROLLING • PRODUCT COST CONTROLLING • COST OBJECT CONTROLLING • PRODUCT COST BY PERIOD • PERIOD-END CLOSING • WORK IN PROCESS • DEFINE RESULTS ANALYSIS VERSIONS. This menu path is displayed in Figure 16.5.

Extended Control Off	

Extended Control

- [ ] Split Creation/Usage
- [ ] Generate Line Items
- [ ] Legacy Data Transfer
- [ ] Deletion Allowed
- [ ] Assignment/RA Key
- [x] Update/RA Key
- [x] Update Plan Values

Calculate WIP or Results Analysis For

- [ ] Orders in Sales-Order-Related Production
- [ ] Orders in Engineer-to-Order Production
- [ ] Mfg Orders w/o Settlement to Material
- [ ] Internal and Service Orders w/o Revenue

Status Control `A`

Cutoff Period for Actual RA/WIP `1,2008`

- (●) Actual RA
- ( ) Actual and Plan RA
- ( ) Simulate Actual w/ Plan

Planned Results Analysis

- [ ] Version Relevant to Settlement

Plan Version

Cutoff Period for Planned RA `0`

Cost Elements Off	

Cost Elements: Results Analysis Data

Valuated Actual Costs	675300
Calculated Costs	675300

Cost Elements: Down Payment Allocation

Reduction in REB	675300
Down Payment Surplus	675300

Cost Elements: Plan Values of Valuation

Plan Costs of Valuation	675300
Plan Revenue of Valuation	675300

Figure 16.4 Advanced Results Analysis Settings

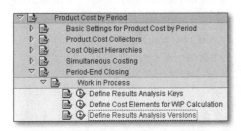

Figure 16.5 Define Results Analysis Versions Menu Path

Click the paper and glasses icon to the left of Define Results Analysis Versions to display standard documentation on setting up and leveraging this advanced results analysis functionality. We'll discuss some of these fields in more detail in following sections.

> **Note**
>
> You can find documentation on any configuration transaction using the same technique.

16.1.3 Define Valuation Method (Target Costs)

You define valuation methods with Transaction OKGD or by following the menu path CONTROLLING • PRODUCT COST CONTROLLING • COST OBJECT CONTROLLING • PRODUCT COST BY PERIOD • PERIOD-END CLOSING • WORK IN PROCESS • DEFINE VALUATION METHOD (TARGET COSTS). The screen shown in Figure 16.6 is displayed.

Change View "Valuation Method for Work in Process": Ov

New Entries

CO Area	RA Versi	RA Key	Status	Status	RA Type
0001	0	FERT	REL	1	WIP Calculation on Basis of Actual Costs
0001	0	FERT	DLV	2	Cancel Data of WIP Calculation and Results Ana
0001	0	FERT	TECO	3	Cancel Data of WIP Calculation and Results Ana
0001	0	FERT-P	REL	0	WIP Calculation on Basis of Target Costs

Figure 16.6 Valuation Method for Work in Process

The first three lines in this screen are typical for WIP based on order status for actual costs:

▶ Order status REL (released) results in WIP calculation based on actual costs at period-end.

▶ Order status DLV (delivered) or TECO (technically complete) results in cancellation of WIP and results analysis data.

This screen is relatively easy to configure. Click the New Entries button in Figure 16.6 to display the dialog box shown in Figure 16.7.

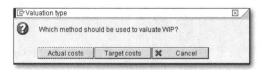

Figure 16.7 WIP Valuation Method Dialog Box

Click the relevant button to valuate WIP either at actual or target costs. The dialog box shown in Figure 16.8 is displayed.

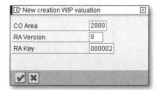

Figure 16.8 Create New WIP Valuation Entries

Fill in the fields and press Enter, and the required entries will appear automatically as shown in Figure 16.6. Now let's consider the next WIP configuration transaction.

16.1.4 Define Valuation Variant for WIP and Scrap (Target Costs)

The valuation variant allows a choice of cost estimates to valuate scrap and WIP. Prior to SAP R/3 Release 4.5 you could use only the standard cost estimate. If the structure of a routing was changed after a costing run, WIP could not be valuated, and an error message resulted. The system then posted all product cost collector costs as variances.

The error message can only be eliminated by creating and releasing another standard cost estimate. Because releasing a standard cost estimate can change inventory valuation, many companies prefer to only release standard cost estimates during main costing runs in a controlled and supervised environment. Costing runs are explained in detail in Chapter 10. WIP at target eliminates the need to create and release new standard cost estimates, because valuation is based on the preliminary cost estimate, which does not affect inventory valuation.

WIP at target allows the product cost collector preliminary cost estimate to valuate WIP, even if the routing structure is changed. If the valuation variant for scrap and WIP is not defined, scrap and WIP valuation are based on the current standard cost estimate.

Refer to Chapter 11 for more information on preliminary cost estimates

You define the valuation variant for WIP and scrap (target costs) by following the IMG menu path CONTROLLING • PRODUCT COST CONTROLLING • COST OBJECT CONTROLLING • PRODUCT COST BY PERIOD • PERIOD-END CLOSING • WORK IN PROCESS • DEFINE VALUATION VARIANT FOR WIP AND SCRAP (TARGET COSTS). The screen shown in Figure 16.9 is displayed.

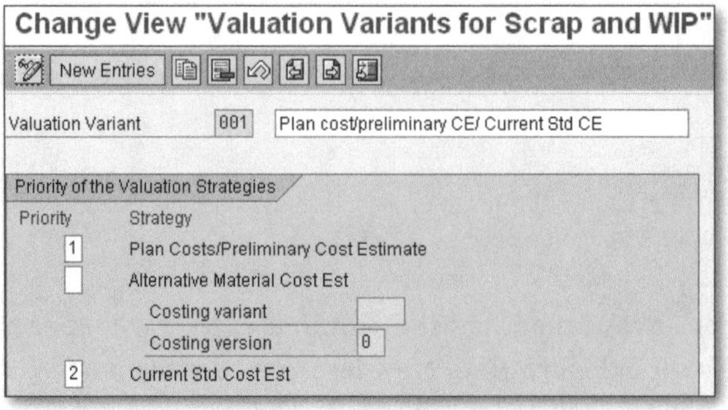

Figure 16.9 Define Valuation Variant for Scrap and WIP

The valuation strategies indicate that WIP calculation will first search for a preliminary cost estimate, and if unsuccessful, it will search for a current standard cost estimate. This strategy is useful because if for any reason a preliminary cost estimate is not created, the current standard cost estimate can still be used to valuate WIP, avoiding an error message that would otherwise be generated.

WIP at target is used by product cost collectors in repetitive manufacturing. Repetitive manufacturing eliminates the need for production or process orders in manufacturing environments with production lines and long production runs. It reduces the work involved in production control and simplifies confirmations and goods receipt postings.

Production orders can also be assigned to product cost collectors starting with SAP R/3 Release 4.5. Assignment to a product cost collector occurs automatically when a production order is created in this scenario. At period-end, target costs (planned costs adjusted for confirmed yield not yet delivered to inventory) are temporarily moved from product cost collectors to WIP financial accounts. Variance is calculated and posted at the same time.

> **Note**
>
> In Product Cost by Order, WIP and scrap are valuated at actual, so there is no need to calculate WIP and scrap. The valuation variant for WIP does not apply in this environment.

16.1.5 Assignment of Valuation Variant for WIP

You assign valuation methods by following the IMG menu path CONTROLLING • PRODUCT COST CONTROLLING • COST OBJECT CONTROLLING • PRODUCT COST BY PERIOD • PERIOD-END CLOSING • WORK IN PROCESS • ASSIGNMENT OF VALUATION VARIANT FOR WIP. The screen shown in Figure 16.10 is displayed.

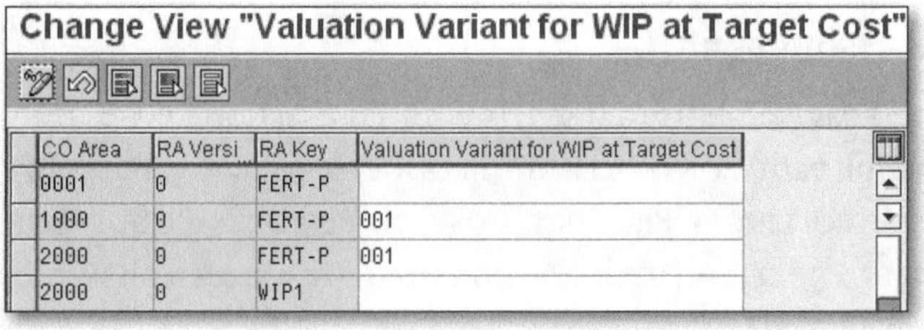

Change View "Valuation Variant for WIP at Target Cost"

CO Area	RA Versi	RA Key	Valuation Variant for WIP at Target Cost
0001	0	FERT-P	
1000	0	FERT-P	001
2000	0	FERT-P	001
2000	0	WIP1	

Figure 16.10 Assignment of Valuation Variant for WIP

In this screen you can assign a valuation variant for WIP at target cost to a combination of CO area (controlling area), RA version, and RA key. The only RA keys that are relevant here are those used to calculate WIP at target costs.

16.1.6 Define Line IDs

You create line IDs by following the IMG menu path CONTROLLING • PRODUCT COST CONTROLLING • COST OBJECT CONTROLLING • PRODUCT COST BY PERIOD • PERIOD-END CLOSING • WORK IN PROCESS • DEFINE LINE IDs. The screen shown in Figure 16.11 is displayed.

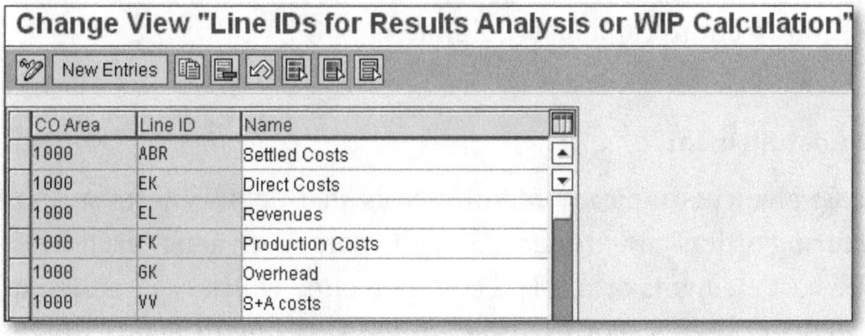

Change View "Line IDs for Results Analysis or WIP Calculation"

CO Area	Line ID	Name
1000	ABR	Settled Costs
1000	EK	Direct Costs
1000	EL	Revenues
1000	FK	Production Costs
1000	GK	Overhead
1000	VV	S+A costs

Figure 16.11 Define Line IDs for Results Analysis and WIP Calculation

Line IDs allow you to group together similar types of costs for results analysis and WIP calculation and postings. WIP calculation updates the WIP and reserves for unrealized costs on the order, grouped by line ID. To transfer the data to Financial Accounting, we'll define posting rules that associate the data with general ledger (G/L) accounts as described in Section 16.1.9.

16.1.7 Define Assignment

You assign source cost elements to line IDs with Transaction OKG5 or by following the menu path CONTROLLING • PRODUCT COST CONTROLLING • COST OBJECT CONTROLLING • PRODUCT COST BY PERIOD • PERIOD-END CLOSING • WORK IN PROCESS • DEFINE ASSIGNMENT. The screen shown in Figure 16.12 is displayed.

Change View "Assignment of Cost Elements for WIP and Results Analysis"

New Entries

CO	RA V	RA Key	Masked Cost Element	Ori	Masked Cost Center	Masked Activity	Business Proc.	C	V	Appor	Acco	Valid-Fr.	ReqToC
1000	0		00004+++++	++++			+++++++++++++	+	+	++	++	001.1993	EK
1000	0		00006+++++	++++	++++++++++	++++++	+++++++++++++	+	+	++	++	001.1993	FK
1000	0		0000655+++	++++	++++++++++	++++++	+++++++++++++	+	+	++	++	001.1993	VV
1000	0		00006551++	++++	++++++++++	++++++	+++++++++++++	+	+	++	++	001.1993	GK
1000	0		00008+++++	++++			+++++++++++++	+	+	++	++	001.1993	EK
1000	0		000080++++	++++			+++++++++++++	+	+	++	++	001.1993	EL
1000	0		000081++++	++++			+++++++++++++	+	+	++	++	001.1993	ABR
1000	0		0000895+++	++++			+++++++++++++	+	+	++	++	001.1993	ABR

Figure 16.12 Assignment of Cost Elements for WIP and Results Analysis

Completing this screen is typically an exercise of mapping source cost elements in the Masked Cost Element column to line IDs in the ReqToC... (requirement to capitalize) column.

Masked Cost Element

Source cost elements typically identify costs that debit objects such as manufacturing orders and product cost collectors. You can enter individual source cost elements or masked cost elements, which is a method of grouping cost elements. For example, in the first line in Figure 16.12, masked cost element 00004+++++ represents all cost elements that start with the numbers 00004.

Masked Cost Center

When more detail is required in Order Detail reports such as KKBC_PKO, you can also enter individual cost centers in the Masked Cost Center column. This level of detail is not normally required, but you can enter individual entries in any of the masked columns in Figure 16.12.

Requirement to Capitalize

Usually, you are required to capitalize total WIP and enter the line IDs corresponding to the cost elements in the ReqToC... (requirement to capitalize) column. In more complex projects you may not be legally allowed to capitalize certain costs, and must make entries in columns to the right in Figure 16.12 as shown in Figure 16.13.

Valid-Fr	ReqToC	OptToCap	CannotBeCap	% OptToCap	% CannotBeCap
001.1993	EK				
001.1993	FK				
001.1993	VV				
001.1993	GK				
001.1993	EK				
001.1993	EL				
001.1993	ABR				
001.1993	ABR				

Figure 16.13 Option to Capitalize WIP Columns

In more complicated cases you can place these line IDs in the OptToCap (option to capitalize) and CannotBeCap (cannot be capitalized) columns together with the relevant percentages in the last two columns in the screen in Figure 16.13.

You can update the following data with reference to a line ID:

▸ WIP

▸ Reserves for unrealized costs

▸ Reserves for cost of complaints

▸ Cost of sales

Now let's consider the next WIP configuration transaction, which involves assigning line IDs to WIP and results analysis cost elements.

16.1.8 Define Update

You assign line IDs to WIP and results analysis cost elements with Transaction OKGA or by following the IMG menu path Controlling • Product Cost Controlling • Cost Object Controlling • Product Cost by Period • Period-End Closing • Work in Process • Define Update. The screen shown in Figure 16.14 is displayed.

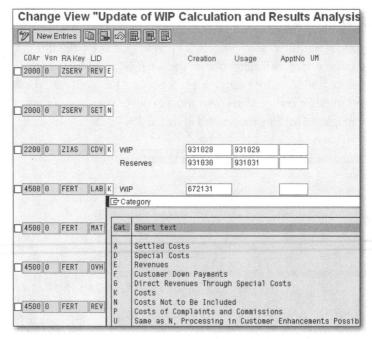

Figure 16.14 Update of WIP Calculation and Results Analysis

In this screen you map line IDs to WIP cost elements for reporting purposes.

Line ID

You assign each line ID in the LID column to a category shown in the next column. Right-click a category and select Possible Entries to display the list of categories shown in Figure 16.14. Certain categories such as E (revenues) and N (costs not to be Included) do not require assignment of WIP cost elements, and no fields are available to enter cost elements.

Creation

You enter WIP cost elements in the Creation column for categories such as K (costs).

Usage

If you selected Split Creation/Usage in the Extended Control section of the results analysis version previously shown in Figure 16.2, you must enter a usage WIP cost element (type 31) in Figure 16.14. This provides more detailed WIP reporting capability.

> **Note**
>
> You can assign WIP cost elements to cost components as described in Chapter 7, and report WIP as cost components. If you don't assign the WIP cost elements to cost components, the costs appear in a not assigned category in standard reports.

Assigning line IDs to WIP and results analysis cost elements is for reporting purposes only. The next configuration step defines which G/L accounts are posted to during settlement.

16.1.9   Define Posting Rules for Settling Work in Process

You define posting rules for settling WIP to financial accounts with Transaction OKG8 or by following the IMG menu path Controlling • Product Cost Controlling • Cost Object Controlling • Product Cost by Period • Period-End Closing • Work in Process • Define Posting Rules for Settling Work in Process. The screen shown in Figure 16.15 is displayed.

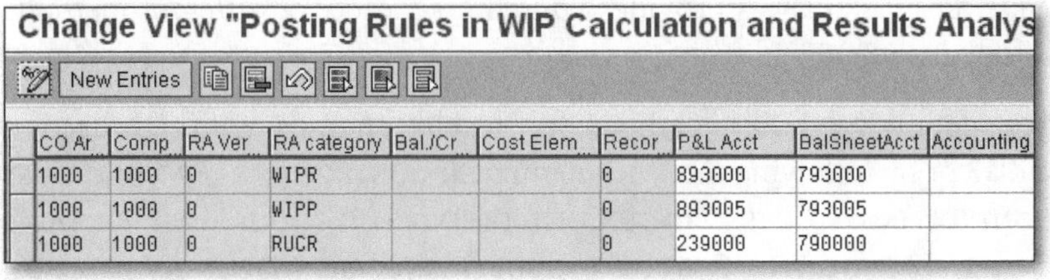

Change View "Posting Rules in WIP Calculation and Results Analys

New Entries

CO Ar	Comp	RA Ver	RA category	Bal./Cr	Cost Elem	Recor	P&L Acct	BalSheetAcct	Accounting
1000	1000	0	WIPR			0	893000	793000	
1000	1000	0	WIPP			0	893005	793005	
1000	1000	0	RUCR			0	239000	790000	

Figure 16.15 Posting Rules for WIP and Results Analysis

In this screen you define the WIP financial accounts for settlement in the P&L Acct and BalSheetAcct columns. There are six main RA categories that you can enter in the RA category column:

- **WIPR:** WIP with the requirement to capitalize costs
- **WIPO:** WIP with an option to capitalize costs
- **WIPP:** WIP with a prohibition to capitalize costs
- **RUCR:** Reserves for unrealized costs (group must be capitalized)
- **ROCU:** Reserves for unrealized costs (group can be capitalized)
- **RUCP:** Reserves for unrealized costs (group cannot be capitalized)

You can define separate reserve accounts if production credit exceeds costs (more costs are expected).

> **Note**
>
> You can calculate WIP as often as required during a period. Posting to WIP G/L accounts only occurs during settlement.

Now that we've discussed WIP configuration for reporting and posting, let's look at results analysis configuration.

16.2 Results Analysis Configuration

WIP is calculated on manufacturing orders and product cost collectors. In sales order costing, and when you use nonvaluated customer stock, an additional step is required to settle these costs. Results analysis calculates cost of sales (COS) and revenue on sales order line items.

Accounting principles require you to match recognition of COS and revenue. Results analysis provides you with a variety of different methods to calculate COS and match revenue.

You define valuation methods for results analysis with Transaction OKG3 or by following the IMG menu path Controlling • Product Cost Controlling • Cost Object Controlling • Product Cost by Sales Order • Period-End Closing • Results Analysis • Define Valuation Methods for Results Analysis. The screen shown in Figure 16.16 is displayed.

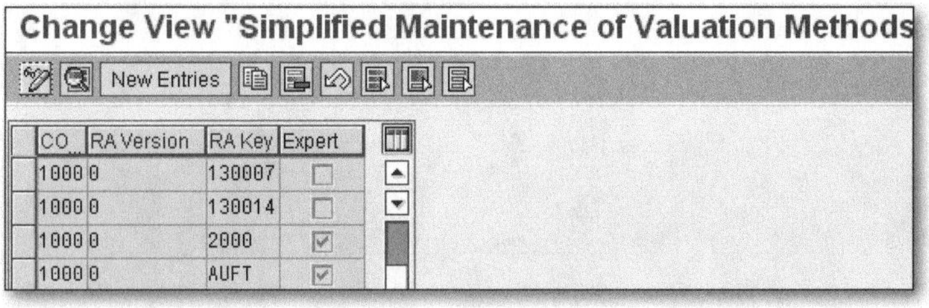

Figure 16.16 Simplified Maintenance List of Valuation Methods

You can configure results analysis in either simplified or expert mode depending on the checkbox in the Expert column:

▶ In simplified mode you can choose from a list of standard valuation methods.

▶ In expert mode you can modify any of the standard valuation methods to suit any special requirements you may have.

Double-click the first line in Figure 16.16 to display the screen shown in Figure 16.17.

In this screen you choose a results analysis method, and you can change the sales order line item status control, which determines when results analysis is calculated or inventory is canceled. You can display a list of standard results analysis methods by right-clicking the field and selecting Possible Entries. The screen in Figure 16.18 is displayed.

Select the results analysis method you require from the descriptions shown in Figure 16.18. If none of the standard valuation methods meets your requirements, click the Expert Mode button in Figure 16.17. An example of an expert mode screen is shown in Figure 16.19.

Many specialized fields and checkboxes are available in the expert mode screen. If you're not experienced with configuring results analysis, you may need to test different settings in this screen until they meet your results analysis requirements.

Now that we've configured WIP and results analysis, let's examine the WIP period-end process.

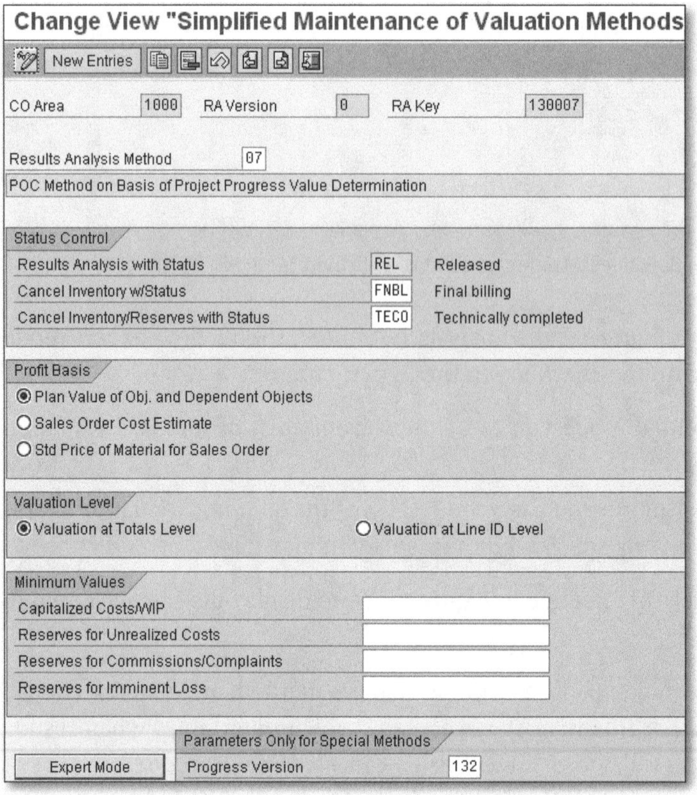

Figure 16.17 Simplified Maintenance of Valuation Methods

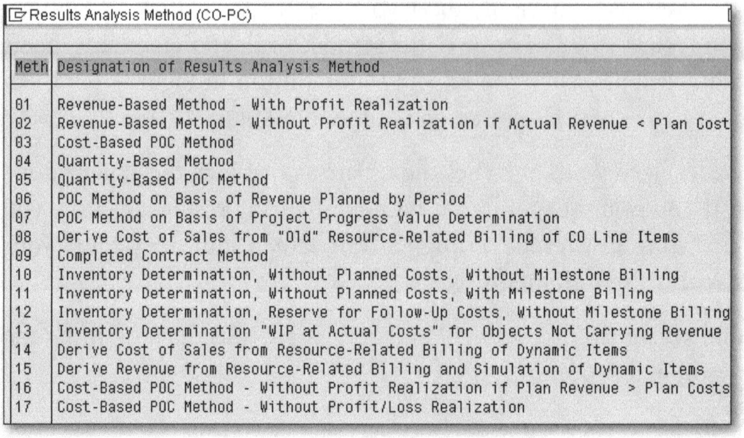
Results Analysis Method (CO-PC)

Meth	Designation of Results Analysis Method
01	Revenue-Based Method - With Profit Realization
02	Revenue-Based Method - Without Profit Realization if Actual Revenue < Plan Cost
03	Cost-Based POC Method
04	Quantity-Based Method
05	Quantity-Based POC Method
06	POC Method on Basis of Revenue Planned by Period
07	POC Method on Basis of Project Progress Value Determination
08	Derive Cost of Sales from "Old" Resource-Related Billing of CO Line Items
09	Completed Contract Method
10	Inventory Determination, Without Planned Costs, Without Milestone Billing
11	Inventory Determination, Without Planned Costs, With Milestone Billing
12	Inventory Determination, Reserve for Follow-Up Costs, Without Milestone Billing
13	Inventory Determination "WIP at Actual Costs" for Objects Not Carrying Revenue
14	Derive Cost of Sales from Resource-Related Billing of Dynamic Items
15	Derive Revenue from Resource-Related Billing and Simulation of Dynamic Items
16	Cost-Based POC Method - Without Profit Realization if Plan Revenue > Plan Costs
17	Cost-Based POC Method - Without Profit/Loss Realization

Figure 16.18 Results Analysis Method Possible Entries

Change View "Valuation Methods": Details

New Entries ▭▭▱▱▱▱

CO Area	1000	RA Version	0	Status Profile
RA Key	130007	Status	REL	Status Number	1

RA Type	L	Results Analysis Using Earned Values
Profit Indicator	Q	Percentage-of-Completion

Valuation

Valuation Basis	0
Plan Version	0
Version f. Sim.	0
Progress Versio	132
Updated Costs	
Valuation Level	S
Profit Basis	C
Base Quantity	
Loss Realiztion	E
Final RA	
Project Struct.	A
SalesOrderStruct	E
Profit %	
ResultsRes	A
Commitments	
☐ No Valuation	

Cancell. | Meth. of Appt

☑ WIP	I
☑ Res. Unreal Cost	D
☑ Res. Complaints	D
☑ Res. Immin. Loss	C
☑ Other Apportionment	
Redistribution	A
Cost of Sales	

Planned Values

Overall Plan	E
Line ID Costs	
Line ID Revenue	
Overrun	B
Line ID Overrun	

Minimum Values

WIP	
Reserves	
ResrvCompl	
ResImmLoss	

Extended Control

Cutoff	D	Special Funct.	
End	E	Time Frame	
Manual RA	Z	☑ Only Periodic	
Enhance 1			
☐ UserDefCOS			
Quantities			

Figure 16.19 Valuation Methods Expert Mode

16.3 WIP Period-End

We'll discuss WIP calculation for product cost collectors in detail and then discuss the differences for WIP calculation for manufacturing orders, because there are many similarities between the two processes.

16.3.1 Product Cost by Period

WIP is valuated at target cost for Product Cost by Period. Operation quantities confirmed for manufacturing orders are valuated at the target cost of the operation, minus scrap and goods receipt quantities. WIP at target value is not based on actual costs. Instead, it is based on what value WIP should be according to a cost estimate. You specify which cost estimate is used to calculate target costs in the valuation variant for scrap and WIP, as discussed in Section 16.1.4. For product cost collectors, SAP recommends calculating target costs based on the product cost collector preliminary cost estimate.

One of the main advantages of WIP at target is that variance and WIP can be posted at the same time. If production orders remain open for multiple periods, variance reconciliation is usually easier using WIP at target.

Case Scenario

The price of natural gas used in drying kilns increases unexpectedly one month. If the production order is delivered three months later, the production order variances in Controlling (CO) are posted after the primary expenses occurred in Financial Accounting (FI). This makes reconciliation between CO and FI difficult during any one period. With product cost collectors, WIP and variance are posted together during the period in which they occur. Variance is posted in the same period as the primary financial postings that caused the variance, simplifying reconciliation between CO and FI.

Another advantage of WIP at target is that variance analysis is based on material or product, usually a key reporting requirement. Variance comparison of different products allows analysis of which product is made more efficiently, improving product profitability. This analysis is usually more beneficial than analyzing variance per production order.

You run period-end WIP calculation with Transactions KKAS (individual) and KKAO (collective) or by following the menu path ACCOUNTING • CONTROLLING • PRODUCT COST CONTROLLING • COST OBJECT CONTROLLING • PRODUCT COST BY PERIOD • PERIOD-END CLOSING • SINGLE FUNCTIONS: PRODUCT COST COLLECTOR • WORK IN PROCESS. A selection screen is displayed, as shown in Figure 16.20.

Note

You carry out WIP calculation for production and process orders with Transactions KKAX (individual) and KKAO (collective). You run period-end results analysis calculation with Transaction KKA3 (individual) and KKAK (collective).

In this example, we calculate WIP only for product cost collectors by selecting the With Product Cost Collectors checkbox. You can include other objects in the calculation, without running another transaction, by selecting the relevant checkbox.

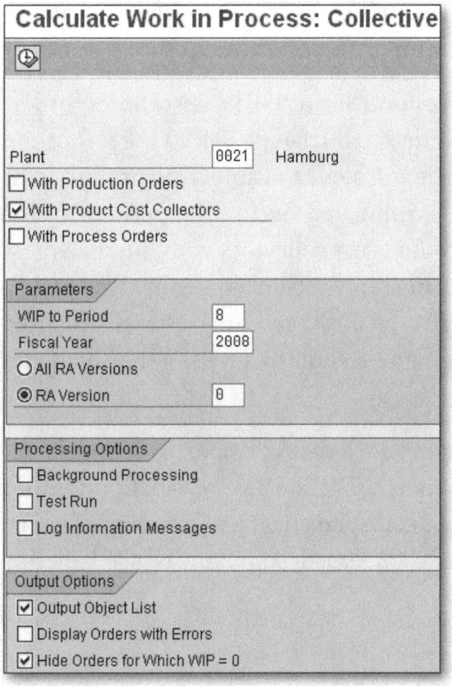

Figure 16.20 Work in Process Selection Screen

Complete the selection screen using the settings shown in Figure 16.20 as an example and click the execute icon to display the screen shown in Figure 16.21.

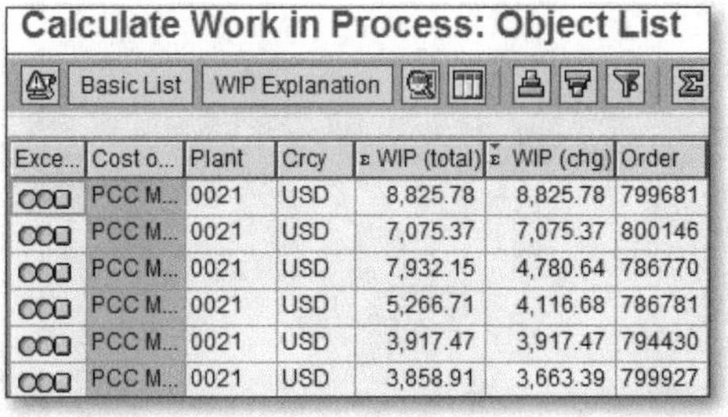

Calculate Work in Process: Object List

Basic List | WIP Explanation

Exce...	Cost o...	Plant	Crcy	Σ WIP (total)	Σ WIP (chg)	Order
	PCC M...	0021	USD	8,825.78	8,825.78	799681
	PCC M...	0021	USD	7,075.37	7,075.37	800146
	PCC M...	0021	USD	7,932.15	4,780.64	786770
	PCC M...	0021	USD	5,266.71	4,116.68	786781
	PCC M...	0021	USD	3,917.47	3,917.47	794430
	PCC M...	0021	USD	3,858.91	3,663.39	799927

Figure 16.21 Calculate Work in Process Object List

You can display messages by clicking the red triangle icon. You should analyze all messages and take corrective action where necessary. If you identify specific materials with several messages, it can be easier to calculate WIP for the individual materials separately with Transaction KKAS, and then analyze messages for a specific material.

In Figure 16.21 the WIP (chg) column is sorted in descending order. This is indicated by the small red inverted triangle just to the left of the WIP (chg) column header text. This provides visibility of product cost collectors with the largest WIP accumulated during the period of WIP calculation. If you analyze the product cost collectors with the six largest positive and negative values of change in WIP during each period, you'll find that the number and severity of messages progressively reduces each period-end. You can use the same technique on the WIP (total) column if necessary.

To analyze WIP calculated for a product cost collector in more detail, click the corresponding line and then click the WIP Explanation button. The screen shown in Figure 16.22 is displayed. (The English spelling of the word *labor* is used because a UK-based company is used in this example.)

Calculate WIP: Explanation

Activity	Cost Ele...	Name	Origin	∑ WIP (total)	Input qty	Unit	GR qty	Yield	Rel. scrap	∑	Ref. qty
	690420	Labour Overhead	1600	24.42							
	690410	Quality Overhead	1400	7.97							
	690420	Labour Overhead	1600	119.77							
	690410	Quality Overhead	1400	39.11							
				▪ 191.27							
0010						EA	90.000	90.000			
						EA	50.000	50.000			
	690020	Set-Up	1650/SET	8.89	0.250	HR					
	690010	Labour	1650/RUN	53.36	1.5	HR					
						EA		50.000			50.000
0010				▪ 62.25		EA				▪	50.000
						HR					
0020						EA	90.000	90.000			
						EA	50.000	50.000			
	690020	Set-Up	1650/SET	8.89	0.250	HR					
	690010	Labour	1650/RUN	296.40	8.333	HR					
						EA		50.000			50.000
0020				▪ 305.29		EA				▪	50.000
						HR					
0022						EA					
				▪▪ 558.81		EA				▪▪	100.000
						HR					

Figure 16.22 Calculate WIP Explanation Screen

Numbers shown in the Activity (first) column correspond to operations in the routing. WIP at target is based on quantities confirmed at each operation. The first four rows correspond with overhead allocated to the product cost collector due to WIP quantities, and do not correspond to operations.

A quantity in the Ref. qty (last) column indicates that this is a reference quantity for calculating WIP. If you look to the left of the first quantity of 50 in the Ref. qty column, you will see a quantity of 50 in the Yield column. This indicates that there has been a confirmed yield of 50 for a partial assembly from operation 0010, which has not yet been consumed in operation 0020. Looking further to the left and one row down, in the WIP (total) column, you can see that the value of the partial assemblies is 62.25. This corresponds to the value of WIP at target residing on operation 0010 during the period. The same process is used to determine WIP at each operation. The WIP value at each operation is added to the corresponding overhead value to determine the total WIP value for the period of 558.81.

Values in the GR qty column in Figure 16.22 correspond to goods receipt quantity of finished assemblies into inventory. In the first line of operation 0010, you can see that there has been a goods receipt quantity of 90 for the finished assembly and a corresponding yield of 90 for operation 0010. All subsequent operations show a corresponding first line and no WIP. As long as the sum of the Yield and Rel. scrap columns equals the GR qty column, there will be no corresponding WIP for that row.

> **Note**
>
> WIP cannot be canceled by changing the status of underlying manufacturing orders to technically complete (TECO). This status prevents any further processing or costs posting to the product cost collector through the manufacturing order.
>
> However, a status of TECO does not remove existing WIP, which remains associated with the product cost collector. Setting the manufacturing order deletion flag, corresponding with status DLFL, will cancel existing WIP. You can set the deletion flag while viewing a production order in change mode by selecting FUNCTIONS • DELETION FLAG • ACTIVATE from the menu bar. The deletion flag can be revoked if necessary by selecting FUNCTIONS • DELETION FLAG • REVOKE from the menu bar.

No financial postings occur during WIP calculation. You can run the WIP transaction as often as you like, and carry out analysis and fixes progressively during a fiscal period. Financial postings only occur during settlement, which is normally carried out as the last step at period-end.

16.3.2 Product Cost by Order

The Product Cost by Order scenario involves working with manufacturing orders. We'll now look at the differences between WIP calculation for manufacturing orders and product cost collectors.

WIP is valuated at actual cost in Product Cost by Order. All order debits are considered WIP until valuated goods receipt into inventory occurs. At period-end, the actual balance of incomplete manufacturing orders not fully delivered to inventory is determined during WIP calculation. During settlement, calculated WIP is posted to a WIP balance sheet account and an offsetting profit and loss account.

WIP calculation is based on manufacturing order status:

▸ **REL (released):** Calculate WIP

▸ **DLV (delivered):** Cancel WIP

▸ **TECO (technically complete):** Cancel WIP

WIP is calculated each period until the status of the order is set to fully delivered or technically complete, and then the WIP is canceled and variance is calculated.

This concludes the WIP chapter, so let's review what we've covered.

16.4 Summary

In this chapter we configured and calculated WIP and results analysis. This process calculates the cost of incomplete assemblies on the production floor. Let's now look at the next period-end process, variance calculation, in Chapter 17.

Variance calculation assigns the difference between order debits and credits into categories for analysis.

17 Variance Calculation

In the Chapters 15 and 16 we studied the period-end processing steps of overhead and work in process. In this chapter we'll discuss in detail the variance calculation step.

Variance calculation provides information to assist you during analysis of production variance. It helps you determine the reason for the difference between order debits and credits. It does this by analyzing causes of the variance and assigning categories. The following sections present an overview of the types of variance calculation, configuration, and period-end processing.

17.1 Types of Variance Calculation

There are three main types of variance categories which we will discuss in the following sections.

17.1.1 Total Variance

Total variance is the difference between actual cost debited to the order and credits from deliveries to inventory. You calculate total variance with target cost version 0, which determines the basis for calculation of target costs. Target costs are the expected costs when a quantity is delivered to inventory. Total variance is the only variance relevant to settlement. The difference between debits and credits is settled to Financial Accounting, Profit Center Accounting, and Profitability Analysis.

17.1.2 Production Variance

Refer to Chapter 11 for more information on preliminary cost estimates

Production variance is the difference between net actual costs debited to the order and target costs based on the preliminary cost estimate and quantity delivered to inventory. You calculate production variances with target cost version 1. Production variances are for information only and are not relevant for settlement.

17.1.3 Planning Variance

Planning variance is the difference between costs on the preliminary cost estimate for the order and target costs based on the standard cost estimate and planned order quantity. You calculate planning variances with target cost version 2. Planning variances are for information only and are not relevant for settlement.

Now that we've looked at the three main types of variance calculations, let's examine the configuration required for variance analysis to assist in understanding the calculations that occur during variance analysis.

17.2 Variance Configuration

Variance configuration for Product Cost by Period and Product Cost by Order are similar. Let's look at variance configuration for Product Cost by Period, and highlight the differences along the way.

17.2.1 Define Variance Keys

You define variance keys with Transaction OKV1 or by following the IMG menu path CONTROLLING • PRODUCT COST CONTROLLING • COST OBJECT CONTROLLING • PRODUCT COST BY PERIOD • PERIOD-END CLOSING • VARIANCE CALCULATION • VARIANCE CALCULATION FOR PRODUCT COST COLLECTORS • DEFINE VARIANCE KEYS. The screen shown in Figure 17.1 is displayed.

This overview screen displays a list of available variance keys. Double-click a variance key in the Variance Key column to display the details screen shown in Figure 17.2.

Figure 17.1 Define Variance Keys

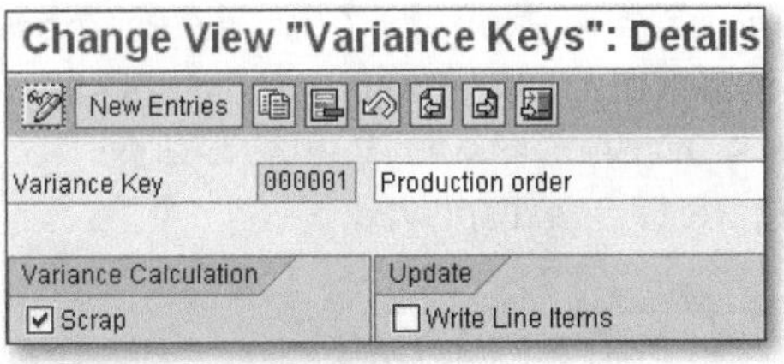

Figure 17.2 Edit Variance Keys

This screen allows you to change the variance key description and maintain two checkboxes.

Scrap

Select the Scrap checkbox to ensure that the value of scrap is calculated and subtracted from total variances during variance calculation. Any difference between planned and actual scrap is shown as scrap variance. If planned scrap equals actual scrap, there is no scrap variance. Target costs for the valuation of scrap are calculated according to the valuation variant for work in process (WIP) and scrap, as discussed in Chapter 16. If a valuation variant for WIP and scrap is not defined, target costs are valuated on the basis of the standard cost estimate.

Write Line Items

Select the Write Line Items checkbox shown in Figure 17.2 to ensure that a document is created when variances or target costs are calculated. The line items document records when the target costs or variances were calculated and who created them. It also displays which target costs or variances were changed. The Write Line Items checkbox is not selected by default, because this level of detail is not generally needed and increases system load requirements.

Now that we've defined variance keys, let's examine the next variance configuration step.

17.2.2 Define Default Variance Keys for Plants

You define default variance keys per plant with Transaction OKVW or by following the IMG menu path CONTROLLING • PRODUCT COST CONTROLLING • COST OBJECT CONTROLLING • PRODUCT COST BY PERIOD • PERIOD-END CLOSING • VARIANCE CALCULATION • VARIANCE CALCULATION FOR PRODUCT COST COLLECTORS • DEFINE DEFAULT VARIANCE KEYS FOR PLANTS. The screen shown in Figure 17.3 is displayed.

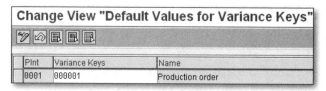

Figure 17.3 Default Variance Keys per Plant

When a material master is created, a default variance key is proposed for the Costing 1 view field, based on the Variance Keys field entry in Figure 17.3. When a manufacturing order or product cost collector is created, a default variance key is proposed based on the variance key entered in the material master Costing 1 view.

17.2.3 Define Variance Variants

You define variance variants with Transaction OKVG or by following the IMG menu path CONTROLLING • PRODUCT COST CONTROLLING • COST OBJECT CONTROLLING • PRODUCT COST BY PERIOD • PERIOD-END CLOSING • VARIANCE CALCULATION • VARIANCE CALCULATION FOR PRODUCT COST COLLECTORS • DEFINE VARIANCE VARIANTS. The screen shown in Figure 17.4 is displayed.

Variance variants determine which variance categories are calculated. Variances are calculated for all variance categories that are selected in this view. If a variance category is not selected, variances of that category are assigned to remaining variances. Scrap variances are the only exception to this rule. If Scrap Variance is not selected, these variances enter all other variances on the input side.

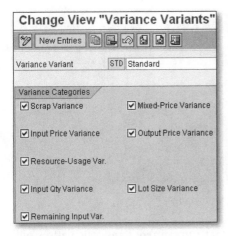

Figure 17.4 Define Variance Variants

You specify whether scrap variances are calculated by selecting the Scrap checkbox in the variance key in Figure 17.2. You control whether scrap variances are displayed by selecting the Scrap Variance checkbox in the Variance Variant in Figure 17.4.

You can assign different variance variants to each target cost version. As long as you have specified that scrap variances are to be calculated in the variance key, you could, for example, use a variance variant with the Scrap Variance checkbox selected for target cost version 0 and deselected for target cost version 3. This would allow you one view of variances in target cost version 0 with scrap displayed separately and another view of variances in target cost version 3 without scrap variances displayed separately.

17.2.4 Define Valuation Variant for WIP and Scrap (Target Costs)

You define the valuation variant for WIP and unplanned scrap (target costs) by following the IMG menu path Controlling • Product Cost Controlling • Cost Object Controlling • Product Cost by Period • Period-End Closing • Variance Calculation • Define Valuation Vari-

ANT FOR WIP AND SCRAP (TARGET COSTS). The screen shown in Figure 17.5 is displayed.

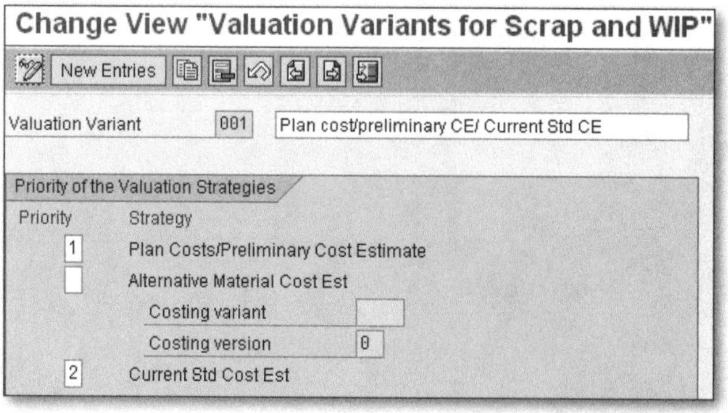

Figure 17.5 Define Valuation Variant for Scrap and WIP

Refer to Chapter 16 for more information on the valuation variant for WIP and scrap

The valuation strategy indicates that unplanned scrap calculation will first search for a preliminary cost estimate, and if unsuccessful, will then search for a current standard cost estimate. This strategy is useful because if for any reason a preliminary cost estimate is not created, the current standard cost estimate can still be used to valuate unplanned scrap, avoiding an error message that would otherwise be generated.

17.2.5 Define Target Cost Versions

You define target cost versions with Transaction OKV6 or by following the IMG menu path CONTROLLING • PRODUCT COST CONTROLLING • COST OBJECT CONTROLLING • PRODUCT COST BY PERIOD • PERIOD-END CLOSING • VARIANCE CALCULATION • VARIANCE CALCULATION FOR PRODUCT COST COLLECTORS • DEFINE TARGET COST VERSIONS. An overview screen is displayed, as shown in Figure 17.6.

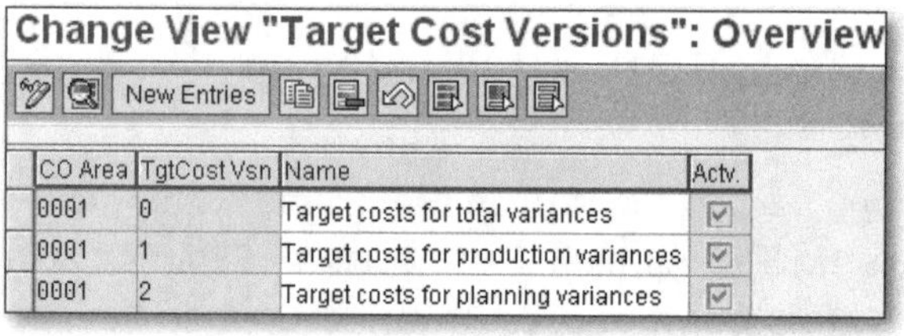

Figure 17.6 Define Target Cost Versions

This overview screen presents a list of all available target cost versions. Let's examine each of these target cost versions in detail.

Target Cost Version 0

Double-click target cost version 0 to display the details screen shown in Figure 17.7.

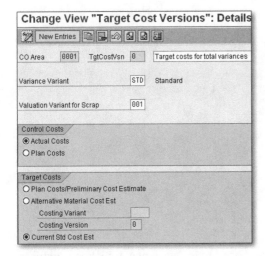

Figure 17.7 Target Cost Version 0 Details Screen

Control costs are based on actual costs, or, in other words, actual debits. Target costs are based on the current standard cost estimate (Current Std Cost Est), or, in other words, actual credits.

Target cost version 0 calculates total variance and is used to explain the difference between actual debits and credits on an order. It is the only target cost version that can be settled to Financial Accounting, Profit Center Accounting, and Profitability Analysis.

You can specify a valuation variant for scrap (and WIP) with target cost version 0. This allows you to control which cost estimate is used to valuate scrap, as previously discussed in Section 17.2.4. The valuation variant for scrap is not changeable in other target cost versions.

Now that we've examined target cost version 0 configuration, let's look at other target cost versions.

Target Cost Version 1

Double-click target cost version 1 in the screen shown in Figure 17.6 to display the details screen shown in Figure 17.8.

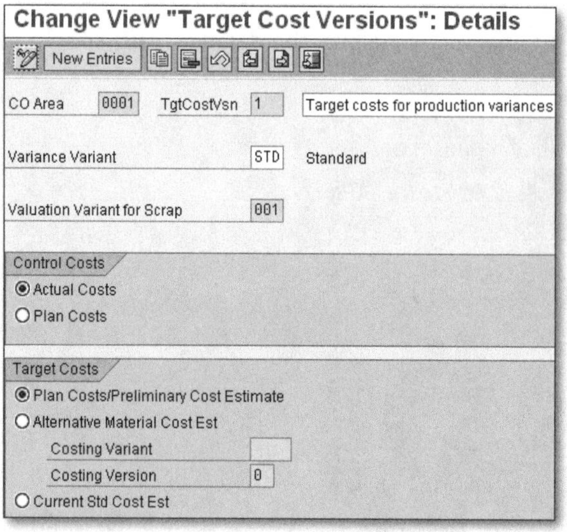

Figure 17.8 Target Cost Version 1 Details Screen

Target cost version 1 calculates production variance, which is the difference between net actual costs and target costs based on the preliminary cost estimate. This allows you to exclude variances that occurred because a different quantity structure was used during production compared to the standard cost estimate quantity structure.

Although this target cost version is for information only and cannot be settled, it is useful for analyzing production performance and efficiency.

Target Cost Version 2

Double-click target cost version 2 in the screen shown in Figure 17.6 to display the details screen displayed in Figure 17.9.

Target cost version 2 calculates planning variance, which is the difference between plan costs based on the preliminary cost estimate of a manufacturing order and target costs based on the current standard cost estimate (Current Std Cost Est).

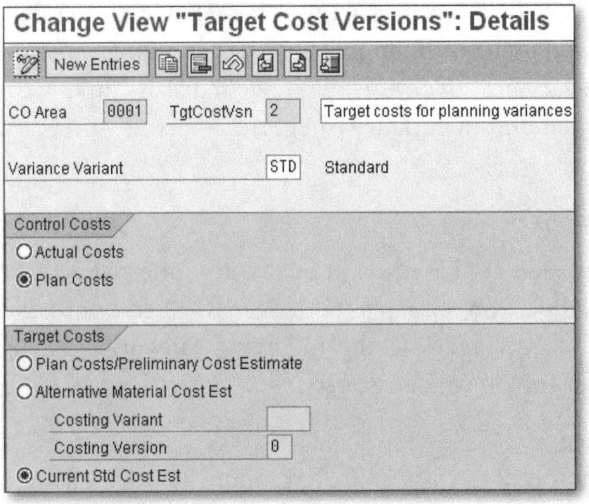

Figure 17.9 Target Cost Version 2 Details Screen

You can use target cost version 2 to decide whether to manufacture an order with a particular quantity structure. Although this target cost version is for information only and cannot be settled, it is useful for analyzing production planning performance and efficiency.

The system does not allow calculation of a planning variance between a current standard cost estimate and a preliminary cost estimate for product cost collectors. Therefore, you cannot calculate variances with target cost version 2 for product cost collectors.

So far in this chapter we've analyzed types of variance calculation and configuration. Next we'll discuss variance categories and then follow a typical period-end processing scenario.

17.3 Variance Categories

During variance calculation, the order balance is divided into categories on the input and output sides. Variance categories provide reasons for the cause of the variance, which you can use when deciding what corrective action to take. No financial postings are made during variance calculation, and it can be run as often as necessary to control production processes. The frequency can be daily if variances are high and many corrective actions are necessary. Continual improvements in master data and user knowledge and skills through frequent variance analysis usually results in reduced variances over time. First, we'll discuss input variance categories, and then output variance categories.

17.3.1 Input Variances

Variances on the input side are based on goods issues, internal activity allocations, overhead allocation, and general ledger (G/L) account postings. Input variances are divided into the following categories during variance calculation, according to their source.

▸ **Input price variance**
Input price variance occurs as a result of component price changes after the higher-level assembly cost estimate is released. This occurs in one of two ways:

  ▹ If the component valuation is based on standard price control, a standard cost estimate for the component could be released after the cost estimate for the assembly is released.

  ▹ If the component valuation is based on moving average price control, a goods receipt of the component could change the component price after the cost estimate for the assembly is released.

▸ **Resource-usage variance**
Resource-usage variance occurs as a result of substituting components. This could occur if a component is not available and another component with a different material number is used instead. The costs for both components are reported as resource-usage variances.

▸ **Input quantity variance**
Input quantity variance occurs as a result of a difference between planned and actual quantities of materials and activities consumed.

▸ **Remaining input variance**
Remaining input variance occurs when input variances cannot be assigned to any other variance category.

17.3.2 Output Variances

Variances on the output side result from too little or too much planned order quantity being delivered, or because the delivered quantity was valuated differently. Output variances are broken down into the following categories during variance calculation:

▶ **Mixed-price variance**

Mixed-price variance occurs when inventory is valuated using a mixed cost estimate for the material. If you want to perform mixed costing, create a procurement alternative for each production version and then define a mixing ratio. Refer to Chapter 5 for more information on the procurement alternative.

The mixed cost estimate calculates a mixed price. This price can be written to the material master as the standard price. The target credit is based on the confirmed quantity times the standard cost of the procurement alternative. The actual cost is based on the confirmed quantity times the standard price, where the standard price corresponds to the mixed price.

The mixed price variance is caused by a difference between target and actual costs. If you don't select the Mixed-Price Variance checkbox in the variance variant, as discussed in Section 17.2, mixed-price variances are shown as output price variances.

▶ **Output price variance:** Output price variance can occur in three situations:

   ▷ It occurs if the standard price is changed after delivery to inventory and before variance calculation.

   ▷ It occurs if the material is valuated at moving average price and it is not delivered to inventory at standard price during target value calculation. You control how the target value is calculated for delivery to stock when the price control checkbox is set to V (moving average price) in customizing with Transaction OPK9 or by following the IMG menu path CONTROLLING • PRODUCT COST CONTROLLING • COST OBJECT CONTROLLING • PRODUCT COST BY PERIOD • SIMULTANEOUS COSTING • DEFINE GOODS RECEIVED VALUATION FOR ORDER DELIVERY.

▸ It can occur if you don't select the Mixed-Price Variance checkbox in the variance variant, as discussed in Section 17.2.

▸ **Lot size variance**
Lot size variance occurs if a manufacturing order lot size is different from the standard cost estimate costing lot size. Setup time does not usually change with lot size, so a different lot size will either increase or decrease the unit cost. Whenever a portion of manufacturing cost does not change with output quantity, such as setup or tear-down time, lot size variance can occur.

▸ **Remaining variance**
Remaining variance occurs if variances cannot be assigned to any other variance category. Rounding differences or overhead applied to costs that do not vary with lot size are reported as remaining variances.

Remaining variance is also reported when target costs cannot be calculated, such as when a standard cost estimate does not exist, or if a goods receipt for the order has not taken place. All variance is also reported as remaining variance when no variance categories have been selected in the variance variant. Scrap variances are an exception to this rule. If the Scrap Variance checkbox is not selected in the variance variant, scrap variances can be reported against any other relevant variance on the input side.

Now that we've examined types of variance calculations, configuration, and variance categories, let's follow a typical period-end processing scenario.

17.4   Variance Period-End

There are differences in variance calculation for product cost collectors and manufacturing orders. Variance is calculated every period-end for product cost collectors, whereas the timing is dependent on order status for manufacturing orders. WIP and scrap variances are subtracted from actual costs to determine control costs for product cost collectors. Only scrap variances are subtracted from actual costs to determine control costs for manufacturing orders.

We'll now discuss variance calculation for product cost collectors in detail. Then we'll discuss only the differences for variance calculation for manufacturing orders, because there are many similarities between the two processes.

17.4.1 Product Cost by Period

You run period-end variance calculation with Transactions KKS6 (individual) and KKS5 (collective), or by following the menu path ACCOUNTING • CONTROLLING • PRODUCT COST CONTROLLING • COST OBJECT CONTROLLING • PRODUCT COST BY PERIOD • PERIOD-END CLOSING • SINGLE FUNCTIONS: PRODUCT COST COLLECTOR • VARIANCES. A selection screen is displayed, as shown in Figure 17.10.

Note
You can also carry out variance analysis for production and process orders with Transactions KKS2 (individual) and KKS1 (collective).

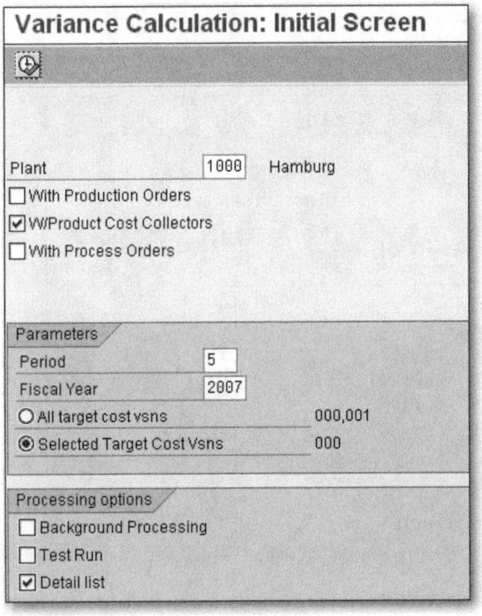

Variance Calculation: Initial Screen

Plant   1000   Hamburg
☐ With Production Orders
☑ W/Product Cost Collectors
☐ With Process Orders

Parameters
Period   5
Fiscal Year   2007
○ All target cost vsns   000,001
◉ Selected Target Cost Vsns   000

Processing options
☐ Background Processing
☐ Test Run
☑ Detail list

Figure 17.10 Variance Calculation Selection Screen

In this example, we will calculate variance only for product cost collectors by selecting the W/Product Cost Collectors checkbox. You can include other objects in the calculation, without running another transaction, by selecting the relevant indicator in Figure 17.10.

Target cost versions selected in this screen determine whether only total variances (target cost version 0) or all selected variances are calculated. You can adjust the selected target cost versions by selecting EXTRAS • SET TARGET COST VERSIONS from the menu bar.

Collective processing time can be reduced by deselecting the Detail list indicator. Although variances are calculated, you do not see any variance calculation details in the following screens. You can then use summarized reporting to analyze the aggregated data. Orders that caused high variances can be identified by sorting on variance columns or by using exception rules. To find detailed information for an order that caused high variances, recalculate variance for the individual order with the Test Run and Detail list checkbox selected.

Complete the selection screen using the settings in Figure 17.10 as an example and click the execute icon to display the screen shown in Figure 17.11.

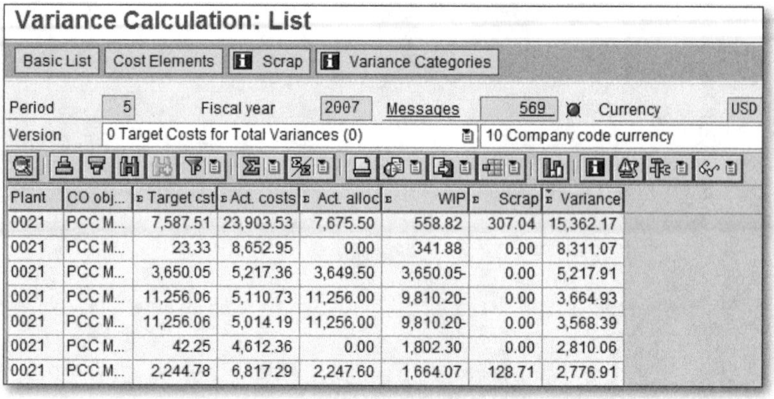

Variance Calculation: List

Plant	CO obj...	Σ Target cst	Σ Act. costs	Σ Act. alloc	Σ WIP	Σ Scrap	Σ Variance
0021	PCC M...	7,587.51	23,903.53	7,675.50	558.82	307.04	15,362.17
0021	PCC M...	23.33	8,652.95	0.00	341.88	0.00	8,311.07
0021	PCC M...	3,650.05	5,217.36	3,649.50	3,650.05-	0.00	5,217.91
0021	PCC M...	11,256.06	5,110.73	11,256.00	9,810.20-	0.00	3,664.93
0021	PCC M...	11,256.06	5,014.19	11,256.00	9,810.20-	0.00	3,568.39
0021	PCC M...	42.25	4,612.36	0.00	1,802.30	0.00	2,810.06
0021	PCC M...	2,244.78	6,817.29	2,247.60	1,664.07	128.71	2,776.91

Period: 5 Fiscal year: 2007 Messages: 569 Currency: USD
Version: 0 Target Costs for Total Variances (0) 10 Company code currency

Figure 17.11 Variance Calculation Results Screen

You should analyze all messages and take corrective action where necessary. You can display messages by clicking on the red traffic light icon. If you identify specific materials with several messages, it may be easier to calculate variance for the individual materials separately with Transaction KKS6 and analyze the messages for the specific materials.

The formula for calculating variance in Figure 17.11 is:

Variance = Actual Costs – Actual Costs Allocated (credits) – WIP – Scrap

The Variance column is sorted in descending order. This is indicated by the small red inverted triangle just to the left of the Variance column header. Sorting provides visibility of product cost collectors with large variances during the period. Let's follow an example that demonstrates how to analyze the causes of the largest variances. We'll analyze the product cost collector corresponding to the first line in Figure 17.11, because it has the largest unfavorable variance.

To display more details of the product cost collector variance calculation, click the first row shown and then click the Cost Elements button. The screen shown in Figure 17.12 is displayed. If you don't see variance category columns as shown in Figure 17.12, click the select layout (grid) icon and select Variance Categories layout.

Cost ...	Cost Elem.	Origin	≡	Variance	≡ Price Var.	≡ ResU...	≡	Qty var.	≡ RemInputVa	≡ MxdPrcVar	≡ OutPricVar	≡ OtptQtyVar	≡ LotSizeVar	≡ Rem. var.
500100	Comp Mts - ...	0021/M...		0.24	0.24	0.00		0.00	0.00	0.00	0.00	0.00	0.00	0.00
500100	Comp Mts - ...	0021/P3..		3.98-	0.00	0.00		3.98-	0.00	0.00	0.00	0.00	0.00	0.00
690010	Labour	1650/R...		10,059.09	0.05	0.00		10,059.04	0.00	0.00	0.00	0.00	0.00	0.00
690010	Labour	1660/R...		47.86-	0.00	47.86-		0.00	0.00	0.00	0.00	0.00	0.00	0.00
690020	Set-Up	1650/SET		155.81	0.03	0.00		155.78	0.00	0.00	0.00	0.00	0.00	0.00
690020	Set-Up	1660/SET		16.52-	0.01-	16.51-		0.00	0.00	0.00	0.00	0.00	0.00	0.00
690030	Rework	1650/R...		14.41	0.00	14.41		0.00	0.00	0.00	0.00	0.00	0.00	0.00
690400	Material Over...			0.36-	0.00	0.00		0.00	0.36-	0.00	0.00	0.00	0.00	0.00
690410	Quality Overh...			1,301.63	0.00	0.00		0.00	1,301.63	0.00	0.00	0.00	0.00	0.00
690420	Labour Overh...			3,987.70	0.00	0.00		0.00	3,987.70	0.00	0.00	0.00	0.00	0.00
Debit			▪	**15,450.16** ▪	**0.31** ▪	**49.96-** ▪		**10,210.84** ▪	**5,288.97** ▪	**0.00** ▪	**0.00** ▪	**0.00** ▪	**0.00** ▪	**0.00**
500600	Fin Goods - I...	0021/M...		32.68	0.00	0.00		0.00	0.00	0.00	0.08	0.00	0.00	32.60
690020	Set-Up	1650/SET		91.17-	0.00	0.00		0.00	0.00	0.00	0.00	0.00	91.17-	0.00
690020	Set-Up	1660/SET		29.50-	0.00	0.00		0.00	0.00	0.00	0.00	0.00	29.50-	0.00
Delivery			▪	**87.99-** ▪	**0.00** ▪	**0.00** ▪		**0.00** ▪	**0.00** ▪	**0.00** ▪	**0.08** ▪	**0.00** ▪	**120.67-** ▪	**32.60**

Figure 17.12 Cost Elements Breakdown of Variance Calculation

The sum of input and output variances in the Variance column shown in Figure 17.12 is equal to the total variance shown in the Variance column of the first row of Figure 17.11. Most of the variance is due to an input quantity variance in the Qty var. column of the third row in Figure 17.12. More actual labor time was confirmed than planned in the cost estimate. This could be due to an incorrect confirmation entry or because it took longer than planned. You can display a more detailed view of variances and target costs by clicking the Variances and Target Costs buttons shown in Figure 17.12.

You can analyze input quantity variance further by displaying a detailed analysis of the product cost collector for the period with Transaction KKBC_PKO or by following the menu path ACCOUNTING • CONTROLLING • PRODUCT COST CONTROLLING • COST OBJECT CONTROLLING • PRODUCT COST BY PERIOD • INFORMATION SYSTEM • REPORTS FOR PRODUCT COST BY PERIOD • DETAILED REPORTS • FOR PRODUCT COST COLLECTORS. A selection screen is displayed, as shown in Figure 17.13.

Note

Use Transaction KKBC_ORD for production and process orders.

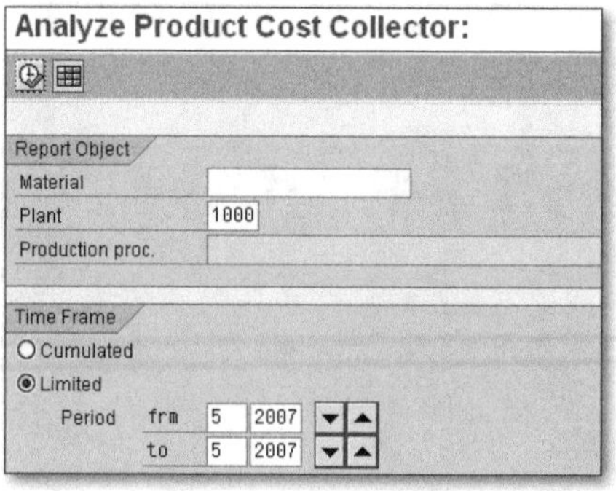

Figure 17.13 Analyze Product Cost Collector Selection Screen

Complete the fields as required and click the execute icon to display the screen shown in Figure 17.14.

BusTran.	Origin	Origin (Text)	Σ Total tgt	Σ Ttl actual
Confirmations	1650/RUN	Sewing / Run Time	4,706.44	15,127.19
	1650/SET	Sewing / Set Time	47.41	218.71
	1650/REW...	Sewing / Rework	0.00	14.41
	1660/RUN	Painting / Run Time	46.02	0.00
	1660/SET	Painting / Set Time	15.34	0.00

Figure 17.14 Analyze Product Cost Collector Results Screen

Double-click the first row to display the confirmations line item details that caused the large input quantity variance in the third row in Figure 17.12. The screen shown in Figure 17.15 is displayed.

Cost Elem.	CElem.name	Σ Val.in RC	Quantity	PUM	Off.acct	Offst.acct
690010	Labour	266.60	449.717	MIN		
690010	Labour	266.31	449.233	MIN		
690010	Labour	266.21	449.050	MIN		
690010	Labour	265.49	447.833	MIN		
690010	Labour	264.85	446.750	MIN		
690010	Labour	264.75	446.600	MIN		

Figure 17.15 Confirmation Line Items

The Quantity column is sorted in descending order. This provides visibility of confirmations with the largest time bookings. By double-clicking any line, you can drill down to individual activity confirmations. From the detailed confirmation screens, you can determine the original cause of the large input quantity variance.

In this example, we examined the cause of an input quantity variance due to labor confirmations. You can use the same technique to analyze any variance category, by sorting line items and drilling down to original transactions.

We've discussed variance calculation for product cost collectors in detail. We'll now discuss the differences for variance calculation for manufacturing orders, because there are many similarities between the two processes.

17.4.2 Product Cost by Order

In this section we'll examine variance calculation for Product Cost by Order, which means working with manufacturing orders. We'll analyze the differences between variance calculation for manufacturing orders and product cost collectors.

Variance calculation for manufacturing orders is also known as cumulative variance. Cumulative variance compares target costs and cumulative control costs. As previously shown in the configuration for target cost version 0 in Section 17.1, target costs for total variance are based on the standard cost estimate, or, in other words, the valuated goods receipt. Control costs are equal to actual costs less scrap variances. The manufacturing order must meet the following two conditions to calculate variance:

▸ Settlement type FUL (full settlement) in the settlement rule

▸ Status DLV (delivered) or TECO (technically complete)

Settlement type FUL allows all unsettled WIP and variance from the current and previous periods to be settled in the current settlement period. WIP and variances are calculated based on order status, not period. You normally settle manufacturing orders every period.

Status DLV is determined automatically when posting valuated goods receipts during manufacturing order confirmation. Status TECO is determined manually and indicates that processing is complete even though the order is not fully delivered. When either status is detected during period-end processing, WIP in canceled and variance is calculated.

During variance calculation, target and control costs are compared, and variance categories are assigned. Variance categories are assigned in the following sequence:

▸ Input price variance

▸ Resource-usage variance

▸ Input quantity variance

▸ Remaining input variance

▸ Mixed-price variance

▸ Output price variance

▸ Lot size variance

▸ Remaining variance

Variance categories were discussed in detail in Section 17.3.

This concludes the variance calculation chapter, so let's review what we've covered.

17.5   Summary

In this chapter we studied the types of variance calculation, configuration, and period-end processing. We'll examine the final period-end process of settlement in Chapter 18.

Settlement transfers work in process and variances to Financial Accounting, Profit Center Accounting, and Profitability Analysis.

18 Settlement

Work in process (WIP) and variances are transferred to Financial Accounting, Profit Center Accounting, and Profitability Analysis during settlement. Variance categories can also be transferred to value fields in Profitability Analysis.

Let's discuss settlement configuration and then settlement period-end processing.

18.1 Settlement Configuration

Settlement configuration for Product Cost by Period and Product Cost by Order are similar. Let's look at settlement configuration for Product Cost by Period and highlight the differences along the way.

18.1.1 Create Settlement Profile

A settlement profile contains settlement control parameters on how orders settle. You enter the settlement profile in the order type definition with Transaction KOT2 or by following the IMG menu path CONTROLLING • PRODUCT COST CONTROLLING • COST OBJECT CONTROLLING • PRODUCT COST BY ORDER • MANUFACTURING ORDERS • CHECK ORDER TYPES. When you create an order, the settlement profile contained in the order type defaults into the order settlement rule. To display the settlement profile in a production order, display a production order with Transaction CO02 and select HEADER • SETTLEMENT RULE from the menu bar. You will see a list of distribution rules that define where the costs are to settle. Select GOTO • SETTLEMENT PARAMETERS from the menu bar to display the screen shown in Figure 18.1.

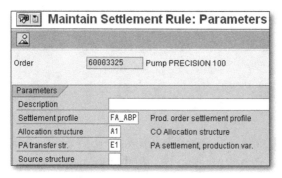

Figure 18.1 Settlement Rule Parameters

The Settlement profile field in the Settlement Rule Parameters defaults from the order type that you configure with Transaction KOT2. The Allocation structure, PA transfer struct., and Source structure fields default from the settlement profile, which we'll examine in detail in this chapter.

> **Note**
>
> Even though the Settlement Rule Parameters default from the order type and settlement profile, you can manually change the default values.

You create settlement profiles with Transaction OKO7 or by following the IMG menu path CONTROLLING • PRODUCT COST CONTROLLING • COST OBJECT CONTROLLING • PRODUCT COST BY PERIOD • PERIOD-END CLOSING • SETTLEMENT • CREATE SETTLEMENT PROFILE. The screen shown in Figure 18.2 is displayed.

The overview screen displays a list of available settlement profiles. Double-click a settlement profile to display the details screen shown in Figure 18.3.

You maintain settlement profile details in this screen. Let's examine the fields and checkboxes of each section of the screen.

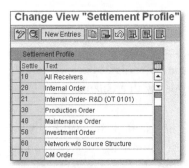

Figure 18.2 Settlement Profile Overview Screen

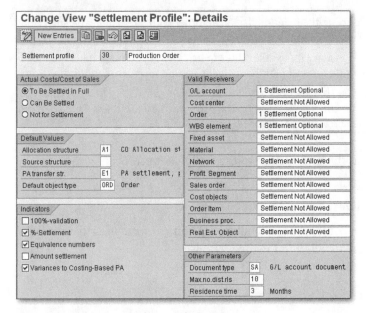

Figure 18.3 Settlement Profile Details Screen

Actual Costs/Cost of Sales

The Actual Costs/Cost of Sales section controls how actual costs or cost of sales (COS) are to be settled.

▶ **To Be Settled in Full**

This is the default setting. If you try to close an order, or set the deletion flag, the system displays an error message if the balance of the object is not zero.

▶ **Can Be Settled**
You can settle actual costs and COS, but you do not have to. When you try to close the object or set the deletion flag, the system displays a warning message if the balance in the object is not zero. You can, however, set the deletion flag on an order with a balance.

▶ **Not for Settlement**
Actual costs, COS, and variances are not settled, but WIP can be. When you close the object or set the deletion flag, the system does not display a message if the balance in the object is not zero.

> **Tip**
>
> If you need to set the deletion flag on an order with a remaining balance, you will receive an error message until you either:
>
> ▶ Settle the balance if possible. This can be difficult at times if there are problems with the order or if it hasn't been settled for many periods.
>
> ▶ Change the To Be Settled in Full setting to Can Be Settled in the settlement profile, set the deletion flag on the order, and then reselect To Be Settled in Full in the settlement profile.

Let's look at the next section of the settlement profile.

Default Values

This section contains default values for control structures that we'll discuss in more detail in following sections.

Indicators

This section contains checkboxes that control the amount to be settled:

▶ **100 %-validation**
This checkbox controls whether the system checks percentages in the settlement rule. A settlement rule determines which portions of a sender's costs are allocated to which receivers. A settlement rule is contained in a manufacturing order or product cost collector header data.

If you have defined percentage distribution rules for a particular settlement rule, the system checks the total percentage either when you save the settlement rule or if you use the percentage check function.

▶ If the checkbox is set, the system issues a warning if the total is less or more than 100 %.

▶ If the checkbox is not set, the system issues a warning if the total is more than 100 %.

In both cases, you can ignore the warning and save the settlement rule. However, to be able to run the settlement, you must first correct the settlement rule. The settlement run itself prevents you from settling more than 100 %.

▶ **%-Settlement**
If you set this checkbox, you can use the settlement rule to determine the distribution rules governing the percentage costs to be settled.

▶ **Equivalence numbers**
If you set this checkbox, you can define distribution rules in the settlement rule, according to which costs are settled proportionally.

▶ **Amount settlement**
If you set this checkbox, you can define distribution rules in the settlement rule, which allow costs to be settled by amount. For example, you can settle a specific amount such as $5000 of the costs incurred on an order to cost center 4711.

▶ **Variances to Costing-Based PA**
If you set this checkbox, variances are sent to costing-based Profitability Analysis (CO-PA) during order settlement.

Tip
If you need to set the deletion flag on an order with unsettled variances, you will receive an error message until you either: ▶ Settle the variances to Profitability Analysis if possible. This can be difficult if there are problems with the order or if it hasn't been settled for many periods. ▶ Deselect the Variances to Costing-Based PA checkbox in the settlement profile, set the deletion checkbox on the order, and then reset the checkbox in the settlement profile.

Now let's look at the Valid Receivers section of the selection profile.

Valid Receivers

In this section of the settlement profile, you choose whether settlement to certain types of receivers is optional, required, or not allowed.

> **Example**
>
> In Figure 18.3 we have allowed production orders to optionally settle to a G/L account, an order, or a WBS element (project system). We do not want settlement to occur to any other object type, so they are set to Settlement Not Allowed.

Now let's examine the Other Parameters section of the settlement profile.

Other Parameters

In this section you maintain the following fields:

- **Document type**
  You can assign individual document types for each settlement rule to assist in identifying settlement documents separately. You create and maintain document types with customizing Transaction OBA7.
- **Maximum number of distribution rules**
  This determines the maximum number of distribution rules possible for each settlement rule.
- **Residence time**
  This determines the minimum amount of time necessary between setting the order deletion flag (revocable) and deletion indicator (not revocable).

Now that we've examined settlement profiles, let's look at the next settlement configuration transaction, the allocation structure.

18.1.2   Create Allocation Structure

An allocation structure allocates the costs incurred on a sender by cost element or cost element group. The allocation structure is used for settlement and for assessment. Each allocation structure contains a number of assignments of cost element or cost element group to a settlement or assessment cost element.

Each allocation structure must fulfill the following criteria:

▶ **Completeness**
An allocation structure is assigned to each order to be settled. All cost elements that incur costs (source cost elements) must be represented in the allocation structure.

▶ **Uniqueness**
Each cost element that incurs costs can only appear once in an allocation structure. Only one settlement cost element can be assigned to a source within a particular allocation structure.

You create an allocation structure with Transaction OKO6 or by following the IMG menu path CONTROLLING • PRODUCT COST CONTROLLING • COST OBJECT CONTROLLING • PRODUCT COST BY PERIOD • PERIOD-END CLOSING • SETTLEMENT • CREATE ALLOCATION STRUCTURE. The screen shown in Figure 18.4 is displayed.

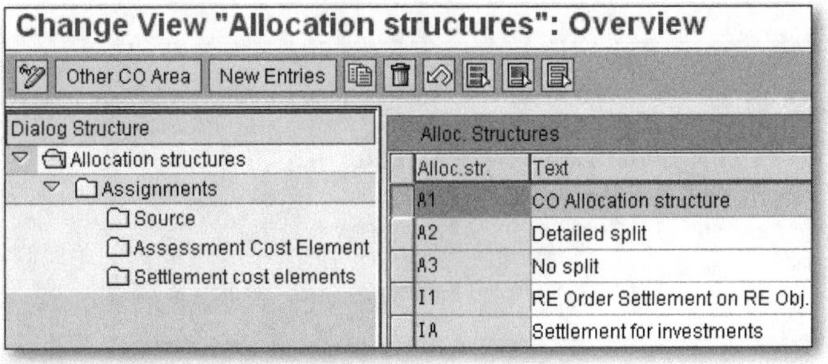

Figure 18.4 Allocation Structures Overview Screen

Available allocation structures are listed on the right side of this overview screen. You can use any allocation structure or copy one and create your own. Let's choose allocation structure A1 as shown in Figure 18.4 and examine its components.

Select allocation structure A1 and double-click Assignments to display the screen shown in Figure 18.5.

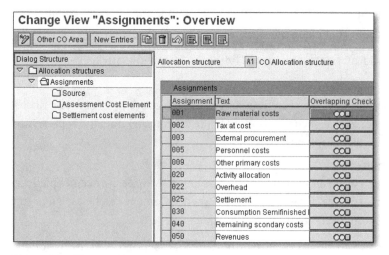

Figure 18.5 Allocation Structure Assignments Overview Screen

Available allocation structure assignments are listed on the right side of the Overview screen. Select an assignment and double-click Source to show the screen displayed in Figure 18.6.

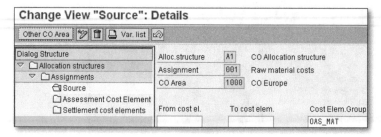

Figure 18.6 Source Cost Element Details

Three methods are available to assign source cost elements:

▶ A single cost element

▶ A range of cost elements

▶ A cost element group

Double-click the cost element group (Cost Elem.Group) OAS_MAT shown in Figure 18.6 to display the details as shown in Figure 18.7.

The cost elements included in the cost element group are displayed.

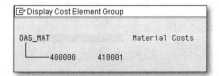

Figure 18.7 Display Cost Element Group

> **Tip**
>
> If a new source cost element is introduced, for example, to identify a new external processing cost, you must ensure that the source cost element is included in the allocation structure, or an error message will occur when you run the settlement transaction.
>
> The easiest way to include new source cost elements in an allocation structure is to assign a cost element group, even if the group includes only one cost element. A cost element group is master data that you can maintain with Transaction KAH2 or by following the menu path ACCOUNTING • CONTROLLING • COST CENTER ACCOUNTING • MASTER DATA • COST ELEMENT GROUP • CHANGE.
>
> If you do not assign a cost element group, you may need to add the new cost element as a configuration change in the allocation structure, which generally takes more documentation, procedures, and time than to carry out a simple master data change to a cost element group.

Double-click Assessment Cost Element in Figure 18.6 to display the screen shown in Figure 18.8.

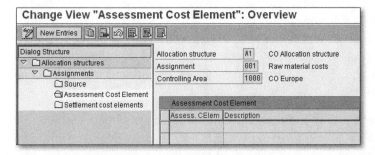

Figure 18.8 Assessment Cost Element Overview

Allocation structures can be used for both assessments and settlements.

▶ Assessments allocate costs between cost centers.

▶ Settlements allocate costs from orders to other objects.

You generally set up allocation structures for either assessments or settlements. In this case, because we are configuring a settlement, there is no need to enter assessment cost elements.

Double-click Settlement cost elements in Figure 18.8 to display the screen shown in Figure 18.9.

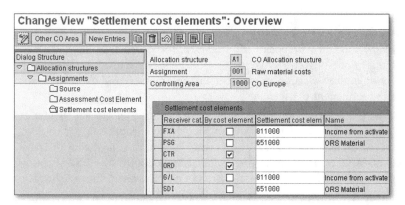

Figure 18.9 Settlement Cost Elements Overview

Let's examine the Settlement cost elements section of this settlement profile, beginning with the first column.

Account Assignment Category

When assigning settlement cost elements, the first field you maintain is Receiver cat. (account assignment category), which specifies the object types allowable for the settlement receiver. Click and then right-click a category and select Possible Entries to display the screen shown in Figure 18.10.

This screen lists all possible entries for account assignment category. By entering the account assignment category in the settlement rule, you specify how the entry is interpreted in the general receiver field.

> **Example**
>
> If you enter CTR as the account assignment category and 1000 as the receiver, the system will settle to cost center 1000. If, however, you enter ORD and 1000, the order with number 1000 is the settlement receiver.

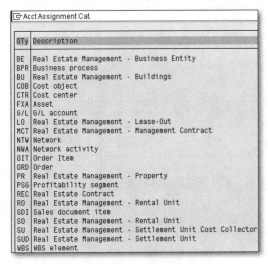

Figure 18.10 Account Assignment Categories Possible Entries

The F4 help in the general receiver field is influenced by the account assignment category. If, for example, you enter CTR as the account assignment category, the system will offer you F4 help for the selection of cost centers.

Example

Display a production order with Transaction CO02 and select HEADER • SETTLEMENT RULE from the menu bar. Enter CTR in the first available account assignment rule field. Then click the Settlement Receiver field and press the F4 key to display the screen shown in Figure 18.11.

The list of possible entries is restricted to cost center because the category (Cat.) entered is CTR (cost center).

Let's now examine the next column in the Settlement cost elements section of the settlement profile shown in Figure 18.9.

By Cost Element

If you select the By cost element checkbox in Figure 18.9, the settlement cost element will be the same as the source or debit cost element. You only select this checkbox if you need the original debit cost element appear on the settlement object such as a cost center.

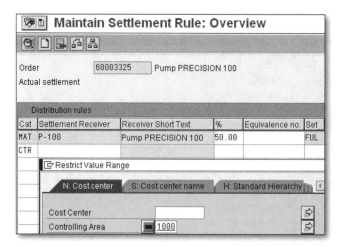

Figure 18.11 Settlement Rule Receiver Possible Entries by Category

This is not normally necessary. You typically group source cost elements to settle with one settlement cost element. If you require more details of the source costs when viewing the object settled to, you simply double-click the settlement cost element to take you directly to the sender details.

If you select this checkbox, you cannot enter a settlement cost element in the next field because the settlement cost element has already been defined as the source cost element.

Settlement Cost Element

The settlement cost element credits the sender and debits the receiver during settlement. Settlement cost elements are secondary cost elements of category 22. If you press the F4 key in this field, you will see a list of secondary cost elements of category 22.

Name

The text in this field is the name of the settlement cost element that transfers automatically from the cost element master data.

Now that we've examined allocation structures, let's look at the next settlement configuration transaction, the source structure.

18.1.3 Create Source Structure

You define source structures when settling and costing joint products. Joint production involves the simultaneous production of many materials in a single production process. A source structure contains several source assignments, each of which contains the individual cost elements or cost element intervals to be settled using the same distribution rules.

In the settlement rule for the sender, you can define one distribution rule, in which you specify the distribution and receivers for the costs for each source assignment.

> **Note**
>
> Check whether you need to use source structures in your settlement procedures. If you are settling to cost elements, you do not need a source structure. Otherwise, create a source structure with the following procedure.

Create a source structure with Transaction OKEU or by following the IMG menu path CONTROLLING • PRODUCT COST CONTROLLING • COST OBJECT CONTROLLING • PRODUCT COST BY PERIOD • PERIOD-END CLOSING • SETTLEMENT • CREATE SOURCE STRUCTURE. The screen shown in Figure 18.12 is displayed.

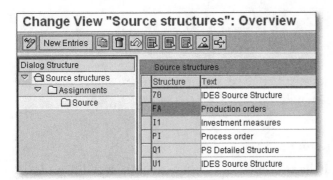

Figure 18.12 Source Structures Overview Screen

Available source structures are listed on the right side of this overview screen. You can use any available source structure or copy one and create your own. Let's choose source structure FA, shown in Figure 18.12, and examine its components.

Select source structure FA and double-click Assignments to display the screen shown in Figure 18.13.

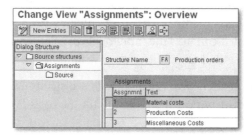

Figure 18.13 Source Structure Assignments Overview

Available source structure assignments are listed on the right side of the overview screen. Select an assignment and double-click Source to show the screen displayed in Figure 18.14.

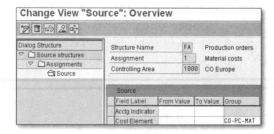

Figure 18.14 Source Structure Sources

You enter the source structure source in this screen. Let's examine the rows in this screen in detail.

Accounting Indicator

The accounting indicator serves as another criterion in addition to cost element, discussed in the next section. Incurred costs and earned profits can, for example, be identified by sales volume, warranty, or good will.

Cost Element

You can enter an individual cost element, range, or group. You maintain cost element groups with Transaction KAH2.

Example

An order has incurred both direct and overhead costs. The direct costs are to be divided 50 % each between a fixed asset and a cost center, whereas the overhead is to be settled in full to an administration cost center. To do this, you create a source structure with two source assignments:

▸ Direct cost elements

▸ Overhead cost elements

Now that we've examined settlement profiles, allocation structures, and source structures, let's look at the final settlement configuration transaction, the PA transfer structure.

18.1.4 Create PA Transfer Structure

Settlement lets you transfer costs, revenues, sales deductions, and production variances to costing-based Profitability Analysis (CO-PA). The PA transfer structure defines which quantities or values of a sender are to be transferred and which value fields in CO-PA are part of settlement. You use value fields to report on CO-PA values.

Example

For a marketing order, you can assign the cost element group Personnel costs to value field VTRGK (sales overhead).

CO-PA enables you to evaluate market segments, which can be classified according to products, customers, orders, or any combination of these, or strategic business units, such as sales organizations or business areas, with respect to your company's profit or contribution margin.

You create a PA transfer structure with Transaction KEI1 or by following IMG menu path CONTROLLING • PRODUCT COST CONTROLLING • COST OBJECT CONTROLLING • PRODUCT COST BY PERIOD • PERIOD-END CLOSING • SETTLEMENT • CREATE PA TRANSFER STRUCTURE. The screen shown in Figure 18.15 is displayed.

Available PA transfer structures are listed on the right side of this overview screen. You can use any PA transfer structure or copy one and create your own. Let's choose PA transfer structure E1, shown in Figure 18.15, and examine its components.

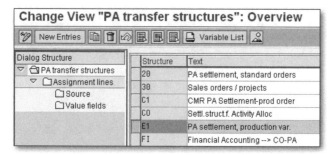

Figure 18.15 PA Transfer Structures Overview

Select PA transfer structure E1 and double-click Assignment lines to display the screen shown in Figure 18.16.

Change View "Assignment lines": Overview

Assgnmnt	Text	Qty billed/delivered	Source assigned	Value field a
10	Scrap	☐	☑	☑
20	Price variance	☐	☑	☑
25	Mixed-price variance	☐	☐	☑
30	Quantity variances material	☐	☑	☑
35	Quantity variances productio	☐	☑	☑
40	Resource usage variance	☐	☑	☑

Figure 18.16 PA Transfer Structure Assignment Lines Overview

The PA transfer structure allows you to define the level of detail of production variances you require to be transferred to CO-PA. You can transfer all production variance categories to separate value fields or just one value field for reporting in CO-PA, depending on the level of detail you require in variance reporting in CO-PA.

Select an assignment and double-click Source to show the screen displayed in Figure 18.17.

Let's examine the fields of this source details screen.

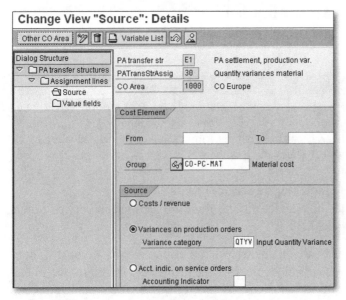

Figure 18.17 Assignment Lines Source Details

Cost Element

In these fields you can enter an individual source cost element, range, or group. Click the glasses icon to display cost elements in a cost element group if required.

> **Note**
>
> It is easier to maintain a cost element group than individual cost elements or ranges entered in this screen. This is because a cost element group is master data, which is relatively easy to maintain. Maintaining values directly in Figure 18.17 requires a configuration change, which generally takes more documentation and testing than master data changes.

Source

In this section you define the source information transferred to CO-PA depending on your selection:

▶ **Costs/revenue**
Costs posted to the cost elements listed in the Cost Element section will transfer to a value field.

▶ **Variances on production orders**
This allows you transfer production variances by variance category to individual value fields.

> **Note**
>
> You can differentiate between material and labor input quantity variance by transferring material and labor cost elements to different value fields. This is one of the only ways you can differentiate between material and labor input quantity variance in standard reporting.

▶ **Accounting indicator on service orders**
Costs posted to the accounting indicator defined in service orders post to a value field.

To maintain the value fields to which the source costs are posted, double-click Value fields in Figure 18.17 to display the screen shown in Figure 18.18.

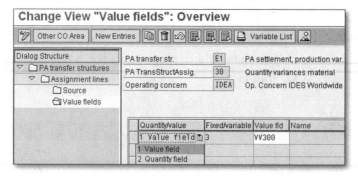

Figure 18.18 Assignment Lines Value Fields

This screen allows you to maintain details of the CO-PA fields to which the source information is transferred.

Quantity/value

Click this field to see the two possible entries as shown in Figure 18.18. You have the following choices:

▶ **Value field**
You transfer monetary amounts to this field.

▶ **Quantity field**

You transfer quantity amounts to this field.

Now let's look at the next value field column.

Fixed/variable

This field allows you to enter the following three options depending on the level of detail you require to transfer to individual value field in CO-PA:

1. Fixed amounts

2. Variable amounts

3. Sum of fixed and variable amounts

Now let's look at the next value field column.

Value Field

In this field you enter the value field that is to receive the amount or quantity from the source. You can display a list of available value fields by clicking the field and pressing the F4 key, as shown in Figure 18.19.

Field Name	Description
VV010	Revenue
VV020	Quantity discount
VV030	Customer discount
VV040	Material discount
VV060	Other rebates
VV070	Cash discount
VV090	Accrued bonus
VV100	Outgoing freight
VV110	Accrued freight
VV120	Dispatch packaging
VV130	Internal sales Comm.
VV140	Cost of goods sold
VV150	Material Input

Figure 18.19 Value Field Possible Entries

Standard value fields are available, or you can freely define your own. Value fields you manually create typically have a VVxxx format. You can maintain value fields with Transaction KEA6 or by following the IMG menu path Controlling • Profitability Analysis • Structures • Define Operating Concern • Maintain Value Fields.

Now that we've finished examining settlement configuration settings, let's look at the period-end process.

18.2 Settlement Period-End

You run period-end settlement with Transactions KK87 (individual) and CO88 (collective) or by following the menu path Accounting • Controlling • Product Cost Controlling • Cost Object Controlling • Product Cost by Period • Period-End Closing • Single Functions: Product Cost Collector • Settlement. A selection screen is displayed, as shown in Figure 18.20.

> **Note**
>
> Carry out settlement for production and process orders with transactions KO88 (individual) and CO88 (collective).

Actual Settlement: Production/Process Orders

Plant   8821   Hamburg
☐ With Production Orders
☐ With Process Orders
☑ With Product Cost Collectors
☐ With QM Orders

☐ With Orders for Projects/Networks
☐ With Orders for Cost Objects

Parameters
Settlement period   6   Posting period   ____
Fiscal Year   2007
Processing type   1 Automatic

Processing Options
☐ Background Processing
☐ Test Run
☑ Detail List   [Layouts]
☑ Check trans. data

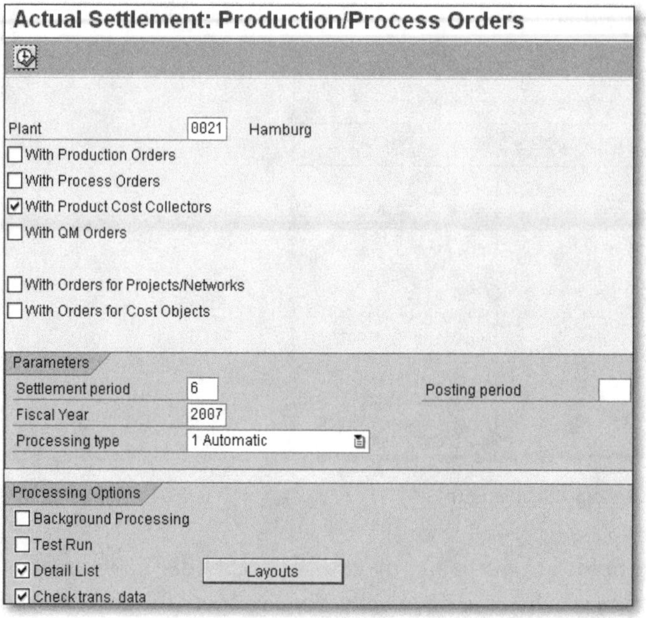

Figure 18.20 Actual Settlement Selection Screen

In this example, we'll carry out settlement only for product cost collectors by selecting the With Product Cost Collectors checkbox. You can include other objects in the settlement, without running another transaction, by selecting the relevant checkbox.

Product Cost by Period requires each period to be settled sequentially, which can lead to difficulties if a prior period needs to be reversed. By using the Posting period field shown to the right in Figure 18.20, you can make reversals, corrections, and resettlements in prior periods by posting to the present or previous period.

If you select the Detail List checkbox, a detail list becomes available for analysis following settlement (as shown later, in Figure 18.22). If you do not select the checkbox, only the basic list is available following settlement, as shown in Figure 18.21. You can also analyze settlement postings by viewing and sorting the settlement G/L account line item report in financial accounting with transaction FBL3N.

If you select the Check trans. data checkbox, the system checks whether any transaction data was posted to the product cost collector or manufacturing order since the last settlement. If no transaction data was posted, sender processing is stopped. This improves processing time. Error messages that could have been issued during settlement are not issued. This improves message analysis by reducing the number of redundant messages.

Complete the selection screen using the settings shown in Figure 18.20 as an example and click the execute icon to display the screen shown in Figure 18.21.

This screen provides you with basic information on the parameters you entered in the previous selection screen, such as period and fiscal year. Click the detail lists (grid) icon to proceed to a detailed list of settlement values, as shown in Figure 18.22.

In Figure 18.22 the Value ObjCurr (value in object currency) column is sorted in descending order. This provides visibility of product cost collectors with the largest settlement amounts. You can reconcile the sum of values settled at the bottom of Figure 18.22 with the sum of the collective variance calculation discussed in Chapter 17. You can also reconcile Figure 18.22 with postings to settlement financial accounts, by sorting the settlement account line item report in financial accounting (Transaction FBL3N).

Actual Settlement: Production/Process (	
Selection	
Selection Parameters	Value
Plant	0021
With Production Orders	X
With Product Cost Collectors	X
With Process Orders	X
With QM Orders	X
Period	006
Posting period	006
Fiscal Year	2007
Processing type	1
Posting Date	09/30/2006

Processing category	Ʃ	Number
Settlement executed		401
No change		643
Not relevant		
Inappropriate status		1
Error		
	▪	1045

Figure 18.21 Actual Settlement Basic Screen

Senders	Ʃ	Value ObjCurr	ObCur
ORD 794932		7,948.67-	USD
ORD 799681		9,340.19-	USD
ORD 799017		10,336.32-	USD
ORD 796989		21,502.64-	USD
ORD 787034		22,918.86-	USD
ORD 786865		39,884.74-	USD
ORD 795323		39,898.28-	USD
ORD 787033		56,253.42-	USD
	▪	139,100.12-	USD

Figure 18.22 Actual Settlement Detail List

Settlement is the last step in period-end closing for product cost collectors and manufacturing orders. Let's review what we've covered in this chapter.

18.3   Summary

In this chapter we examined the settlement configuration transactions including the settlement profile, which defaults from the order type and includes parameters, such as a requirement for the order to be settled in full before it can be deleted, and the default values for other settlement transactions. It also defines valid receivers such as G/L accounts and cost centers.

We also examined the allocation structure, which allocates the costs incurred on a sender by cost element or cost element group. An assignment assigns a cost element or cost element group to a settlement cost element.

We examined the source structure, which you define when settling and costing joint products. A source structure contains several source assignments, each of which contains the individual cost elements or cost element intervals to be settled using the same distribution rules.

We also looked at the PA transfer structure, which assigns source costs to value fields in CO-PA.

Finally, we looked at the settlement period-end processing step. In Chapter 19 we'll look at special processes.

Special topics cover specialized areas within Product Cost Controlling.

19   Special Topics

Product Cost Controlling covers a range of topics that are continuously being developed and improved. Whereas previous chapters covered the foundation subject areas of integrated planning, master data, configuration, cost estimates, and period-end processing, there are too many other specialized and varied topics to cover in detail in one book.

This chapter covers some additional topics that may be useful in some more specialized areas that fall under the umbrella of Product Cost Controlling.

19.1   Sales Order Controlling

Sales order costing scenarios involve customer orders that require components to be procured or assemblies to be manufactured specifically for individual customers or orders. This sometimes involves configurable materials, where the customer can choose between component or assembly options when placing an order. Because the customer sales order involves special requirements, costing of sales orders needs to be treated on an individual basis.

There are three possible options for costing sales order scenarios:

- Sales orders without Controlling and valuated inventory
- Sales orders with Controlling and valuated inventory
- Sales orders with Controlling and nonvaluated inventory

Let's first look at the configuration required for these sales order costing scenarios, and then examine postings and period-end processing requirements.

19.1.1 Configuration

The first indication that sales order controlling is involved in a process is the requirements type, which is displayed in the procurement tab of a sales order line item. You can display a sales order with Transaction VA03 or by following the menu path LOGISTICS • SALES AND DISTRIBUTION • SALES • ORDER • DISPLAY. Click the Procurement tab to display the screen shown in Figure 19.1.

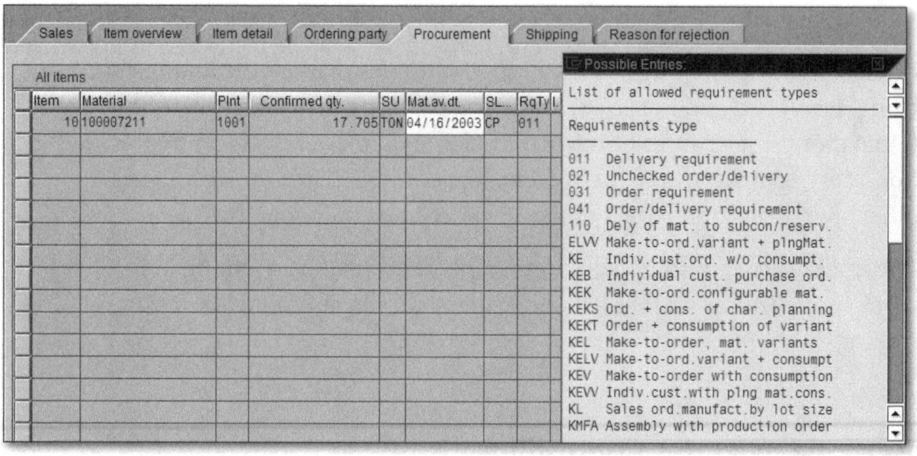

Figure 19.1 Sales Order Requirements Types Possible Entries

Click the RqTy (requirements type) field, and then right-click and select Possible Entries to display a list of available requirements types similar to the one shown in Figure 19.1. Requirements type KEK is typically used in a make-to-order environment with configurable materials. This is just one of many requirements types that can be used, depending on the planning strategy determined by the production department.

You configure the requirements type with Transaction OVZH or by following the IMG menu path CONTROLLING • PRODUCT COST CONTROLLING • COST OBJECT CONTROLLING • PRODUCT COST BY SALES ORDER • CONTROL OF SALES-ORDER-RELATED PRODUCTION/PRODUCT COST BY SALES ORDER • CHECK REQUIREMENTS TYPES. The screen shown in Figure 19.2 is displayed.

This screen shows a mapping of requirements type to requirements class (ReqCl). In this example requirements type KEK is mapped to requirements class 046. You can view the configuration settings for a requirements class with Transaction OVZG or by following the IMG menu path Controlling • Product Cost Controlling • Cost Object Controlling • Product Cost by Sales Order • Control of Sales-Order-Related Production/Product Cost by Sales Order • Check Requirements Classes. Double-click requirements class 046 to display the screen shown in Figure 19.3.

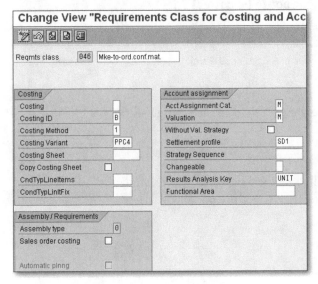

Change View "Requirement Types": Overview

RqTy	Requirements type	ReqCl	Description
011	Delivery requirement	011	Delivery requirement
021	Unchecked order/delivery	021	Unchecked order/dlv
031	Order requirement	031	Order requirements
041	Order/delivery requirement	041	Order/delivery reqmt
110	Dely of mat. to subcon/reserv.	110	Delivery w/o MRP
BSF	Gross planned indep. reqmts	102	Gross reqmts pinning
ELVV	Make-to-ord.variant + plngMat.	061	Mk->O. MatVar.PlgMat
KE	Indiv.cust.ord. w/o consumpt.	040	MkToOrdNoValW/o cons
KEB	Individual cust. purchase ord.	KEB	Cust.- individual PO
KEK	Make-to-ord.configurable mat.	046	MMTO config. value.
KEKS	Ord. + cons. of char. planning	043	Mke-ord.cons.charPlg
KEKT	Order + consumption of variant	042	Mke-ord.cons plgVar.
KEL	Make-to-order, mat. variants	047	MkToOrd.-mat.variant

Figure 19.2 Mapping of Requirements Type to Requirements Class

Change View "Requirements Class for Costing and Acc

Reqmts class 046 Mke-to-ord.conf.mat.

Costing
Costing	
Costing ID	B
Costing Method	1
Costing Variant	PPC4
Costing Sheet	
Copy Costing Sheet	☐
CndTypLineItems	
CondTypLinItFix	

Account assignment
Acct Assignment Cat.	M
Valuation	M
Without Val. Strategy	☐
Settlement profile	SD1
Strategy Sequence	
Changeable	
Results Analysis Key	UNIT
Functional Area	

Assembly / Requirements
Assembly type	0
Sales order costing	☐
Automatic plnng	☐

Figure 19.3 Requirements Class Configuration

461

The checkboxes and fields in this screen determine the sales order costing and inventory valuation scenario. Let's examine each relevant field and indicator.

Costing

This field determines if a sales order cost estimate is to be created. Listed below are the possible entries:

- **X (sales document item to be costed)**
  You must create a sales order cost estimate. Subsequent functions such as delivery and billing are only allowed when costing has been carried out with no errors.

- **A (costing to be simulated)**
  Costing of the sales document item is only simulated. The simulation is not saved in the system. The status is not updated. Subsequent functions such as delivery and billing can be carried out at any time.

- **Blank (costing allowed but not necessary)**
  If you do cost the sales document item, then subsequent functions such as delivery and billing are only allowed if there were no errors during costing.

- **B (sales document not to be costed)**

> **Note**
>
> To create a sales order line item cost estimate select EXTRAS • COSTING when displaying a sales order.

Now let's examine the next field in the Costing section.

Costing ID

This field determines if the sales order cost estimate is to be created automatically. Listed below are the possible entries:

► **A**

Cost estimate is to be created automatically when saving a sales order.

► **B**

Cost estimate is to be created automatically and marked when saving a sales order. This is particularly useful if you want the marked sales order to evaluate sales order stock.

► **Blank**

Cost estimate is to be created manually for a sales order line item.

Now let's look at the next field in the Costing section.

Costing Method

This checkbox controls whether the items in the sales document are costed automatically in product costing or manually in unit costing. Refer to Chapter 12 for more information on unit costing.

Costing Variant

The costing variant determines how the sales order cost estimate determines prices. You can maintain costing variants for sales orders with Transaction OKY9 or by following the IMG menu path CONTROLLING • PRODUCT COST CONTROLLING • COST OBJECT CONTROLLING • PRODUCT COST BY SALES ORDER • PRELIMINARY COSTING AND ORDER BOM COSTING • PRODUCT COSTING FOR SALES ORDER ITEMS/ORDER BOMS • COSTING VARIANTS FOR PRODUCT COSTING • CHECK COSTING VARIANTS FOR PRODUCT COSTING. Refer to Chapter 8 for more information on costing variants.

Costing Sheet

The costing sheet determines the calculation of overhead. The costing sheet in the valuation variant defaults to the sales order line item. Refer to Chapter 6 for more information on costing sheets.

Copy Costing Sheet

This checkbox determines if the costing sheet is copied to production orders generated by the sales order line item requirements.

Condition Type for Copying Costs from Line Items

If you enter the condition type into the requirements class, this condition type is used for all sales and distribution document items containing a requirements type, which contains this requirements class.

The condition type indicates, for example, whether during pricing the system applies a price, a discount, a surcharge, or other pricing elements, such as freight costs and sales taxes.

Two standard condition types are available for the cost transfer of line items:

▶ **EK01**
The result of the sales order costing is first printed to the pricing screen for the item. The value can be used as the basis for price calculation.

▶ **EK02**
The result of the sales order costing is simply a statistical value, which you can compare with the price.

Condition Type for Fixed Cost Transfer from Line Items

The fixed cost part is determined statistically. The transfer of the fixed cost part makes it easier for the system to predict the profit margin. Standard condition type EK03 is provided for transfer of the fixed cost part.

The condition type for determining the fixed cost part is maintained with the condition type for the cost transfer of line items in the previous field.

Assembly Type

In assembly processing a manufacturing order is generated together with the sales order. There are two methods of assembly processing:

▶ **Static**
A single manufacturing or planned order is generated for a sales order line item.

▸ **Dynamic**

  Multiple manufacturing or planned orders are generated for a sales order line item.

Two static (1 and 2) and two dynamic (3 and 4) processing options are available. If you choose a static option, you can use the preliminary cost estimate of the manufacturing order for setting the standard price of the sales order line item.

Sales Order Costing

You select this checkbox to generate a sales order cost estimate for setting the standard price of the sales order line item. You can only select this indicator if you select option 2 for the previous assembly type field.

> **Note**
>
> One of the considerations when deciding whether to use the preliminary cost estimate of the manufacturing order or a sales order cost estimate is the timing of changes to the sales order item and the manufacturing order. This depends on how long after the sales order is placed you allow the customer to make changes to the sales order item. It also depends on how long after the manufacturing order is created that production takes place.
>
> The standard price of the sales order stock is determined by the relevant cost estimate price at the time of first goods receipt of sales order stock into inventory.

Let's discuss the next checkbox in this section of the requirements class.

Automatic Planning

If you select this checkbox, the system automatically carries out single-item, multilevel planning for a sales order if a sales order item is either created or changed. This function can only be used for make-to-order production.

Now that we've finished discussing the assembly and requirements fields, let's look at the fields in the final section in the requirements class.

Account Assignment Category

This checkbox controls if costs are maintained on the sales order line item with sales order controlling as follows:

▶ **E**

Sales order controlling is active. Therefore, revenues and costs are maintained on the sales order line item, and there is an associated settlement process at period-end.

▶ **M**

Sales order controlling is not active. No costs are maintained on the sales order, and there is no associated settlement process. This is the setting you normally choose for sales order costing because it is the simplest, and no period-end process is involved.

> **Note**
>
> Two of the most commonly used account assignment categories for sales-order-related costing are listed above. You can maintain existing account assignment categories or create your own with Transaction OME9 or by following the IMG menu path CONTROLLING • PRODUCT COST CONTROLLING • COST OBJECT CONTROLLING • PRODUCT COST BY SALES ORDER • CONTROL OF SALES-ORDER-RELATED PRODUCTION/PRODUCT COST BY SALES ORDER • CHECK ACCOUNT ASSIGNMENT CATEGORIES.

Now let's look at the next field in the account assignment section.

Valuation

This field determines if sales order stock is managed on a valuated or non-valuated basis as follows:

▶ **Blank**

Sales order stock is not valuated. With this option you need to choose sales order controlling as active in the previous field. You also need to run period-end results analysis to determine revenue and cost of sales and then settle the values to general ledger (G/L) accounts or Profitability Analysis (CO-PA).

▶ **M**

Sales order stock is valuated, based on either the sales order line item cost estimate or the manufacturing order preliminary cost estimate at the time of first goods receipt into inventory. You can display valuated special stocks using report RM07MBWS.

▶ **A**
Sales order stock is valuated based on the standard price of the material, and the stock is managed together with anonymous warehouse stock.

> **Note**
>
> Valuated sales order stock is treated in a similar way to make-to-stock production. Account postings occur at the time of goods movements of the sales order inventory based on the standard price of the customer segment stock.
>
> Valuated sales order stock became available as of R/3 release 4.0. It is now usually the preferred method of dealing with sales order stock because it eliminates several period-end processing steps associated with non-valuated sales order stock.

Without Valuation Strategy

Set this checkbox to valuate the valuated sales order stock with the standard price of the non-allocated warehouse stock. This can be used, for example, if you are producing the same material as a non-allocated stock item as well as for sales order-related mass production.

Settlement Profile

A settlement profile contains the parameters necessary to create a settlement rule that determines which portions of a sender's costs are allocated to which receivers. You only need a settlement profile if you intend to settle the sales order line item.

Strategy Sequence

During automatic generation of a settlement rule, a settlement rule is created as specified by the strategies in the strategy sequence. You can prioritize the strategies in this sequence, and can also have more than one strategy with the same priority. Evaluation of more than one strategy with the same priority results in a settlement rule with more than one distribution rule.

Changeable

This setting determines the behavior of a settlement rule after a change to the master data. During generation of settlement rules, another settlement rule could already exist for an object. The checkbox determines how the system should continue if this is the case. It can differentiate between the following:

▶ Manually created or changed distribution rules

▶ Automatically generated distribution rules

Normally, the system does not modify manually created or changed rules.

If a rule was originally created by the system, but then you modified it manually, it qualifies as a manually changed rule.

Results Analysis Key

Refer to Chapter 16 for more information on results analysis

You normally enter a results analysis key for non-valuated inventory to determine the revenue and cost of sales values at period-end.

Functional Area

A functional area is required to create a profit and loss account in Financial Accounting using cost-of-sales accounting.

Now that we've considered configuration for sales order costing, let's look at period-end processing and posting.

19.1.2 Period-End Processing

There are three possible scenarios for sales order costing. Let's examine each in turn in the following sections.

Sales Orders Without Controlling with Valuated Inventory

Valuated sales order inventory has been available since R/3 version 4.0. This is the preferred scenario because it's the simplest. Cost of sales (COS) and revenue postings occur in real time because sales order stock is valuated. The sales order stock standard price is based on either the sales order line item cost estimate or the manufacturing order preliminary cost estimate, based on the sales order costing checkbox as discussed in Section 19.1.1. Period-end processing including work in process (WIP) and variance analysis is based on manufacturing orders and not the sales order, as discussed in Chapters 15 to 18.

This scenario is applicable if detailed margin analysis on each sales order, or deferred postings to costing-based CO-PA, are not required. If more detailed margin analysis of each sales order line item is required, you can consider using the scenario described in the next section.

Sales Orders with Controlling and with Valuated Inventory

This option may be useful if you need to closely monitor the profit margin for each sales order, for example, if you have high-value individual sales orders. It should also be considered if you need to defer billing until the customer has received and accepted the product, as determined in customer contracts.

In this scenario, postings to G/L financial accounts occur at the time of goods movement because the sales order inventory is valuated. Postings to costing-based CO-PA, however, occur during period-end settlement. This process has two advantages:

▶ Real-time postings to G/L financial accounts during goods movements and billing

▶ Detailed reporting analysis available per sales order line item in CO-PA

A disadvantage is that you are required to run two additional period-end processing steps of RA and settlement as described in the following scenario. Let's follow seven steps in an example scenario as shown in Figure 19.4.

Below is a description of each of the seven steps in this scenario:

1. The sales order cost estimate can be used as the basis for the standard price of the sales order stock when produced. For configurable products, customer choices (e.g., red or blue color for a car) are saved with the sales order.

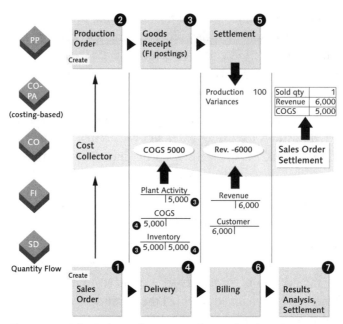

Figure 19.4 Sales Order Without Controlling with Valuated Inventory

Refer to Section 19.1.1 for more information on assembly processing

2. The production order preliminary cost estimate also can be used as the basis for the standard price of the finished good when produced. (Note that this is the only option when using assembly processing, i.e., when a production order is created automatically when the sales order is saved.)

3. Financial account postings are generated when finished goods are received into inventory. A finished goods inventory account is debited, a plant activity P/L account is credited, and postings to account-based CO-PA occur. The production order is credited with the quantity produced times the standard price determined by either the sales order or production order preliminary cost estimate. Once the first goods receipt occurs, the standard price is set and cannot be changed. There are no postings to the sales order at this stage.

4. A posting to a COS account is made when removing the sales order stock from inventory for delivery to the customer. The sales order is debited with the COS amount.

5. During production order settlement, the production variances are settled to costing-based CO-PA. Individual variance categories can be

settled to different value fields if required. It is standard practice to also settle the total production variance to two P/L accounts, such as a production variance and plant activity accounts.

6. Billing results in immediate postings to financial accounts, account-based CO-PA, and the sales order. If there are no postings to deferred accounts (described in the next step), billing is normally carried out on the same day as sales delivery in order to match COS and revenue postings.

7. Period-end RA and sales order settlement do not result in postings to financial accounts in this scenario, because all required postings to G/L accounts have already occurred during steps 4 and 6. If, however, billing occurs much later than sales delivery, RA can be used to ensure that COS and revenue post to CO-PA at the same time, at period-end. Though RA and sales order settlement are normally period-end processes, you have an option to run these as batch jobs once a week or even daily.

You can run period-end RA with Transactions KKA3 (individual) and KKAK (collective), and period-end settlement with Transaction VA88 or by following the menu path Accounting • Controlling • Product Cost Controlling • Cost Object Controlling • Product Cost by Sales Order • Period-End Closing • Single Functions.

Now that we've discussed and followed an example of sales order controlling with valuated inventory, let's examine the third and final possible sales order costing scenario.

Sales Orders with Controlling and Without Valuated Inventory

This was the only option available prior to R/3 Release 4.0. You can use it after Release 4.0 if non-valuated inventory is necessary, for example, if you need to track asset quantities in inventory. The asset already has its own balance sheet valuation, so valuated inventory would lead to double counting on the balance sheet. This scenario can occur if the company manufactures its own assets, which are then leased or loaned to customers. Let's follow the seven steps in the example scenario shown in Figure 19.5.

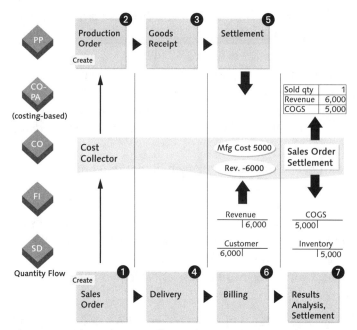

Figure 19.5 Sales Order Controlling with Non-Valuated Sales Order Stock

Below is an explanation of each of the seven steps that occur during this scenario:

1. The process starts with the creation of a sales order line item that acts as a cost collector in sales order controlling. For configurable products, customer choices (e.g., red or blue color for a car) are saved with the sales order.

2. The production order is either created automatically when the sales order is created (called assembly processing) or created manually later. The production order preliminary cost estimate is created from bill of materials (BOM) and routing information supplied by the sales order.

3. There are no accounting entries during finished goods receipt into inventory from the production order, because sales order stock is non-valuated.

4. There are also no accounting entries when the finished goods are removed from inventory and issued to the customer during sales order delivery.

5. During production order settlement, all production costs are transferred from the production order to the sales order. This is a movement of costs only within the controlling module. No Financial Accounting entries result from production order settlement in this scenario.

6. Billing results in immediate postings to financial accounts and account-based CO-PA. A revenue posting is also made to the sales order.

7. At period-end, the RA transaction determines sales order billing status. The financial G/L accounts for COS and WIP postings during the following settlement step are determined. If a sales order has a status of finally billed, the full production costs received from the production order are posted to a COS G/L account. A status of partially billed may result in a portion of the production costs posted to COS, and the remainder to WIP. There are many possible RA methods to determine the portions posted. Two of the most common are revenue-based results analysis and cost-based percentage of completion (POC).

Refer to Chapter 16 for more information on RA methods

> **Note**
>
> Detailed variance analysis is not possible with the sales order controlling and non-valuated inventory scenario because there is no standard price to compare with the actual costs of purchase or manufacture. All costs are posted to the sales order and compared with revenue to determine profitability.
>
> This is an advantage of using valuated sales order stock. You can carry out variance analysis on the cost of manufacturing the sales order stock because you can compare it with either the sales order cost estimate or the manufacturing order preliminary cost estimate.

Now that we've discussed sales order controlling, let's move onto the next special topic.

19.2 Subcontracting

The process of subcontracting involves sending components to an external vendor where the assembly is manufactured. The vendor then returns the completed assembly, and during goods receipt the components are issued from subcontract inventory.

Let's examine the main processes involved in subcontracting in the following sections.

19.2.1 MRP 2 View

Refer to Chapter 4 for more information on MRP views

The special procurement type field in the material master Material Requirements Planning (MRP) 2 view determines if a material is to be manufactured with a subcontracting process. You can view or change material master views with Transaction MM02 or by following the menu path LOGISTICS • PRODUCTION • MASTER DATA • MATERIAL MASTER • MATERIAL • CHANGE • IMMEDIATELY. Select the MRP 4 tab to display the screen shown in Figure 19.6.

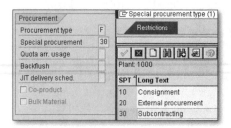

Figure 19.6 MRP 2 View Subcontracting Special Procurement Type

Right-click in the Special procurement field and select Possible Entries to display a list of special procurement types as shown in Figure 19.6. This tells MRP to create a purchase requisition or order to issue to the sub-contract vendor. The system first searches for a subcontract purchasing info record.

19.2.2 Purchase Order

You create a subcontract purchase order with Transaction ME21N or by following the menu path LOGISTICS • MATERIALS MANAGEMENT • PUR-CHASING • PURCHASE ORDER • CREATE. Enter the subcontract material purchasing information to display the screen shown in Figure 19.7.

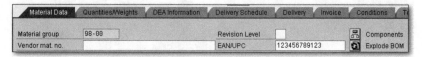

Itm	A	I	Material	Short Text	PO Quantity	O.	C	Deliv. Date	Net Price		Curr.	Per
10		L	8161	Product	10	KG	D	09/25/2008	100.00		USD	1

Figure 19.7 Subcontract Purchase Order Line Item

You indicate that this material is to be procured by subcontracting by entering item category L (third column) when creating the purchase order line item. When you press Enter after entering a subcontract item category, two new icons appear in the Material Data tab of the item details as shown in Figure 19.8.

| Material Data | Quantities/Weights | DEA Information | Delivery Schedule | Delivery | Invoice | Conditions | T |

Material group	98-00	Revision Level		Components
Vendor mat. no.		EAN/UPC	123456789123	Explode BOM

Figure 19.8 Components and Explode BOM in Material Data Tab

Click the Components icon to display the screen shown in Figure 19.9.

Processing Components: Collective Entry

| Component overview | Detailed entry |

Material	8161	Product		
Plant	1000	Release Date	09/24/2008	
Quantity	10.000	Delivery date	09/25/2008	

Component Overview

Material	Description	Requirement qty	U	Q	Plant	Pro
				☐		
				☐		
				☐		

Figure 19.9 Subcontract Components Entry Screen

In this screen you enter the subcontract components that are sent to the vendor for assembly into finished goods. You can also create a BOM for the subcontract components that can automatically populate this screen.

19.2.3 Monitoring Stocks Provided to Vendor

You can monitor stocks issued to a subcontract vendor with Transaction ME2O or by following the menu path LOGISTICS • MATERIALS MANAGEMENT • PURCHASING • PURCHASE ORDER • REPORTING • SC STOCKS PER VENDOR. The selection screen shown in Figure 19.10 is displayed.

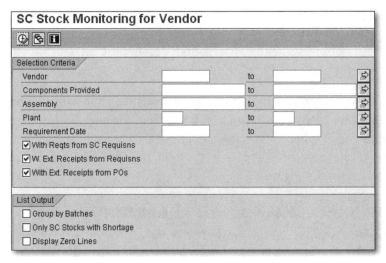

Figure 19.10 Subcontract Stock Monitoring for Vendor

Complete the fields you need information on and click the execute icon to display the screen shown in Figure 19.11.

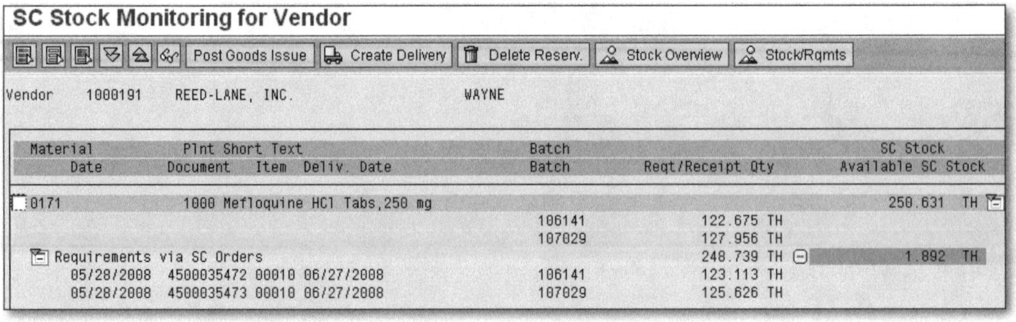

Figure 19.11 Subcontract Stock Monitoring for Vendor

From this screen you can determine the status of subcontract stock. The components that are provided to the subcontractor are managed as stock provided to vendor. You can carry out a transfer posting from unrestricted-use stock to the stock of material provided to vendor. Components in a subcontract order that are consumed can only be debited from the stock of the material provided to the particular vendor.

19.2.4 Goods Receipt of End Product

You post the goods receipt for the end product with reference to the subcontract order item. At goods receipt, a consumption posting for the components is also made from the stock of material provided to vendor. For each goods receipt item, the system copies the components with their quantities as goods issue items. If the vendor (subcontractor) consumed a greater or smaller quantity than was planned in the purchase order, you can adjust the component quantity at goods receipt.

> **Note**
>
> Here's the difference between subcontracting and external processing:
> - Subcontracting involves supplying components. The vendor does all the manufacturing, and the finished good is placed in inventory.
> - External processing involves single operations in a manufacturing order that are performed by an external vendor. Selecting a subcontracting indicator available in the external operation allows you to send components for assembly by the vendor during the external operation.
>
> Subcontracting involves only purchasing, whereas external processing involves both operations and purchasing.

Now that we've reviewed the subcontracting process, let's examine the material ledger.

19.3 Material Ledger

The material ledger has two basic functions:

- To carry material prices in multiple currencies and valuations
- Actual costing

Let's discuss each of these functions in detail.

19.3.1 Multiple Currencies or Valuations

Without the material ledger, inventory valuations are only carried in company code currency. The material ledger enables the system to carry inventory in two additional currencies or valuations. With the material

Refer to Chapter 4 for more information on the material ledger settings

ledger active, all goods movements are updated in up to three currencies or valuations. Currency amounts are translated into foreign currencies at historical exchange rates directly at the time of posting.

> **Note**
>
> If you use transfer prices when moving materials between internal legal entities, the material ledger allows you to view inventory valuations both including transfer pricing for legal reporting purposes and excluding transfer pricing for internal management and consolidated reporting requirements.

If you just want to use the material ledger to carry material inventory values in multiple currencies or valuations, you must activate the material ledger. In addition, you can choose transaction-based price determination (price determination checkbox in the material master record = 2). Refer to Chapter 4 for more information on the price determination checkbox in the material master Accounting 1 view.

You must be clear and fully test which currencies or valuations you need to use before activating the material ledger because you cannot change these settings later in a production system.

19.3.2 Actual Costing

Actual costing generates a material ledger document and valuates all goods movements within a period at the standard price (preliminary valuation). At the end of the period, an actual price is calculated for each material based on the actual costs of the period. This actual price is called the periodic unit price and can be used to revaluate the inventory for the period to be closed. In addition, you can use this actual price as the standard price for the next period.

Actual costing determines what portion of the variance is to be debited to the next-highest level using material consumption. The actual BOM enables variances to be rolled up over multiple production levels all the way to the finished product. Additionally, you can choose to have variances from cost centers and business processes taken into account.

If you want the system to calculate a periodic unit price for your materials based on the actual costs incurred in a period, you need to activate actual costing in addition to activating the material ledger. We'll discuss the configuration required to activate the material ledger in the next section.

In addition, you must choose single-level or multilevel price determination for your materials (price determination checkbox in material master record = 3). In this case, you must use price control standard price for all materials that you want to use in actual costing. Refer to Chapter 4 for more information on the price determination checkbox in the material master Accounting 1 view.

19.3.3 Configuration

Now let's consider the configuration steps required to set up the material ledger.

Activate Valuation Areas for Material Ledger

You activate the material ledger with Transaction OMX1 or by following the IMG menu path CONTROLLING • PRODUCT COST CONTROLLING • ACTUAL COSTING/MATERIAL LEDGER • ACTIVATE VALUATION AREAS FOR MATERIAL LEDGER. Double-click the Activate Material Ledger text to display the screen shown in Figure 19.12.

Change View "Activation of Material Ledger": Overview

Valuation Area	Company Code	ML Act.	Price Deter.	Price Det. Binding in Val Area
0001	0005	☐		☐
0005	0005	☐		☐
0006	0006	☐		
0007	0007	☐		
0008	0008	☐		
001	FAB1	☐		
0099	1000	☐		
1000	1000	☐		

Material Price Determination: Control

Price Det.	Short text
2	Transaction-Based
3	Single-/Multilevel

Figure 19.12 Activate Material Ledger

We'll now consider the available checkboxes:

▶ **Material ledger activated**
Select the ML Act. (material ledger active) checkbox to activate the

material ledger for a valuation area (plant) and company code combination.

▶ **Price determination**
Click the Price Deter. (price determination) field, and then right-click and select Possible Entries to display the list shown in Figure 19.12. This setting determines the proposed material price determination when creating a new material master. This entry is ignored at production startup. The system automatically sets the indicator to 2 in the material master for all materials present. Refer to Chapter 4 for more information on the price determination checkbox in the material master Accounting 1 view.

▶ **Price determination binding in valuation area**
Select this checkbox if you want to prevent the price determination for the materials in the valuation area from being changed. Do not select this checkbox if you want to enable the price determination for the materials in the valuation area to be changed upon creation of the material at a later time.

> **Note**
>
> If you use multiple valuation approaches, the material ledger must be active in all valuation areas within a company code.

Assign Currency Types to Material Ledger Type

You assign currency types to the material ledger type with Transaction OMX2 or by following the IMG menu path CONTROLLING • PRODUCT COST CONTROLLING • ACTUAL COSTING/MATERIAL LEDGER • ASSIGN CURRENCY TYPES TO MATERIAL LEDGER TYPE. The screen shown in Figure 19.13 is displayed.

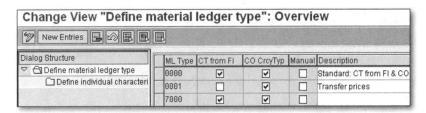

ML Type	CT from FI	CO CrcyTyp	Manual	Description
0000	☑	☑	☐	Standard: CT from FI & CO
0001	☐	☑	☐	Transfer prices
7000	☑	☑	☐	

Figure 19.13 Assign Currency Types to Material Ledger Type

This screen allows you to determine currency types either automatically or manually depending on the material ledger type (ML Type). The standard system contains the material ledger type 0000, which uses currency types from accounting. Let's consider each indicator in this screen.

If you select the CT from FI (use currency types from financial accounting) checkbox, the system uses the currency types that were defined in Financial Accounting customizing as additional local currencies for a company code. You set the additional local currencies in Financial Accounting with Transaction OB22 or by following the IMG menu path FINANCIAL ACCOUNTING • FINANCIAL ACCOUNTING GLOBAL SETTINGS • COMPANY CODE • PARALLEL CURRENCIES • DEFINE ADDITIONAL LOCAL CURRENCIES. The screen shown in Figure 19.14 is displayed.

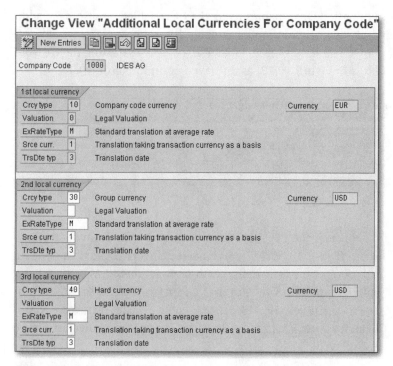

Figure 19.14 Define Additional Local Currencies for Company Code

It's mandatory to define at least one local currency in Financial Accounting as shown in the first local currency section of Figure 19.14. This local currency includes company code currency type and legal valuation. These fields are grayed out and cannot be changed.

If you define additional local currencies as shown in the second and third local currency sections of Figure 19.14, every Financial Accounting document will include the postings in the additional local currencies. You may need to add additional document layout columns to display the additional currencies in Financial Accounting documents.

> **Note**
>
> The material ledger does not have to be activated to define additional local currencies in Financial Accounting. The material ledger only refers to postings related to inventory transactions, whereas the settings in Figure 19.14 refer to all Financial Accounting postings.

Most multinational companies using the material ledger also have additional local currencies defined in Financial Accounting. You would normally copy these settings to the material ledger by selecting the CT from FI checkbox in Figure 19.13, as displayed again in Figure 19.15.

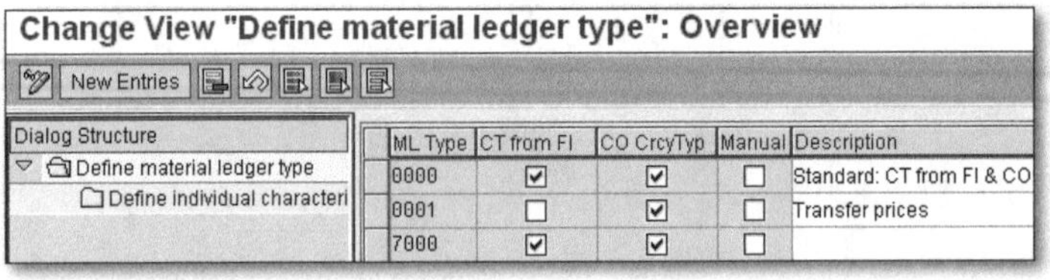

Figure 19.15 Assign Currency Types to Material Ledger Type

Now let's consider the CO CrcyTyp (use currency type from controlling) checkbox in Figure 19.15. When you select this checkbox, the system uses the currency types you define with Transaction 8KEM or by following the IMG menu path CONTROLLING • GENERAL CONTROLLING • MULTIPLE VALUATION APPROACHES/TRANSFER PRICES • BASIC SETTINGS • MAINTAIN CURRENCY AND VALUATION PROFILE. The screen shown in Figure 19.16 is displayed.

A list of available currency and valuation profiles (C+V Prof.) is displayed in this overview screen. To maintain the details of a profile, select one and double-click Details. The screen shown in Figure 19.17 is displayed.

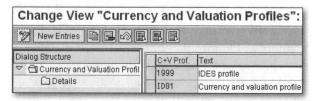

Figure 19.16 Maintain Currency and Valuation Profile Overview

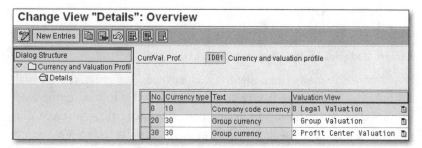

Figure 19.17 Maintain Currency and Valuation Profile Details

In this screen you can define additional currency types for all documents that post within the Controlling component. You only need currency and valuation profiles if you want to manage various valuations in parallel in your system. You would normally set up additional currency types in Controlling equivalent to your additional currency types in Financial Accounting.

After you've created a currency and valuation profile, you assign it to a controlling area with Transaction 8KEQ or by following the IMG menu path CONTROLLING • GENERAL CONTROLLING • MULTIPLE VALUATION APPROACHES/TRANSFER PRICES • BASIC SETTINGS • ASSIGN CURRENCY AND VALUATION PROFILE TO CONTROLLING AREA.

> **Note**
>
> You can also assign a currency and valuation profile directly to a controlling area with Transaction OKKP.
>
> You can check the currency and valuation profile in a controlling area when you maintain versions with Transaction OKEQ. Select a version, double-click controlling area settings, and click the valuation button.

Referring back to Figure 19.15, you would normally select the checkbox to use the currency type from the currency and valuation profile. If you set up Financial Accounting and Controlling additional currency types to be the same, and select the two copy checkboxes in Figure 19.15, you'll be able to make useful comparisons between Financial Accounting, Controlling, and the material ledger postings.

Now let's move onto the next material ledger configuration setting in the following section.

Assign Material Ledger Types to Valuation Area

Now that we've maintained material ledger types, we assign these to valuation areas (plants) with Transaction OMX3 or by following the IMG menu path CONTROLLING • PRODUCT COST CONTROLLING • ACTUAL COSTING/MATERIAL LEDGER • ASSIGN MATERIAL LEDGER TYPES TO VALUATION AREA. The screen shown in Figure 19.18 is displayed.

Change View "Assignment of Material Ledger

Valuation area	Mat. ledger type	
6000	0000	
6100	0000	
7000	0000	

Figure 19.18 Assignment of Material Ledger Types to Valuation Area

This screen shows a typical example of assigning the system supplied standard material ledger type (Mat. Ledger type) 0000. This setting ensures that Financial Accounting and Controlling currency types are copied to the material ledger settings for a plant.

We've now discussed the main configuration transactions required to use the material ledger for multiple valuation approaches. Let's now discuss the additional configuration required for actual costing.

Activate Actual Costing

You activate the material ledger actual costing by following the IMG menu path CONTROLLING • PRODUCT COST CONTROLLING • ACTUAL COST-

ING/MATERIAL LEDGER • ACTUAL COSTING • ACTIVATE ACTUAL COSTING. The screen shown in Figure 19.19 is displayed.

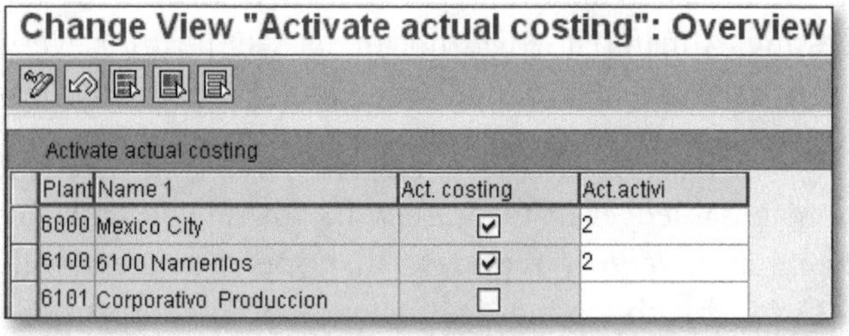

Change View "Activate actual costing": Overview

Plant	Name 1	Act. costing	Act.activi
6000	Mexico City	☑	2
6100	6100 Namenlos	☑	2
6101	Corporativo Produccion	☐	

Figure 19.19 Activate Actual Costing

You activate actual costing in a plant by selecting the Act. costing (actual costing) checkbox.

The Act.activi (update of activity consumption in the quantity structure) field is for updating the consumption of activities and processes in the actual quantity structure. Three settings are available:

▶ **0**

Update is not active.

▶ **1**

Update is active but not relevant to price determination. Consumption is updated in the quantity structure but not taken into account upon price determination.

▶ **2**

Update is active and relevant to price determination. Variances between the activity prices and process prices posted during the period and the actual price at the end of the period are adjusted subsequently.

Now that we've discussed the main configuration settings for the material ledger, let's discuss the final material ledger topic in this chapter.

19.3.4 Period-End Processing

There are three main period-end possibilities if you've activated the material ledger, which we'll discuss in the following sections.

485

No Period-End Processing

If you've activated the material ledger with only one currency type, and you're not using the actual costing functionality, there is no need for period-end processing. A material ledger document will post for every inventory-related transaction in the legal valuation approach in company code currency.

Activation of the material ledger in this case will provide you with the advantage of additional inventory reporting that you can access with Transaction CKM3 or by following the menu path ACCOUNTING • CONTROLLING • PRODUCT COST CONTROLLING • ACTUAL COST/MATERIAL LEDGER • MATERIAL LEDGER • MATERIAL PRICE ANALYSIS. The screen shown in Figure 19.20 is displayed.

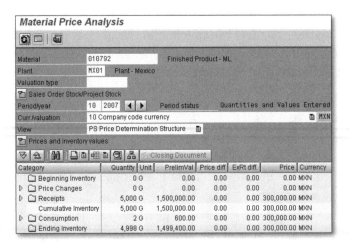

Figure 19.20 Material Price Analysis Screen

This screen allows you to access all material transactions for a period. Transactions are grouped by category, which you can progressively expand to display all transaction documents within a category.

Now let's look at the next level of period-end processing.

Single-Level Price Determination

Single-level refers to an individual material and its procurement process. A simple example with three levels within the material ledger includes purchased materials, subassemblies, and finished products. When you use actual costing, all materials are valued with a *preliminary* periodic unit price that remains constant during a given period. This price can be, for example, a standard price or an actual price from the previous period determined by the material ledger.

During a period the material ledger posts differences to a price difference account and updates them separately for each material. At the end of a period you can use single-level price determination to assign the variances for each material. This allows the cumulative price differences to be assigned proportionally to the ending inventory quantity and the material consumption of the period.

To carry out period-end processing in the material ledger you need to create an actual costing run with Transaction CKMLCP or by following the menu path ACCOUNTING • CONTROLLING • PRODUCT COST CONTROL-LING • ACTUAL COST/MATERIAL LEDGER • ACTUAL COSTING • EDIT COSTING RUN. The screen shown in Figure 19.21 is displayed.

Create Cost Estimate								
Flow step	Authorizn	Parameters	Execute	Log	Status	Successful	Errors	Still open
Selection		▶▯▶		▤		0	0	0
Determine Sequence		▶▯▶		▤		0	0	0
Single-Level Pr. Determination	🔓	▶▯▶		▤		0	0	0
Multilevel Pr. Determination	🔓	▶▯▶		▤		0	0	0
Revaluation of Consumption		▶▯▶				0	0	0
Post Closing	🔓	▶▯▶		▤		0	0	0
Mark Material Prices		▶▯▶				0	0	0

Figure 19.21 Edit Actual Costing Run

The functionality of the actual costing run screen is similar to the standard cost estimate costing run screen we discussed in Chapter 10. You first assign plants to the actual costing run, and then you follow the rows listed in the Flow step column of Figure 19.21. To carry out single-level price determination, you first carry out the selection and determine sequence steps and then the single-level price determination steps.

Actual costing run

The system calculates periodic unit prices for the period and updates them (for information) in all valuation approaches in the material price analysis shown in Figure 19.20. The system also updates the price in company code currency in the material master record for the period.

Multilevel Price Determination

During multilevel price determination you assign the differences calculated during single-price determination progressively to the next-highest levels of the production process using a multilevel actual quantity structure, which is a type of actual BOM. For example, purchase price differences for raw materials are rolled up to subassemblies and then to finished products.

The system calculates periodic unit prices for the period and updates them (for information) in all valuation approaches in the material price analysis. The system also updates the price in company code currency in the material master for the period.

At period-end during actual costing inventory can either:

▸ Be revaluated with the actual price of the period (the periodic unit price). The material stock account is debited with the proportional price differences, and the price differences account is credited with the same amount.

▸ Remain with the same value, and price differences are posted to an accrual account. If you decide not to revalue inventory with the actual price, the amount that would have been posted to the material stock account is posted to another price difference account.

Price differences allocated to consumption remain on the price difference account at this point.

You decide to revalue inventory or not according to which financial G/L accounts are posted to during automatic account determination with configuration Transaction OBYC.

To proceed with multilevel price determination, execute the remaining steps following single-level price determination in Figure 19.21.

Now that we've examined the material ledger, that completes the special topics chapter, so let's review what we've covered.

19.4   Summary

In this chapter we discussed three special topics within the Product Cost Controlling component. First, we looked at sales order controlling and the options for handling customer stock. We looked at the configuration steps required to choose sales order cost estimate options and how to valuate sales order stock. We also looked at the possible combinations of sales order controlling and valuated sales order stock.

The second special topic we discussed was subcontracting and how purchasing controls this process. Components are issued to a vendor for assembly, and the assembled product is then received into inventory. All financial postings occur at the point of goods receipt of the assembly into inventory.

The third special topic discussed was the material ledger and the two functions it can perform. We looked at how you can carry inventory in three parallel valuations and how actual costing rolls up differences from purchased materials to finished products.

The only topic left to discuss in our examination of Product Cost Controlling is reporting and information system, which we'll look at in Chapter 20.

The information system provides many standard reports to help leverage the transactional processing power of your system.

20 Information System

There are standard information system reports for:

▸ Product Cost Planning

▸ Cost Object Controlling

We'll examine reports in both these modules in this chapter.

In Product Cost Planning there is a great deal of information available when displaying an individual cost estimate as previously discussed in Chapter 10, including the:

▸ Costed multi-level bill of material (BOM)

▸ Cost components and views

▸ Itemization list

▸ Dates, quantity structure, valuation, and history

In addition to the information available in an individual cost estimate, there are reports available which list cost estimates according to multiple criteria. There are also reports to analyze costing run data, similar to the analysis section of the costing run step we discussed previously in Chapter 10. We'll look at these reports in detail in this chapter.

20.1 Product Cost Planning

Let's start with the summarized reporting available for cost estimates. This involves analyzing costing runs which are a mass processing of cost estimates.

20.1.1 Analyze Costing Runs

You can analyze costing runs from two locations:

▸ When you create or maintain a costing run with Transaction CK40N

▸ From the information system menu path

We previously discussed analyzing a costing run with Transaction CK40N in Chapter 10. Let's now look at doing the analysis with the information system. You analyze a costing run with Transaction S_ALR_87099930 or using menu path ACCOUNTING • CONTROLLING • PRODUCT COST CONTROLLING • PRODUCT COST PLANNING • INFORMATION SYSTEM • SUMMARIZED ANALYSIS • ANALYZE COSTING RUN. The selection screen in Figure 20.1 is displayed.

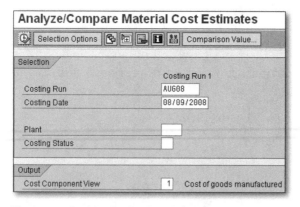

Figure 20.1 Analyze Costing Runs Selection Screen

This selection screen is useful for analyzing one costing run with limited selection criteria. Enter a Costing Run and Date and click the execute icon to display the results screen shown in Figure 20.2.

This screen displays a list of cost estimates generated during the costing run depending on your selection criteria. You can double click any line to display the corresponding individual cost estimate details. You can display different columns in this screen by clicking the grid icon.

To view more selection fields and compare two costing runs click the plus sign icon in Figure 20.1. The screen in Figure 20.3 is displayed.

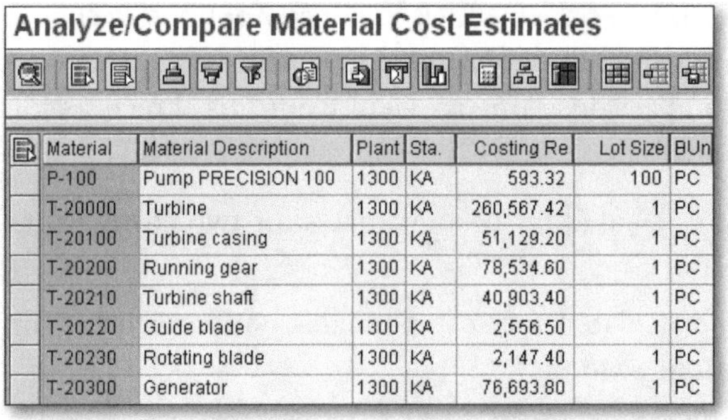

Analyze/Compare Material Cost Estimates

Material	Material Description	Plant	Sta.	Costing Re	Lot Size	BUn
P-100	Pump PRECISION 100	1300	KA	593.32	100	PC
T-20000	Turbine	1300	KA	260,567.42	1	PC
T-20100	Turbine casing	1300	KA	51,129.20	1	PC
T-20200	Running gear	1300	KA	78,534.60	1	PC
T-20210	Turbine shaft	1300	KA	40,903.40	1	PC
T-20220	Guide blade	1300	KA	2,556.50	1	PC
T-20230	Rotating blade	1300	KA	2,147.40	1	PC
T-20300	Generator	1300	KA	76,693.80	1	PC

Figure 20.2 Analyze Material Cost Estimates

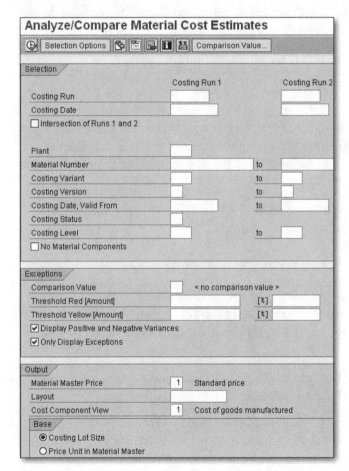

Figure 20.3 Analyze Costing Runs With Expanded Selection Fields

This expanded selection field screen allows you many options to choose cost estimates from a costing run or two compare costing runs. There are four main types of comparisons you can view from this screen as follows:

- ▶ Compare the value calculated for cost estimates for two costing runs in the Selection section
- ▶ Compare the value calculated for cost estimates with a Comparison value in the Exceptions section
- ▶ Compare the calculated values with Threshold amounts in the Exceptions section
- ▶ Compare the calculated values with a Material Master price in the Output section

Let's examine each of these screen sections in detail.

Selection

The easiest option is to enter two costing runs in the Costing Run 1 and Costing Run 2 fields with corresponding Costing Dates and click the execute icon to see a comparison of the cost estimates in the two costing runs.

Select the Intersection of Runs 1 and 2 indicator to view only cost estimates that occur in both costing runs.

Exceptions

The Exceptions section allows you to decide which values to compare with the cost estimate values and to display exceptions beyond certain percentages you set in Threshold values. Let's examine these fields in more detail.

Right click the Comparison Value field and select Possible Entries to display the screen shown in Figure 20.4.

After you select a Comparison Value option you set a Threshold Amount or percentage in the subsequent fields which will highlight value differences greater than you set with either Red or Yellow traffic light icons in the output report.

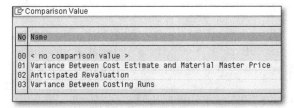

Figure 20.4 Comparison Value Possible Entries

Output

Right click the Material Master Price field in Figure 20.3 and select Possible Entries to display the list shown in Figure 20.5.

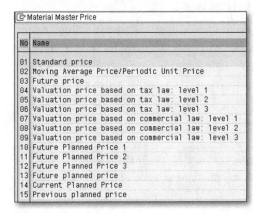

Figure 20.5 Material Master Price Possible Entries

The selection you make in this field determines the Material Master Price which appears as a column in the report results screen. You can compare the Material Master Price field you choose with the cost estimate calculation proposed price. You can also review exceptions which you defined in the Exceptions section.

The default selection for this field is the Standard Price. You can see from the list of possible entries in Figure 20.5 that you can also choose from any of fifteen material master price fields to compare with the cost estimate values.

Let's now examine the two possible entries you can select in the Base section of the screen in Figure 20.3.

Base

The default selection for the Base section is Costing Lot Size. This means, for example, if the costing lot size is 1,000 for a material, you will see the prices in the results screen displayed in units of 1,000.

Depending on your costing lot size settings, it can sometimes be more useful to display the results screen with the Price Unit in Material Master setting.

Now that we've analyzed costing runs in detail, let's look at analyzing cost estimate lists in the next Product Cost Planning report.

20.1.2 List Material Cost Estimates

For each material in a plant there can be many cost estimates created over time. You can display a list of cost estimates for materials with Transaction S_P99_41000111 or using menu path ACCOUNTING • CONTROLLING • PRODUCT COST CONTROLLING • PRODUCT COST PLANNING • INFORMATION SYSTEM • OBJECT LIST • FOR MATERIAL. The selection screen shown in Figure 20.6 is displayed.

> **Note**
>
> If you click the plus sign icon you see the same selection fields as displayed in Figure 20.3.

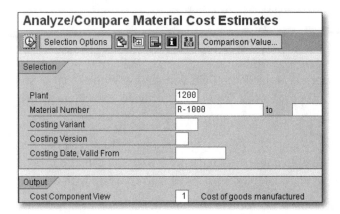

Figure 20.6 Display Cost Estimate List Screen

Make your entries in this selection screen and click the execute icon to display the result screen shown in Figure 20.7.

Analyze/Compare Material Cost Estimates

Material	Material Description	Plant	Status	Costing Re	Lot Size	BUn	Valid from
R-1000	Maxitec-R 375 Personal computer	1200	KA	717.52	1	PC	07/20/2008
R-1000	Maxitec-R 375 Personal computer	1200	KA	718.95	1	PC	07/23/2008
R-1000	Maxitec-R 375 Personal computer	1200	KA	718.95	1	PC	07/19/2008
R-1000	Maxitec-R 375 Personal computer	1200	FR	718.31	1	PC	01/09/2006

Figure 20.7 Material Cost Estimate List

Double click any line to display the corresponding cost estimate details. There can be many cost estimates in this list and the quickest method to locate the latest released standard cost estimate is to click the Current cost estimate button in the material master Costing 2 view.

Now that we've looked at cost estimate list reports let's discuss the next section in the information system.

20.1.3 Detailed Reports

Most of the reports in the detailed reports section of the Product Cost Planning information system display individual sections of an individual cost estimate such as the costed multilevel BOM, cost component and itemization views. We previously discussed these cost estimate sections in Chapter 10. The menu path to locate these reports within the information system is ACCOUNTING • CONTROLLING • PRODUCT COST CONTROLLING • PRODUCT COST PLANNING • INFORMATION SYSTEM • DETAILED REPORTS.

20.1.4 Object Comparisons

The reports available in the object comparisons section of the information system allow you to compare costs between cost estimates and sections of cost estimates. The first report we'll look at allows you to a compare standard cost estimate with a preliminary cost estimate.

For Material

You can compare standard cost estimates with preliminary cost estimates with Transaction S_ALR_87013046 or using menu path ACCOUNTING • CONTROLLING • PRODUCT COST CONTROLLING • PRODUCT COST PLANNING • INFORMATION SYSTEM • OBJECT COMPARISONS • FOR MATERIAL • MATERIAL COST ESTIMATE VS. PRELIMINARY ORDER COST ESTIMATE. The selection screen in Figure 20.8 is displayed.

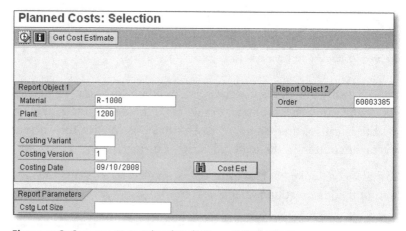

Figure 20.8 Compare Material and Preliminary Cost Estimates

This selection screen is divided into two sections:

▶ **Reporting Object 1:** Enter the standard cost estimate information

▶ **Reporting Object 2:** Enter the manufacturing order number associated with the preliminary cost estimate

Click the execute icon to display a comparison report similar to the one shown in Figure 20.9.

This report can be useful when analyzing the details of the cause of the production variance of an order.

Material vs. Material

You can compare the difference between components of material cost estimates with Transaction S_ALR_87013047 or using menu path ACCOUNTING • CONTROLLING • PRODUCT COST CONTROLLING • PRODUCT

COST PLANNING • INFORMATION SYSTEM • OBJECT COMPARISONS • FOR MATERIAL • MATERIAL VS. MATERIAL • COST COMPONENTS. The selection screen in Figure 20.10 is displayed.

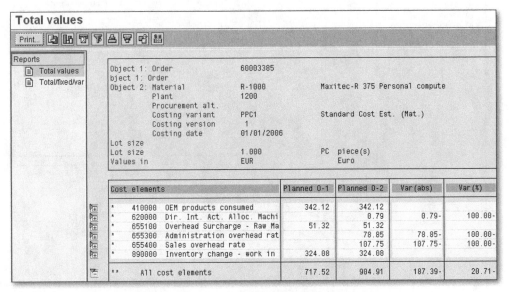

Figure 20.9 Compare Material and Preliminary Cost Estimates Results

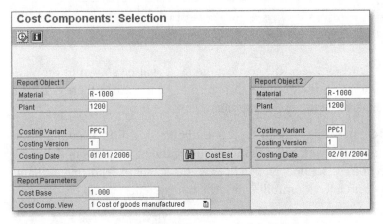

Figure 20.10 Compare Material Cost Components Selection Screen

Complete the selection screen with the material cost estimates you wish to compare and click the execute icon to display the screen shown in Figure 20.11.

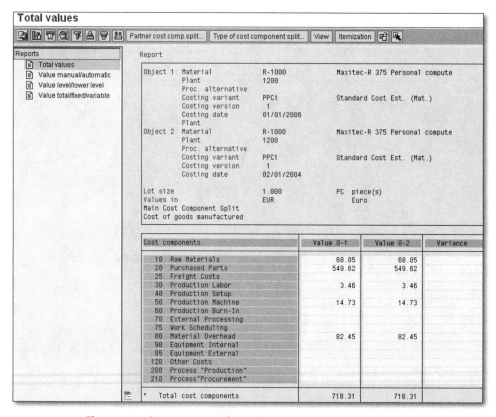

Figure 20.11 Compare Material Cost Components Results Screen

Any variance between the cost components will be shown in the Variance column. In the example displayed in Figure 20.11 there is no difference between the cost components.

There are more specialized reports in the Product Cost Planning information system, which you can locate using the menu paths in the previous sections as a guide. Now let's examine standard reporting available in the Cost Object Controlling information system.

20.2 Cost Object Controlling

In the Cost Object Controlling information system there are three main areas of reporting:

- Summarized
- Detail
- Line item

These reports allow you to analyze plan, target, and actual costs on objects such as manufacturing orders and product cost collectors at a summarized level across plants or company codes, and then drill down to a more detailed view of any areas of interest, including source documents.

You can expand the summarization level to display the next level, e.g., material group. You can then expand individual material groups, to display a list of materials within material groups. You can set up exception rules and traffic light icons to highlight individual materials with high variances as required in this report.

When you have identified product cost collectors or manufacturing orders, which require further analysis, detailed reports provide analysis at a cost element level. Cost elements appear as rows in detailed reports and identify costs such as raw materials, activities, and overhead.

You can drill down on a row in a detailed report to a line item report. The line item report displays a list of all line item postings, identified by the cost element, to the order. You can sort the Value or Quantity columns in a line item report to identify large line item postings that may need further investigation. To analyze a line item posting further, double click on it to display the source document, such as Material Document in the case of a goods issue.

Example

Production managers, production planners, and Material Requirements Planning (MRP) controllers typically run summarized reports and detailed and line item reports weekly or even daily. They look for, and analyze, large variances indicating problems such as incorrect activity confirmations or incorrect master data settings. Experienced plant personnel realize the importance of not leaving variance analysis until period-end, when it may be too late to correct some errors, or there may be too many errors to correct within the period-end closing time frame, and postings to the previous period are blocked.

Period-end processing and analysis is usually restricted to a time frame of just a couple of days, at the start of the following period. At the end of the time frame, postings to the previous period are blocked so the data underlying the previous period reports already supplied to managers does not change. If variances are not corrected within the narrow period-end time frame, they will remain in the previous period and need to be explained, even if they were due to mistakes, e.g., activity confirmations.

Now that we've introduced the standard reports and explained who is likely to use them and the purpose for using them, let's examine summarized analysis and detailed and line item reports in more detail in the following sections.

20.2.1 Product Drilldown Reports

Summarization analysis in Cost Object Controlling is based on hierarchy structures (like pyramids), with manufacturing orders or product cost collectors at the wide base, and progressively higher and narrower levels based on, e.g., material group and plant, on the way up to the Controlling area at the peak.

You regularly run a data collection program, which rolls up the order cost information from the base, through the nodes and levels, to the top of the hierarchy.

You then run a summarization report, which reads the information stored on the hierarchy nodes and presents the output either in a product drilldown report, which allows you to navigate between summarization levels, or in a summarization hierarchy report, with the hierarchy nodes presented as expandable and collapsible rows based on the hierarchy levels, and cost information presented in columns such as Target, Actual, and Variance.

Now that we've discussed summarization reports at a basic level, let's look more closely at the types of summarization reports available, and how they are set up and maintained. There are two types of summarization reports available:

- ▶ Product Drilldown Reports which we'll discuss in this section
- ▶ Summarization Hierarchy Reports which we'll discuss in the following section

Product drilldown reports allow you to slice and dice data based on characteristics such as product group, material, plant, cost component, and period. You can easily navigate between characteristics and drill down to lower-level characteristics. The navigation methods used for product drilldown reports are similar to those used with Profitability Analysis reports.

Product drilldown reports use predefined summarization levels, which means they are already set up for you. The predefined summarization levels are suitable for most scenarios. However, if they do not fully meet your requirements, you can create your own hierarchies, as we will examine in Section 20.2.2.

Now that we've introduced product drilldown reports, let's look in detail the three steps necessary to display the reports.

Configuration

You can run product drilldown reports without this configuration step. Its only purpose is to add a group, such as material group, to drilldown reports. You can try running the reports first, to see if you have a requirement to add a group.

This configuration step is required only once. You do not need to change product drilldown configuration after making the initial settings with the following procedure.

You can change the configuration setting with Transaction OKN0 or using IMG menu path CONTROLLING • PRODUCT COST CONTROLLING • INFORMATION SYSTEM • CONTROL PARAMETERS. Select the Data Extraction/ Product Drilldown tab to display the screen shown in Figure 20.12.

Click the Prod. group type (product group type) field to display a list of possible entries as shown in Figure 20.12. Select your choice and save your work.

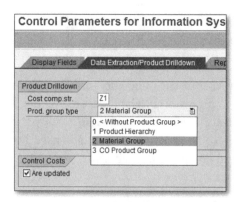

Figure 20.12 Product Drilldown Setting in Control Parameters

Product Hierarchies and Material Groups may already be defined and assigned in your material masters. If so, making the selection in the screen shown in Figure 20.12 will cause the group to appear in product drilldown reports with associated summarized data.

> **Note**
>
> You create CO product groups with Transaction KKC7 or using menu path ACCOUNTING • CONTROLLING • PRODUCT COST CONTROLLING • COST OBJECT CONTROLLING • PRODUCT COST BY PERIOD • INFORMATION SYSTEM • TOOLS • SUMMARIZED ANALYSIS: PREPARATION • PRODUCT GROUP • CREATE.

Now that we've assigned a group to the product drilldown report in configuration, the next step is to populate the predefined summarization hierarchy with data collection.

Data Collection

Product drilldown reports access a dataset, which must first be populated during a data collection run and saved. You run data collection for product drilldown reports with Transaction KKRV or using menu path ACCOUNTING • CONTROLLING • PRODUCT COST CONTROLLING • COST OBJECT CONTROLLING • PRODUCT COST BY PERIOD • INFORMATION SYSTEM • TOOLS • DATA COLLECTION • FOR PRODUCT DRILLDOWN. The screen shown in Figure 20.13 is displayed.

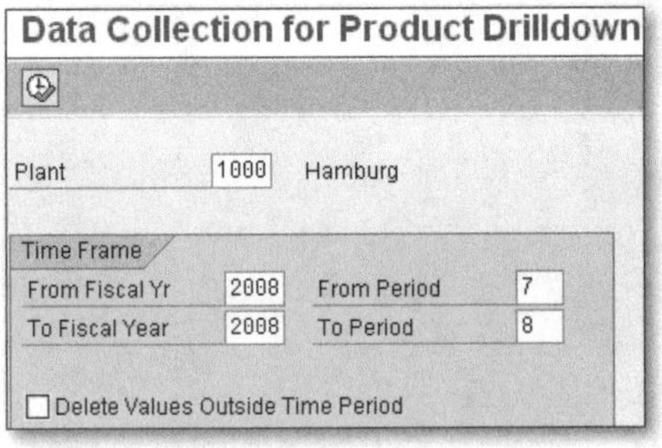

Figure 20.13 Data Collection for Product Drilldown Reports

You normally run data collection following period-end closing for the current and previous period, since data on orders can change within open financial periods. If data collection has already been run, the system resets and recalculates all data within the summarization time frame of the new data collection run. Data outside the time frame is retained, unless you select the DELETE VALUES OUTSIDE TIME PERIOD indicator.

Complete the fields using Figure 20.13 as an example and save your work. A subsequent data collection results screen indicates the number of records read.

Now that we've populated the hierarchy, the next step is to run the report, as described in the next section.

Run Report

Following data collection, you can run product drilldown reports with Transaction S_ALR_87013139 or using menu path ACCOUNTING • CONTROLLING • PRODUCT COST CONTROLLING • COST OBJECT CONTROLLING • PRODUCT COST BY PERIOD • INFORMATION SYSTEM • REPORTS FOR PRODUCT COST BY PERIOD • SUMMARIZED ANALYSIS • WITH PRODUCT DRILLDOWN • VARIANCE ANALYSIS • TARGET/ACTUAL/PRODUCTION VARIANCES • CUMULATIVE. The screen shown in Figure 20.14 is displayed.

You can run the report with a wide period range, as shown in Figure 20.14, or you can restrict the period range to improve performance if you only need to report on one or two periods. Complete the fields and click the execute icon to display the product drilldown report shown in Figure 20.15.

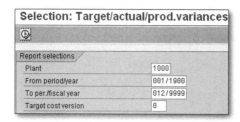

Figure 20.14 Product Drilldown Report Selection Screen

Navigation	Tgt (deb.)	Act.(deb.)	Scrap	Var.w/oScr
Product group	37,889.59	165,837.94	0.00	128,425.97
Material	173.03	91,809.67	0.00	91,809.67
Period/year	40,247.26	44,644.87	0.00	50,408.95
Cost Compon	2,025.05	2,782.17	0.00	28,609.58
	29,874.35	56,917.42	348.38	28,261.86

Figure 20.15 Product Drilldown Report Results Screen

In Figure 20.15, each line represents a Material, and the Var.w/oScr (variance without scrap) column is sorted in descending order. This provides visibility to materials with the largest accumulated variance. You can drill down on any line in this report to find out more details by Period/year and Cost Compon (cost component). You can analyze variance per Material further by displaying a detailed report of the individual product cost collector with transaction KKBC_PKO, or transaction KKBC_ORD for manufacturing orders, as described later in Section 20.2.3.

In addition to the *cumulative* drilldown report discussed above, a *periodic* drilldown report is available in the same menu path. In periodic drilldown reports, results are shown by period, enabling fast navigation across multiple periods. With cumulative drilldown reports you can summarize results across multiple periods, such as by quarter or fiscal year.

Now that we've examined product drilldown reporting, let's examine another type of summarized reporting.

20.2.2 Summarization Hierarchy Reports

Summarization hierarchies allow you flexibility in setting up and displaying summarized data. A summarization hierarchy groups together manufacturing orders or product cost collectors at the lowest-level summarization nodes, which in turn are grouped together at higher-level nodes, to create a pyramid structure.

You set up each summarization level manually in configuration. The hierarchy levels are presented as expandable and collapsible rows in the reports. Here is an example of hierarchy levels, starting at the top of the pyramid: Controlling area, profit center, plant, material group, and material number. Since you can display summarized data at each node, you may decide to define hierarchy levels based on responsibility at lower management levels, e.g., profit center, material groups, or order types. You may also decide to create an alternate summarization hierarchy with levels based on profitability reporting requirements, such as profit center, division, and sales document.

After you define the summarization hierarchy in configuration, you run a data collection transaction, which populates the hierarchy with current data. During a data collection run, the following cost data is collected for all orders included in the run and rolled upwards through the hierarchy nodes and levels:

▸ Plan

▸ Target

▸ Actual

▸ Variances

▸ Work in process

Following the data collection run, the above cost data is available to be added as columns to the summarization report. You then run a summarization report, which displays the data summarized at each of the hierarchy levels. You may typically display the following cost data as columns at each level: Target, Actual, and Variance. This allows you to display total variance for a plant and then at each of the lower hierarchy levels, by expanding the levels as required. At the lowest level, you can display variance details of individual orders. You can then display a detailed report with cost element rows and drill down to line item reports and source documents if necessary.

Now that we've described how summarization hierarchy reports work, we'll examine in detail the three steps necessary to display the reports.

Configuration

The configuration step is required only once. You only need to change the configuration if you need an additional hierarchy or need to change an existing hierarchy.

You maintain summarization hierarchies with Transaction KKRO or using menu path Accounting • Controlling • Product Cost Controlling • Cost Object Controlling • Product Cost by Period • Information System • Tools • Summarized Analysis: Preparation • Create Summarization Hierarchy. The screen shown in Figure 20.16 is displayed.

Change View "Summarization hierarchy
New Entries
Dialog Structure
Summarization hierarch
Data scope (object ty
Data Scope (Totals F
Hierarchy levels
Hierarchy
Hierarchy Descript
Z001
Summarization 01
Z002
Summarization 02

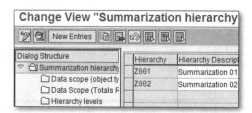

Figure 20.16 Change Summarization Hierarchy Initial Screen

This screen displays the existing Hierarchy list and allows you to define new hierarchies. Select an existing Hierarchy and double click Data scope (object types) to display hierarchy details, as shown in Figure 20.17.

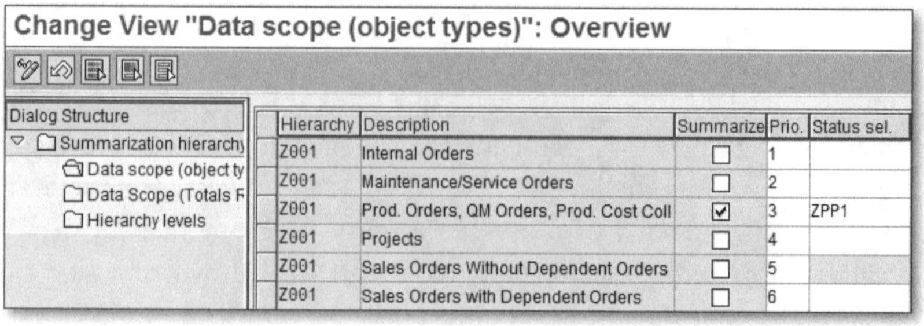

Change View "Data scope (object types)": Overview
Dialog Structure
Summarization hierarch
Data scope (object ty
Data Scope (Totals F
Hierarchy levels
Hierarchy
Description
Summarize
Prio.
Status sel.
Z001
Internal Orders
1
Z001
Maintenance/Service Orders
2
Z001
Prod. Orders, QM Orders, Prod. Cost Coll
3
ZPP1
Z001
Projects
4
Z001
Sales Orders Without Dependent Orders
5
Z001
Sales Orders with Dependent Orders
6

Figure 20.17 Change Data Scope Object Types Overview

In this screen you specify which object types are summarized in the hierarchy. Read the Description in the row with the Summarize indicator selected to understand the purpose of the hierarchy.

You can also specify a status selection profile in the Status sel. column. Enter a status selection profile if you want to select only objects with a status that matches the selection criteria in the status selection profile. For example, you may be interested in only summarizing production orders with a status of fully delivered or technically complete. You can achieve this with a status selection profile.

To display further details of the hierarchy, double click Hierarchy levels. The screen shown in Figure 20.18 is displayed.

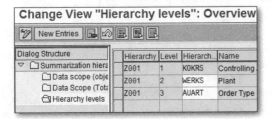

Figure 20.18 Change Hierarchy Levels

In this screen you specify the hierarchy levels of the summarization hierarchy. You can display a list of possible levels by right clicking in any row in the Hierarch... (hierarchy field) column and clicking Possible Entries. Some typical hierarchy levels are Plant, Order Type, profit center, material, and order number.

Now that we've maintained a hierarchy, let's examine how to maintain a status selection profile to narrow the selection of summarized orders.

You maintain status selection profiles with Transaction BS42 or using IMG menu path CONTROLLING • PRODUCT COST CONTROLLING • INFORMATION SYSTEM • COST OBJECT CONTROLLING • SETTINGS FOR SUMMARIZED ANALYSIS/ORDER SELECTION • DEFINE STATUS SELECTION PROFILES. The screen shown in Figure 20.19 is displayed.

This screen shows the existing SelProf (selection profile) list and allows you to define new profiles. Select an existing selection profile and double click Selection conditions to display selection profile details, as shown in Figure 20.20.

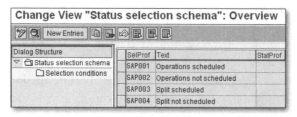

Figure 20.19 Status Selection Profile Overview Screen

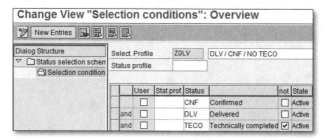

Figure 20.20 Selection Profile Selection Conditions Screen

This screen is where you define the Status of orders for selection. The selection conditions displayed in Figure 20.20 result in a selection of orders with a Status of Confirmed and Delivered and not Technically completed.

Now that we've defined the summarization hierarchy and looked at how to create a status selection profile, the next step is to populate the summarization hierarchy with the data collection step.

Data Collection

Summarization hierarchy reports access a dataset, which must first be populated during a data collection run and saved. You run data collection for summarization hierarchy reports with Transaction KKRC or using menu path ACCOUNTING • CONTROLLING • PRODUCT COST CONTROLLING • COST OBJECT CONTROLLING • PRODUCT COST BY PERIOD • INFORMATION SYSTEM • TOOLS • DATA COLLECTION • FOR SUMMARIZATION HIERARCHY. The screen shown in Figure 20.21 is displayed.

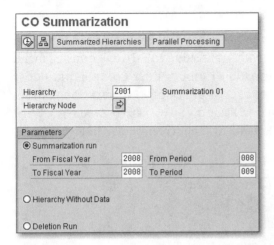

Figure 20.21 Data Collection for Summarization Reports

You normally run data collection following period-end closing for the current and previous period, since data on orders can change within open financial periods. If data collection has already been run, the system resets and recalculates all data within the summarization time frame of the new data collection run. Data outside the time frame is retained.

Complete the fields in Figure 20.21 and click the Hierarchy Node (right-pointing arrow) icon. The screen shown in Figure 20.22 is displayed.

☞ Enter Subhierarchy		
Hierarchy	Z001	Summarization 01
Description	Value	
Plant	0021	
Order Type		

Figure 20.22 Hierarchy Node Screen

You can narrow the data collection run to specific objects by entering the object number in a Value field. Click the Confirm button to return to the screen in Figure 20.21, and then click the execute icon. A data collection results screen appears, indicating the number of records read.

Run Report

Following data collection, you can execute summarization reports. You run summarization reports with Transaction KKBC_HOE or using menu path ACCOUNTING • CONTROLLING • PRODUCT COST CONTROLLING • COST OBJECT CONTROLLING • PRODUCT COST BY PERIOD • INFORMATION SYSTEM • REPORTS FOR PRODUCT COST BY PERIOD • SUMMARIZED ANALYSIS • WITH DEFINED SUMMARIZATION HIERARCHY. The screen shown in Figure 20.23 is displayed.

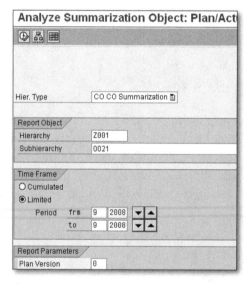

Figure 20.23 Summarization Report Selection Screen

You can run the report with a wide period range, or you can restrict the period range to improve performance if you only need to report on one period. Complete the fields and click on the hierarchy icon to display the report shown in Figure 20.24.

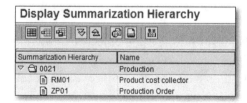

Figure 20.24 Display Summarization Hierarchy Screen

You can see the hierarchy levels we defined in the previous Configuration section, which are plant (0021) and order type (RM01 and ZP01). To display the Target, Actual, and Variance columns in this report, select SETTINGS • LAYOUT • CHOOSE from the menu bar and select the Target/Actual Comparison layout (not shown). The screen shown in Figure 20.25 is displayed.

Summarization ...	Total tgt costs	Actual debit	Target/actual var.
▽ 🗁 0021	9,063.34	3,317.24	5,746.10-
📄 RM01	9,063.34	3,317.24	5,746.10-

Figure 20.25 Target, Actual, and Variance Columns Displayed

This report indicates that the Actual debit for all orders of order type RM01 is 3,317.24. To see details of individual orders reporting to this node, click node RM01 and select GOTO • SINGLE OBJECTS from the menu bar. The screen shown in Figure 20.26 is displayed.

OTy	Object	Σ Actl	Σ Tgt	Σ Variance
ORD	786960	246,064.96	154,738.43	91,365.08
ORD	786855	110,826.72	90,673.79	65,850.97
ORD	786865	385,201.21	347,858.60	30,004.12
ORD	787063	292,255.35	235,662.70	27,700.51
ORD	786838	27,749.27	20,683.21	22,509.88

Figure 20.26 Single Objects Results Screen

In Figure 20.26, the Variance column is sorted in descending order. Sorting provides visibility to product cost collectors or orders with the largest variances during the time frame selected. Double click any line to display a cost element analysis report for the product cost collector or order. You can change the target cost version selecting SETTINGS • TARGET COST VERSION from the menu bar.

Alternate Summarization Hierarchies

An advantage of summarization reporting is that you can create multiple hierarchies. In the example hierarchy in the previous Configuration section, we chose plant and order type as hierarchy levels. You can create hierarchies with an additional level of, say, order or material number and see more details directly in the results screen in Figure 20.24, without branching to the single objects screen in Figure 20.26. An advantage of the single objects report is that the columns are easily sorted and rearranged.

If you add more detail in hierarchy levels, you can create exception rules and display traffic light symbols in the results screen shown in Figure 20.24. This helps you quickly find nodes that require further analysis. You can create exception rules using IMG menu path CONTROLLING • PRODUCT COST CONTROLLING • INFORMATION SYSTEM • COST OBJECT CONTROLLING • SETTINGS FOR SUMMARIZED ANALYSIS/ORDER SELECTION • DEFINE EXCEPTION RULES. You include exception rules during data collection with transaction KKRC by selecting EXTRAS • EXCEPTION • DEFINE RULE from the menu bar.

Now that we've looked at summarization reports, let's examine detailed reports for reporting on individual cost objects.

20.2.3 Detailed Reports

If you use summarized analysis, you'll often drill down to detailed reports. You can also display detailed reports directly from the material or manufacturing order to be analyzed. You typically run a detailed report directly if you identify a material with large variances during variance analysis. Since you can't drill down to line item details from the variance calculation output screen, you need to take note of the material number and run the detailed report to drill down to line item reports and source documents.

Detailed reports are useful during variance analysis because they provide cost element details by row, and target, actual, and variance by column for an individual product cost collector or manufacturing order. You can display the costs for one or multiple periods, or cumulatively (all periods). The cost element rows can be grouped together by similar business transactions, such as confirmations, goods issues, and goods receipts in the detailed report.

This style of report is particularly useful when analyzing variance for an order. You search for the cost element with the largest variance and drill down to line item details by double clicking the line. You then sort the line item list and double click the line item with the largest value to display the source document. The source document should contain all the information needed to find the cause of the largest variances.

You can display and analyze target vs. actual costs in detailed product cost collector reports with transaction PKBC_PKO or using menu path ACCOUNTING • CONTROLLING • PRODUCT COST CONTROLLING • COST OBJECT CONTROLLING • PRODUCT COST BY PERIOD • INFORMATION SYSTEM • REPORTS FOR PRODUCT COST BY PERIOD • DETAILED REPORTS. A selection screen is displayed, as shown in Figure 20.27.

> **Note**
>
> A similar report is also available for production and process orders with transaction PKBC_ORD.

Figure 20.27 Analyze Product Cost Collector Selection Screen

You can display costs for one period, a range of periods, or cumulatively (all periods). Complete the fields and click the execute icon to display the screen shown in Figure 20.28.

BusTran.	Origin	Origin (Text)	Σ Total tgt	Σ Ttl actual
Confirmations	1650/RUN	Sewing / Run Time	4,706.44	15,127.19
	1650/SET	Sewing / Set Time	47.41	218.71
	1650/REW...	Sewing / Rework	0.00	14.41
	1660/RUN	Painting / Run Time	46.02	0.00
	1660/SET	Painting / Set Time	15.34	0.00

Figure 20.28 Analyze Product Cost Collector Results Screen

You are presented with a detailed report with cost elements as rows and Total tgt (total target), Ttl actual (total actual), and Variance (not shown) as columns. Sort a column in descending order and double click the row containing the largest value to display line item details, as shown in Figure 20.29.

Cost Elem	CElem.name	▵ Val.in RC	▾ Quantity	PUM	Off.acct	Offst.acct
690010	Labour	266.60	449.717	MIN		
690010	Labour	266.31	449.233	MIN		
690010	Labour	266.21	449.050	MIN		
690010	Labour	265.49	447.833	MIN		
690010	Labour	264.85	446.750	MIN		
690010	Labour	264.75	446.600	MIN		

Figure 20.29 Confirmation Line Items

In Figure 20.29, the Quantity column is sorted in descending order. This highlights confirmations with the largest time bookings. By double clicking a line in the screen shown in Figure 20.29, you can drill down to individual activity confirmations and analyze the reasons for confirmations with the largest Quantity.

Now that we've examined how to run and analyze detailed reports for individual product cost collectors and manufacturing orders, let's look at line item reports. Although you often drill down to line item reports from detailed reports, it's possible to display them directly. I'll explain how to do that next.

20.2.4 Line Item Reports

You often drill down to line item reports for an individual object from summarized analysis and detailed reports. This is useful because there can be many line items. Just as summarization reports group together product cost collectors by characteristics for management reporting, detailed reports group together line items. Analyzing a detailed report for a product cost collector and drilling down on the cost element with the largest variance is a more efficient method of variance analysis than searching through many line items directly. However, if you are in a situation where you need to display line items directly, the procedure is as follows.

Display and analyze line item reports with Transaction KRMI or using menu path ACCOUNTING • CONTROLLING • PRODUCT COST CONTROLLING • COST OBJECT CONTROLLING • PRODUCT COST BY PERIOD • INFORMATION SYSTEM • REPORTS FOR PRODUCT COST BY PERIOD • LINE ITEMS • PRODUCT COST COLLECTORS • ACTUAL COSTS. A selection screen is displayed, as shown in Figure 20.30.

> **Note**
>
> A similar report is also available for production and process orders with Transaction KOB1.

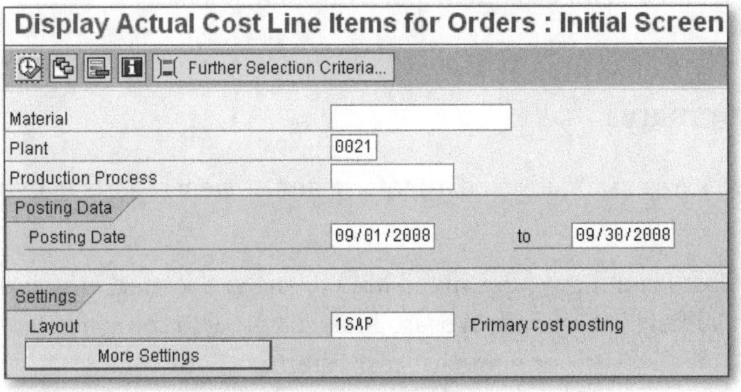

Figure 20.30 Line Item Report Selection Screen

When displaying line items directly, it's important to restrict the Posting Date range sufficiently to avoid long runtimes, since there can be large numbers of line items. It's usually best to tightly restrict the Posting Date range initially, and then gradually increase it if required.

Complete the fields and click the execute icon. The screen shown in Figure 20.31 is displayed.

Cost Elem.	CElem.name	Σ Val.in RC	Quantity	PUM	Off.acct	Offst.acct
690010	Labour	266.60	449.717	MIN		
690010	Labour	266.31	449.233	MIN		
690010	Labour	266.21	449.050	MIN		
690010	Labour	265.49	447.833	MIN		
690010	Labour	264.85	446.750	MIN		
690010	Labour	264.75	446.600	MIN		

Figure 20.31 Confirmation Line Items

You typically sort line item lists by Val.in RC (value in reporting currency) or Quantity and analyze the lines with the largest and smallest values by double clicking through to the source documents. In the case of confirmation line items, the source documents are activity confirmations. In the case of goods receipt and goods issue line items, the source documents are material documents.

Now that we've examined how to run line item reports directly without drilling down from a detailed report, we've reached the end of this chapter, and of this Product Cost Controlling book. In the following summary section, we'll review a summary of this chapter and also review some of the main take-home points from the book.

20.3 Summary

In this chapter we examined standard information system reports in two modules.

In Product Cost Planning we examined how to analyze costing runs and create cost estimate list reports. We also looked at how to compare standard cost estimates with preliminary cost estimates, and compare two standard cost estimates by cost components, cost elements and itemization.

In Cost Object Controlling we looked at how product drilldown reports are supplied with a predefined reporting hierarchy. We saw how to run data collection and the report. We also looked at summarization hierarchy reports which allow you to create your own reporting hierarchies. We saw how you can create your own nodes in the hierarchy, run data collection and how to run the reports. We also saw how you can create multiple alternate reporting hierarchies.

Summarized reports allow selection of individual orders for further analysis. Individual orders can be analyzed at a cost element level with detailed reports. When you double-click a cost element, you are presented with a line item report. Line item reports can also be run directly with a transaction, without drilling down, although this is often not necessary. We examined a method to display line item reports directly, sort the rows based on value and drill down on the largest values to examine the source documents, such as activity confirmations and material documents.

20.4   Book Summary

Product Cost Controlling allows you to carry out budget planning for future fiscal periods and years, post actual costs, and compare plan, target, and actual costs and to analyze variances. This module integrates with many other modules by receiving and analyzing costs. We'll summarize the integration aspects of product costing by looking at the three different parts of this book. Let's first revisit integrated planning.

20.4.1   Integrated Planning

There are many areas in R/3 and ECC 6.0 where planning can be carried out. We looked at one typical best practice flow starting with entering sales plan data into either Profitability Analysis (CO-PA) or Sales and Operations Planning. These modules, as in many other areas of SAP, allow you to enter different versions for scenario based planning and budgeting. Sales managers test the profitability of different sales plan quantities for products or product groups and determine a preferred sales plan, which is then converted into a production plan.

The production plan is then transferred to Demand Management which involves the planning of requirement quantities and dates for finished products and important assemblies and definition of the strategy for planning and producing or procuring a finished product.

Long-term planning accesses the assembly and finished product requirements data from demand management and determines the requirements of lower-level components and activities by accessing bill of material (BOM) and routing master data. These planned requirements can then be transferred to both the purchasing information system and Cost Center Accounting.

Data from long-term planning is transferred to the purchasing information system to determine request for quotations (RFQ) which are sent to vendors to determine procurement prices for components to meet the sales plan data. The preferred vendor quotation prices for components are then stored as data in purchasing info records per material.

Activity data from long-term planning is then analyzed on a work center capacity planning basis and work level load leveled across work centers where appropriate. This activity quantity data can then be transferred to cost center and activity type combinations which can then be used to determine activity prices.

The next part of the book examined Product Cost Planning, which we'll now summarize.

20.4.2 Product Cost Planning

This module determines the planned cost to manufacture products based on the preferred sales plan, master data setup and configuration settings.

Controlling master data setup includes cost elements, cost centers and activity types which are maintained by cost accounting personnel. Material master data views relevant to Product Cost Planning are MRP, Costing and Accounting which are setup by the corresponding departments. Logistics master data includes BOM's, work centers and routings which provide the quantity structure information for cost estimates. Purchasing info records supply the price information for cost estimates.

For configuration settings we looked at costing sheets which contain overhead setup, and cost components which identify costs of similar types such as material labor and overhead by grouping cost elements. We also examined the configuration of costing variants which are the primary source of information on how a cost estimate calculates the standard price.

We then created standard, preliminary and unit cost estimates and examined how they determine planned procurement and manufacture prices. We also looked at how standard cost estimates can be used to update the standard price and revaluate inventory.

The next part of this book then examined Cost Object Controlling as summarized in the next section.

20.4.3 Cost Object Controlling

Cost objects are entities such as cost centers and production orders which collect planned and actual costs. Preliminary costing determines the planned costs for each cost object. Actual costs then are collected during purchasing and manufacturing in a process called simultaneous costing. During period-end processing, overhead, work in process and variances are calculated and settlement carried out.

We also looked at three more specialized processes. Sales order costing involves costing sales order line items for individual customer requirements. Subcontracting is a purchasing process which involves sending components to an external vendor which assembles the components and returns the finished good into inventory. The material ledger allows up to three different valuations to be stored at the same time. It also allows actual costing which involves allocating all purchasing and manufacturing difference postings upwards through BOM to assembly levels to finished goods.

Finally, in the last chapter we looked at the many standard summarized, detailed and line item reports available to analyze costs and explain variances. A best practice method of period-end reporting is to analyze summarized costing reports to determine overall manufacturing plant performance. You then drill-down from summarized reports to analyze specific objects further by cost element with detailed reports. You can obtain even more detailed analysis by drilling-down to line item reports, sorting on the largest values, and then accessing source documents to assist in determining the cause of the variance. You can then take corrective action as required.

20.5   Looking Ahead

The Product Cost Controlling module is integrated with many other modules since most activities in a company involve costs. The core functionality of setting up master data and configuration, creating cost estimates and analyzing variances on cost objects has stayed relatively constant over several R/3 SAP versions. Two major improvements have included:

- The costing run cockpit, which allows you to mass process cost estimates within the one screen with Transaction CK40N.

- Valuated sales order stock reduces period-end processing requirements by eliminating the need to run results analysis and settlement. You can also carryout variance analysis by comparing the sales order cost estimate with actual costs.

There are many other improvements introduced with each new version which you can review by selecting HELP • RELEASE NOTES from the menu bar from any SAP screen. You can also display customizing release notes with Transaction SPRO, clicking the SAP Reference IMG button, and then clicking the Release Notes button. Any IMG menu paths with new functionality will then include an information icon.

> **Note**
>
> You can access online help documentation directly from any transaction by selecting HELP • APPLICATION HELP from the menu bar.

One of the aims of this book is to provide you with a detailed reference guide for the core functionality of Product Cost Controlling, including basic overviews and concepts, as well as detailed master data and configuration setup information. You've also been provided with many notes, examples and real life case scenarios to assist in understanding how the many product costing settings can improve your system.

In many cases it is helpful to understand and effectively utilize the core product costing functionality before implementing the most recent added features. One of the exceptions to this rule is additional standard reporting available with new versions of SAP. It is always useful to explore and analyze any addition standard reporting available.

One of the best ways to keep up with the constant improvements made to Product Cost Controlling in new system versions is to routinely attend seminars and conferences run by user groups and SAP affiliated companies. These events also provide you with excellent opportunities to exchange information with colleagues from other companies on different approaches available to solve similar issues.

A   Glossary

Active Pharmaceutical Ingredient An active pharmaceutical ingredient (API) is the substance in a drug that is pharmaceutically active, and is by far the highest cost ingredient in pharmaceutical products. One way to identify these costs is with a separate cost component by creating an API origin group and assigning it to API material masters with Transaction MM03, and an API cost component in the cost component structure with Transaction OKTZ.

Activity Input Planning Just as cost centers can provide planned output services based on activity quantities with Transaction KP26, you can plan cost center activity input quantities from other cost centers with activity input planning using Transaction KP06.

Activity Type An activity type identifies activities provided by a cost center to product cost collectors and manufacturing orders. The secondary cost element associated with an activity type identifies the activity costs on cost center and detailed reports.

Actual Costing Actual costing determines what portion of the variance is debited to the next-highest level using material consumption. All purchasing and manufacturing difference postings are allocated upward through the

BOM to assemblies and finished goods. Variances can be rolled up over multiple production levels to the finished product.

Actual Costs Actual costs debit a product cost collector or manufacturing order during business transactions such as general ledger account postings, inventory goods movements, internal activity allocations, and overhead calculation.

Additive Cost Estimate This is a material cost estimate in which you can enter costs manually in the form of a unit cost estimate (spreadsheet formant) so that manual costs can be added to an automatic cost estimate with quantity structure.

Allocation Structure An allocation structure allocates the costs incurred on a sender by cost element or cost element group. The allocation structure is used for settlement and assessment. An assignment assigns a cost element or cost element group to a settlement or assessment cost element. Each allocation structure contains a number of such assignments.

Alternative Bill of Material There can be multiple methods of manufacturing an assembly, and many possible bills of material (BOM). The alternative BOM allows you to identify one BOM in a BOM group.

Alternative Sequence An alternative sequence is a sequence of operations that can be used as an alternative to a number of consecutive operations from the standard sequence. Alternative sequences are used, for example, if the production process differs according to lot size.

Alternative Unit of Measure This is a unit of measure defined in addition to the base unit of measure. Examples of alternative units of measure are order unit (purchasing), sales unit, and unit of issue.

Apportionment Method An apportionment method distributes the total costs of a joint production process to the primary products. The costs of the individual primary products may vary. They are apportioned by means of an apportionment structure.

Apportionment Structure An apportionment structure defines how costs are distributed to co-products. The system uses the apportionment structure to create a settlement rule that distributes costs from an order header to the co-products. For each co-product, the system generates a further settlement rule that assigns the costs distributed to the order item to stock.

Assembly Scrap Assembly scrap is the percentage of assembly quantity that does not meet required production quality standards. The plan quantity of the assembly is increased. Assembly scrap is an output scrap, since it

affects the planned output quantity of items in the production process. You plan assembly scrap in the material master MRP 1 view. It can be ignored by selecting the Net ID indicator in the basic data tab of a bill of material item.

Automatic Account Assignment Automatic account assignment allows you to enter a default cost center per cost element within a plant.

Auxiliary Cost Component Split Only the main cost component split can update the results of the standard cost estimate to the material master. A second cost component split, called the auxiliary cost component split, is used for statistical information purposes and can be used in parallel to the main cost component split.

You define an auxiliary cost component split when assigning cost component structures to organizational units with Transaction OKTZ.

Backflush Backflushing is the automatic posting of a goods issue for components some time after their actual physical issue for use in an order. The goods issue posting of backflushed components is carried out automatically during confirmation.

Backflushing is used to reduce the amount of work in warehouse management, especially for low value parts. To use backflushing effectively, the material components from the BOM that are required in the operation should be assigned to the operations in the routing.

Base Quantity All component quantities in a BOM relate to the base quantity. You can increase the accuracy of component quantities by increasing the base quantity, similar in concept to the price unit.

Base Planning Object This is a simple reference object that can be used for the development of new products before any master data exists.

Base Unit of Measure Stocks of the material are managed in the base unit of measure. The system converts all quantities you enter in other units of measure (alternative units of measure) to the base unit of measure.

Bill of Material A bill of material (BOM) is a structured hierarchy of components necessary to build an assembly. BOM's together with purchasing info records or vendor quotations, provide cost estimates with the information necessary to calculate material costs of assemblies.

BOM Application BOM application is a component within a costing variant representing a process for automatic determination of alternative BOMs in the different organizational areas within a company.

BOM Item Component Quantity This is the quantity of a BOM item which is entered in relation the base quantity of the product.

BOM Item Status These six indicators, such as Production relevant and Costing Relevancy, are contained in the Status/Long Text tab of each BOM item. Whether this field is active depends on the BOM usage you selected on the initial screen when maintaining a BOM.

BOM Group A BOM group is a collection of BOMs for a product or number of similar products.

BOM Status This controls the current processing status of the BOM. For example, a BOM may have a default status of *not active* when initially created, which then may be changed to *active* when the BOM is available for use in material requirements planning (MRP) and released for planned orders.

BOM Usage This determines a specific section of your company, such as production, engineering or costing. You can define which item statuses can be used in each BOM usage. For example, all items in BOMs with a certain usage may be relevant to production.

Bulk Material Bulk materials are not relevant for costing in a cost estimate, and are instead expensed directly to a cost center. The bulk material indicator can be maintained in the material master MRP 2 view, and also in the bill of material (BOM) item. The indicator in the material master has higher priority. If a material is always used as a bulk material set the indicator in the material master. If a material is only used as a bulk material in individual cases, set the indicator in the BOM item.

Business Area A business area is an organizational unit of financial accounting that represents a separate area of operations or responsibilities within an organization. You can create financial statements for business areas, and you can use these statements for internal reporting purposes.

Calculation Base A calculation base is a group of cost elements to which overhead is applied. The calculation base is a component of a costing sheet which summarizes the rules for allocating overhead.

Capacity Category Capacity category enables you to differentiate between machine and labor capacity. Machine capacity is the availability of a machine based on planned and unplanned outages and maintenance requirements. Labor capacity is the number of workers who can operate a machine at the same time based on the factory calendar and shift schedule.

CAPP Data The CAPP (Computer Aided Process Planning) data on a work center Technical Data tab is relevant to the calculation of standard values.

Chart of Accounts A chart of accounts is a group of general ledger (G/L) accounts and must be assigned to each company code. This chart of accounts is the operative chart of accounts and is used in both financial and cost accounting. All companies within the one controlling area must have the same operative chart of accounts.

Other charts of accounts include the country specific chart of accounts (required by individual country legal requirements) and the group chart of accounts (required by consolidation reporting).

Co-Product You select the co-product indicator located in the material master MRP 2 and Costing 1 views if a material is a valuated product that is produced simultaneously with one or more other products. Setting this indicator allows you to assign the proportion of costs this material will receive in relation to other co-products within an apportionment structure.

Company Code A company code is the smallest organizational unit of financial accounting for which a complete self-contained chart of accounts can be drawn up for purposes of external reporting.

Component Scrap Component scrap is the percentage of component quantity that does not meet required production quality standards before being inserted in the production process. The plan quantity of components is increased. Component scrap is an input scrap, since it is detected before use in the production process. You can plan component scrap in the material master MRP 4 view and the Basic Data tab of the bill of material (BOM) item. An entry in the BOM item field takes priority over an entry in the material master MRP 4 view.

Condition Conditions are stipulations agreed with vendors such as prices, discounts, surcharges, freight, duty and insurance. You maintain purchasing conditions in quotations, purchasing info records, outline agreements, and purchase orders.

Condition Type A condition type is a key that identifies a condition. The condition type indicates, for example, whether during pricing the system applies a price, a discount, a surcharge, or other pricing elements, such as freight costs and sales taxes. For each of these pricing elements there is a condition type defined in the system.

Confirmation A confirmation documents the processing status of orders, operations, sub-operations and individual capacities. With a confirmation you specify the operation yield, scrap and rework quantity produced, the activity quantity consumed, work center, and who carried out the operation.

Consignment Material Consignment is a form of business in which a vendor maintains a stock of materials at a customer site. The vendor retains ownership of the materials until they are withdrawn from the consignment stores.

Controlling Level The controlling level determines the level of detail of procurement alternatives. The standard setting of controlling level is determined by the characteristics material/plant. You perform the following functions at the controlling level for a material:
- Calculate planned values
- Collect actual values
- Determine target values
- Analyze costs

The production process has characteristics values unique to that production process. You specify which characteristics are updated for the production process by means of the controlling level.

Currency Type This identifies the role of the currency such as local or global.

Current Cost Estimate A current cost estimate is based on the current quantity structure and current prices, and is used for the costing of materials during the fiscal year in order to analyze cost changes and developments.

Cost Component A cost component identifies costs of similar types, such as material, labor and overhead by grouping together cost elements in the cost component structure.

Cost Component Group Cost component groups allow you to display cost components in standard cost estimate list reports. In the simplest implementation you create a cost component group for each cost component, and assign each group to each corresponding cost component. The cost component groups become available to assign as columns in cost estimate list reports and costed multilevel BOMs.

Cost Component Split The cost component split is the combination of cost components that makes up the total cost of a material. For example if you need to view three cost components (material, labor and overhead) for your reporting requirements, then the combination of these three cost components represents the cost component split.

Cost Component Structure You define which cost components make up a cost component split by assigning them to a cost component structure. Within the cost component structure you also assign cost elements and origin groups to cost components.

The cost component structure allows you to define cost component views, assign cost component structures to company codes and plants, and create and assign cost component groups.

Cost Component View Each cost component is assigned to a cost component view. When you display a cost estimate you choose a cost component view which filters the cost components you see in the cost estimate. In the simplest case, you assign all cost components in a cost component structure to one cost of goods manufactured or sold view, and this is the only view you use when displaying a cost estimate.

Cost Center A cost center is master data which identifies *where* the cost occurred. There is usually a responsible person assigned to the cost center that analyzes and explains cost center variances at period-end.

Cost Element A cost element is master data which identifies *what* the cost is. Primary cost elements correspond to financial accounting G/L accounts, and identify external costs. Secondary cost elements identify costs allocated

within Controlling, such as activity allocations from cost centers to manufacturing orders.

Cost Estimate A cost estimate calculates the plan cost to manufacture a product, or purchase a component. It determines material costs by multiplying bill of material quantities by material standard price, labor costs by multiplying operation standard quantities by plan activity price, and overhead values by costing sheet configuration.

Costed Multilevel BOM A hierarchical overview of the values of all items of a costed material according to the material's costed quantity structure (BOM and routing). You normally see a costed multilevel BOM on the left when you display a cost estimate. You can also display a costed multilevel BOM directly with Transaction CK86_99.

Costing BOM Costing BOMs are assigned a BOM usage of Costing and are usually copied from BOMs with a usage of Production at the start of each fiscal year before the main costing run. You can make adjustments to Costing BOMs if you require them to be different from Production BOMs.

With the system supplied settings, standard cost estimates search for Costing BOMs before Production BOMs. If no Costing BOM exists, which is usually the case, standard cost estimates will be based on Production BOMs.

Costing Lot Size The costing lot size in the material master Costing 1 view determines the quantity cost estimate calculations are based on. The costing lot size should be set as close as possible to actual purchase and production quantities to reduce lot size variance.

Costing Run A costing run is a collective processing of cost estimates. You generally create and access costing runs with transaction CK40N.

Costing Sheet A costing sheet summarizes the rules for allocating overhead from cost centers to cost estimates, product cost collectors and manufacturing orders. The components of a costing sheet include the calculation base (group of cost elements), overhead rate (percentage rate applied to base), and credit key (cost center receiving credit).

Costing Type The costing type is a component of the costing variant, and determines if the cost estimate is able to update the standard price in the material master.

Costing Variant The costing variant contains information on how a cost estimate calculates the standard price. For example, it determines if the purchasing info record price is used for purchased materials, or an estimated price manually entered in the Planned price 1 field of the material master Costing 2 view.

Demand Management This involves the planning of requirement quantities and dates for finished products and important assemblies and definition of the strategy for planning and producing or procuring a finished product.

Demand Planning Demand Planning is an application component in Advanced Planner and Optimizer (APO) that allows you to forecast market demand for a company's products and produce a demand plan. APO Supply Network Planning (SNP) can be seamlessly integrated with planning modules in SAP such as Sales and Operations Planning (SOP).

Dependent Requirements Dependent requirements are planned material requirements caused by higher-level dependent and independent requirements when running material requirements planning (MRP). Independent requirements, generally created by sales orders or manually planned independent requirement entries in Demand Management, determine all lower-level dependent material requirements.

Detailed Reports Detailed reports display cost element details of manufacturing orders and product cost collectors. You can drill-down on cost elements to display line item reports during variance analysis.

Distribution Rule This is part of the settlement rule, and defines the following for a settlement sender:

▶ Settlement receiver
▶ Settlement share (percentage or proportional)
▶ Settlement type (periodic or total)
▶ Validity period of the distribution rule

You maintain distribution rules in settlement rules in cost objects such as manufacturing orders and product cost collectors.

External Processing External processing of a manufacturing order operation is performed by an external vendor. This is distinct from subcontracting which involves supplying material parts to an external vendor who manufactures the complete assembly via a purchase order.

Factory Calendar The factory calendar is defined on the basis of a public holiday calendar. The validity period of a factory calendar must be within the validity period of the public holiday calendar. The weekdays that are working days must also be specified in this calendar.

An example of a factory calendar is: Monday through Friday are working days while Saturday, Sunday and public holidays are non-working days.

Finite Scheduling Finite scheduling calculates the start and finish dates for operations in a manufacturing order taking capacity loads into account. Only those capacities for which the indicator finite scheduling is set are taken into account in the capacity availability check.

A distinction is made between *lead time* scheduling in which capacity loads are not taken into account, and *finite* scheduling in which capacity loads are taken into account.

Functional Area A functional area allows you to create a profit and loss account in financial accounting using cost-of-sales accounting, which compares the sales revenue for a given accounting period with the manufacturing costs of the activity. Expenses are allocated to the functional areas e.g. production, sales and distribution, and administration.

Group Counter A group counter identifies a unique routing within a task list (routing) group.

Initial Cost Split The initial cost split is based on a cost component structure for raw materials which contains separate cost components for all procurement costs such as purchase price, freight charges, insurance contributions and administrative costs.

With an additive cost estimate you can enter a cost component split for costs such as freight and insurance charges for a specific material. These costs are added to the price from the material master record if the valuation variant allows this.

Input Variance Variances on the input side are based on goods issues, internal activity allocations, overhead allocation, and general ledger account postings. The four input variances are: input price, resource-usage, input quantity and remaining input variance.

Inventory Cost Estimate An inventory cost estimate accesses tax-based and commercial prices in the material master Accounting 2 view for purchased parts, uses these prices for valuation, and then updates the costing results for finished and semi-finished products in the same fields. You can enter values such as the determination of lowest value in the tax-based and commercial price fields of purchased parts.

Itemization Itemization provides detailed cost estimate data about the resources necessary to produce a product. The costing information for each item includes details such as the quantity, unit of measure and value.

Joint Production Joint production involves the simultaneous production of many materials in a single production process. Click the **Joint production** button located in the material master MRP2 and Costing 2 views to assign apportionment structures which define how costs are distributed between co-products. You must first select the Co-product indicator adjacent to the Joint production button in order to be able to access apportionment structures.

Lead-Time Scheduling Lead-time scheduling performed using the routing calculates the start and finish dates and times of the operations.

Lead-time scheduling can be performed in MRP using the times specified in the material master. In this case, it calculates the production start and finish dates, but does not calculate capacity requirements.

A distinction is made between *lead-time* scheduling in which capacity loads are not taken into account, and *finite* scheduling in which capacity loads are taken into account.

Line Balance Line balance is the reconciliation of the time capacity with the time requirements on a production line.

Line Item Reports Line item reports display a list of postings to a cost object within a time frame. You can sort the value or quantity columns to find the largest postings during variance analysis.

Long-Term Planning Long-term planning allows you to enter medium- to longer-term production plans, and simulate future production requirements with long-term material requirements planning (MRP). You can determine future purchasing requirements, for vendor requests for quotations, and update purchasing info records prior to a costing run, and also transfer planned activity requirements to Cost Center Accounting.

Main Cost Component Split The main cost component split is the principal cost component split used by the standard cost estimate to update the standard price. The main cost component split can be a cost component split for cost of goods manufactured or a primary cost component split.

You define the main cost component split when assigning cost component structures to organizational units with Transaction OKTZ.

Mark Standard Cost Estimate After a standard cost estimate is saved without errors it can be marked, which moves the cost estimate into the Future column in the material master

Costing 2 view. You can create and mark standard cost estimates many times before release. Within the same fiscal period new standard cost estimates overwrite existing marked cost estimates.

Manufacturing Order Manufacturing order is an umbrella term for production and process orders.

Master Data Master data is information that stays relatively constant over long periods of time. For example, vendor info records contain vendor information such as business name, which usually doesn't change.

Material Assignment You use material assignment to determine which material is to be produced with a routing. On the basis of this assignment, the routing can be used for Sales and Operations Planning, material requirements planning, creating production orders and cost estimates for this material.

Material Ledger The material ledger consists of the following two parts:

Firstly it allows inventory to be carried in up to three different valuation approaches.

Secondly, actual costing determines what portion of the variance is debited to the next-highest level using material consumption. All purchasing and manufacturing difference postings are allocated upwards through the actual BOM to assemblies and finished goods. Variances can be rolled up over multiple production levels to the finished product.

Material Master A material master contains all the information required to manage a material. Information is stored in views, each corresponding to a department or area of business responsibility. Views conveniently group information together for users in different departments e.g. sales and purchasing.

Material Origin The material origin indicator in the material master Costing 1 view determines if the material number is displayed in detailed controlling reports. This is one of the single most important indicators in providing greater visibility to the causes of variances. If you have already created material master records without the material origin indicator selected, you can use report RKHKMAT0 to select the indicator.

Material Type A material type groups together materials with the same basic attributes such as raw materials, semi-finished products, or finished products. Material types also determine whether materials are quantity and/or valuation relevant per plant with configuration Transaction OMS2.

Material Price Determination Material price determination is displayed in the material master Accounting 1 view and is only applicable if the material ledger is active. Activity-based material price determination (indicator 2 in the material master) allows price control to either be set at moving average price (V) or standard price (S). This is the setting you use if you are using multiple currencies and/or valuation approaches for transfer pricing reporting, but not the actual costing functionality. A typical scenario is that you are interested in reporting on global inventory valuation with and without mark up i.e. internal company profit.

Single-/multi-level price determination (indicator 3 in the material master) is only available for materials with standard price control (S) which remains unchanged during a period. A periodic unit price is updated for information during the period, and used for material valuation in a closed period. This setting is only recommended if you are also using multiple currencies and/or valuations.

Material Requirements Planning
Material requirements planning (MRP) guarantees material availability by monitoring stocks and generating planned orders for procurement and production.

Milestone Confirmation The system automatically confirms all preceding operations up to the preceding milestone operation during confirmation of a milestone operation. An operation is marked as a milestone operation in the confirmations field of its control key.

If several operations are marked as milestones, they must be confirmed in the order in which they appear in the processing sequence.

Modified Standard Cost Estimate A modified cost estimate is based on the latest quantity structure and planned prices, and is used for the costing of

materials during the fiscal year in order to analyze cost developments.

Moving Average Price The moving average price (MAP) in the material master Costing 2 view determines the inventory valuation price if price control is set at moving average (V). The MAP is updated during goods receipt.

Multiple BOM A group of bills of material (BOMs) that lets you record different combinations of materials (alternatives) for the same product.

Operation An operation is a work-step in a plan or work order.

Operation Scrap Operation scrap is the percentage of assembly quantity that does not meet required production quality standards. Operation scrap is an output scrap, since it reduces the planned output quantity in the production process. You can plan operation scrap in the routing operation details view, and the Basic Data tab of the BOM item.

Order Type Order types categorize orders according to their purpose and allow you to allocate different number ranges and settlement profiles to different types of orders.

Organizational Unit This represents the organizational structure of a customer such as a sales organization in sales and distribution, company code in financial accounting and Asset Accounting, and plant in materials management and sales and distribution.

Origin Group An origin group enables you to separately identify materials assigned to the same cost element, allowing them to be assigned to separate cost components. The origin group can also be used to determine the calculation base for overhead in costing sheets.

Outline Agreement This is a longer-term arrangement between a purchasing organization and a vendor for the supply of materials or provision of services over a certain period based on predefined terms and conditions. The two types of outline purchase agreements are contracts and scheduling agreements.

Output Variance Variances on the output side result from too little or too much of planned order quantity being delivered, or because the delivered quantity was valuated differently. Output variances are divided into the following categories during variance calculation: mixed price, output price, lot size, and remaining variance.

Overhead Group An **overhead group** is used to apply different overhead percentages to individual materials, or groups of materials. You assign an overhead group directly to an overhead key in configuration Transaction OKZ2. You assign the overhead key in the overhead rate component of a costing sheet.

Overhead Key An overhead key is used to apply different overhead percentages to individual orders, or groups of orders. You assign the over-head key in the overhead rate component of a costing sheet.

PA Transfer Structure A PA transfer structure allows you to assign costs and revenues from other modules to value and quantity fields in Profitability Analysis.

Phantom Assembly A phantom assembly is a logical assembly created for efficient maintenance of a single BOM which is part of many higher-level assemblies. It is neither a physical assembly nor an inventory item. A phantom assembly is not included in a costing run however you can create an individual cost estimate with Transaction CK11N.

Pipeline Material Pipeline materials, such as oil or water, flow directly into the production process. Stock quantities are not changed during withdrawal.

Plan Reconciliation This allows you to compare and overwrite the plan *activity quantity* manually entered in the second column of Transaction KP26, with the *scheduled activity* quantity automatically entered in the second last column of Transaction KP26. Scheduled activity quantities are transferred from Sales and Operations Planning, MRP or Long-term planning with Transaction KSPP.

You carry out plan reconciliation with Transaction KPSI, which you can run in test mode first to compare proposed changes to the plan activity quantity. You can select the *plan quantity set* indicator in the activity type master data to default as selected when planning activity prices and quantities with Transaction KP26. This ensures the activity quantity manually planned will not be overwritten during plan reconciliation.

Planned Order Planned orders are created automatically by material requirements planning (MRP) when it encounters a material shortage. A planned order may also be created manually by a planner. Planned orders are converted into production orders for in-house production and into purchase requisitions for external procurement.

Planned Independent Requirements Planned independent requirements are either created by sales orders or manually by entering quantities and dates in Demand Management. You may need to make manual entries to generate requirements for purchased components or assemblies with long delivery times in order to satisfy demand by sales orders which you expect, but are not yet entered in the system. An example of this is long-term government defense contracts which can specify several years before the first planned delivery to the customer.

Planned Price 1, 2 and 3 You can manually enter prices in these fields in the Costing 2 view. These are generally used to estimate the purchase price of components early in the life-cycle of a new or modified product.

Planning Plant This is the plant in which the goods receipt takes place for the manufactured material. If the planning plant and production plant are identical then you need not enter the planning plant as well. The production plant is copied automatically.

Planning Variance Planning variance is a type of variance calculation based on the difference between costs on the preliminary cost estimate for the order and target costs based on the standard cost estimate and planned order quantity. You calculate planning variances with target cost version 2. Planning variances are for information only, and are not relevant for settlement.

Preliminary Cost Estimate A preliminary cost estimate calculates the planned costs for a manufacturing order or product cost collector. There can be a preliminary cost estimate for every order or production version, while there can only be one released standard cost estimate for each material. The preliminary cost estimate can be used to valuate scrap and work in process (WIP) in a WIP at target scenario.

Preliminary Costing Preliminary costing is carried out when you create a cost estimate for a manufacturing order or product cost collector. It is generally based on a quantity structure which consists of a Bill of Material (BOM) and routing.

In Cost Object Controlling you compare preliminary costing with simultaneous costing during variance analysis.

Price Control The price control field in the material master Costing 2 view determines whether inventory is valuated at standard (S) or moving average (V) price.

Price Indicator The price indicator field in an activity type determines how the system automatically calculates the price of an activity for a cost center.

Price Unit The **price unit** is the number of units to which the **price** refers. You can increase the accuracy of the price by increasing the price unit. To determine the unit price divide the price by the price unit.

Primary Cost Component Split The primary cost component split provides an alternative view of cost components based on cost center primary costs. This allows you to more readily analyze changes to your more significant primary costs such as wages, energy and depreciation primary costs by displaying each as a cost component. These costs would normally be divided between cost components as activities are consumed during manufacturing.

This functionality is only normally required if you have significant primary costs that you need to analyze separately from the manufacturing process. To set this up you need to create a primary cost component split in Cost Center Accounting when calculating the activity price. You can only use the primary cost component split to break apart your activity costs into components if you automatically calculate the activity price.

Procurement Alternative A procurement alternative represents one of a number of different ways of procuring a material. You can control the level of detail in which the procurement alternatives are represented through the controlling level. Depending on the processing category, there are single-level and multilevel procurement alternatives. For example, a purchase order is single-level procurement, while production is multilevel procurement.

Procurement Type The procurement type defines if the material is assembled in-house, purchased externally or both.

An in-house production entry (E) in the procurement type field in the material master MRP 2 view means a cost estimate will search for a bill of material and routing.

An external procurement type (F) results in the system searching for purchasing information such as a purchasing info record price.

A procurement type of both (X) means a planned order can be converted into either a production or purchase order.

Product Cost Collector A product cost collector collects target and actual costs during the manufacture of an assembly. Product cost collectors are necessary for repetitive manufacturing, and optional for order-related manufacturing.

Product Drilldown Reports Product drilldown reports allow you to slice and dice data based on characteristics such as product group, material, plant, cost component and period. Product drilldown reports are based on predefined summarization levels.

Production Campaign In production campaigns you combine process orders to manufacture products on a production line without having to perform major setup and/or teardown and cleaning activities for each individual order.

Production Line A production line is used in repetitive manufacturing, and typically consists of one or more work centers.

Production Process From SAP R/3 release 4.5A on, product cost collectors are created with reference to a production process which describes the way a material is produced i.e. quantity structure used. The quantity structure is taken from the production version, which is noted during the production process. The production process is determined by the following characteristics: material, production plant and production version. One production process can be created for each production version.

Production Resource/Tool A moveable operating resource used in production or plant maintenance.

Production Variance Production variance is a type of variance calculation based on the difference between net actual costs debited to the order and target costs based on the preliminary cost estimate and quantity delivered to inventory. You calculate produc-

tion variances with target cost version 1. Production variances are for information only, and are not relevant for settlement.

Production Version A production version describes the types of production techniques that can be used for a material in a plant. It is a unique combination of bill of material, routing and production line and is maintained in the MRP 4, Work scheduling and Costing 1 views of the material master.

Profit Center A profit center receives postings made in parallel to cost centers and other master data such as orders. Profit Center Accounting is really a separate ledger which enables reporting from a profit center point of view. You normally create profit centers based on areas in a company that generate revenue and have a responsible manager assigned.

If Profit Center Accounting is active, you will receive a warning message if you do not specify a profit center, and all unassigned postings are made to a dummy profit center. You activate Profit Center Accounting with configuration Transaction OKKP which maintains the controlling area.

Profitability Analysis Profitability Analysis (CO-PA) enables you to evaluate market segments, which can be classified according to products, customers, orders or any combination of these, or strategic business units, such as sales organizations or business areas, with respect to your company's profit or contribution margin.

Public Holiday Calendar This is a combination of an annual calendar and a list of all public holidays in a year. The public holiday calendar gives an overview of all working days and days off for a calendar year. It can be created to cover a validity period of several years.

Purchase Price Variance When raw materials are valued at standard price, there will be a purchase price variance posting during goods receipt if the purchase price is different to the material standard price.

Purchasing Info Record A purchasing info record stores all the information relevant to the procurement of a material from a vendor. It contains the purchase price field, which the standard cost estimate usually searches for when determining the purchase price.

Purchasing Organization A purchasing organization procures materials and services, and negotiates conditions of purchase with vendors.

Quantity Structure A quantity structure typically consists of a bill of materials (BOM) and a routing. In the process industries a master recipe is used instead of a BOM, and in repetitive manufacturing a rate routing is used instead of a routing. A quantity structure is used by a standard cost estimate to determine the quantities of components and activities.

Quantity Structure Control Quantity structure control is a costing variant component which automatically

searches for alternatives if multiple BOMs and/or routings exist for a material when a cost estimate is created.

Quantity Structure Date The quantity structure date determines which BOM and routing are selected when initially creating a cost estimate. Since these can change over time, it is useful to be able to select a particular BOM or routing by date when developing new products, or changing existing products.

Quantity Structure Determination Quantity structure determination is the process that determines a valid quantity structure when creating a cost estimate. Quantity structure can be determined via settings in quantity structure control or through default values in the material master.

Reference Operation Set A reference operation set is a routing type that defines a sequence of operations that is repeated regularly which simplifies entering data in a routing.

Reference Variant A reference variant is a costing variant component which allows you to create material cost estimates or costing runs based on the same quantity structure for the purpose of improving performance or making reliable comparisons.

Release Standard Cost Estimate When you release a material standard cost estimate the results of the cost estimate are written to the material master Costing 2 view as the current planned price and current standard price. Inventory is revalued during this process and accounting documents are posted. A standard cost estimate must be marked before it can be released and can be released only once per fiscal period.

Repetitive Manufacturing Repetitive manufacturing eliminates the need for production or process orders in manufacturing environments with production lines and long production runs. It reduces the work involved in production control and simplifies confirmations and goods receipt postings.

Request for Quotation A request for quotation (RFQ) refers to the request made to a vendor to submit a quotation for materials or services.

Requirement This is the quantity of material needed in a plant at a certain point in time.

Results Analysis Key Each product cost collector or order for which you want to create work in process (WIP) must contain a results analysis key. The presence of a results analysis key means that the product cost collector or order is included in WIP calculation during period-end closing. You define results analysis keys with configuration Transaction OKG1.

Rework Assemblies or components that do not meet quality standards may either become scrap, or require rework. Depending on the problem, cheaper items may become scrap, while more costly assemblies may justify rework.

Routing A routing is a list of tasks containing standard activity times required to perform operations to build an assembly. Routings, together with planned activity prices, provide cost estimates with the information necessary to calculate labor and activity costs of products.

Routing Header A routing header contains data that is valid for the entire routing. Select DETAILS • HEADER from the menu bar when displaying a routing to display the routing header.

Sales and Operations Planning This allows you to enter a sales plan, convert it to a production plan, and transfer the plan to long-term planning.

Scale A scale represents vendor quotations containing reduced prices for greater purchase quantities. Scales are entered when maintaining purchasing info record conditions with Transaction ME12.

Scheduled Activity Scheduled activity quantities are transferred from Sales and Operations Planning, MRP or long-term planning with Transaction KSPP to cost center/activity type planning. The scheduled activity quantity appears in the second last column when planning activity prices and quantities with Transaction KP26. You can compare and overwrite a manual plan activity quantity with the scheduled activity quantity during plan reconciliation.

Scheduling During scheduling the system determines the start and finish dates of orders or of operations in an order. Scheduling is performed in MRP, capacity planning and networks.

Scheduling Agreement A scheduling agreement is a longer-term purchase arrangement with a vendor covering the supply of materials according to predetermined conditions. These apply for a predefined period and a predefined total purchase quantity.

Scheduling Types Scheduling types include *forward scheduling* starting from the start date, *backward scheduling* starting from the finish date, *scheduling to current date* starting from the current date and *today scheduling* for rescheduling an order if the start date is in the past. You maintain scheduling types in the general data tab of a production order with Transaction CO02.

Selection Method The selection method field in the material master MRP 4 view determines the method of selecting an alternate BOM.

Settlement Work in process and variances are transferred to financial accounting, Profit Center Accounting and Profitability Analysis (CO-PA) during settlement. Variance categories can also be transferred to value fields in CO-PA.

Settlement Profile A settlement profile contains the parameters necessary to create a settlement rule for manufacturing orders and product cost collectors, and is contained in the order type.

Settlement Rule A settlement rule determines which portions of a sender's costs are allocated to which receivers. A settlement rule is contained in a manufacturing order or product cost collector header data.

Simultaneous Costing The process of recording actual costs for cost objects such as manufacturing orders and product cost collectors in Cost Object Controlling is called simultaneous costing. Costs incurred typically include goods issues, and receipts to and from an order, activity confirmations and external service costs.

You compare actual costs on cost objects incurred during simultaneous costing and period-end processing with planned costs on cost objects calculated during cost estimate creation during variance analysis.

Source Cost Element Source cost elements identify costs which debit objects such as manufacturing orders and product cost collectors.

Source List A list of available sources of supply for a material, indicating the periods during which procurement from such sources is possible. Usually a source list is a list of quotations for a material from different vendors.

You can specify a preferred vendor by selecting a Fixed Source of Supply indicator. If you do not select this indicator for any source, a cost estimate will choose the lowest cost source as the cost of the component. You can also indicate which sources are relevant to MRP.

Source Structure You define source structures when settling and costing joint products. A source structure contains several source assignments, each of which contains the individual cost elements or cost element intervals to be settled using the same distribution rules.

Special Procurement Type The special procurement type field found immediately below procurement type in the material master MRP 2 view is used to more closely define the procurement type. For example, it may indicate if the item is produced in another plant and transferred to the plant you are analyzing.

Special Procurement Type for Costing If you enter a special procurement type in the material master Costing 1 view, it will be used by costing. If no entry is made in this field, the system will use the special procurement type in the MRP 2 view.

Splitting Rule A splitting rule determines how a splitting structure distributes the cost center costs of an individual cost element, range or group over an activity type, range or group.

Splitting Structure You can allocate activity independent cost center plan costs to activity types either with equivalence numbers or with a splitting structure. A splitting structure contains one or more assignments for which you assign splitting rules for corresponding cost elements and the activity types over which the costs are split. The plan price calculation splits the activity independent costs automatically based on equivalence numbers or a splitting structure if assigned. You can also split the plan costs manually to see how the plan costs are distributed to the activity types.

A splitting structure can also be used to view all cost center costs at the cost center/activity type level during cost center plan/target/actual comparison.

Standard Cost Estimate This is a material cost estimate used to calculate the standard price of a material. The cost estimate must be executed with a costing variant that updates the material master, and the cost estimate must be released. A standard cost estimate can be released only once per period, and is typically created for each product at the beginning of a fiscal year or new season.

Standard Text You can use standard texts as templates to create texts for operations, phases, or secondary resources. The standard text associated with the standard text key defaults from the work center to the operation in a routing.

Standard Price The standard price in the material master Costing 2 view determines the inventory valuation price if price control is set at standard (S). The standard price is updated when a standard cost estimate is released. You normally value manufactured goods at standard price.

Standard Value This is the planned value for executing an operation in a routing. For example you may define that it normally takes five minutes to drill a hole in a metal plate, or that it takes one hour setup time to prepare to manufacture a batch of pharmaceuticals. The standard value is multiplied by the planned activity rate to determine the value of labor and activities in cost estimates.

Standard Value Key The standard value key in the basic data tab of an operation defines and gives a dimension (for example, time or area) to one of up to six standard values available in an operation.

Statistical Key Figure Statistical key figures define values describing cost centers, profit centers and overhead orders such as number of employees or minutes of long-distance phone calls. You can use statistical key figures as the tracing factor for periodic transactions such as cost center distribution or assessment. You can post both plan and actual statistical key figures.

Subcontracting In subcontracting you supply component parts to an external vendor who manufactures the complete assembly. The vendor has previously supplied a quotation which is entered in a purchasing info record with a category of subcontracting.

Summarization Hierarchy Reports Summarization reports are based on data collected at the levels and nodes of a summarization hierarchy. A summarization hierarchy groups together manufacturing orders or product cost

collectors at the lowest-level summarization nodes, which in turn are grouped together at higher-level nodes, to create a pyramid structure. You can create your own multiple hierarchies with Transaction KKR0.

Target Cost Version The target cost version determines the basis for the calculation of target costs. Target cost version 0 calculates total variance and is used to explain the difference between actual debits and credits on an order. It is the only target cost version that can be settled to financial accounting, Profit Center Accounting and Profitability Analysis.

Task List A task list (routing) is a list of tasks containing standard activity times required to perform operations to build an assembly. Task lists, together with planned activity prices, provide cost estimates with the information necessary to calculate labor costs of products.

Task List Group A task list group indentifies routings that have different production steps for the one material.

Task List Type A task list type classifies task lists according to their function. Typical task list types include routing, reference operation set, rate routing and standard rate routing.

Tracing Factor Tracing factors determine the cost portions received by each receiver from senders during periodic allocations such as assessments and distributions.

Transfer Control Transfer control is a costing variant component that requires a higher-level cost estimate to use recently created standard cost estimates for all lower-level materials. Preliminary cost estimates for product cost collectors use transfer control.

Transfer Price This is the price charged for transfer of a material or product from one business unit (company code or profit center) to another. The amount of price mark up is generally determined by tax authorities in each country involved in the transfer, and is the basis of legal inventory valuation.

Global companies are also generally interested in global inventory group valuation excluding transfer pricing in consolidations reporting. This provides a view of inventory valuation based on actual cost of purchase and manufacture for internal reporting and analysis.

Total Variance Production variance is a type of variance calculation based on the difference between actual costs debited to the order and credits from deliveries to inventory. You calculate total variance with target cost version 0, which determines the basis for calculation of target costs.

Under/Over Absorption Cost center balance, otherwise known as under/over absorption, represents the difference between cost center debits and credits during a period or range of periods. Cost center under/over absorption occurs due to differences between plan and actual debits, and plan and actual credits.

Unit Costing Unit costing is a method of costing that does not use BOMs or routings, typically when developing new products. You create a preliminary structure of materials and activities in a view similar to the layout of a spreadsheet.

Valuation Approach A valuation approach describes the values that are stored in accounting as a combination of a currency type (such as the group currency) and a valuation view (such as the profit center valuation view). The combination of various valuation approaches is known as a currency and valuation profile.

Valuation Category The valuation category located in the material master Accounting 1 and Costing 2 views determines which criteria are used to group partial stocks of a material in order to value them separately. The valuation category is part of the split valuation functionality.

Normally you will have only one price per material per plant. Split valuation allows you to valuate, for example, batches separately. Moving average price (V) is the only price control setting available if you activate split valuation and enter a valuation category. You assign valuation types to valuation categories, and valuation categories to plants in configuration Transaction OMWC.

Valuation Class The valuation class in the material master Costing 2 view determines which general ledger accounts are updated as a result of inventory movement or settlement.

Valuation Date The valuation date determines which material and activity prices are selected when initially creating a cost estimate. Purchasing info records can contain different vendor-quoted prices for different dates. Different plan activity rates can be entered per fiscal period.

Valuation Type You use valuation types in the split valuation process which enables the same material in a plant to have different valuations based on criteria such as batch.

You assign valuation types to each valuation category, which specify which individual characteristics exist for that valuation category. For example, you can valuate stocks of a material produced in-house separately from stocks of the same material purchased externally from vendors. Then you select Procurement type as the valuation category and internal and external as the valuation types.

Valuation Variant The valuation variant is a costing variant component that allows different search strategies for materials, activity types, subcontracting and external processing. For example, the search strategy for purchased and raw materials typically searches first for a price from the purchasing info record.

Valuation Variant for Scrap and WIP This valuation variant allows a choice of cost estimates to valuate scrap and work in process (WIP) in a WIP at target scenario. If the structure of a routing is changed after a costing run, WIP can still be valued with the valuation variant for scrap and WIP resulting in a more accurate WIP valuation.

Valuation View In the context of multiple valuation and transfer prices, you can define the following views:
▸ Legal valuation view
▸ Group valuation view
▸ Profit center valuation view

Together with a currency type and a currency, the valuation view creates what is called a valuation approach. You can maintain up to three different valuation approaches in financial accounting, controlling and the material ledger.

Value Field In costing-based Profitability Analysis (CO-PA), value fields store the base quantities and amounts for reporting. Value fields can either be highly summarized (representing a summary of cost element balances, for example) or highly detailed (representing just one part of a single cost element balance).

Variance Calculation Variance calculation provides information to assist you during analysis of how the order balance occurred. In other words, it helps you determine the reason for the difference between order debits and credits. It does this by analyzing variance causes and assigning categories. The three main types of variance calculation are: total, production and planning.

Variance Categories During variance calculation, the order balance is divided into categories on the input and output sides. Variance categories provide reasons for the cause of the variance, which you can use when deciding what corrective action to take.

Variance Key Variances are only calculated on manufacturing orders or product cost collectors containing a variance key. This key is defaulted from the Costing 1 view when manufacturing orders or product cost collectors are created. The variance key also determines if the value of scrap is subtracted from actual costs before variances are determined.

Variance Variant The variance variant (Transaction OKVG) determines which variance categories are calculated. If a variance category is not selected, variances of that category are assigned to remaining variances. Scrap variances are the only exception to this rule. If scrap variance is not selected, these variances enter all other variances on the input side.

Version Versions, formerly known as plan versions, enable you to have independent sets of planning and actual data.

WIP at Actual Work in process (WIP) at actual is valuated based on actual

debits to a manufacturing order or product cost collector.

WIP at Target Work in process (WIP) at target is valuated based on a cost estimate.

Work Center Operations are carried out at work centers representing, for example, machines, production lines or employees. Work center master data contains a mandatory cost center field. A work center can only be linked to one cost center, while a cost center can be linked to many work centers.

Work in Process Work in process (WIP) represents production costs of incomplete assemblies. For balance sheet accounts to accurately reflect company assets at period-end, WIP costs are moved temporarily to WIP balance sheet and profit and loss accounts. WIP postings are canceled during period-end processing following delivery of associated assemblies or finished products to inventory.

Workflow Workflow is a method of automating communications between people and processes in the system. For example you can automatically send an email to a user when the status of an item changes.

B   Bibliography

Janet Salmon: *Use the Primary Cost Component Split to Explain the Factors Behind Your Activity Rates*. FI/CO Expert, Volume 2, Issue 4, April 2003.

Janet Salmon: *Improve Your Cost Center Planning with Driver-Based Planning*. Financials Expert, Volume 6, Issue 3, March 2007.

John Jordan: *Transfer Control Can Produce Unexpected Results in Costing Runs*. FI/CO Expert, Volume 3, Issue 7, July/August 2004.

John Jordan: *Production Variance Analysis in SAP Controlling*. SAP PRESS Essentials, December 2006.

SAP Training Course Guide: *AC412-Cost Center Accounting-Advanced Functions-Release 470*. April 11, 2006.

SAP Training Course Guide: *AC505-Product Cost Planning-Release 470*. April 11, 2006.

SAP Training Course Guide: *AC510-Cost Object Controlling for Products-Release 470*. April 11, 2006.

SAP Training Course Guide: *AC515-Cost Object Controlling for Sales Orders-Release 470*. April 11, 2006.

SAP Training Course Guide: *AC530-Actual Costing/Material Ledger-Release 470*. April 11, 2006.

Sydnie McConnell: *Summarize Your Cost Estimate Analysis View for More Flexible Reporting*. Financials Expert, Volume 6, Issue 8, September 2007.

C   Author Biography

 **John Jordan** is Founder and Principal Consultant at ERP Corp and has worked with many clients worldwide. Specializing in product costing and all associated integration areas, he assists companies gain transparency of production costs, resulting in increased efficiency and profitability. He regularly speaks at conferences and publishes articles, and is considered one of the leading experts in the SAP ERP Controlling Component by clients and peers.

Index

S

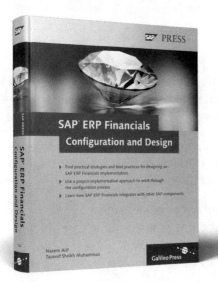

Find practical strategies and best practices for designing an SAP ERP Financials implementation

Use a project-implementation approach to work through the configuration process

Learn how SAP ERP Financials integrates with other SAP modules

Naeem Arif, Sheikh Tauseef

SAP ERP Financials: Configuration and Design

Master the most important issues involved in designing and configuring an SAP Financial implementation using the real-world, holistic business information provided in this comprehensive reference. You'll learn everything from the general areas of SAP Financials and how they fit in the SAP landscape, to how the General Ledger can work for you.
This invaluable guide is the one resource you need to understand the configuration and design process, the enterprise structure, reporting, data migration, Accounts Payable and Receivables, Financials integration with other modules, and all other critical areas of SAP Financials.

467 pp., 2008, 79,95 Euro / US$ 79.95
ISBN 978-1-59229-136-6

>> www.sap-press.de/1462

Get the most out of your SAP ERP Financials
implementation using the practical tips and
techniques provided

Achieve operational efficiencies by adopting
the process-driven approach detailed
throughout the book

Find useful value-added activities and
important strategy ideas in the case studies
and real-world examples

Shivesh Sharma

Optimize Your SAP ERP Financials Implementation

The real work in SAP Financials begins after the implementation is complete. This is when
it's time to optimize and use SAP Financials in the most efficient way for your organization.
Optimization entails understanding unique client scenarios and then developing solutions to
meet those requirements, while staying within the project's budgetary and timeline
constraints. This book teaches consultants and project managers to think about and work
through best practice tools and methodologies, before choosing the ones to use in their own
implementations.

The variety of real-life case studies and examples used to illustrate the business processes and
highlight how SAP Financials can support these processes, make this a practical and valuable
book for anyone looking to optimize their SAP Financials implementation.

676 pp., 2008, 79,95 Euro / US$ 79.95
ISBN 978-1-59229-160-1

>> www.sap-press.de/1583

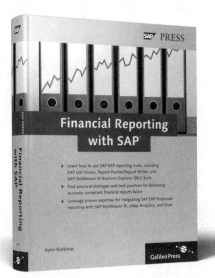

Understand and implement strategies for maximizing Financials reporting capabilities

Learn and apply best practices for simplifying, streamlining, and automating financial and management reporting

Leverage proven expertise concerning the integration of Financials reporting with BI, xApp Analytics, and Duet™

Aylin Korkmaz

Financial Reporting with SAP

This book provides finance and IT teams with best practices for delivering financial reports faster, more accurately, and in compliance with various international accounting standards. Featuring step-by-step coverage of all major FI reporting functions (including Sub-Ledger, Corporate Finance Management, and Governance, Risk & Compliance), this timely book will help you streamline and simplify financial business processes and automate financial and management reporting in SAP ERP Financials. It includes coverage of integrating FI reporting with Business Intelligence, xApp Analytics, and Duet™.

668 pp., 2008, 79,95 Euro / US$ 79.95
ISBN 978-1-59229-179-3

>> www.sap-press.de/1654

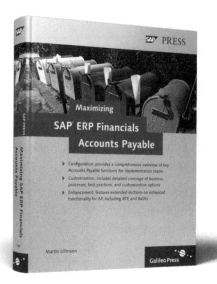

Configuration: provides a comprehensive overview of key Accounts Payable functions for implementation teams, consultants, project managers, and end-users

Customization: includes detailed coverage of business processes, best practices, and customization options

Enhancement: features extended sections on enhanced SAP functionality for Accounts Payable, including BTEs and Badis, among

Martin Ullmann

Maximizing SAP ERP Financials Accounts Payable

Maximizing Accounts Payable in SAP ERP Financials is the definitive, comprehensive guide to implementing, configuring, and enhancing AP for project managers, executives, technical leads, and end-users (functional resources who actually interact on a daily basis with the configured system).Covering the configuration of every AP function, plus strategies for incorporating business processes, best practices, and additional SAP enhancements, this book provides the guidance and experience needed for maximizing the use and potential of the Accounts Payable module.

approx. 488 pp., 79,95 Euro / US$ 79.95
ISBN 978-1-59229-198-4, Nov 2008

>> www.sap-press.de/1754

Interested in reading more?

Please visit our Web site for all
new book releases from SAP PRESS.

www.sap-press.com